W9-BDN-613

LOWE'S®
Home Improvement Warehouse

Texas Gardening Handbook

Dale Groom

Copyright© 1999 Dale Groom

All rights reserved. No part of this book may be reproduced or transmitted in any form or by any means, electronic or mechanical, including photocopying, recording, or by any information storage and retrieval system, without permission in writing from the publisher.

Groom, Dale
    Lowe's Texas Gardening Handbook / Dale Groom

    p.   cm.
    Includes bibliographical references (p.) and index.
    ISBN 1-888608-30-7
    1. Landscape plants -- Texas 2. Landscape gardening -- Texas.
    3. Gardening -- Texas I. Title.

First printing 1999
Printed in the United States of America
10 9 8 7 6 5 4 3 2 1

Horticultural Nomenclature Editor: Andrew Bunting

Map (p.25) provided by Agricultural Reasearch Service, USDA

DEDICATION

*T*HIS BOOK IS LOVINGLY DEDICATED to Judy Claire Lewis Groom, my wife of thirty years, my partner in life. She has made my walk wonderful and is a true blessing. How fortunate I am to have her, a dedicated wife to me and mother to our three children, Aaron, Angela, and Ashley.

FOREWORD

*F*OR YEARS, DALE GROOM, known as The Plant Groom™, has shared his special knowledge and expertise of Texas landscapes and gardens with college students and gardeners alike. The author uses a multimedia approach including television, radio, and newspapers, along with public demonstrations to reach Texans in every area of the state. Through many years of study, research and practical application, Dale Groom has compiled an impressive amount of knowledge on gardening in the diverse and challenging regions of Texas.

Finally this valuable material has been gathered and compiled into one complete source of information—the book you now hold in your hands. This book is for everyone, regardless of experience level; no matter if you garden as a hobby or design landscapes as a professional.

Space does not permit me to magnify each aspect of the *Lowe's Texas Gardening Handbook*. I can, however, assure you that every type of plant material suitable for Texas gardening is carefully discussed: from native plants to roses, annuals to perennials, bulbs to grasses; to the best shrubs and trees that are in concert with Texas conditions. This book outlines in great detail the best plants to select, how to plant and how to maintain them to ensure that your piece of Texas is as magnificent as Texas itself.

I have had the privilege of a special friendship with Dale for 20 years—he is like a little brother to me. I am certain that the love he has for Texas gardening, for Texas and for Texans will shine through this book and make this a treasured volume in good gardeners' libraries all across the state.

Enjoy the wonderful world of gardening and

Bon Appétit!

David Wade
'The Gourmet'

ACKNOWLEDGMENTS

I'D LIKE TO GRATEFULLY ACKNOWLEDGE the following friends and associates in "the wonderful world of green" we have in Texas. I appreciate these knowledgeable and experienced individuals who reviewed my manuscript and offered their suggestions. I've often said, "No one individual knows all there is about gardening or horticulture." My associates greatly helped me in my attempt to bring you usable and reliable information about landscape gardening in Texas. Thank you all, very much.

— Dale Groom, The Plant Groom™

My bill of friends and associates:

Andrew Bunting, Scott Arboretum, Swarthmore College, Swarthmore, Pennsylvania

David Creech, Director, SFA Arboretum, SFA State University, Nacogdoches, Texas

Calvin Finch, Bexar County Horticulturist, San Antonio, Texas

Greg Grant, Cherokee County Horticulturist, Rusk, Texas

Dwight Hall, Horticulturist, Whitehouse, Texas

Starley Hand, Pres., Hand Rose Farm, Tyler, Texas

Keith Hanson, Smith County Horticulturist, Tyler, Texas

Keith Mills, Rosarian, City of Tyler, Tyler, Texas

Debbie Rothermel, Landscape Designer, Carrollton, Texas

Doug Welsh, Horticulturist, Texas A. & M. University, College Station, Texas

Doug Williams, Executive Director, Mercer Arboretum and Botanical Garden, Humble, Texas

A super thank you to Roger Waynick, Publisher, Cool Springs Press, for coming to Texas to meet and recruit me for this project, for "making things happen," and for being a friend.

CONTENTS

Introduction 8

Annuals 26

Bulbs, Corms, Rhizomes and Tubers 68

Grasses: Lawn and Ornamental 92

Groundcovers 124

Native Texas Plants 146

Perennials 226

Roses 252

Shrubs 276

Trees 350

Vines 390

Sources 405

Index 419

About the Author 423

TEXAS GARDENING

*W*E TEXANS HAVE EXCELLENT OPPORTUNITIES for establishing all kinds of gardens in our great state. We are quite diverse as far as soils and climatic zones are concerned, and there are wonderful plants available to all of us. This book will give you an introduction to the many plants you can select and enjoy for a Texas home landscape. Most of the plants are readily available, and all are worth seeking out. Follow the suggestions in this book for help in enjoying your Texas gardening experience.

CLIMATIC ZONES

Texas has five different climatic zones, as seen on the United States Department of Agriculture Climatic Data Zone map (page 25). The state reaches from Zone 6 in the Panhandle where minus 10 degrees Fahrenheit is common, all the way down to Zone 10 in the valley, where freezes are the exception. There is no other place in the country that has this diversity.

The colder zones are in the northwest areas of Texas, including Wheeler, Randall, and Bailey counties in the Panhandle. The warmer zones are in the south and include Cameron, Hidalgo, and Starr counties of our Rio Grande Valley. Keep in mind that the USDA Plant Hardiness Zone map doesn't tell the whole story of temperatures in our state. Temperatures in urban areas can be 10 degrees warmer than those in rural areas due to asphalt, concrete, masonry, and a denser population, all of which create what are called "microclimates."

Microclimates can also be created in our own home landscapes by fencing, by shrubbery, and by our homes and structures. You may discover that your yard has a location where particular plants will survive due to a microclimate that you have created, while your neighbor may not be able to grow the same plants.

Temperature range and rate of change greatly affect gardening in Texas. If, for example, one area was to drop down to a sub-freezing temperature for a short period of time and climb right back up, plants in that area would most likely receive little harm. But if the temperature dropped suddenly and remained there for several days, great damage could occur. A recent example is the freezing spell that struck North Texas; some of its live oak trees, which would normally be considered quite hardy in that area, were severely damaged.

The USDA Plant Hardiness Zone map gives us an idea of the temperatures in each of the zones. Plant hardiness refers to each plant's ability to withstand the freezing temperatures in the various zones. A plant that is barely able to withstand the temperatures in Zone 8 should not be planted in the colder Zone 7. Plants that will grow in Zone 6 will often grow in Zone 9.

One of the problems that we sometimes encounter when plants are brought in from Northeastern places of the country where summers are relatively mild is damage by our prolonged high summer temperatures. While such plants will withstand all of our freezing temperatures, they will not be able to handle the heat that we have. Make sure all plants you buy will be able to handle Texas summertime heat. Even the temperatures in our shade can be too hot for these plants, and they may not receive the sunlight needed to grow properly. Texas sun in July and August, for example, will fry some plants that can be grown in full sun in other parts of the country. I noticed an example of this when I was in Winnipeg, Canada, taping a television show in July, and I saw impatiens being grown in full sun. If those impatiens were growing in full Texas sun in July, they would be "cooked" very quickly. When you read that particular plants can be grown in full sun, make sure the writer is referring to full-sun locations in Texas.

WIND

Wind can also affect gardening activities. Make sure that the plants that you select will be able to withstand the wind that is common in your area. Many Texans experience prevailing southwestern breezes, and in some locations they can be quite strong. I have seen some rather significant landscape plants growing at a 45-degree angle due to these prevailing breezes. Make sure that trees or other tall shrubs are staked temporarily until large enough to withstand the strong breezes and can begin growing in a vertical position. Select trees that are resistant to the type of wind that is common in your particular location. Trees that are properly selected and placed can serve beautifully as breaks to block out strong winds.

MULCHING

Mulching can be a confusing topic for Texas gardeners. But whether it is compost, ground-bark mulch, or another type of material, "mulch" simply means a blanket on top of the soil. Whether we are planting vegetables, perennials, trees, or any other plant, mulch is that blanket we put on top of the ground.

Generally we recommend a minimum of 2 to 4 in. of such items as pine bark mulch. Perhaps you prefer hardwood bark, or maybe you like to use shredded cypress. When using a high-density mulch, 3 to 4 in. is quite sufficient. You may also use materials such as pine needles or clean hay. These are rather lightweight, but 6 in. placed between plants is sufficient. All the roses in The City of Tyler's Rose Garden are mulched with pine needles.

Mulching has several benefits. Perhaps the most important is conserving water. Plants that are properly mulched require less frequent watering, maintain an even soil moisture content, and respond with better overall growth. Mulching is especially important in the root zone. If you take a walk through the woods, you will notice that our native vegetation is mulched by woodland floor debris or natural mulch. When you add mulch to your finished plantings, you are helping to approximate that natural environment.

Mulching is something that I encourage every gardener to do yearly. There are lots of mulching materials—select the one that you like best. In addition to those mentioned above, you may use peanut hulls, pecan hulls, cocoa hulls, shredded sugar cane, and many other

Introduction

different kinds of materials. In my opinion, the best mulches are the organic mulches.

FERTILIZING

Fertilization supplies nutrients to the soil for the plant to pick up. This process is sometimes misunderstood. While many say they are feeding the plant, they are actually adding nutrients to the soil for the plant to absorb. If soils lack sufficient amounts of naturally occurring plant nutrients, then our plants will not grow as well as we would like.

We can fertilize our plants with various materials, including water-soluble, liquid, encapsulated, and premium-quality, slow-release fertilizers. Many different forms and types are available. Make sure that you read and understand the directions before you apply any type of fertilizer. When a container of fertilizer specifies an amount, we Texas gardeners may say, "Well, if that works well, then double that amount ought to be really great!" But it doesn't work that way with fertilizers. Make sure you apply only the amount specified on the label. My granny said that my granddad was known to burn up crops in the vegetable garden by putting on too much cottonseed meal. Cottonseed meal is a 100 percent natural organic fertilizer, but just because something is all organic does not mean that you cannot have problems with it.

Plants do not have the ability to determine where nutrients come from. As far as they are concerned, nutrients come from the soil reservoir. With the proper application of fertilizers, you can make sure that the soil has the nutrients necessary for good plant growth.

Soil nutrients are sometimes categorized as major or minor. Plants need more of the major nutrients than they do of the minor. This doesn't mean that major nutrients are more important, just that plants use more of them. Nitrogen (N), phosphorus (P), and potassium (K) are considered the three major nutrients. Some horticulturists classify sulfur and calcium as secondary nutrients and call the remaining nutrients micronutrients because they are used by plants in extremely small amounts.

Nutrients occur naturally in our soil. They come from various materials, including stone and/or organic matter in the soil itself. Perhaps you have heard someone say, "The soil is just worn out." We don't really wear soils out, but we can deplete them of nutrients and damage soil structure. By supplying nutrients to those that we have depleted and keeping soil structure in good shape, we can continue to grow in the same soils for generation after generation. If soils are deficient in naturally occurring nutrients, then we can apply those nutrients in the form of fertilizers. I always recommend that you water thoroughly after applying any type of fertilizer.

Select the fertilization program with which you feel most comfortable. When fertilizing your lawn, apply the fertilizers when the grass blades are dry. Follow label directions and then water thoroughly. You will be rewarded with a nice, thick vigorous lawn, if you also mow properly and water as you should.

Don't forget that your lawn may also need to be aerated if your soils are compacted or are the heavy clay types. Aeration allows oxygen, water, and nutrients to penetrate the soil and reach the root zones.

WATERING

Water has been described as "the essence of life"—we must have water in order to survive. The drought of 1996 in Texas reminded us just how important water is to us. Water is not available in unlimited quantities. (See the precipitation map on page 13 for the annual rainfall for areas of Texas.) Not only is our population growing, but we now have large international corporations with their "straws" in our underground water supply.

Certainly there are some plants that require very little water. Others like to be moist at all times. Unfortunately, some areas may not be desirable for gardening because the water in those areas may be too high in soluble salts.

PRECIPITATION MAP

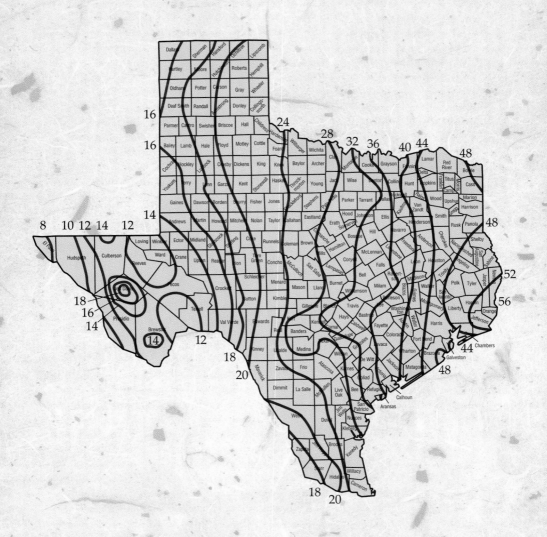

Mean annual total precipitation (inches) in Texas.
Adapted from Griffiths and Orton (1968).

Introduction

Don't set any of your plants, including your lawn, on a watering schedule. I have seen folks who want to turn on their lawn sprinklers, for example, every morning at 6:38 for 10 minutes. That is not desirable for individual plants, grass, shrubbery, or any other plant. Water your plants when they need it, deeply and thoroughly. Lawns, for example, need to be watered a minimum of 6 in. deep, and they prefer to be watered to 8 in. After watering, don't go back to rewater until your plants tell you they need to be rewatered. Grass will tell you when it needs to be watered by changing from a nice pleasant green color to a kind of bluish gray. Or perhaps its sides will roll up, or it will lie flat when you walk across it, not springing back. When you see these signs, water the lawn thoroughly. You can tell when shrubs need to be watered by simply sticking your finger in the soil. If the soil is dry, then irrigate or apply water thoroughly.

It is important to water thoroughly. Be sure that you soak the entire root zone of your plants when watering. If you water your plants frequently and very lightly, they will develop undesirable shallow root systems. When watering shrubbery or containers of color, water until there are no more air bubbles coming out of the pots or containers. You will then know that all the pores have been saturated with moisture. The excess water will drain out. Be sure that all your pots or containers drain properly.

Certain methods of irrigation can be good for water conservation, others can be quite wasteful. Sprinklers that throw a lot of water high in the air before striking lawns, or shrubs are not as efficient as other methods. Drip irrigation is the most efficient method of delivering water to landscape plants, including trees, shrubs, vines, groundcovers, annuals, and perennials.

Drip irrigation can conserve as much as 50 percent of overall water usage. This water conservation translates into cost savings, plus it helps provide a beneficial environment for overall healthy plant growth. I have seen side-by-side comparisons of landscape beds that were planted and irrigated by drip irrigation and sprinkler irrigation. Drip irrigation is far superior. Many hardware stores, sprinkler supermarkets, and nurseries carry drip irrigation systems, and they can help you select the best one for your home application.

If watered at midday, especially with sprinklers that disperse the water high into the air before it falls to the soil, lawns can lose a significant amount of moisture through evaporation. Early-morning watering helps to prevent some of the evaporation.

PEST CONTROL

Pest control has several meanings. Weeds, insects, and diseases are all considered pests by most Texas gardeners.

Weeds in our landscape beds can be controlled by the use of mulches. Mulching beds heavily with a 3- to 4-in. layer makes it difficult for weed seeds to germinate and grow.

Weeds can also be controlled by making sure our lawns are well fertilized, mowed, and watered. A healthy, actively growing, thick lawn will naturally have fewer problems with weeds.

A well-selected and well-cared-for landscape will have fewer insect problems and fewer disease problems. For example, when crape myrtles are properly selected and planted in ideal locations in the landscape, there will be few or no problems with powdery mildew. When improperly selected, placed in areas where there is poor air circulation, and watered frequently, crape myrtles present a perfect environment for growth of this fungus.

Before you buy plants at local nurseries, ask about potential disease and insect problems. If it sounds as if a plant may have too many problems for your taste, then make another selection. Remember that plants that tend to have problems in certain locations (such as the crape myrtles) may have few problems when placed in other locations.

Introduction

SOIL PREPARATION

Before planting anything in your home landscape, be sure you understand the soil that you have, and properly prepare that soil. It is very important that you know whether you have well-drained soil, sandy soil, clay soil, etc. You will certainly want to know the soil pH.

Whether for annuals, shrubs, perennials, vines, or groundcovers, preparing the soil includes breaking it up in some way. If you are planting in a small area, you may choose a shovel or digging fork. Those planting in larger areas traditionally use various types of tillers. The incorporation of organic matter into these areas will greatly improve the soil's drainage and moisture- and nutrient-holding capacity.

The positive benefits of organic matter cannot be overemphasized. You may use compost that you have made or purchased. Brown Canadian sphagnum peat moss, ground bark, composted sawdust, and other types of organic matter will greatly improve the soil. Annuals and perennials usually require more extensive preparation than do shrubs and trees. I recommend that 3 in. or more of quality organic matter be blended with native Texas soils when prepared for bedding plants.

Our trees require a simple loosening of the soil. In most cases, it is impossible to amend the soil in an area wide enough or deep enough for a tree's root system. Simply loosen the soil thoroughly before planting your trees, and be sure that you have selected the right trees for your soil type. The oak tree is the number one shade tree grown in Texas, but some oaks do well in all areas, while others are very selective. For example, a water oak will grow in all areas of East Texas, but if you put it in the highly alkaline soils of Central or North Texas, results will be less than desirable.

PROPER PLANT SELECTION

Proper plant selection is extremely important for long-term success when gardening in Texas. You will see many plants in magazines, in catalogs, and on television that excite the gardener in you. They may look wonderful, but you must make sure these plants will grow in your area before you go out and spend your money on them.

You can get additional information on some of the newer varieties and some that have been tested rather extensively by visiting your local County Agent's Office for a list of trees, shrubs, vines, groundcovers, annuals, and perennials that are well adapted to your home area.

Make sure that you select the proper plant for long-term success with minimal maintenance. There are some wonderful plants from which to choose. If you select trees that need to be grown as understory plants and you put these out in full Texas sun, they will "cook." If a plant needs shade, give it some shade. The aucuba shrub, for example, is wonderful in shaded areas in Texas, but it will not tolerate our sun. It will burn like my red-headed, fair-skin wife, Judy.

Here are some questions to ask before purchasing any type of plant:

- How tall and wide does this plant usually grow in my area?
- How much sun or shade is required . . . full sun, morning sun with afternoon shade, dappled sun/shade, or full shade?
- Does this plant have special soil requirements? Does it require well-drained soils or will it grow in poorly drained or damp soils?
- Does it bloom? If so, when, for how long, and in what color? Spring, summer, fall, or winter? For 2 weeks, 6 months, or longer?
- Does it have fall color? If so, what are the colors?
- Is it resistant to insect and disease pests that usually occur in our area? (This is very important information to gather when considering plants.)
- What is the watering or soil moisture requirements? Moist at all times? Tolerant of relatively dry soils?

- How often should it be fertilized, with what, and when?
- Are there any special pruning requirements? (Roses and certain other landscape plants require special pruning and/or training to realize maximum benefits.)

SOILS

Soil is the foundation for all of our successful gardening experiences. It is very important that we take care of our soils so that they can help take care of us as we work to achieve our gardening goals.

Some Texas gardeners want to have the most luxurious lawn possible to run our bare toes through in July and August. Others would like to have the most gorgeous roses, azaleas, marigolds, irises, or other plants. Soil testing is a very important tool that will help us accomplish our gardening goals.

It is worth performing soil tests every two years. If you are sampling several areas, they will need to be segregated. For example, your lawn needs to be separated from your landscape shrub bed and perennial garden and annual plantings. Each soil test stands alone.

When we test the soil, we may find that some of the efforts that we have been putting into soil care are not necessary. It is always pleasing to find that we can do more with less, and a soil test is a great way to find that out about managing your soil.

You may have your soil tested through our Agricultural Extension Service. Most of us call the local representative of the Texas Agricultural Extension Service "The County Agent." To find his or her phone number, look in the directory where all the County office numbers are listed for your county. Your agent can mail you instruction and information sheets and soil sample bags, or you can go by the offices and pick them up. The offices are usually located in the County Courthouse, County Annex, or another County Office location. A phone call can determine specific locations. The County Agent's offices in Texas are always worth visiting in person because you will have the opportunity to meet some good people that can be very helpful to you and your gardening goals. The Stephen F. Austin State University Soil Testing Laboratory is also available to you for complete soil testing. Contact the lab directly at: (409) 468-4500. There are also some private soil-testing labs throughout Texas, but be prepared to pay higher fees.

Make sure that the soil grade in the area you wish to landscape is correct. If grading is necessary on new landscapes, complete the activity before installing grass or landscape beds or any other plants. Grading can be done with small tractors, hand tools, or other methods. It is more effective to correct any grades that need it before planting is done. It is much more difficult to go back and correct a drainage problem after thick turf is established on a lawn area.

If you don't feel comfortable performing the grading, contact a landscape contractor. In most communities there are one or more members of the Texas Association of Landscape Contractors (TALC). When a contractor supplies an estimate, be sure that you understand exactly what work is to be done and that you have it in writing.

Drainage is very important and is one of the reasons that we do grading in our landscape. Drainage can be improved in certain locations with the addition of raised beds, which may necessitate additional soil and/or lots of organic matter. In some cases, it may be necessary to use French drain systems in landscape beds to drain off excess water that may be a problem from time to time.

Soils that drain poorly tend to be oxygen starved. Oxygen-starved soils will not allow plants to grow healthy roots, and plants in these soils will suffer. Certainly there are plants that grow in damp to wet soils, including bald cypress, water-loving plants, bog plants, and weeping willow—but these are exceptions. The general rule is that a very high percentage of our landscape plants, including trees, need a well-drained soil in order to be healthy.

Sample Information Box

EXPOSURE
F. Sun to Semi-

COLD HARDINESS
Annual

WATER USAGE
Semi-Moist

GROWTH RATE
Fast

AVG. HT × WIDTH
6–40″ × 6–12″

SPACING
15–18″

(This sample box shows the information for *Zinnia elegans*.)

   EXPOSURE

Note these icons for a quick read on the plant's light requirements. The filled-in sun icon indicates Full Shade; the unfilled sun indicates Full Sun. The half-filled sun means the plant will tolerate a range of light conditions between these two extremes. Be sure to check the text under each icon for a fuller explanation.

 WATER USAGE

Note these icons for a quick read on the plant's moisture requirements. Check the text under each icon for a fuller explanation.

 COLD HARDINESS

The plant is expected to be cold hardy to temperatures as low as the indicated temperature. An **Annual** is not expected to survive over winter and will have to be replaced every year. **All Texas** indicates a plant that is cold hardy in all Texas growing zones.

   GROWTH RATE
Fast Medium Slow

Check these icons to determine how quickly your plant is expected to grow.

Introduction

 Avg. Ht X Width

The first number or range refers to the plant's expected height; the second number or range refers to the plant's expected width. If measurements are followed by **(v.)**, height and width vary greatly or are dependent on the variety of the plant you have selected. If size varies so much that it would not be helpful to give possible measurements, the icon may simply be labeled: **Varies.**

 **Spacing**

When planting, space plants according to these suggested measurements.

Abbreviations

D.T.	Drought Tolerant	**F.**	Full
Ann.	Annual	**(v.)**	Varies, or Variety-Dependent
Mst.	Moist		

Buying Plants

There are many different sizes of landscape plants available and sometimes they tend to get confusing. Someone once wrote to my garden column about nursery container sizes: "Plants advertised as 1-gallon plants do not necessarily measure 1 gallon fluid measurement of a gallon container." This may be true, but we use adopted trade size measurements in the industry that are relatively close to the actual gallon size. You will also find plants in 2-, 3-, 5-, 7-, 10-, 15-, 20-gallon, and larger-sized containers. Certainly the larger sizes will be quite large, almost tree-type shrubs or trees. Sizes larger than 20 gallons are most likely trees. We home gardeners can generally handle containers up to a 20-gallon size. If larger than that, it is almost a sure bet that we need to have a landscape contractor plant it for us. Smaller-sized plants require less investment from us, but in most cases they do take longer to reach the size we want.

Tall-growing shrubs such as crape myrtles and trees are sometimes sold according to height, or they may be sold using caliper
measurement, which is the diameter of the trunk. According to the
American Association of Nurserymen (AAN), the caliper measurement of trees should be made approximately 12 in. above the soil
line. This measurement gives you the thickness, thus the diameter,
of the trunk. You will see advertisements offering an oak tree of 3 in.
This is the thickness measurement of the trunk 12 in. above the soil
line. You may also find plants sold in 6- to 8-ft., 8- to 10-ft., and 10-
to 12-ft. height ranges. Certainly the tall crape myrtles, tall hollies,
and some of the smaller-growing trees are classified in these ways.

PRUNING

From time to time our landscape plantings will require some pruning. But we want to prune for a purpose; we don't want to prune
haphazardly. You may be pruning to shape a plant. You may want
more light coming down through trees. You may be pruning to do
some specialized training. Perhaps you are training a tree into an
espalier or maybe you are training a rose for a particular type of
growth or pruning to enhance selected blooms for shows. We often
prune the tips out of garden mums to induce branching and therefore thickening of the overall planting so we have loads of buds that
bloom in the fall. There are quite a few reasons for pruning. The timing of pruning can be important. If you have a spring-blooming
plant such as azalea, you certainly don't want to do any pruning
until after the blooming season is completed in the spring. If you
happen to have a group of overgrown azaleas that you wish to
rework, do it after all blooming is complete, just as you see the flush
of spring growth beginning.

When pruning shrubs, select buds that are pointed outward
and upward and then remove the branch just above the buds. That
will give direction to the plant's branches. You can do similar types
of pruning fairly often with certain types of roses. Pruning can be
kept to a minimum if you select specific plants and place them prop-

Introduction

erly in your home landscape to minimize pruning maintenance. Shrubs often look best when allowed to grow into their natural form.

This book is an introduction to the plants that thrive in our great gardening state. We begin with a look at annuals, different varieties that offer fine possibilities. All can be tried in the home landscape—and don't forget to let "little gardeners" try their hand with annuals.

Texas gardeners grow a lot of bulbs, though there are some wonderful lesser-used bulbs that have been around for generations. We need to be on the lookout for these and incorporate them again into our landscapes.

Nearly all Texas gardeners like to grow grasses in the home landscape. Not all lawn grasses will grow in all areas of the state, but I've included grasses for every area of Texas. Also try some of the ornamental grasses that are on the market, such as blue fescue or fountain grass.

Gardeners may not pay much attention to groundcovers., but if you need an alternative for lawn grass in a heavily shaded area, groundcovers are the answer. I've included some of the best available in Texas for your consideration.

Texans like to talk about our native plants. We have a reputation for being the wildflower state because we have such a broad palette of wonderful color. We also have shrubs, trees, and vines that are all native to Texas, and this book offers a good selection.

Perennial is that group of plants which bloom for three years or more. Some of them grow for generations in our home landscapes. Some are very tough and durable plants that can stand up to our Texas environment, including achillea or yarrow.

We have the world's headquarters for roses in Tyler, but we can grow roses in all areas of Texas. The American Rose Society (ARS)

lists over fifty different classifications. I have grouped them together into nine of the most popular and fun groups.

There are many different types of shrubs available. I have listed thirty-nine for your consideration, from abelia to viburnum. These are actually thirty-nine separate families, and in those families you will find many different varieties.

Trees are near and dear to my heart. I like to climb trees, I build treehouses for my children, and I like to rest in the shade from trees. I've put together information on nineteen trees for you to review. These are generally what we call shade trees, including some that have been used in our landscapes for generations.

We will also take a look at vines and different ways to use them.

For additional information, contact me at my current web site: **www.cleaf.com\~plantgrm** or e-mail me at **plantgrm@cleaf.com.** Should my web-site or e-mail address change, contact me at my permanent mailing address:

Dale Groom P.O. Box 365 Eustace, TX 75124

When requesting information, always send a long, stamped, self-addressed envelope. I hope you enjoy the information I have put together for you.

Great Gardening . . . to YOU!

—Dale Groom, The Plant Groom™

USDA HARDINESS ZONE MAP

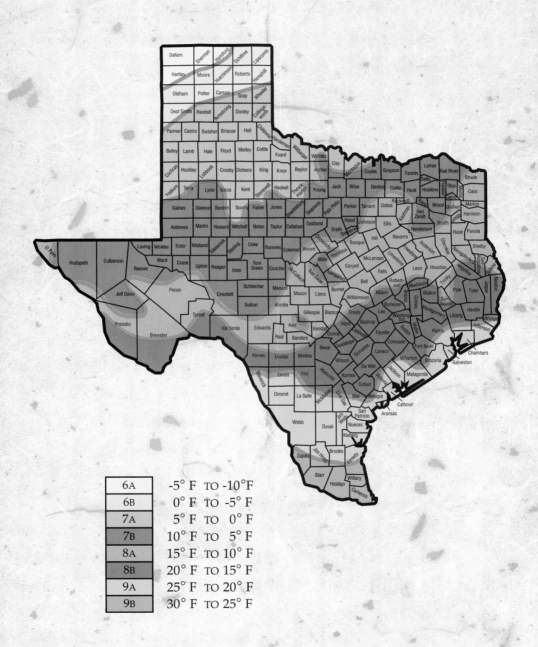

6A	-5° F TO -10° F
6B	0° F TO -5° F
7A	5° F TO 0° F
7B	10° F TO 5° F
8A	15° F TO 10° F
8B	20° F TO 15° F
9A	25° F TO 20° F
9B	30° F TO 25° F

CHAPTER ONE

ANNUALS

To FRAME BEDS AND HELP ACCENT LOCATIONS, annuals give us the most spectacular color—there is absolutely nothing that grabs our attention like color.

We plant most annuals in the springtime and we hope that they stay with us all summer long. Some will and some will not; it all depends on selection and care. One of the better annuals to plant in springtime is gomphrena, or globe amaranth, *Gomphrena globosa*. It will remain through the entire spring and summer seasons up until the first fall frost. My granny used to call these plants bachelor buttons. For low-growing color, you can't beat periwinkle, *Catharanthus roseus*, which is also known as annual vinca. Today there are several periwinkle colors on the market, from solid white and white with pink or red "eyes" (centers) to pinks and purples.

Zinnia, *Zinnia eleganus*, is the most popular flower grown from seed in the United States. It is as easy to grow today as it has been for generations, but there are new varieties on the market, making it even more versatile.

Sunflowers, *Helianthus annuus*, are annuals that a lot of folks have been growing for a long time, particularly the tall-growing varieties. While the tall yellow ones are still available, there are many other different sizes and colors of sunflowers on the market today. It is possible to create a complete outdoor room for your children by selecting and planting sunflowers and some complementary annuals. Work on this project together—it's a fun thing for kids to do!

Annuals are often broken down into various categories. Spring and summer annuals are traditionally planted in the springtime after all danger of frost is past. Some varieties of annuals will cease to bloom when our July-August blast furnace heat arrives. Others continue blooming all season long.

We also have fall and winter annuals. The most prominent family to look for is pansies, *Viola × wittrockiana*. We plant those strictly for cool-season growth in Texas. Two members of the *Brassica* family, ornamental flowering kale and cabbage, are good in the cool season as well as in the spring. Dianthus, *Dianthus barbatus* is absolutely great during the fall and early spring, plus it provides wonderful fragrance.

Annuals may also be grouped into sun or shade categories. Some can grow in both sun and shade. Wax leaf begonias, *Begonia* × *semperflorens-cultorum*, particularly those with bronze leaves and red flowers, will grow in full sun as well as shade if they are set out early in the springtime. Some varieties of coleus, *Coleus* × *hybridus*, will also grow in full sun. (Traditionally, coleus is a very colorful foliage annual grown by Texas gardeners only in shaded areas.)

Soil preparation is important for successful long-term growth of annuals. Be sure to prepare your beds properly before planting your first seed or transplant. When buying fresh seed, be sure to purchase those packaged for the current season, and get the named variety you want. All of this information, as well as planting instructions, will be found on the seed package itself.

Not all annuals are grown for their flowers. There are some colorful foliage annuals, including flowering kale, flowering cabbage, coleus, and copper plant.

Some plants that are perennials in tropical regions are grown as annuals in Texas. Because of our winter freezes, these plants complete their life-cycle in one season.

Because of space limitations, I have included only twenty annuals in this book, but you will find outstanding varieties and colors among these twenty. Don't forget to visit Lowe's to see the other annuals that are available including the latest varieties.

Bachelor Buttons
Gomphrena globosa

EXPOSURE

Full Sun

COLD HARDINESS

Annual

WATER USAGE

Arid to Semi-Mst.

GROWTH RATE

Fast

AVG. HT × WIDTH

9"–12' × 6–9"

SPACING

8–18"

Grows upright and has globe-shaped flowers that come in purple, pink, white, orange, and yellow.

The most important flower grown by my Granny in her old-fashioned non-irrigated garden at Indian Creek, Texas, was bachelor buttons, also known as globe amaranth or, simply, gomphrena. Whatever name you choose, Granny made a good choice when she planted it every year. Granny Miller had one of those old-fashioned Texas country gardens that many rural living landscape gardeners had before the turn of the century and that continued to be enjoyed by succeeding generations. Most had no grass or water systems as we know them today. If any of Granny's plants received water, it was hauled to them one bucket at a time. Needless to say, her plants had to be tough and quite drought tolerant to make it through our blazing summers. Gomphrena is one surefire tough-blooming Texas annual that every Texan should have in the garden. They continue to bloom all summer long until the first fall frost puts them to rest for the year.

WHEN TO PLANT

When planting from transplants, make sure all frost danger is past and wait till nighttime temperatures have been at or above 70 degrees Fahrenheit for a couple of weeks. If starting from seed, plant indoors in very sunny windowsills approximately 6 weeks before transplanting outside. I prefer to purchase fresh packs of globe amaranth transplants at area nurseries. This allows me to select the colors and the number of plants I want.

WHERE TO PLANT

Plant in well-drained locations which receive at least 6 to 8 hours "of sun per day. Don't plant in shady or poorly drained spots. The shorter varieties may be used in border plantings while the taller ones are great for background color. You might also "stair-step" from the shorter to the taller varieties for an interesting effect that is easy to care for. If you like to have some pots of color, give bachelor buttons a try. A dark-purple gomphrena in the center of a large terracotta container with a solid white periwinkle or annual vinca planted around the pot's edge is most pleasing. Other plants and color combinations are equally pleasing to the eye. Try these beauties for summer-long color in areas where you have tried other annuals that can't tolerate the Texas heat.

HOW TO PLANT

While globe amaranth will do well under adverse conditions, for best results, plant in improved soils. Add approximately 3 in. of high-quality organic matter and blend with the top 3 in. of your soil. Then install the transplants no deeper than the top of the root-ball, firm, water thoroughly, and apply a root stimulator. After planting is completed, mulch the entire planting area with 3 in. of a material like pine bark mulch.

CARE AND MAINTENANCE

This plant has no serious pests. You may deadhead if desired, but it is not required. To ensure good results, water enough to prevent soil dryness. Do not overwater. Maintaining a season-long thick mulch layer will greatly aid in soil moisture conservation. Season-long encapsulated "bedding plant" fertilizers may be applied at planting time. Liquid, water-soluble, and specialty granular fertilizers may be applied as needed throughout the season. Remember to read and follow label directions when using any gardening aid.

ADDITIONAL INFORMATION

Globe amaranth is one of the "everlasting" annuals. It makes excellent cut dried flowers that often last for years. To dry, cut shortly after the blooms are fully open, and hang upside down indoors till fully dried. Then use in any arrangement or potpourri desired.

ADDITIONAL SPECIES, CULTIVARS, OR VARIETIES

G. globosa Mixed, 'Amber Glow', 'Blushing Bride', 'Innocence', 'Lavender Lady', 'Professor Plum', 'Strawberry Fayre', 'Buddy', and the 'Gnome' Series, including 'White Gnome'.

Cockscomb
Celosia cristata

EXPOSURE

Full Sun

COLD HARDINESS

Annual

WATER USAGE

Semi-Moist

GROWTH RATE

Fast

AVG. HT × WIDTH
6–36" × 8–12"

SPACING

8–16"

Has tiny, brightly colored flowers of yellow, orange, red, pink, or purple in a plume or cockscomb type of arrangement.

*T*here are basically two types of cockscomb or celosia. One is considered the plume type and looks much like feathery flowers. The second type is considered crested and has very tight flowers that resemble the comb of a rooster. Cockscomb is the older of the two types that are used by Texas gardeners. They are great for use in cut gardens. They are wonderful in masses or as border plants. The tall 3-ft. varieties look wonderful as background plants, while the very low-growing dwarf types in the 6- to 12-in. range are wonderful by themselves. All cockscomb needs to be planted in full-sun locations that receive at least 6 to 8 hours of sun per day and well-drained soil. Try some of these beauties in containers along with some other plants. For a spectactular look, plant an apricot-colored plume in the center of a large container, with solid white annual vinca or periwinkle drooping down the sides.

WHEN TO PLANT
The best time to plant cockscomb or celosia is in the early spring after all danger of frost is past from your particular area. If you are not familiar with the last average killing frost dates in your area, check with your local retail garden centers or County Extension Agent. Either can give you the correct dates.

WHERE TO PLANT

In Texas, celosia or cockscomb does best when planted in improved soil—do not plant in heavy clay soil unless improved with organic matter or areas of poor drainage. Cockscomb works well when used in color gardens to outline other varieties, types, and colors often used in Texas gardens. I believe the most spectacular use of cockscomb is in large numbers of single colors. It also works very well in containers to provide color in outdoor entertainment areas. These areas may include benches, decks, gazebos, or swimming pools.

HOW TO PLANT

Plant celosia in soils that have been improved with the addition of organic matter. Incorporate 3 in. of high-quality organic matter such as ground bark, brown sphagnum peat moss, or compost into the top 3 in. of your existing native soil. I prefer planting celosia from transplants purchased at local retail garden centers. This gives me control over which varieties, colors, and even sizes of containers I desire to select and plant. After your selections are made, install them in your improved planting bed no deeper than the plant's soil-ball top. Firm the soil, water thoroughly, and apply root stimulator according to label directions. After the entire planting is complete, mulch the bed well with approximately 3 in. of mulch.

CARE AND MAINTENANCE

This plant usually has no serious pests. Very little pruning, if any, is required. You may remove any damaged or spent blooms or leaves if desired. Maintain a moist, not wet, soil throughout the entire growing season. Maintaining a season-long layer of mulch will greatly aid in soil moisture conservation. If a season-long, granulated, bedding plant–type fertilizer is applied at planting time, no additional fertilization should be necessary. If you prefer water-soluble or liquid fertilizers, apply according to label directions as needed through the season. Remember, always read and follow label directions.

ADDITIONAL INFORMATION

Celosias of all types work well as cut flowers when used indoors. Select your cut flowers in early morning before midday heat.

ADDITIONAL SPECIES, CULTIVARS, OR VARIETIES

Some of the popular cultivars, or cultivated varieties, include 'Jewel Box', 'Corona', 'Century Mixed', 'Apricot Brandy', 'Red Fox', 'Forest Fire', 'Flamingo Feather', 'Dwarf Fairy Fountains', 'Prestige Scarlet', and 'Kimono Mixed'.

Coleus
Coleus × hybridus

EXPOSURE

F. Sun to Shade

COLD HARDINESS

Annual

WATER USAGE

Semi-Moist

GROWTH RATE

Fast

AVG. HT × WIDTH

8–36″ (v.)

SPACING

1–3′

A foliage plant with colors of chartreuse, red, pink, white, maroon, bronze, and yellow.

*I*n my hometown of Brownwood, Texas, on Oakland Drive, our yard was blessed with many shade trees. When I was in the Navy, I mentioned to a sailor from New Jersey that my family had 73 oak trees in our yard. He thought this was a "Texas tale," but it was absolutely true. Because of the shade in the yard, Mom had to look for plants that would grow in shady conditions, and coleus was one of those. She once grew a particular variety of the old-fashioned coleus that was nearly 6 ft. high. Most of the varieties that we use and grow today in our home, as well as in commercial landscapes, are not of the old varieties; they are hybrids. Though hybrids are not quite as tall, we do enjoy a vast array of colors, textures, and forms because of hybridization. Some varieties available today will grow not only in shaded areas, but also in full-sun locations. If you plan to grow coleus in the Texas summer sun, make sure that you purchase varieties that are propagated by cuttings. The seed-grown coleus does not hold up in the Texas sun as well as do those grown from cuttings.

WHEN TO PLANT
The best time for installing coleus in your home landscape is when all danger of frost is past in the early spring.

WHERE TO PLANT

Coleus are often used in shaded areas. This is wonderful in our Texas landscapes, because in these areas we are rather limited as far as good color is concerned. They work well in front of evergreen shrubbery in these shaded areas. They work equally well in beds in and among shade trees. Certain varieties work well in containers. These containers may be terracotta, plastic, wood, or any other materials of your choosing. Try hanging baskets of coleus. I've done this for many years and they work marvelously well. Some varieties will grow in full-sun locations, but they require more care because coleus has a high moisture requirement.

HOW TO PLANT

Plant your selected transplants in well-prepared beds. If your beds are not thoroughly improved, here is what you can do: blend 3 in. of top-quality organic material including compost, brown sphagnum peat moss, and ground bark into the top 3 in. of the existing soil. Install your transplants no deeper than their soilball, firm the soil around your newly planted plants, water thoroughly, apply root stimulator according to label directions, and after the planting is complete, mulch the entire area with approximately 3 in. of bark mulch.

CARE AND MAINTENANCE

Sucking insects may visit coleus throughout the growing season. If they visit your plantings, take a trip to your local retail garden center, which will offer several control possibilities. Remember, always read and follow label directions on any product you decide to purchase and use. Keep blooms pinched from your coleus plantings. Maintain a moist soil throughout the entire growing season. Do not let the plants dry out. Continue to maintain the 3-in. layer of mulch throughout the entire growing season to reduce the need for and conserve water. Proper plant nutrition can be accomplished by adding an encapsulated season-long fertilizer at planting time or by applying water-soluble fertilizers as needed.

ADDITIONAL INFORMATION

You may find some coleus that you would like to enjoy through the fall and winter. In late fall, before any frost, use lightweight potting soil and place several in containers to grow indoors on sunny windowsills.

ADDITIONAL SPECIES, CULTIVARS, OR VARIETIES

Here are some varieties that you might want to try: 'Molten Lava', 'Scarlet Poncho', and 'Dragon Sunset'. There is an entire group called 'Wizard' which includes 'Pink', 'Pastel', 'Pineapple', 'Scarlet', and 'Golden Wizard'. 'Milky Way' is a dwarf variety. Try these sun coleus varieties: 'Alabama Sunset', 'Burgundy Sun', and 'Plum Parfait'.

Copper Plant
Acalypha wilkesiana

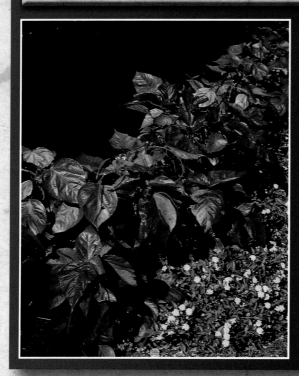

EXPOSURE	COLD HARDINESS
F. Sun to Semi-	Annual

WATER USAGE	GROWTH RATE
Arid to Semi-Mst.	Fast

AVG. HT × WIDTH	SPACING
2–4' × 3–4'	3–4'

Grown for its coppery color foliage. Very tolerant of Texas summer heat and sun.

*T*he sun-loving copper plant is one of my favorite summertime color plants. These are wonderful as background plants and they will take all the heat that the sun can dish out. I often utilize them in containers as the center planting in large 15-gallon nursery containers. I plant some solid white periwinkle around the outside edges, allowing them to cascade down. These particular plants are used on our driveway. These are in black nursery containers set out on black asphalt, and they continue to grow and give us outstanding color all season long. A color plant for Texas gardeners doesn't get much tougher.

WHEN TO PLANT
Copper plants love warmth, so do not set them out until the air temperature is consistently above 65, preferably 70, degrees Fahrenheit at night. I usually set mine out after Easter. The plants will give you color all the way to the first hard freeze in the fall.

WHERE TO PLANT
You may use copper plant virtually anywhere in your home landscape where you have full-sun locations that receive at least 6 to 8 hours of sun per day. Do

not plant in heavily shaded areas—it will not grow properly, nor will you see the great coppery color. It is wonderful in background settings with an array of color in front of them. Use it as a background, and place salvia, periwinkle, lantana, or other Texas heat-tolerant color plants in front. It may be used to divide areas, or it may be used as a specimen plant. I have even seen these plants trained into small annual trees. If space is limited and you have a sunny area, consider a tree-form copper plant.

How to Plant

When grown as bedding plants, make sure that the soil is well improved. Here is how you can accomplish that: add 3 in. of high-quality organic matter to the native soil in your beds. Blend the organic matter with the top 3 in. of your existing soil. High-quality organic matter includes compost (homemade or commercial), ground-bark mulch, and brown sphagnum peat moss. After blending the soil with your organic matter, the bed will be ready to plant. Install your selected copper plant no deeper than the soilball. Firm the soil well around your newly transplanted selections, water thoroughly, and apply a root stimulator according to label directions. After the planting is complete, mulch with 3 in. of high-quality selected shredded bark; I usually use pine bark. In containers, use a lightweight premium-quality potting soil of your choice. Plant at the same depth you would plant in a bed.

Care and Maintenance

I have experienced no serious pest problems in my years of growing copper plants outdoors. If desired, you may shape or prune to specific forms throughout the growing season. You may take cuttings from your copper plant to be rooted for additional plant materials. To ensure good results with copper plants, water sufficiently to prevent soil dryness. Do not overwater or keep wet. Maintain a season-long layer of mulch to conserve soil moisture, therefore reducing the need for watering. You may fertilize with several different types of fertilizer products, including water-solubles, liquids, specialty granular fertilizers, or encapsulated season-long fertilizers. Whatever type of fertilizer you choose, remember to read and follow label directions.

Additional Information

Copper plants are usually available in 4- to 6-in. and 1-gallon containers. To achieve immediate visual impact, select larger containers. When planting masses of copper plants, go for the 4-in. pot.

Additional Species, Cultivars, or Varieties

Varieties include common and 'Louisiana Red', which looks like its parent but has much larger leaves, making for a showy foliage of red, bronze, and pink. Additional varieties exist, but Common and 'Louisiana Red' are the most widely available varieties.

Dianthus or Sweet William

Dianthus chinensis and *barbatus*

EXPOSURE

F. Sun to Semi-

COLD HARDINESS

Cool-Season Ann.

WATER USAGE

Semi-Moist

GROWTH RATE

Fast

AVG. HT × WIDTH

4–18″ × 6–12″ (v.)

SPACING

8–12″

Has fine green to gray-green foliage and small "pinked' blooms in white, pink, red, and blends.

"**P**inks" (as dianthus is often called in Texas) are staples of cool-season color in our Texas gardens. While it is true their color is pink, they are also available in white, red, and blends—so not all pinks are pink. Why are they called pinks? Here are a couple of possible answers. You decide which one is most likely to be correct. The first species used in our gardens may indeed have been pink and subsequent species and varieties simply retained the name. Another possibility: the bloom edges look as if they have been "pinked" by a pair of pinking shears. But no matter how this family received its name, dianthus, or pinks, are wonderful additions to our Texas color gardens. Some are classified as biennial and others as short-lived perennials, but they often behave and are used as annuals in our landscapes. Pinks do best in cool weather. They are often planted in the fall or very early spring. Not only are they colorful, nearly all are fragrant.

WHEN TO PLANT

For color during fall and mild winters, plant transplants in very late summer after high temperatures are gone for the year, or plant in very early fall. For spring to early summer color, set out transplants in late winter/early spring after the danger of hard freezes and killing frosts. Start seeds for transplants approximately 6 weeks before planting in the landscape.

WHERE TO PLANT

For best results, plant in areas of good soil drainage with morning sun and afternoon shade. They may be grown in daylong full-sun locations, but their blooming season will be shortened. The shorter varieties are excellent as border plants, while the taller ones are great background plants and cut flowers. They may be grown and enjoyed in large containers by themselves or mixed with additional flowering plants such as lobelia and verbena. The fragrance of dianthus is most pleasing, and we Texas gardeners like to use them near our entryways. In these applications, pinks may be utilized in containers or beds. Both work well. They are also pleasant in containers around decks, pools, benches, swings, or other garden spots we enjoy.

HOW TO PLANT

I prefer setting dianthus out from transplants. Set the selected transplants into well-amended beds at the same depth as their soilball, firm the soil, water thoroughly, and apply root stimulator. After the entire planting is complete, mulch with 3 in. of bark mulch. Improve the soil by blending 3 in. of high-quality organic matter with the top 3 in. of the native soil. Do not plant in poorly drained, wet or difficult-to-water soils.

CARE AND MAINTENANCE

Aphids may visit tender growth, but this usually isn't a serious problem. If the need arises, you may have to use some kind of chemical control. Remember, always read and follow label directions when applying any aid. Maintain a moist, but not wet soil, and maintain a season-long 3-in. layer of bark mulch. This helps to conserve soil moisture, control weeds, and moderate soil temperatures. When transplanting, fertilize with a season-long encapsulated fertilizer, or as needed with water-soluble fertilizers. Always read and follow label directions. You may remove spent blooms if desired.

ADDITIONAL INFORMATION

Have some fun and introduce a little one to "Lady Di." Little gardeners enjoy Lady Di, or dianthus, so be sure to let them plant some.

ADDITIONAL SPECIES, CULTIVARS, OR VARIETIES

Some *D. barbatus* varieties are 'Roundabout', 'Indian Carpet', 'Summer Beauty', 'Dunnets Dark Crimson', 'Harlequin', and 'Dwarf Double Pinnochio'. You may wish to try *D. chinensis* 'Fire Carpet', 'Raspberry Parfait', 'Snowfire', 'Telstar', and 'Lilliput' as well as the 'Ideal Series' and the 'Floral Lace Series'.

Flowering Cabbage
Brassica oleracea

EXPOSURE

F. Sun to Semi-

COLD HARDINESS

0°–10°

WATER USAGE

Semi-Moist

GROWTH RATE

Medium

AVG. HT × WIDTH

10–18″ × 10–12″ (v.)

SPACING

12″

Forms high round heads. Masses of very colorful leaves in white, carmine, purple, and cream.

*S*ometimes you will find flowering (sometimes called ornamental) cabbage or kale listed as "edible." Of course taste is a subjective thing and beauty is in the eye of the beholder. My taste may not be the same as yours, so try the taste of flowering cabbage or kale and see if you like it. Some folks feel it is a bit too bitter. One of the best uses of flowering kale and cabbage is in masses of single color. If you like the purple one, plant masses of that. You might also use them to outline beds of other cool-season plants such as calendula, pansies, or dianthus.

WHEN TO PLANT

The best time to plant flowering kale and cabbage for most Texas gardeners is in very early fall when things are cool.

WHERE TO PLANT

Flowering kale and cabbage are wonderful when used near front entries or back entries or any place where you want eye appeal. They may also be used in beds near the curb and are quite attractive when used this way. For best color, do not plant in the shade. They perform much better in full-sun locations which provide at least 6 to 8 hours of sunlight per day. Do not plant in heavy clay soil without first improving with organic matter, and do not plant in poorly drained areas. Flowering kale and cabbage also work well in large containers. They may serve as a central focal point or be part of a mass color pot.

HOW TO PLANT

Flowering kale and cabbage do best in improved soil. Here is how to do it: Blend 3 in. of high-quality organic matter such as brown sphagnum peat moss, compost, and ground-bark mulch with the top 3 in. of your existing soil. In the well-prepared planting bed, insert your transplants no deeper than they were originally grown in the container. Firm the soil around them, water thoroughly, and apply root stimulator according to label directions. After the entire planting is complete, mulch the bed with 3 in. of bark mulch. If planting in containers, use a premium-quality, lightweight potting soil.

CARE AND MAINTENANCE

Cabbage loopers or aphids may visit your flowering kale and cabbage but normally are not serious problems, although some type of control may be necessary. Remember, always read and follow label directions when using any gardening aid. Very little pruning is required. You may wish to remove an unsightly leaf from time to time. Apply sufficient water to ensure moist growing conditions, but do not overwater. Maintaining a season-long mulch layer will greatly aid in soil moisture conservation. If a season-long encapsulated bedding plant fertilizer was applied at planting time, no additional fertilization will be necessary. But if you prefer water-soluble fertilizers, apply according to label directions as needed through the season. Remember to read and follow label directions when using fertilizers.

ADDITIONAL INFORMATION

In the southern part of our state in Zones 8 and 9, flowering kale and cabbage may give winter color all through the season till spring heat arrives. In Zones 6 and 7, they are still worth planting because they give you some spectacular early fall colors.

ADDITIONAL SPECIES, CULTIVARS, OR VARIETIES

Flowering kale and cabbage normally are sold as just white, pink, or mixed. The 'Northern Lights' Series is available in white, pink, rose, and mixed. 'Cherry Sundae' is available in patterns of carmine and cream. Flowering kale is available in Red and White Peacock as well as 'Nasoya'. These are sometimes described as looking like snowflakes.

Geranium
Pelargonium × hortorum

EXPOSURE

Semi-Shade

COLD HARDINESS

Annual

WATER USAGE

Semi-Moist

GROWTH RATE

Fast to Med.

AVG. HT × WIDTH

12–24″ × 10–12″ (v.)

SPACING

10–12″

Upright to open, medium- to dark-green fuzzy-leaved annual. Flowers normally held in clusters of pink, red, bronze, maroon, and white.

*E*very year when springtime rolls around, my wife Judy needs to have some geraniums, and I'm sure that if you have a chance to enjoy their beauty, you like to have some too. Geraniums may be grown as bedding plants in masses, or in individual containers such as large terracotta pots, planters, and hanging baskets. While red tends to be the traditional color of geraniums, today there are wonderful varieties of coral, pink, white, and blends. Some even have very colorful foliage. Some geraniums not only come with colorful blossoms and interesting foliage, but are also scented; this group of geraniums is simply called scented geraniums.

WHEN TO PLANT
Plant geraniums in the early spring after all danger of frost is past in either 4- or 5-in. pots.

WHERE TO PLANT
Some references will refer to geranium as a full-sun plant. Writers of these guides must be writing about Canada or some other northern climate, but not

Texas. In Texas, plant geraniums where they receive morning sun, but shade them from the hot west afternoon sun. Plants grown this way should give you long bloom periods. But even some of the plants grown in shaded areas will stop blooming in midsummer due to our tremendous heat. Geraniums can be successfully grown in containers. I have grown them in 14-in. terracotta pots and have had some as long as 5 years. They work well not only in terracotta, but in plastic or even in wooden planters that you may design and fashion yourself.

How to Plant

In order for geraniums to do well, do not plant them in poorly drained areas or heavy clay soil, but plant in well-drained, improved beds. Incorporate 3 in. of high-quality organic matter into your existing native soil. Part of your organic matter may consist of ground-bark mulch, brown sphagnum peat moss, or compost. I prefer a little of all three. Remove your geraniums from the container and insert them into the soil to the depth of the plant's soilball. Firm the soil around the plant. Water thoroughly and apply root stimulator according to label directions. After planting is complete, mulch with 3 in. of bark mulch. When planting in containers, use a good-quality, lightweight premium potting soil.

Care and Maintenance

I have experienced no serious pests with geraniums planted outdoors. If pests do become a problem on your geraniums, consider some control possibilities. Remember to read and follow label directions on any product you use. Remove spent bloom heads to help ensure continuous blooming throughout the entire season. Water deeply and thoroughly, but do not overwater. Geraniums will not tolerate a wet soil. Maintain a thick layer of bark mulch throughout the entire growing season. Geraniums need to be well nourished in order to do their best. This can be accomplished by applying slow-release granular-type fertilizers, water-soluble fertilizers, or encapsulated fertilizers that last throughout the growing season. The choice is yours, but remember to read and follow label directions.

Additional Information

There are many different types of geranium. Take a look at some of the more unusual or different types such as 'Martha Washington'.

Species, Cultivars, or Varieties

Try some of these: 'Avante', 'Salmon', 'Break Away Salmon', 'Classic Scarlet', 'Eye Right', 'Hollywood Star', 'Apple Blossom', 'Violet', 'Improved Scarlet', 'Playboy Speckles', 'Raspberry Ripple', 'Tango Orange', 'Vogue Apple Blossom', 'Summer Showers', 'Summertime Lilac', 'Cherry Border', 'Designer Series', 'Showcase', 'Starburst', 'Galleria', and 'Scarlet Border'—and don't forget the scented cousins.

Impatiens
Impatiens walleriana

EXPOSURE

Shade

COLD HARDINESS

Annual

WATER USAGE

Moist

GROWTH RATE

Fast

AVG. HT × WIDTH

6–18″ × 10″–2′

SPACING

12″

Succulent, multiflowered plant in white, red, scarlet, mauve, orchid, purple, and bicolors. Perennial, but grown as an annual.

*O*ne of the most enjoyable plants in my gardening experience for shaded areas is impatiens, also known as busy Lizzie or sultana. Whatever name you choose to call this very colorful plant, try some in the shaded areas of your home. If you've read guides that say impatiens can be used in full-sun locations, it is not in reference to Texas. While shooting a television show in Winnipeg, Canada, one July, I had an opportunity to see impatiens grown in full-sun in that area. They were magnificent. Their colors were outstanding and the foliage was gorgeous. But that was Canada. Impatiens may be used in beds of single colors, most striking in a landscape. They are also extremely effective in hanging baskets or other containers.

WHEN TO PLANT
The best time to plant impatiens is in the spring, approximately 2 weeks after all danger of frost is past.

WHERE TO PLANT
The very best locations for impatiens in our Texas summertime gardens is in the shade in planting beds where they are easily watered. The shorter varieties

make excellent border plants. Short, low-growing varieties of impatiens can be used in a border with taller-growing varieties of coleus as background plants. Both have similar watering requirements. They make interesting statements of color when used in color beds around trees or other shaded structures. Windowboxes in shady locations are often successfully filled with impatiens.

How to Plant
Impatiens need to be planted in an improved, moisture-holding soil. For soil improvement, use a combination of compost and brown sphagnum peat moss. Use about 1$\frac{1}{2}$ in. of each of these two with 3 in. of the native soil, tilled together for a high-quality planting bed. Insert your transplants into the well-prepared bed at soilball depth. Water thoroughly. Apply root stimulator according to the label and mulch the bed; when planting is complete, mulch with 3 in. of bark. When planting in containers, use a premium-quality lightweight potting soil and plant at the same depth.

Care and Maintenance
Mealybugs may visit impatiens but I have not had a serious problem with any insects on these plants. If insects become a problem that requires treatment or control, be sure to consult with your Lowe's customer service associate. Remember to always read and follow label directions when using any garden aid. Midsummer pruning may be necessary with impatiens in order to improve their overall struc-ture. Maintain a moist soil throughout the growing season. Impatiens are considered a high-water-requirement plant and will be one of the first to wilt in the landscape. Drip irrigation will help to maintain an even soil moisture throughout the growing season, and may even save you up to 50 percent on your water bill. Maintain a thick layer of mulch to conserve soil moisture. Impatiens respond quite favorably to seasonal applications of water-soluble fertilizers, liquid fertilizers, or specially granulated fertilizers when applied according to label directions.

Additional Information
Impatiens are easy to propagate from cuttings. Make your cuttings in early spring.

Additional Species, Cultivars, or Varieties
The following are just a few to try: 'Accent Bright Eye', 'Blitz Orange', 'Blue Pearl', 'Cleopatra', 'Dazzler', 'Deco Red', 'Deco Pink', 'Fiesta', 'Impulse Apple Blossom', 'Mega Orange Star', 'Mosaic Lilac', 'Star Bright', 'Super Swirl', 'Apricot', 'Blush', 'Burgundy', 'Lavender', 'Rose', 'Salmon', 'Scarlet', and 'White'. Among the New Guinea varieties, which also have colorful foliage, are 'Blake', 'Spectra Salmon', 'Celebration', and 'Tango'.

Marigold
Tagetes erecta and *patula*

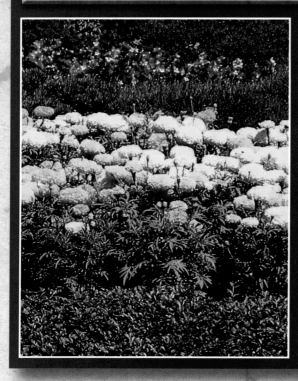

EXPOSURE	COLD HARDINESS
F. Sun to Semi-	Annual

WATER USAGE	GROWTH RATE
Arid to Semi-Mst.	Fast

AVG. HT × WIDTH	SPACING
6–36″ × 10–18″	12″

Tall, upright annual with dark-green, finely cut foliage and flowers of orange, yellow, mahogany, gold, lemon, and near-white.

*M*arigolds are without a doubt my favorite annual blooming plant. Mom and Granny Miller started their marigolds from seeds. These plants are among the easier annuals to start from seed if you choose to begin your season of color this way. Marigolds have been grown for centuries in various cultures, and today there are even more interesting forms and exciting colors available.

WHEN TO PLANT
Marigolds are subject to frost and freeze, so don't plant until all danger of frost has passed in your part of Texas.

WHERE TO PLANT
Marigolds require full sun at least 6 to 8 hours per day in order to do well. They will grow in sandy or clay soil, as long as that soil is improved.

HOW TO PLANT
Here is how you can improve the soil for marigolds, no matter what type of plant you have. Add approximately 3 in. of good-quality organic matter,

including compost, ground-bark mulch, and brown sphagnum peat moss, and till into the native soil. I like to purchase my marigolds ready to set out. I do not necessarily look for those that have lots of buds on them or blooms, just nice, dark-green transplants that are short, compact, and healthy. After making your selections, insert the transplants into your improved bed, no deeper than the soilball. Firm the soil, water thoroughly, and apply root stimulator. After the planting is complete, apply a 3-in. layer of bark mulch. Marigolds also work well in all manner of container plantings, be they large bathtubs, barrels cut in half, large nursery containers, pots, or hanging baskets. The smallest container that I would attempt to grow marigolds in for the season is 12 in. in diameter. Plant in the containers at the same depth you would if you were planting in an entire bed.

CARE AND MAINTENANCE

The marigold pest most prevalent in Texas is spider mites. When it gets hot and dry late in the season, spider mites may visit your plants. If this becomes a problem, ask your Lowe's customer service associate about control possibilities. Read and follow label directions when using any lawn and garden aid. Deadhead (remove spent blossoms) if desired. Water enough to prevent soil dryness and to better ensure good results in growth as well as blooms. Maintain an even soil moisture, but do not overwater. It is easier to maintain an even soil moisture if your beds are properly mulched with 3 in. of bark mulch. Marigolds benefit from a fertile soil. This can be accomplished by the use of special granular fertilizers, water-soluble fertilizers, liquid fertilizers, or encapsulated fertilizers that you apply one time at the beginning of the season. Remember, read and follow label directions.

ADDITIONAL INFORMATION

Try some marigolds in hanging baskets. The short bushy variety of marigolds works very well in hanging baskets.

ADDITIONAL SPECIES, CULTIVARS, OR VARIETIES

Some of the varieties and types you may wish to try include 'Cracker Jack' varieties, gold and vanilla, and the Inca colors of 'Gold', 'Orange', 'Super Yellow', 'Moonbeam', 'Sumo', 'Aurora Yellow Fire', 'Fire Flame', 'Golden Gate', 'Gold Finch', 'Gypsy Sunshine', 'Honeycomb', 'Mr. Majestic', 'Queen Sophia', 'Scarlet Sophia', 'Red Southern Star', 'Safari Volero', 'Spanish Brocade', 'Striped Marble', 'Tiger Eyes', 'Susie Wong', 'Golden Gem', 'Lemon Gem', 'Paprika', and 'Star Fire'. Normally we do not plant marigolds late in the season, but horticulturist Greg Grant's trials in San Antonio were instrumental in selecting marigolds for this use. The two types found to work well are 'Discovery' and 'Voyager'. They are often called mari-mums and may be labeled as such at your local nursery. Try some, they are great!

Morning Glory
Ipomoea purpurea

EXPOSURE

F. Sun to Semi-

COLD HARDINESS

Annual

WATER USAGE

Semi-Moist

GROWTH RATE

Fast-Vine

AVG. HT × WIDTH

Varies

SPACING

As Trained

Vining, large-leaved, flowering plant with colors of white, purple, pink, red, and blue, as well as scarlet and crimson; perennial to annual.

Morning glories are flowers that Texas gardeners have grown in our land-scapes for generations, raising them successfully since the 1700s, if not before. You won't find an easier flowering vine to grow. There are many different colors and forms of morning glory. Some in the frost-free areas will remain with us year after year, and we call those perennials. Use the same plant in areas where it is not hardy, and it will freeze out in the wintertime. We call those half-hardy perennials and grow them as annuals.

WHEN TO PLANT
The best time to plant morning glories is in the springtime after all danger of frost is past and the soil is warm.

WHERE TO PLANT
Morning glory starts very easily when directly seeded into the soil. It requires a well-drained location, and sandy soils are preferred. To do well, it needs a location with a minimum of 6 hrs. of full sun. Don't plant in heavily shaded areas or poorly drained soils. These plants are extremely useful for summer-

time flowering screens. They may be used on any type of structure such as trellises, gazebos, fences, and other gardening structures. You may work with your little ones at home and help them construct a simple trellis of some scrap lumber and string. They will enjoy their structure with morning glory plantings.

HOW TO PLANT

Seeds planted directly will germinate in 7 to 30 days. That is quite a long time, and germination can be hastened by nicking each of the large seeds with a pocket knife, grinder, or hacksaw. An alternative to nicking the seeds is to soak them 24 to 48 hours in warm water. These procedures will greatly speed up and increase the percentage of germination. If you live in an area of Texas that has clay soil, be sure to improve it greatly so that it drains rapidly. These plants will not tolerate wet locations, poorly drained locations, or heavy soils that are not amended. To improve your heavy soils, incorporate 3 in. of high-quality organic matter into the top 3 in. of the soil. If you wish to start from transplants, insert them in your prepared bed no deeper than they were originally grown in their containers. Firm the soil well, water thoroughly, apply root stimulator, and mulch with about 3 in. of bark mulch. Morning glory is excellent in large containers, especially if you have erected an upright structure. Use a premium-quality lightweight potting soil for container planting.

CARE AND MAINTENANCE

Morning glory is virtually insect and disease free. No pruning is necessary, but you may wish to train your morning glory to grow in a specific direction. Water as necessary to prevent wilting. Morning glory requires a minimum amount of nutrition in order to do well. One application of fertilizer early in the spring is beneficial. Remember to read and follow label directions.

ADDITIONAL INFORMATION

There are many different varieties and types of morning glory. It is one of those old-fashioned plants that you may have forgotten. It is extremely tough and durable.

ADDITIONAL SPECIES, CULTIVARS, OR VARIETIES

Try these: *I. nil, I. purpurea, I. alba, I. tricolor,* and the cultivars 'Mini Sky-blue', 'Scarlet Star', 'Heavenly Blue', 'Roman Candle', 'Early Call Mixed', 'Pearly Gates', and 'Scarlett O'Hara'.

Pansy
Viola × wittrockiana

EXPOSURE

F. Sun to Semi-

COLD HARDINESS

Cool-Season Ann.

WATER USAGE

Semi-Moist

GROWTH RATE

Fast

AVG. HT × WIDTH

8–12" × 12"

SPACING

8–10"

Bushy form, perennial, can be grown as an annual in a rainbow of colors.

*P*ansies are a long-time staple of Texas gardens. If you are new to our area and want to plant pansies at the beginning of summer: don't do it. Spring/summer planting works fine if you are in Indiana, the Northeastern states, or Canada, but not in Texas. Pansies provide outstanding fall and winter color in Zones 7, 8, and 9. They are most striking in the landscape when one color is used in masses, as is often seen at botanical gardens.

WHEN TO PLANT

The best time to plant pansies is early fall when nighttime temperatures have cooled to the 60s. In most of Texas, this plant group will give us some color through the entire winter. Even though they look awful after a hard freeze, give them a little sunlight and time. They will pop right back out and continue to grow and bloom right on through the wintertime.

WHERE TO PLANT

In the fall and through the winter, there is nothing more spectacular than mass plantings of pansies at theme parks or botanical gardens. The average Texas gardener can pick up hints from the way these pansies are used. Pansies are tops when planted as a splash of color by the entryways to our homes. They also work well in large containers on the front porch, back porch, or other areas that need some color during the fall, winter and early spring. Do not plant pansies in shaded areas or where the soil drains poorly.

HOW TO PLANT

Blend 3 in. of high-quality organic matter with the top 3 in. of your existing soil. High-quality organic matter includes compost, brown sphagnum peat moss, and ground-bark mulch. After your bed is improved, set your transplants approximately 6 to 8 in. apart, in a checkerboard pattern for outstanding impact. Plant no deeper than the soilball. Firm the soil around the transplants, water thoroughly, apply root stimulator according to the label directions, and mulch with 2 in. of bark mulch. To grow pansies in containers: Select the type of container desired, fill with a loose premium-quality lightweight potting soil, and follow the same procedures as in ground plantings.

CARE AND MAINTENANCE

Aphids or slugs and snails may visit your pansies. If they become a problem, ask your Lowe's customer service associate about control possibilities. Remember to read and follow label directions when you use any gardening aid. Deadheading is beneficial and tidies up the planting. Maintain a moist soil during the growing season to ensure better pansy growth, bloom, health, and vigor. Nutrition may be supplied by the use of water-soluble, special granular, liquid, or encapsulated fertilizers. Remember to read and follow label directions.

ADDITIONAL INFORMATION

Pansies are considered a tough plant in Texas. They have been used for decades and decades in our home landscapes. Pansies are often said to have funny faces on them. Certain types of pansies do have faces, and the little gardeners at your home love funny-faced flowers. Let them try growing some pansies this year.

ADDITIONAL SPECIES, CULTIVARS, OR VARIETIES

Some of the larger-flowered varieties are 'Burning', 'Clear Sky Primrose', 'Scarlet Crown', 'Yellow Splash', 'Imperial Flame Princess', 'Blackberry Rose', 'Frost Rose', 'Pink Shades', 'Raspberry Rose', 'Silver Princess', 'Joker Viola Gold', 'Jolly Joker', 'Love Duet', 'Maximum Marina', 'Melody Sunrise', 'Paper White', 'Wine Gold', 'Rippling Waters', 'Silver Wings', 'Spanish Sun', 'Majestic Giant' series, and also try the 'Crystal Bowl' series for outstanding bloom color and the 'Bingo' series.

Periwinkle
Catharanthus roseus

EXPOSURE

F. Sun to Semi-

COLD HARDINESS

Annual

WATER USAGE

Semi-Moist, D.T.

GROWTH RATE

Fast

AVG. HT × WIDTH

6–12" × 12–14"

SPACING

12"

Dark-green foliage with blooms of white, pink, and purple, slightly mounding to spreading in form.

*P*eriwinkle is also called annual vinca. This is because it is similar in foliage and bloom shape to the groundcover vinca. If you happen to be looking for a heat- and sun-tolerant plant that will provide color throughout the entire season, periwinkle is the answer. It is often used in masses to create outstanding groundcover effects. These plants are excellent as filler plants and work equally well when container grown. I use solid white periwinkles in large black plastic containers of a 10- to 15-gallon size with copper plants in the center. This combination gives lasting outstanding color. I believe it can truly be said that periwinkles are "Texas flameproof." They continue to bloom and do well in spite of all the heat thrown at them throughout the entire state.

WHEN TO PLANT
The best time to plant periwinkles is in the spring after all danger of frost is past from your area. If you don't know when the last average killing frost date is, ask your Lowe's customer service associate or Extension Agent.

WHERE TO PLANT

Periwinkles are versatile, but they do have a couple of requirements that must be met. Do not plant in heavy clay soil, wet locations, poorly drained locations, or heavily shaded areas. To do their best, periwinkles need a full-sun location providing at least 6 hours of sunlight per day and a well-draining soil that is fertile yet moist. They may be planted along entryways to your home or along your driveway. They work equally well in large containers on a deck, around a pool, and near water features, gazebos, and garden benches, or any place in your home landscape where you wish to enjoy containers of outstanding color. They are also great in various bed applications. Whether used as border plants or cascading down rock gardens, you will find them very useful in the home landscape.

HOW TO PLANT

Blend 3 in. of organic matter into the top 3 in. of your existing soil. High-quality organic matter includes brown sphagnum peat moss, compost, and ground-bark mulch. Till or blend the organic matter into the soil with your favorite shovel or digging fork and you will be ready to plant. Select your periwinkles and remove them from their containers. Set the new transplants into the prepared bed at the same level they were growing in their containers, and firm the soil. Water thoroughly, apply root stimulator according to label directions, and mulch thoroughly with 2 to 3 in. of bark mulch. To plant in containers, fill near the top with a premium-quality, lightweight potting soil. Plant as when planting in beds.

CARE AND MAINTENANCE

In years of growing periwinkles, I have had no insect or disease problems in my plantings. Should pests or diseases decide to invade your plantings, investigate some control possibilities. Remember to read and follow label directions on any product you use. No pruning should be necessary. Water often enough to prevent soil dryness and ensure good growth and bloom all season long. Periwinkles need to be nourished throughout the entire growing season with water-soluble, special granular, liquid, or encapsulated fertilizers applied according to label directions.

ADDITIONAL INFORMATION

When looking for a plant that virtually anyone can grow—even the person who says he or she can't grow anything—try periwinkles. They are just about foolproof.

ADDITIONAL SPECIES, CULTIVARS, OR VARIETIES

Try some of these periwinkles in your home landscape: 'Apricot Delight', 'Pacifica Red', 'Parasol', 'Peppermint Cooler', 'Velvet Rose', 'Tropica', 'Terrace Vermilion' and the 'Cooler' series.

Petunia
Petunia × hybrida

EXPOSURE
F. Sun to Semi-

COLD HARDINESS
Annual

WATER USAGE
Arid to Semi-Mst.

GROWTH RATE
Fast

AVG. HT × WIDTH
6–18" × 12–24"

SPACING
12–18"

Mounding, cascading, and upright in form, medium- to dark-green, fuzzy-leaved annual in a rainbow of color blooms.

My experience with petunias in Texas is that the single-petal varieties tend to be more heat resistant. Two of these groups are 'Summer Madness' and 'Carpet' series. Petunias are usually a cool-season plant in Texas. They like the cool spring, early summer, and early fall for growing. I've had several complaints on my call-in radio shows about the petunias in midsummer that just fizzle out. My suggestion: if you are looking for petunias that grow all season, ask for heat-resistant varieties. Otherwise, grow these gorgeous annuals in the cooler seasons of the year in containers or landscape beds. When they reach a stage when they're no longer active, remove them and install heat-resistant summer annuals.

WHEN TO PLANT
The best time to plant petunias is very early spring, approximately 2 weeks after the last average killing frost in your area. If you don't know this date, check with your local nursery people or County Extension Agent. Some gardeners also enjoy planting petunias in very early fall. Petunias will resist light frost and stay with you up until the first hard freeze.

WHERE TO PLANT

In order for petunias to thrive, they need to be planted in a moist, fertile soil that drains well. Petunias work wonderfully as beds of color early in the year or even during early fall. Certain varieties are often used in hanging baskets or other hanging containers, or in large containers. The most striking petunia effect is accomplished by using many of one variety or color together, a practice common at arboretums throughout our great state.

HOW TO PLANT

Add organic matter to your soil in the form of brown sphagnum peat moss, compost, and ground-bark mulch. Add approximately 1 in. of each one of these three to the top 3 in. of your soil. Blend thoroughly and you will have a bed approximately 6 in. deep, ready for petunia planting. Remove your selected petunias from their containers and insert them soilball-deep into the prepared bed. Firm the soil well, water thoroughly, apply root stimulator, and mulch the entire planting with approximately 2 in. of bark mulch. When planting in containers, fill near the top with a premium lightweight potting soil and follow directions given for planting in a bed.

CARE AND MAINTENANCE

My petunias have suffered no pest problems. If pests decide to visit your planting, seek help from your Lowe's customer service associate, who can offer you several possibilities for control. Remember to read and follow label directions on any product you choose to control insect pests. Minimal to no pruning is required. Water petunias sufficiently to maintain a moist, but not wet, soil throughout the entire season. Nutrition can be added one of several ways, including long-lasting slow-release, specialty-type granular, water-soluble, liquid, or encapsulated fertilizers that are applied once at planting time. Be sure to read and follow label directions.

ADDITIONAL INFORMATION

Petunias are known to be flowers loved by children. You may want to let your favorite little gardener try some petunias in the springtime. Red seems to be their favorite color, so a single-petal, red-blooming, heat-resistant variety is ideal for these little ones.

ADDITIONAL SPECIES, CULTIVARS, OR VARIETIES

Among the many varieties are 'Merlin', 'Big Daddy', 'Blue Sky', 'Celebrity Pink Morn', 'Cloud Mix', 'Flame Carpet', 'Madness Plum Crazy', 'Madness Series', 'Pastel Salmon', 'Plum Purple', 'Starship', 'Summer Sun', 'Summer Cascade Series', 'Ultra Star Series', 'Wave Series', 'Purple Waves', 'Pink Waves', 'White Magic', 'Double Delight', 'Caprice', 'White Swan' and 'V.I.P.'.

Portulaca
Portulaca grandiflora

EXPOSURE

Full Sun

COLD HARDINESS

Annual

WATER USAGE

Arid to Semi-Mst.

GROWTH RATE

Fast

AVG. HT × WIDTH

4–12″ × 8–12″

SPACING

10–12″

Low-growing, spreading annual, small mosslike green leaves, and multitudes of extremely colorful blooms.

*G*ranny Miller always had moss growing in her Indian Creek garden in Brown County, Texas. Years later, I found out that the "moss" Granny grew was portulaca, moss rose, or rose moss—though it was just moss to her. It is a plant that is extremely easy to care for. Granny grew it in an old dishpan that she had discarded. Her garden was an old-fashioned country garden with no grass of any kind in it except for some ornamental grass in the corner. It didn't have a watering system of any kind. If a plant received water, it was carried one bucket at a time, and that would normally be at establishment time. I think we can safely say that moss rose or portulaca is a plant for Texas gardens. It is tough and durable, and quite versatile. It will even grow in pavement cracks.

WHEN TO PLANT
The best time to get your initial start with portulaca is in the spring after all danger of frost is past.

WHERE TO PLANT

Moss rose does well in areas which many other color plants can't tolerate. Moss rose can stand the heat! It can even stand the heat in nearly pure-sand locations. It is marvelous in outlying beds in your home landscape and sunny locations, all the way up to your door so you can enjoy the flowers each morning when they put out their beautiful bright heads for you. They work as well in containers as they did in Granny Miller's big dishpan. They may also be grown successfully in hanging baskets of all sizes.

HOW TO PLANT

While moss rose is quite tolerant of relatively dry areas, it will not tolerate prolonged wet-soil conditions. Don't plant in poorly drained or full-shade locations. To improve the soil, add organic matter in the form of compost, ground bark, or brown sphagnum peat moss. Add approximately 1 in. of one of these 3 ingredients to the soil. Till the organic matter into the top 3 in. of your soil and you will have a bed fit for moss rose the entire season. Remove your transplants from their containers and insert them to the depth of the top of the soilball. Firm soil, water thoroughly, and apply root stimulator. After planting is complete, add an inch or two of bark mulch in and around the planting. When planting in containers, fill with premium-quality lightweight potting soil near the top.

CARE AND MAINTENANCE

I have experienced no insect problems with moss rose through decades of growing it. No pruning is necessary to maintain a good-looking bed. Water enough to prevent soil dryness and to ensure good growth and great blooms throughout the entire season. Apply water-soluble, liquid, or specialty granular fertilizers through the season. Be sure to read and follow label directions.

ADDITIONAL INFORMATION

Moss rose usually closes up in the afternoon.

ADDITIONAL SPECIES, CULTIVARS, OR VARIETIES

There are new varieties of moss rose that stay open longer, in some cases all day. One group is called 'Cloud Beater'. 'Swan Lake' is a stunning, large-flower double. 'Sun Dial Peppermint' is another wonderful one. 'Sun Kissed Hybrid' is one of those that will stay open longer. Some other great-looking ones are 'Double Flowered', 'Rose Colored', 'Daytime', and the 'Sundial Series'.

Salvia
Salvia splendens

EXPOSURE

F. Sun to Semi-

COLD HARDINESS

Annual

WATER USAGE
Semi-Moist

GROWTH RATE
Fast

AVG. HT × WIDTH
6–12" × 8–10"

SPACING
15–20"

Upright-growing, multi-stemmed, medium-green annual with brightly colored blooms.

*T*here are over 750 different types of salvias around the world. In Texas, the one we think of as the bedding salvia is called salvia splendens, red salvia, or sometimes scarlet sage. Whatever name you wish to apply to it, it is a striking plant when used in the home landscape. Salvia may be used in masses in a sunny location where the soil drains well. It is not a color plant for heavily shaded areas, but it will tolerate some light shade. It is equally as striking when used in containers 12 in. or larger of ceramic, terracotta, or plastic, or you may wish to use some planters that you have made. I have seen them used in masses inside hanging baskets for an outstanding color combination with a dark-green basket.

WHEN TO PLANT
The best time to plant salvia is in the early spring after all danger of frost is past.

ANNUALS

WHERE TO PLANT

Salvia splendens requires a well-drained, rich, moist soil. Do not plant in hot, dry locations that are difficult to water, in poorly drained or wet locations, or in shade. For best results, plant salvia where it will receive morning sun with afternoon shade. Salvia is often used in masses in parks of all sorts, including theme parks and municipal parks, as well as arboretums. Try using them the same way in your home landscape. Masses of salvia with their bloom spikes raised high are eye-stoppers, and children love to pause and admire the beauty of salvia when touring parks or visiting homes. Salvia may be planted in entryways and yard beds. They may be used in various types of containers on decks, gazebos, or swings, or in any other area where the outdoors is enjoyed through the use of containers.

HOW TO PLANT

Incorporate 3 in. of high-quality organic matter into the top 3 in. of your soil, using a tiller, digging fork, or shovel. After soil improvement is complete, remove existing plants from their containers and insert them into the soil at soilball level. Firm them in and water thoroughly. Apply root stimulator according to directions, and mulch the entire planting when complete. When planting in containers, be sure to use high-quality lightweight potting soil.

CARE AND MAINTENANCE

Spider mites may appear during hot, dry summers. Should such pests become a problem on your plantings, ask about proper controls. Remember to read and follow label directions. Pruning off spent bloom spikes may be necessary to maintain a more compact and desirable plant. This will also ensure better growth and bloom during the late summer/early fall bloom period. Be sure to maintain even soil moisture—do not keep it wet and do not keep it dry. A drip irrigation system can help in this operation. To help maintain and conserve soil moisture plus moderate some of the extremities in soil temperatures, be sure to maintain about a 3-in. layer of bark mulch over your planting throughout the entire season. Properly nourished salvia will survive stressful situations. Apply the fertilizer of your choice according to label directions.

ADDITIONAL INFORMATION

There are many different types of salvia today. In Texas, there are some salvias that are considered woody, shrubby plants.

ADDITIONAL SPECIES, CULTIVARS, OR VARIETIES

Some varieties are white, pink, rose, red, violet, or cream, or you may wish to try 'Victoria', which is a kind of violet-blue. *S. coccinea* 'Lady In Red' is excellent for Texas gardeners and one of my favorites. It's very easy to grow, will bloom all season long, and tolerates drought conditions.

Snapdragon
Antirrhinum majus

EXPOSURE

F. Sun to Semi-

COLD HARDINESS

Cool-Season Ann.

WATER USAGE

Semi-Moist

GROWTH RATE

Fast

AVG. HT × WIDTH

15" × 12"

SPACING

10–12"

Upright growing, has medium- to dark-green foliage with multitudes of colorful blooms.

*M*any flowering annuals that we use in our Texas landscape are also extremely popular across the rest of the country. Among these are zinnias, marigolds, petunias, and snapdragons. When I have given gardening talks for children, I have learned that children think the snapdragons are very "neat." They enjoy planting them and opening the flowers and looking on the inside. If you have little gardeners around, let them plant some snapdragons in the fall or early spring.

WHEN TO PLANT

Snapdragon is best used as a cool-season annual planted in the fall. It may also be planted in late winter or early spring and enjoyed up until our summertime heat takes them out.

WHERE TO PLANT

Snapdragons need a very rich, moist, well-drained soil in order to do well. Do not plant in dry soil, heavy clay soils, or areas that tend to drain poorly and remain moist. Snapdragons do best in daylong full sun, but they will perform satisfactorily in most cases with 6 to 8 hours of sun per day. The shorter varieties may be grouped in plantings for mass effect. They are also excellent as border plants. The taller varieties work very well as background, or they may be used in combination with other plants. The color palette is wide and it includes red, white, yellow, carmine, and pink. You can create all sorts of effects simply by using various types, colors, and sizes of snapdragons in masses. Snapdragons may also be grown in containers near an entryway or any other place that you would like some outstanding color in the cooler season of the year.

HOW TO PLANT

Using your favorite shovel or digging fork, till 3 in. of high-quality organic matter into 3 in. of your existing soil. Once this is blended together you will have a 6-in.-deep bed ready for planting snapdragons. Install your snapdragons in the improved bed no deeper than they were growing in the containers and firm the soil around them. Water thoroughly, apply root stimulator according to label directions, and spread 3 in. of bark mulch over the entire area. If you are planting in containers, use a premium-quality lightweight potting soil filled to within 2 in. of the pot's top.

CARE AND MAINTENANCE

Tender new growth may be visited by aphids, but this is usually not a serious problem. If aphids do become a problem, ask your Lowe's customer service associate about control possibilities. Remember to read and follow label directions when using any gardening aid. Rust may also become a problem for snapdragons. The best control for this disease is to plant rust-resistant varieties. Pruning spent blossoms is beneficial to the long-term bloom of your snapdragons. Water sufficiently to maintain a moist soil, but don't overwater. Good nutrition may be accomplished by fertilizing with water-soluble, liquid, special dry granular, or encapsulated season-long fertilizers. No matter what type you use on your snapdragons, be sure to read and follow label directions.

ADDITIONAL INFORMATION

There are many different kinds of snapdragons. If you have never planted them, you will find it is a fun-filled experience. I don't know any child, from age 6 to 106, who doesn't enjoy planting them.

ADDITIONAL SPECIES, CULTIVARS, OR VARIETIES

Try some of these varieties: 'Madame Butterfly', 'Giant Forerunner', 'Liberty', 'Black Prince', 'Lipstick', 'Monarch', 'Purple King', 'White Wonder', 'Double Sweetheart', 'Dwarf Trumpet', 'Dwarf Bedding Mixed', 'Floral Showers', 'Lavender Bicolor', 'Li'l Darling Mixed', 'Peaches and Cream', and 'Royal Carpet'.

Sunflower
Helianthus annuus

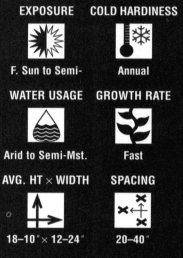

EXPOSURE
F. Sun to Semi-

COLD HARDINESS
Annual

WATER USAGE
Arid to Semi-Mst.

GROWTH RATE
Fast

AVG. HT × WIDTH
18–10" × 12–24"

SPACING
20–40"

Large fuzzy leaves with blossoms in colors of gold, lemon, bronze, mahogany, and white.

Some 17 years ago I was in Winnipeg, Canada, on a road trip while taping a television show. The production crew was stunned when they saw the gigantic fields of sunflowers in the area. If you have ever seen a field of sunflowers in full bloom, a field that stretches as far as you can see, you know the striking effect of which I speak. Sunflowers are great for children, too. I love to get the little gardeners involved in planting, and you won't find a better flower for planting with little bitty fingers. Sunflower seeds are large enough for children to hold and plant individually. There is a wonderful sunflower variety called 'Teddy Bear' that gets about 2 ft. high and has 6-in. ultra-double blossoms. And what child doesn't like Teddy bears? If you wish to get multiple duty out of your sunflowers, remember that the larger varieties can be grown and harvested to feed our feathered friends. The smaller varieties make great cut flowers, so you can enjoy their beauty indoors as well as outdoors.

WHEN TO PLANT
Plant seeds directly in the soil after temperatures are consistently above 70 degrees Fahrenheit, day and night, for approximately 2 weeks.

WHERE TO PLANT

Today's sunflowers may be used anywhere in the landscape that gets plenty of sun and has soil that drains well. Do not plant in heavily shaded, poorly drained, or damp locations. They may be planted in areas where they receive 6 hours of full sun and shade for the remainder of the day.

HOW TO PLANT

Sunflowers are probably the easiest-to-grow seed-grown annual flower in Texas. All that is required is well-drained soil in a sunny location. If you wish to grow sunflowers in some heavy clay soil, simply improve the soil by incorporating approximately 4 in. of organic matter into the top 4 in. of the soil. Follow the directions on your seed packages for proper spacing and depth. The smaller varieties can be planted in 5- to 20-gal. containers filled with premium-quality, lightweight potting soil.

CARE AND MAINTENANCE

Some insect pests may decide to stop by and visit your beautiful sunflower plantings. If they do, consult your local retail garden center for appropriate controls. Remember to always read and follow label directions. It is usually not necessary to prune sunflowers. The larger varieties may require some staking and tying. The smaller varieties may benefit from the removal of spent blossoms to encourage additional blossoms. Sunflowers are quite drought tolerant and will grow under adverse conditions. In order to prevent wilting and dryness and have great-looking sunflowers through the entire blooming season, supply sufficient moisture. Fertilize sunflowers at planting time with a season-long encapsulated fertilizer, or use specialty type granular, liquid, or water-soluble fertilizers as needed, following label directions.

ADDITIONAL INFORMATION

I can't suggest a better blooming annual flower for first-time gardeners to try than the sunflower.

ADDITIONAL SPECIES, CULTIVARS, OR VARIETIES

Try these: 'Italian White', 'Music Box', 'Orange Sun', 'Mammoth Russian', 'Sunbeam', 'Sunburst Mixed', 'Sun Spot', 'Teddy Bear', 'Valentine', and 'Autumn Beauty'.

Verbena
Verbena × hybrida

EXPOSURE

F. Sun to Semi-

COLD HARDINESS

Annual

WATER USAGE

Semi-Mst./Arid-Dry

GROWTH RATE

Fast

AVG. HT × WIDTH

Varies

SPACING

10–14"

Bushy to trailing in form with relatively small to medium dark-green leaves. Blooms are in colorful masses ranging from white to pink, red, purple, and bicolors.

Some verbena, such as prairie verbena, grows wild throughout our state. Most verbenas found today are hybrids. The hybrid varieties have greater vigor, form, and many more blooms and colors. Verbena is great for border planting, or used in masses to create a spectacular annual groundcover effect that lasts throughout the entire season. Verbena provides a variety of color in areas of your garden where a relatively low-trailing plant is needed. The grayish- or deep-green foliage verbenas frequently have is often aromatic. Excellent in solid beds by themselves, you may also want to try verbena in window-boxes or planters in sunny areas.

WHEN TO PLANT
Plant your favorite selections of verbena in the springtime, approximately two weeks after all danger of frost is past.

WHERE TO PLANT
Verbena may be planted in any sunny location where it receives approximately 6 hours of full sun in well-drained soils. Don't plant in heavily shaded,

poorly drained, or wet areas. Use verbena in any type of bed planting, whether you are looking for a colorful garden or an area to be edged. Due to its trailing nature, verbena also makes a wonderful hanging basket, which is particularly useful if you have limited space or want to create a vertical effect. Terracotta, ceramic, metal, plastic, or wood containers work equally well. You may also wish to use verbena in combination with taller-growing plants.

HOW TO PLANT

Add approximately 3 in. of high-quality organic matter into the native soil with the use of a tiller, digging fork, or your favorite digging shovel. Remove verbena transplants from their containers and insert into your prepared bed at the same level they were originally grown in their containers. Firm the soil around the soilball, water thoroughly, and apply root stimulator according to label directions. When the planting is complete, go back and add 3 in. of mulch on top of the finished bed. If you wish to plant verbena in containers, follow the same planting procedure using lightweight potting soil.

CARE AND MAINTENANCE

Verbenas may be visited with powdery mildew if planted in areas where the air movement is poor and they are kept too damp. To prevent this, plant in areas where the air is of good quality and avoid watering the foliage. Pruning is usually not necessary. Water frequently enough to maintain a moist soil to achieve optimum growth and bloom, but don't overwater. Encapsulated bedding plant fertilizers that last for an entire season may be utilized at planting time. Liquid, water-soluble, and specialty granular fertilizers are other options and may be applied as needed throughout the season. Remember to always read and follow label directions when using any gardening aid.

ADDITIONAL INFORMATION

Verbenas come in solid and bicolored forms, so if you are looking for more than one color from a single plant, look into verbena.

ADDITIONAL SPECIES, CULTIVARS, OR VARIETIES

Try these: 'Sangria', 'Trinidad', 'Blaze', 'Show Time', the 'Quartz Series', and the 'Spirit of 76' mixture of red, white, and blue.

Wax Leaf Begonia

Begonia × Semperflorens-Cultorum Hybrids

EXPOSURE	COLD HARDINESS
F. Sun to Semi- (v.)	30°–40° (v.)
WATER USAGE	**GROWTH RATE**
Arid to Semi-Mst. (v.)	Fast
AVG. HT × WIDTH	**SPACING**
6–16 " × 8–12 "	12–20 "

Relatively compact, bushy annual with green to bronze rounded leaves. Blooms are white, red, pink, and blends.

Wax leaf begonias are the bedding plants of choice for Texans who wish to have color in the shade and sun from the same plant that will last the entire season. I enjoy the color of impatiens, but they don't tolerate our summer heat very well. I've been growing wax leaf begonias for over two decades, and I continue to enjoy them. There are many different choices on the market today. Foliage color ranges from bright green to dark green to green with various colors in the foliage to bronze, mahogany, and chocolate brown. Blooms come in various colors of red and carmine and different shades of pink, rose, and white, even white with tints of pink on the edges. They are excellent top-quality bedding plants for edging in the home or commercial landscape.

WHEN TO PLANT

The best time to plant your favorite selections of wax leaf begonia is early spring, 2 weeks after the last killing frost date in your area.

WHERE TO PLANT

Make sure that the soil in which you plant your wax leaf begonia is rich, deep, fertile, and moist. Do not plant in poorly drained soil, wet locations, or areas that are difficult to water. These plants may be used as bedding plants around your walkways, in your landscape beds, in masses, and in beds away from the home. They are wonderful when used as edging plants with taller-growing plants as background. They may be used to create various color effects in your home landscape. To get the most striking effect, use one color in a mass. This is how you will find them used in most commercial applications. They may also be used in areas where space is very limited, like a deck or patio. If you live in an apartment, townhouse, or condominium where space is limited, but you do have an area in which to set some pots or containers, let them be wax leaf begonias. You really will enjoy them.

HOW TO PLANT

Plant in soil that has been well amended with at least 3 to 4 in. of organic matter. I prefer planting wax leaf begonias from the jumbo tray packs or larger plants. Set the plants into your improved soil no deeper than originally grown in their containers, and firm the soil. Water thoroughly, apply root stimulator, and then mulch with approximately 2 to 3 in. of bark mulch. For container planting, use a premium-quality, loose, lightweight potting soil, and fill the container up to 2 in. from the top.

CARE AND MAINTENANCE

Slugs or snails may visit your wax leaf begonias, but they usually are not a serious problem. If pests do become a problem, be sure to ask about options for control. Remember to read and follow label directions on any products you use for insect control. You may wish to remove any spent blossoms or damaged leaves to simply dress up the plant. Maintain a moist soil throughout the entire growing season, but do not overwater. Maintaining a thick layer of mulch will help to keep soil moisture even. Season-long micro-encapsulated bedding plant fertilizers applied at planting time work well for wax leaf begonias. Liquid, water-soluble, and granular fertilizers work well also. They may be applied as needed throughout the entire growing season. Remember, always read and follow label directions when using fertilizers.

ADDITIONAL INFORMATION

Just about anyone can grow wax leaf begonia. If you feel that your thumb is less than green, give this plant a try this season.

ADDITIONAL SPECIES, CULTIVARS, OR VARIETIES

Try some of these: 'Linda', the 'Cocktail Series', 'Flamingo', 'Party Fun', 'Cocoa Mixed', 'Frilly Dilly Mixed', 'Excel Mixed', 'Options Mixed', 'President', 'Dragonwing', and 'Viva Hybrid'.

Zinnia
Zinnia elegans

EXPOSURE

F. Sun to Semi-

COLD HARDINESS

Annual

WATER USAGE

Semi-Moist

GROWTH RATE

Fast

AVG. HT × WIDTH

6–40" × 6–12"

SPACING

10–18"

Upright growing, dark-green leaves with blooms in colors of red, orange, rose, cherry, pink, salmon, lavender, gold, yellow, cream, white, and green.

Zinnia is the most popular seed-grown bedding plant in America. While it is on the end of the alphabet, it is tops when it comes to producing results from seed. My granny, your granny, everybody's granny, as well as moms and dads, at some time or another have grown zinnias. If you haven't personally tried them, I encourage you to do so. They are widely available at local retail gardening centers in a broad assortment of types and colors, from the low-growing bedding plants to the taller "cut-and-come-again" types. Zinnias are marvelous in full-sun locations with good air circulation and soil drainage.

WHEN TO PLANT
The best time to plant zinnias in your home landscape is in the spring, 2 weeks after all danger of frost is past.

WHERE TO PLANT
Zinnias will not tolerate poorly drained soil conditions. Don't plant in shady areas or locations where air movement is insufficient. Plant in well-drained soil that is fertile and moist for best long-term successful growth, bloom, and overall beauty. They work great when massed as bedding plants, and also

when used in masses with other plants. They may be used in entry-ways, or as background plants in your garden to create an out-standing effect. If you are looking for a plant that the little ones can grow from seed successfully, let them plant some zinnias this year.

HOW TO PLANT
Blend in 3 in. of high-quality organic matter, including peat moss, ground-bark mulch, or compost, with the top 3 in. of your existing soil. I prefer to plant zinnias from transplants. Remove the plants from their containers and insert into the bed at the depth that they were originally grown. Firm the soil. Water thoroughly, apply root stimulator according to the label directions, and after the planting is complete, mulch with 3 in. of pine bark mulch. Zinnias may also be grown in the container of your choosing. When growing them in containers, make sure you use a premium-quality lightweight potting soil filled to within 2 in. of the top.

CARE AND MAINTENANCE
Plant your zinnias in beds that drain well and have good air move-ment, for they may be plagued with powdery mildew if circulation and drainage is poor. Leaf miners also visit occasionally. If this becomes a problem, ask about possibilities for control. Remember to always read and follow label directions on any gardening aid that you use. Be sure to remove spent blossoms on your zinnias to keep them tidy and blooming throughout the growing season. Maintain even soil moisture if at all possible, but don't allow your zinnias to become extremely dry . . . or wet. Season-long encapsulated bedding plant fertilizer and liquid, water-soluble, and specialty granulated fertilizers may also be used successfully throughout the season. Remember, no matter which fertilizer you decide to use, always read and follow label directions.

ADDITIONAL INFORMATION
Zinnias are one of the easiest plants to grow. If you are looking for a plant for your children to try, don't forget zinnias, from seeds or transplants. The small-growing varieties are excellent.

ADDITIONAL SPECIES, CULTIVARS, OR VARIETIES
There are plenty to choose from including 'Envy', 'Peter Pan' group, 'Thumbelina', 'Envy Double', 'Dwarf Double', 'Dwarf Mixed', 'Jack Double Mixed', 'Peppermint Stick Mixed', 'Scabulous Flowered', 'Sun Bowl Mixed', 'Giant Cactus Flower', 'Whirligig Improved Mixed', 'Parasol Mixed', 'Persian Carpet Mixed', 'Classic' series, 'Star' series, Z. *linearis* 'Crystal White', and 'Tropical Snow'.

CHAPTER TWO

BULBS, CORMS, RHIZOMES, AND TUBERS

*C*HILDREN LOVE TO PLANT bulbs, corms, rhizomes, and tubers. Traditionally we lump all of these together and call them "bulbs," and we include all of them in this single chapter. But there are horticultural differences between them.

Bulbs are tough. Some bulbs will survive with minimum care if you select the right ones and plant in the proper spot. There are old homesites where nothing remains, not even the foundation, but flowers from bulbs appear each year for us to enjoy as we drive by.

There are native bulbs as well as imports. Imported bulbs are the ones we find most often at garden centers.

Bulbs, corms, rhizomes, and tubers have bloom seasons or color seasons. Some bloom in early spring or late summer, or even in the fall. Be sure you understand the blooming time of the plants you're considering. It is sometimes said: "If it blooms in the spring or summer, you dig, divide, and transplant or plant in the fall. If it blooms in the fall, then you dig, divide, and transplant or plant in the spring." Some plants in these groups need to be divided every 3 to 4 years, or perhaps sooner for those that are very actively growing. Iris, *Iris* spp., needs to be divided every 3 years in most cases.

Because of our hot Texas weather, certain bulbs benefit from being "chilled," or kept in the bottom of a refrigerator below 45 degrees Fahrenheit for about 6 weeks. The two types of bulbs that need refrigeration are hyacinths, *Hyacinth orientalis*, and especially tulips, *Tulipa* spp. After chilling is complete, plant as soon as possible. No other bulbs require chilling.

Because of their chilling requirements, most tulips do not repeat well for Texans year after year. They simply do not get cold enough long enough here in Texas; hence, Texas gardeners often decide to use tulips as an annual.

Some plants in this group, including gladiolus (*Gladiolus* × *hortulanus*), or glads, are best lifted and stored indoors for the winter and then replanted the following spring. Caladium (*Caladium* × *hortulanum*), a tropical plant grown for its colorful foliage, also benefits from being lifted out of the ground for the winter. It does not tolerate cold soils well, especially soils that tend to be poorly drained. When you store bulbs, corms, rhizomes or tubers, store them in a cool location that has good air circulation. Do not seal them in a plastic bag. Bread trays, citrus bags, and ladies' nylon stockings all work well as storage containers.

Drainage is very important for successful long-term growth of most corms or tubers, so make sure your bed is well prepared and drains thoroughly before planting.

Some plants in this group naturalize easily. They appear to grow in many locations as if nature intended them to be there. Plants in the narcissus (*Narcissus* spp.) family, especially the jonquils, are known to naturalize easily. Gardeners who intend to naturalize jonquils often use this technique: they toss handfuls of the bulbs into the air and plant them wherever they land!

Most bulbs, rhizomes, corms, and tubers prefer to be grown in full sun. Their leaves must gather enough sunlight to manufacture food to be stored for the next year's blooming season. Remember to always plant healthy plants; never plant diseased or shrunken plants.

If your gardening space is limited, try growing bulbs in containers. Indoor bulb forcing is an old method of growing and producing early color. Almost any type of container will work and they may be grown in gravel, premium lightweight potting soil, or other media.

Eleven different bulbs, corms, rhizomes, and tubers are presented in this chapter. Whether grown for foliage or bloom, these plants offer a wide selection of textures, colors, and shapes—and they may open up a whole new gardening experience for you.

Caladium
Caladium × hortulanum

EXPOSURE

F. Sun to Semi- (v.)

COLD HARDINESS

Varies

WATER USAGE

Semi-Moist

GROWTH RATE

Medium

AVG. HT × WIDTH

12–16″× 4–8″(v.)

SPACING

6–8″

Large heart-shaped leaves in blends of green, white, pink, and red. Tuber native to tropical South America.

*H*eart-shaped caladiums have been in use by gardeners since the 1800s, if not earlier. Today's hybridization and plant breeding has resulted in a palette of colors in various shades of red, green, white, and pink. I often recommend the use of caladiums to gardeners who have sought my advice for planting in shaded areas. Not many blooming plants will thrive in shaded areas, but caladiums will give outstanding color that will last through our summers. Caladiums are sometimes referred to as "fancy-leaved caladiums." They work as well when grown in containers as they do when placed directly into well-prepared beds. My first experience growing them in containers was in 1971 when I graduated from Stephen F. Austin University with a horticulture degree. I was employed by a nursery which grew literally thousands of 6-in. pots of caladiums. I have continued to grow and use these colorful beauties through the years and have found them to be relatively easy to grow.

WHEN TO PLANT
Do not plant your caladium tubers until nighttime temperatures are consistently above 65 degrees Fahrenheit for 2 weeks. Use a soil, air conditioning/central heat, or "gourmet" thermometer that has an appropriate scale to take

soil temperatures approximately 3 in. deep. When soil temperatures reach 65 degrees in the springtime, it is time to plant. Do not plant caladiums in the fall.

WHERE TO PLANT

Most caladiums do best in shaded areas. They may be used in background plantings, as edgings, or any other way that works well in your landscape beds. They look good in various sizes of containers and baskets. Before planting, improve your soil and make sure that it drains thoroughly. Do not plant caladiums where soil drainage is poor or in difficult-to-water locations.

HOW TO PLANT

If your soil is heavy clay, be sure to improve it thoroughly before planting caladiums. The best way to do this is to blend 3 in. of organic matter with the top 3 in. of existing soil. After bed improvement is complete, place tubers approximately 1 to 1¹/₂ in. below the surface of the soil and water thoroughly. When planting from pots, remove the plants and place them in holes no deeper than the top of the soil in the containers. Firm well, apply root stimulator according to label directions, water thoroughly, and mulch with approximately 3 in. of bark mulch.

CARE AND MAINTENANCE

Slugs or snails may visit your caladiums. If they become a problem, go to your local retail garden center, which will offer several control solutions. Remember to read and follow label directions on any pest-control product. Prune out all flower stems as they emerge, but no other pruning is necessary. Maintain moist growing conditions at all times. Do not allow the caladiums to become dry, but do not keep the soil saturated or wet. Caladiums benefit from fertilization programs. Apply fertilizer according to label directions—don't over-fertilize. Water-soluble, liquid, specialty, and encapsulated slow-release forms all work well.

ADDITIONAL INFORMATION

The fancy-leaved or heart-shaped caladiums tend to do best in shaded areas, though some light morning sun may not be harmful. If you wish to plant some caladiums in sunnier locations, I strongly suggest you try the strapped-leaf varieties.

ADDITIONAL SPECIES, CULTIVARS, OR VARIETIES

Try some of these fancy-leaved caladiums: 'Pink Cloud', 'Aaron', 'Blaze', 'Candidum', 'Carolyn Whorton', 'Fire Chief', 'Fannie Munson', 'Gypsy Rose', 'Irene Dank', 'John Pead', 'Jubilee', 'June Bride', 'Lord Derby', 'Rosebud', 'Pink Beauty', 'Florida Sunrise', and 'Red Flash'. You may also wish to try some strap-leaf varieties, which include 'Jackie Suthers', 'Miss Muffet', 'White Wing', 'Tropicana', 'Red Frill', 'Pink Gem', 'Clarice', and 'Gingerland'.

Canna
Canna × generalis

EXPOSURE

Full Sun

COLD HARDINESS

10° to -10* (v.)

WATER USAGE

Semi-Moist

GROWTH RATE

Fast

AVG. HT × WIDTH

Varies

SPACING

Varies

Large leaves in bright green, blue-green, bronze, and multicolored. Blooms in various shades of yellow, orange, pink, red, coral, and cream.

*C*annas, while native to tropical and subtropical America, have been grown since Colonial times. Today, we can find cannas growing in old homesites, cemeteries, and other locations where little or no maintenance occurs. Cannas were originally grown not for their blooms, but for their striking foliage. The foliage is still interesting, but breeding has resulted in many different bloom colors. For full-sun locations, you won't find an easier to grow or more colorful plant, whether planted directly in the ground or in large tubs. Cannas often come in a range of sizes, from the standard which can be quite tall (to 7 ft.) down to the dwarf which may run from 2 to 3 ft. Before purchasing, be sure to ask how tall your selected varieties will grow in your location.

WHEN TO PLANT
Cannas are best planted in the springtime after soil temperatures reach 60 degrees and higher. Do not plant in the fall.

WHERE TO PLANT
While cannas will survive rather harsh conditions, they prefer a deep, moist, rich soil. Plant in full-sun, well-drained locations that are relatively easy to

water. Cannas are often set in single rows, but the most striking effect comes from mass plantings in multiple rows.

How to Plant

Be sure to prepare your soil well before planting canna rhizomes. Blend 4 in. of organic matter with the top 4 in. of native soil. After bed improvement is complete, plant rhizomes approximately 4 in. below the soil surface, spacing them from 18 in. to 3 ft. apart. If you wish to plant from containers, set the plants in individual planting holes no deeper than the soilball. Firm the soil mix well around the rootball, water thoroughly, apply root stimulator according to label directions, and mulch with approximately 3 in. of bark mulch.

Care and Maintenance

Slugs, snails, and leaf rollers may visit your cannas. If these pests become problems, consult your Lowe's customer service associate to learn about control possibilities. Remember to read and follow label directions on any product you use to control pests. Prune out each bloom stalk as blooms complete their show for you, and cut off and remove plants' entire tops, after the fall killing freezes. No other pruning should be necessary. Maintain moist growing conditions for best results. Drip irrigation is well suited to cannas, and maintaining a 3- to 4-in. layer of mulch will help conserve soil moisture. Fertilize in the springtime after new growth begins, using encapsulated, slow-release, specialty granular, liquid, or water-soluble fertilizer according to label directions. Reapply as desired.

Additional Information

I encourage you to allow your little ones to plant these long-term summer-blooming plants. The underground structures of rhizomes are large enough for small hands to handle and plant. They will marvel at the color and the leaves through the entire growing season. Later they will have something to dig, divide, and share with others.

Additional Species, Cultivars, or Varieties

There are several varieties and types of cannas available. You can find orange-flowered varieties like 'Wyoming' or vermilion-colored varieties like 'King Humbert'. Others are 'Pfitzer', 'Grand Opera', 'Dwarfs', 'Cozy', and 'French'. 'Tropic Rose' is a recent All-America Selection (AAS) choice. Don't forget to look for those varieties with very striking foliage, including 'Tropicana' and 'Pictoria'.

Crinum
Crinum spp.

EXPOSURE

F. Sun to Semi-

COLD HARDINESS

All Texas

WATER USAGE

Arid-Dry/Semi-Mst.

GROWTH RATE

Fast

AVG. HT × WIDTH

1–4 ' × 2–3 '

SPACING

20–30 "

Flowers on tall stalks are white, pale pink, or dark pink with wine markings.

*C*rinums have been successfully grown by Texas gardeners since the 1800s. They have been the staple in many old-fashioned country and cottage-type gardens. My Granny Miller raised crinums in her relatively dry country garden in Indian Creek, Texas, so they have to be tough and durable plants. She grew them with minimum care and water. Crinums can be found growing on their own in woods, pasture areas, meadows, old homesites, and cemeteries throughout Texas. Due to extensive hybridizing and breeding, it is rather difficult to identify many of the varieties that are on the market today. In his book *Garden Bulbs For The South* from Taylor Publishing of Dallas, Texas, Scott Ogden does the best job of chronicling crinum.

WHEN TO PLANT

The best planting time for crinums is in the springtime after soil temperatures have warmed to 60 degrees or higher. They may be planted earlier, but will not emerge until soil temperatures are warm, and planting too early has the potential to cause bulb rotting. Crinums may also be planted through the summertime and in the early fall.

WHERE TO PLANT

For best results, select a location in which the bulbs will not be disturbed for several years. They prefer a loam soil that drains well. They do best when planted in full sun or receive a minimum of 6 hours of full sun. They may be located in areas where they do receive some shade from the hot western afternoon sun. They may also be grown successfully in tubs.

HOW TO PLANT

Plant in well-prepared beds. Incorporate approximately 4 in. of organic matter into the top 4 in. of native soil. After bed preparation is complete, dig individual planting holes and set the bulbs so that the tops are even with the surface of the soil mix. Firm the soil well, water thoroughly, apply root stimulator according to label directions, and mulch with 3 in. of bark mulch.

CARE AND MAINTENANCE

There are few pests that visit crinum. Snails or mealybugs may appear on occasion. If they become a problem in your planting, learn about control possibilities. Remember to read and follow label directions on any product you use for pest control. Remove spent bloom stalks after blooming is complete. No other pruning is required. Water as necessary to prevent soil dryness. Maintaining a 3- to 4-in. layer of mulch will conserve moisture and greatly reduce the necessity for frequent watering. Fertilize as new growth begins in the springtime with water-soluble, encapsulated slow-release, liquid, or specialty granular fertilizers. Be sure to follow label directions. Reapply as necessary during the growing and blooming season.

ADDITIONAL INFORMATION

Crinums are one of the easiest and most rewarding true bulb plants to grow. In areas that have deer populations, structures may need to be installed to protect the crinums from the deer. Certain crinum varieties will work well in bog plantings and around water gardens.

ADDITIONAL SPECIES, CULTIVARS, OR VARIETIES

There are many types and varieties of crinum to try in Texas. Among them are 'Sacramento', 'Empress of India', '12 Apostles', 'Carroll Abbott', 'Gowenii', 'Ollene', 'Peachglow', 'Sangria', 'Cloud Davis', 'Mrs. James Hendry', and 'Ellen Bosanquet'.

BULBS, CORMS, RHIZOMES AND TUBERS

Daylily
Hemerocallis spp.

EXPOSURE

F. Sun to Semi-

COLD HARDINESS

All Texas

WATER USAGE

Semi-Moist

GROWTH RATE

Fast

AVG. HT × WIDTH

1–4′ × 1–2′

SPACING

12–24″

With grasslike leaves, stalks hold typical lily-shaped blooms in colors of white, pink, red, maroon, orange, and variations.

*D*aylily is a member of the lily family that can be grown in all areas of Texas. It is an old-fashioned plant that you may find growing in abandoned locations, but also in the most modern gardens in the state. They are often used in municipal and botanical garden plantings in addition to home gardens. They will grow in almost any type of soil from heavy clay to loose sand, from damp to relatively dry; they will grow in full sun or relatively shaded areas.

WHEN TO PLANT
It is said that daylilies are so tough and durable they can be dug, divided, and planted any time of the year in Texas. But a good rule of thumb is: if it blooms in the spring and summer, dig, divide, and transplant in the fall. Fall planting of daylilies tuberous roots is normally very satisfactory—but very early spring planting also works well.

WHERE TO PLANT
While daylilies will survive rather harsh conditions, for best results locate in areas where the soil is deep, rich, and moist. Daylilies perform best with full

sunlight or partial shade but not with full shade. They may be used as bedding plants for mass plantings, or planted in tubs or any landscape location.

HOW TO PLANT

Plant daylily tuberous roots in soils that have been improved with organic matter. Incorporate 3 to 4 in. of organic matter into the top 3 to 4 in. of existing soil. After soil improvement is complete, plant tuberous roots approximately 2 in. deep, spaced 24 in. apart. Firm the soil lightly. After planting, water thoroughly, apply root stimulator, and cover with 2 in. of bark mulch. Daylilies may also be set out as transplants in improved soil. Dig individual planting holes no deeper than the top of the plant soilball. Insert the plant after removing from the containers. Firm the soil, water thoroughly, apply root stimulator, and mulch.

CARE AND MAINTENANCE

Daylilies have few pests. If pests do become a problem, learn about the best controls. Remember to read and follow label directions. Remove spent bloom stalks after blooming is complete. You may also wish to remove spent blooms daily to tidy the daylily's appearance. Water as necessary to prevent wilting. This is especially important during the blooming periods. Fertilize in springtime as new growth begins. Granular slow-release premium-quality rose foods work well, but feel free to use your favorite type of fertilizer. Remember to read and follow label directions when using any type of fertilizer.

ADDITIONAL INFORMATION

This is one of the easy-to-plant and easy-to-grow flowering plants that gives nearly 100 percent assurance of good results—in other words, it's another "kid-friendly" plant.

ADDITIONAL SPECIES, CULTIVARS, OR VARIETIES

In today's daylily market, you can find literally hundreds, if not thousands, of varieties available. Just a few of these are 'Bluejay', 'Jean George', 'Victoria Elizabeth Barnes', 'Persian Market', 'Lucille Guidry', 'Big Bird', 'Carolyn Criswell', 'Chicago Arnies Choice', 'Chicago Orchid', 'Little Bumble Bee', 'Mallard', 'Mini Stella', 'Red Poll', 'Sacred Shield', 'Sirocco', 'Sombrero Way', 'Bright Yellow', 'Little Jack', and 'Lusty Leland'. Shop for daylily tuberous roots in the fall. Select the ones that you find most attractive; my wife and I currently enjoy 'Aztec Gold' and 'Stella De Oro' hybrids.

Gladiolus
Gladiolus sp.

EXPOSURE

F. Sun to Semi-

COLD HARDINESS

To 10° F.

WATER USAGE

Semi-Moist

GROWTH RATE

Fast

AVG. HT × WIDTH

8"–6' × 9"–12'

SPACING

12"

Spiked, with grasslike leaves. Blooms range from miniature up to 6 inches wide in all colors except a true blue.

*W*hen looking for some great cut flowers to incorporate into your garden plantings, gladiolus or glads should be at the top of your list. Florists prize these summer-blooming plants because they are easy to use in many arrangements and the cut bloom stalks have a long life. The dwarf varieties may be used with plantings in and among some lower-growing varieties of other plants, while the tall varieties tend to work best grouped together in cut flower gardens. It is said that there are close to 300 species of gladiolus available world-wide. Many are native to South Africa, but others are found in different regions of the world.

WHEN TO PLANT

In Texas, gladiolus corms are best planted in the springtime after soil temperatures warm to 60 degrees. Planting approximately every 2 weeks through midsummer will ensure continuous bloom and color from gladiolus during the normal growing season.

WHERE TO PLANT

Gladiolus prefer a deep sandy loam. If growing in heavy clay, add organic matter to the soil to a minimum depth of 6 in. Glads are often used in formal cut gardens, and this may be the most spectacular use of these plants in the home landscape. The taller-growing varieties may need to be staked and placed out of strong prevailing summer breezes.

HOW TO PLANT

Plant corms in the springtime in well-prepared beds. Incorporate approximately 3 in. of organic matter into the top 3 in. of existing soil. After bed improvement is complete, place corms approximately 4 to 6 in. deep and space 4 to 6 in. apart. Cover the corms and mulch with 2 in. of bark mulch.

CARE AND MAINTENANCE

Thrips may become a problem during warm Texas days. If they do invade your planting of glads, visit Lowe's to find the best control possibilities. Remember to read and follow label directions. No pruning is normally necessary, but staking is usually required with the taller-growing varieties in order to prevent lodging. Water as necessary to maintain a moist soil. Do not allow to dry, especially during blooming periods. Fertilize at planting time with long-lasting slow-release rose food placed approximately 2 in. below the corm, or fertilize through the growing season with high-middle-number liquid or water-soluble fertilizers according to label directions.

ADDITIONAL INFORMATION

Try some gladiolus in your next spring garden plantings for a riot of color. There are so many new varieties being developed on a year-to-year basis that it will benefit you to take a look at what is available each spring.

ADDITIONAL SPECIES, CULTIVARS, OR VARIETIES

Because there are over 300 species, you have a multitude of varieties and colors to choose from. Try *G. alatus*, which normally grows 4 to 10 in. high and has red and yellow flowers. Plant it in a rock garden with good drainage. One of the more hardy varieties is *G. byzantinus*, considered hardy in all Texas zones. *G. × colvillei* is hardy in Zone 7 southward and is sometimes called "dwarf baby glads." Some cultivars are 'Amanda Mahy', 'Peach Blossom', and 'Spitfire'.

Hardy Red Amaryllis
Hippeastrum × johnsonii

EXPOSURE

F. Sun to Semi-

COLD HARDINESS

All Texas

WATER USAGE

Arid-Dry/Semi-Mst.

GROWTH RATE

Fast

AVG. HT × WIDTH

18–24" × 1–3'

SPACING

12–16"

Tall, lily- or amaryllis-shaped bloom.

*I*f you happen to be a fan of old varieties of blooming garden plants, then this beauty is right up your alley. While there are many exciting and gorgeous amaryllis available today, 'Johnsonii' is one of the oldest and hardiest varieties for planting in Texas gardens. They may be found in old home sites as well as current low maintenance plantings. Hardy red amaryllis, which is also known as St. Joseph's lily, produces outstanding crimson trumpet-shaped flowers with minimal maintenance. If you happen to like large, raised planters and are looking for some easy-to-grow bulbs that will bloom reliably each year, give amaryllis a try. Children love to plant them.

WHEN TO PLANT
Hardy red amaryllis is best planted in the springtime when soil temperatures are warm.

WHERE TO PLANT
Plant in a well-drained location that is rich and moist. While it will adapt to growing in full-sun, it does best with a little shade to protect it from the hot

western afternoon sun. Hardy red amaryllis is not suitable for planting in full-shade locations.

HOW TO PLANT
Blend approximately 4 in. of organic matter with the top 4 in. of your existing soil. After bed preparation is complete, place individual bulbs approximately 4 in. deep. Water thoroughly, apply root stimulator according to label directions, and cover with 2 in. of bark mulch.

CARE AND MAINTENANCE
Snails and mealybugs may visit your planting. If these pests become a problem, ask about control possibilities. Remember to always read and follow label directions when using any purchased lawn and garden aid. Prune out spent bloom stalks. Usually, no other pruning is required. Water as necessary to maintain a moist soil, especially during blooming. Fertilize as new growth emerges in the springtime with a premium high-quality, long-lasting granular rose food. Alternatives include encapsulated slow-release fertilizers, water-soluble, and liquid. Remember to always read and follow label directions when applying any fertilizer.

ADDITIONAL INFORMATION
There are many varieties of amaryllis, or *Hippeasterum*. The tropical types are often available beginning in late October for utilization in indoor pots.

ADDITIONAL SPECIES, CULTIVARS, OR VARIETIES
H. × *johnsonii* has been in use for over a century and continues in Texas gardens today. It is the most winter-hardy variety that we know. If you want a reliably-blooming amaryllis season after season, look for this specific variety. Other varieties include: 'Ackermanii', 'Orient Red', 'Sumac Pinini', and many others. Be sure and ask about the winter-hardiness of particular varieties, according to your area. Note: Additional types, varieties, and cultivars are often available for indoor forcing in time for the winter holiday season. They are especially great fun for kids.

Hyacinth
Hyacinthus orientalis

EXPOSURE

F. Sun to Semi-

COLD HARDINESS

Texas

WATER USAGE

Semi-Moist

GROWTH RATE

Fast-Bulb

AVG. HT × WIDTH

8–12" × 4–6"

SPACING

12'

Plants with clusters of open to tightly held, bell-shaped flowers that are very fragrant. Colors include white, pale yellow, pink, red, and blue to purplish.

*T*here is nothing like the heavily perfumed fragrance of hyacinths in bloom in Texas gardens. Some sources say that *H. orientalis* came to us through Europe from the Eastern Mediterranean in the early 1500s. You may find it listed today as 'Dutch Hyacinth', 'Common Hyacinth', or 'Garden Hyacinth'. It has a pleasing look in garden settings when used in groups or as a border of color plants. Texans purchase common hyacinths for use indoors as well as outdoors. All types and colors have a wonderful heavenly fragrance. Some of the unusual bloom colors may be a little difficult to find. These colors are quite different from the blue of the hyacinth cultivars that are often used indoors and for garden plantings, but when you become familiar with their fragrance, there is no doubt that these plants are hyacinth.

WHEN TO PLANT
Plant in the late fall as soon as garden areas are prepared and bulbs are available.

WHERE TO PLANT

Plant in thoroughly improved garden-soil locations where they will receive a minimum of 6 hours of full sun. They favor shade from our hot western afternoon sun. Do not plant in locations that are difficult to water, in heavy clay soils that have not been amended, or in damp locations.

HOW TO PLANT

Incorporate approximately 3 in. of organic matter into the top 3 in. of existing soil. After bed preparation is complete, plant individual bulbs approximately 4 in. deep. Water thoroughly and apply root stimulator according to label directions.

CARE AND MAINTENANCE

H. orientalis, or common hyacinths, are generally considered free of insects and diseases. Remove the bloom stalk upon completion of flowering. No other pruning should be necessary. Water as necessary to prevent soil dryness. This is especially important during blooming and growth cycles. Fertilize at planting time with approximately 1 teaspoon of premium-quality, long-lasting rose food, placed 1 in. below the bottom of the bulb. Fertilize existing beds in the spring as new growth emerges. Water-soluble, liquid, and other fertilizers may be utilized. Remember to read and follow label directions.

ADDITIONAL INFORMATION

When grown in the home, *H. orientalis* will reward you in early spring with faithful bloom and fragrance. Try one or more inside by growing in "hyacinth glasses," containers especially made for this purpose. They're fun to grow and anyone can do it.

ADDITIONAL SPECIES, CULTIVARS, OR VARIETIES

According to some information sources, *H. orientalis* has been used by gardeners for almost 400 years. Due to hybridizing programs, there are many selections available today. Try these beauties: 'Anna-Marie', 'Blue Jacket', 'Jan Bos', 'Carnegie', 'Gipsy Queen', 'Blue Giant', 'Pink Perfection', 'Violet Pearl', 'City of Haarlem', 'Hollyhock', 'Splendid Cornelia', 'Pink Pearl', 'Purple Passion', 'Aeolus', 'Gypsy Queen', 'Rose of Naples', 'Distinction', and mixed colors. *H. orientalis albus*, the 'Roman Hyacinth', has white to blue fragrant blooms. Several stems arise from each bulb and the blooms are more open than those of other hyacinths.

Iris

Iris spp.

EXPOSURE

F. Sun to Semi-

COLD HARDINESS

All Texas

WATER USAGE

Arid-Dry/Semi-Mst.

GROWTH RATE

Fast to Med.

AVG. HT × WIDTH

3–6 ′ × 2–3 ′ (v.)

SPACING
12–15 ″

Plant has narrow, strap-shaped, medium-green leaves.

*I*ris is a long-time staple in Texas gardens as well as throughout the southern part of the United States. The rhizome type which most of us know as bearded iris is the most popular, hardy in all of Texas and the one grown most often. Some of our more mature gardeners may use the name "flags" to describe iris. Bearded iris are classified as miniature dwarfs, standard dwarfs, intermediate, miniature tall, and tall, with heights ranging anywhere from 3 in. to 27 in. This gives us a wonderful selection to choose from and install in our home landscapes.

WHEN TO PLANT

I have been told by the Texas Iris Society that Iris is so tough it can be dug, divided, and transplanted any time of the year. We like to set out the rhizomes and do our initial planting in the fall. Remember this guideline for most spring- and summer-blooming plants grown from bulbs, rhizomes, corms, or tubers: if it blooms in the spring or summer, dig, divide, plant, or transplant in the fall.

WHERE TO PLANT

Iris will grow in almost any type of soil, but for best results plant in prepared beds. Smaller varieties may be used in mass plantings for borders or to create a groundcover effect. Taller-growing varieties matched together make excellent cut-flower plantings. Iris needs a minimum of 6 hours of full sun per day in order to do its best. If you wish to plant in areas where shade is present for part of the day, let it be afternoon shade.

HOW TO PLANT

Incorporate approximately 3 in. of organic matter into the top 3 in. of your soil. Install rhizomes level with or about 1 in. below the soil surface, firm the soil, water thoroughly, apply root stimulator according to label directions, and mulch with approximately 2 in. of bark mulch. Note: In relatively heavy soils, plant rhizomes at soil level and cover with an inch of mulch.

CARE AND MAINTENANCE

Iris borers or grasshoppers may visit your planting. If the pests become a problem, inquire about the best control possibilities available. Remember to read and follow label directions. Remove spent bloom stalks after all blooms have opened and completed their show for you. Do not prune back the blades or leaves severely, as is practiced in some Texas gardens. Iris needs to retain all its leaves as long as possible in order to manufacture the plant food which will be stored in underground structures for next year's blooms. Damaged or dead leaves may be pruned as needed. Fertilize in the springtime as new growth begins with a premium-quality, long-lasting, slow-release rose food, following label directions.

ADDITIONAL INFORMATION

Visit local public gardens and botanical gardens during iris blooming times. In addition to your camera, always take a pad and something to write with so you can write down the varieties you like. Use this information to seek out your favorites.

ADDITIONAL SPECIES, CULTIVARS, OR VARIETIES

A word of caution: while there are many outstandingly beautiful hybridized varieties of iris on the market today, be sure when you purchase them to ask if the varieties you want are known to remain in local landscapes for many years. Some varieties will simply die away very shortly in our warm Texas climate. Consider using 'Superstition', 'Supreme Sultan', 'Sultry Mood', 'Rare Treat', 'Titan's Glory', 'Bride's Halo', 'Proud Tradition', 'Copper Classic', 'Storm Center', 'Beverly Sills', 'Sapphire Hills', 'Lacy Snowflake', 'Cherub's Smile', and 'Lady Friend'.

Narcissus
Narcissus spp.

EXPOSURE

F. Sun to Semi-

COLD HARDINESS

All Texas

WATER USAGE

Arid-Dry/Semi-Mst.

GROWTH RATE

Fast

AVG. HT × WIDTH

3–18" × 4–6"

SPACING

6–9"

Has narrow-bladed leaves. Blooms are yellow, gold, white, orange, red, and pink.

Nothing speaks of spring to Texas gardeners as does narcissus. It is among the most important of all bulb plants we grow. You may hear it called jonquil, daffodil, and narcissus and wonder which is correct. All three names are correct. The group name is narcissus and jonquils and daffodils are both narcissus. Most of the time, the name jonquil refers to the very small-blooming, almost grasslike, narrow-leaved plant. The names daffodil and narcissus are often used interchangeably. Whichever name you use, there is a broad selection available: the Royal Horticulture Society lists narcissus in ten different divisions. Narcissus has been used successfully as bedding and border plants as well as in woodland plantings, rock gardens, and containers. Various narcissus varieties are used to naturalize in Texas gardens. I've seen some outstanding examples of this practice throughout our great gardening state.

WHEN TO PLANT
Plant your selections of narcissus in the fall.

WHERE TO PLANT

Narcissus is best planted in well-drained soils in locations receiving full sunlight or partial shade. Do not plant in poorly drained places or in areas that are difficult to water. Narcissus may be used in mass plantings in order to create a "knock your socks off" color effect in the springtime. Narcissus is not only pleasant to the eye, but it has a wonderful fragrance as well. Everyone who visits a home will enjoy the plantings near an entryway.

HOW TO PLANT

Plant in beds that drain well. If the soil at your location does not drain properly, or if it is very hard and compact, add approximately 3 in. of organic matter to the top 3 in. of native soil. Plant bulbs at approximately twice the depth of their height in prepared beds. Firm the soil, water thoroughly, apply root stimulator according to label directions, and cover with 2 in. of bark mulch.

CARE AND MAINTENANCE

Snails may visit your narcissus planting. If slugs or snails become a problem, ask about appropriate control measures. Remember to read and follow label directions when using any lawn and garden aid. Rot may possibly occur in poorly drained locations. After blooming is complete, remove the bloom stalks. No other pruning should be necessary. Allow the leaves to remain on the plant until they turn brown, for they must make plant food in the form of carbohydrates which is stored for next year's bloom. Water as necessary to prevent soil dryness. Fertilize at planting time with approximately 1 teaspoon of premium-quality, slow-release rose food placed 1 in. below the individual bulb. Fertilize new growth from existing beds in the spring with premium-quality, long-lasting, slow-release rose food according to label directions.

ADDITIONAL INFORMATION

Narcissus is one of our best cut flowers grown from bulbs and will last a long time when used indoors in normal room temperatures. One possible use: Let your little one plant them and when they bloom in the springtime, collect some of the bloom stalks and let them dry for memories. I have some dried narcissus blossoms that my daughter Ashley gave me four years ago.

ADDITIONAL SPECIES, CULTIVARS, OR VARIETIES

There are many different varieties and types of narcissus. Some you may wish to try in a Texas garden are 'Lucifer', 'Carbineer', 'Ceylon', 'Rustom', 'Pasha', 'Mount Hood', 'Ice Follies', 'Peeping Tom', and 'Golden Dawn'. Note: In Texas, the name daffodil usually refers to *N. pseudonarcissus* (yellow single trumpet blooms); narcissus is *N. tazetta* (white fragrant clusters of small blooms); and jonquil refers to *N. jonquilla* (yellow fragrant clusters of small blooms).

BULBS, CORMS, RHIZOMES AND TUBERS

Spider Lily
Lycoris spp.

EXPOSURE

Full to Semi-

COLD HARDINESS

All Texas

WATER USAGE

Arid-Dry/Semi-Mst.

GROWTH RATE

Fast

AVG. HT × WIDTH

1–2 ' × 6–10 "

SPACING

8–12 "

Has small strap-type leaves. Bloom colors are red, pink, white, and yellow, borned on tall, slender stems.

Spider lily, also known as magic lily or resurrection lily, is perhaps best known to Texas gardeners as the lily that seemingly comes from nowhere to make wonderful blooms late summer and early fall. These flowers are often used around the bases of trees and in woodland settings where they do an outstanding job of giving color when many of our bedding plants are on the wane. They may seem to come into bloom during our long, hot, dry summers after a thoroughly drenching late-summer / fall rain.

WHEN TO PLANT
Spider lilies are considered relatively minor as far as bulbs are concerned, and they may be somewhat difficult to locate. My best advice: when you find bulbs, plant them at that time. You may find them in the fall, or you may find them in early spring. A good source may be a relative or neighbor who wishes to share some with you.

WHERE TO PLANT
Spider lilies tend to do their best in sandy loam soils, but if you have a heavy clay soil, with soil improvement they should grow adequately. Some varieties

work great in lawn areas if left undisturbed. Remember to leave grass around these areas, as they will not stand constant mowing. Other varieties will work well when grouped in masses in beds, and they will multiply readily.

HOW TO PLANT

When planting in lawn areas, dig individual holes and set bulbs in the ground so the tops are almost even with the soil. Make sure the soil drains properly. For bed plantings, plant in improved soil beds. The best way to improve the soil is to incorporate 3 in. of organic matter into the top 3 in. of soil. After bed improvement is complete, plant the bulbs at the same depth you would plant them in the lawn. Water thoroughly and add a root stimulator if desired, then mulch with about 2 in. of bark mulch.

CARE AND MAINTENANCE

Slugs or snails may visit your planting of spider lilies. If they become a problem, consult your local retail center for the best control possibilities. Remember to read and follow label directions when using any pest-control products. Prune off blooming stalks when flowering is complete. Water as necessary to maintain moist soil. If planted in beds, mulching will aid in conservation of soil moisture. Fertilize in the springtime with one application of premium-quality, long-lasting, slow-release rose food according to label directions.

ADDITIONAL INFORMATION

Spider lilies of all types make great cut flowers. Try using them in your home during their next bloom season.

ADDITIONAL SPECIES, CULTIVARS, OR VARIETIES

L. radiata, a Japanese spider lily, is coral-colored with very long curving upward stamens. 'Alba' has creamy white flowers and 'Carnea' flowers are tinted pink. *L. squamigara* is usually the hardiest variety and has funnel-shaped pink flowers. *L. traubii* is red-orange in color.

Tulip
Tulipa spp.

EXPOSURE

F. Sun to Semi-

COLD HARDINESS

All Texas

WATER USAGE

Semi-Moist

GROWTH RATE

Fast

AVG. HT × WIDTH

12–40" × 8–10"

SPACING

6–12"

Bloom colors range across the rainbow, except for true blue, and there are many different forms, types, and blends available.

*W*hen we think about spring-blooming bulbs in Texas, the first one we generally think of is the tulip. Most Texas gardeners enjoy tulips, but there is a problem in getting reliable blooms year after year in most areas. In the cold Panhandle area temperatures may be cold enough long enough to allow some tulips to rebloom successfully, but in the remainder of the state, the tulip's beauty may be enjoyed during one springtime, with disappointment in the following years. It is said that in order to ensure good shows of tulips year after year in Texas gardens, treat them as annuals and replant each year. To see some outstanding spring color, visit our botanical gardens throughout the state where they put on magnificent shows of tulips. Theme parks and municipal parks are often good places to catch "tulip color" in the spring. The best shows of tulips are created when masses of single colors are used, a technique often used in public plantings. When mass planting tulips, try various patterns or forms such as kidney, teardrop, zig-zag, and curved. In small-space areas, plant your favorite tulips in planters. Be sure to use a premium-quality lightweight potting soil and containers that have several drainholes.

When to Plant

The best time to plant tulips in Texas is in late fall/early winter. Nearly all varieties and types need to be prechilled approximately 6 weeks before planting. Prechilling may be done by placing in the bottom of your refrigerator.

Where to Plant

Plant in well-drained soils in sunny locations to achieve best results.

How to Plant

In clay soils that drain poorly, incorporate approximately 4 in. of organic matter into your existing soil. Plant bulbs 4 in. deep or at a depth 2 times their height in your prepared bed. Apply approximately 1/2 teaspoon of premium-quality, long-lasting, slow-release rose food 1 in. below the bulb and firm the soil. Water thoroughly after planting and mulch with approximately 2 in. of mulch.

Care and Maintenance

Aphids, mice, rots, and other pests and organisms may visit your tulips. If they become a problem, ask about the best control possibilities. Remember to read and follow label directions when using any gardening product. Remove bloom stalks once blooms are finished. No other pruning is normally necessary. Water as necessary to maintain moist soil. Do not keep the soil wet, nor allow it to become totally dry. Usually fertilizing is required only at planting time. For varieties that do repeat, fertilize once as new growth begins in the springtime with a premium-quality, long-lasting, slow-release rose food, according to label directions.

Additional Information

Many tulips will make excellent cut flowers for you to use indoors in arrangements. Remember that bulbs are among the favorite types of plants of little gardeners, so let your kids plant them in the fall.

Additional Species, Cultivars, or Varieties

There are many different types of tulips available. The best types of repeat-blooming tulips in Texas are classified as Species Tulips. In this category are *T. clusiana* (often called peppermint stick or lady tulip), *T. saxatilis*, *T. undulatifolia*, *T. linifolia*, *T. lutea*, *T. kuschkensis*, *T. kaufmanniana*, *T. fosterana*, *T. greigii*, and *T. montana*. Some named Species Tulips are 'Hageri', 'Toronto', 'Red Riding Hood', 'Persian Pearl', 'Pinocchio', 'Donna Bella', *Tarda*, and 'Snow Glory'. The following tulip classifications are from the *Classified List and International Register of Tulip Names*: Single Early and Double Early (Early); Mendel, Triumph, and Darwin Hybrid (Midseason); Darwin, Lily-flowered, Cottage, Rembrandt, Parrot, and Double Late or Peony-flowered (Late).

CHAPTER THREE

GRASSES: LAWN AND ORNAMENTAL

WE TEXANS SPEND MORE TIME, ENERGY, EFFORT, AND DOLLARS on our lawns than on any other single item in our home landscape. Lawns are very important to most of us. We enjoy their look and feel the special qualities they bring to our home landscapes. Both lawn grasses and ornamental grasses are included in this chapter.

TURFGRASSES

The turfgrass grown by most Texans, especially if they have a full-sun location and children to run and play on the grass, is Bermudagrass, *Cynondon dactylon*. A native grass which has been promoted rather heavily in the state of Texas is buffalograss, *Buchloe dactyloides*. Buffalo is good in prairie soils, but it will not do well in the acid, sandy soils of northeast Texas or in the soils of southeast Texas. Centipedegrass, *Eremochloa ophiuroidea*, is a great turfgrass for the acid soils of eastern Texas, but it will not grow well in the highly alkaline soils such as those often found in the western half of our state. Ryegrass, *Lolium multiflorum*, is used in Texas as a temporary cover during our cold season to allow the appearance of green grass on a year-round basis. St. Augustinegrass, *Stenotaprum secundatum*, is known as the turfgrass that will grow in shaded areas, and it will grow in shaded areas, but it will not grow in complete shade. Tall fescue, *Festuca arundinacea*, is a turfgrass that has recently been promoted in Texas as an alternative to St. Augustine. These tall fescues are primarily northern, cool-season grasses. Some varieties have been reasonably adaptable under close management to the clay soils of Texas. Texans should probably take a closer look at zoysiagrass, *Zoysia japonica*. There are some brand-new varieties that show outstanding test results.

ORNAMENTAL GRASSES

There are many different types of ornamental grasses, including blue fescue, *Festica ovian*. Maidengrass, *Miscanthus sinensis*, is an ornamental bunch grass that you may have seen growing in nice

Chapter Three

wonderful clumps at the State Fair of Texas. The widely available mondo grass, *Ophiopogon japonicus* and monkey grass, *Liriope muscari*, are traditional ornamental "grasses" which are used in clumps, as groundcovers, or for borders. The white-plumed pampas grass, *Cortaderia selloana*, may be the oldest clumping grass used in Texas for ornamental purposes. There is also a pink-plumed variety. Fountain grass, *Pennisstum alopecuroides* is a group of grasses and is perhaps best known as purple fountain grass.

You will find ornamental grasses as well as lawn grasses available at Lowe's.

LAWNS: HISTORY, FUNCTION, AND TIPS

If you go back to some of our early American history, you will find lawns in use. For example when visiting Thomas Jefferson's homesite, Monticello, you can see actual drawings of the lawn. Though it was not the closely clipped lawns that we use today, Mr. Jefferson, family, and visitors did enjoy a lawn.

Lawns, of course, serve as carpets in our yards. Lawns help cool the air, hold the soil, and prevent erosion. We lump our lawn grasses into two basic groups, warm-season and cool-season. The only cool-season grass that is reasonably adaptable in a relatively large percentage of the state is some varieties of tall fescue. One may be able to grow Kentucky Bluegrass, *Poa pratensis* in the Panhandle, under closer irrigation, but this is the only area it could possibly grow during Texas summers.

When overseeding existing warm-season grasses, we generally use annual ryegrass. However, perennial ryegrass, *Lolium perenne*, may be planted in late summer/early fall to provide a green-color lawn through the entire cool/winter season also.

Most of our grasses are imported except for the currently available selections of buffalograss. You can start a lawn from seed, plugs, sodding, or sprigs, or you may have it hydro-mulched.

Chapter Three

Don't try starting seeds too early in the springtime when the soils are still too cool for the warm-season, southern lawn grasses. These seeds require a warm soil to germinate properly.

Certain parts of the state are better adapted to different lawn grasses than others, and soil types have a lot to do with that. Match your grass selection to the part of the state that you're in and the soil type that you have. Make sure you understand the care necessary to maintain your lawn. Obtain this information before purchasing any seed, plugs, sprigs, or sod.

Some turfgrasses are relatively high maintenance such as the very fine blade Hybrid Bermudagrass varieties, while others are considerably less. Lawn grasses are wonderful to have here in Texas. I hope the information that I have put together in this chapter for you will help to make your lawn very enjoyable.

The ornamental grasses are groups of plants that can be added to various aspects of your home landscape in masses of their own or in combination with other ornamentals, annuals, perennials, and shrubs. Take a look at what I have offered here and visit a local retail garden center for additional possibilities.

LAWN CARE

The best way to have fewer weed problems in your home lawn is to grow a healthy thick turf. Here's one way to accomplish this:

• Approximately 2 to 3 weeks after the last killing frost/freeze in your area, apply your favorite 3:1:2 ratio, premium-quality, long-lasting lawn fertilizer according to label directions. Reapply approximately every 8 weeks through the growing season and once in the fall. The fall application is the single most important application of the year. Don't miss it. Always water thoroughly after applying any fertilizer.

Note: 21-7-14, 19-5-9, 18-6-12, 15-5-10, and 12-4-8 are all 3:1:2 ratio lawn fertilizer.

Chapter Three

- Water as needed. Do not set your lawn on a watering schedule. If grass blades are rolling inward from their sides, turning gray-green instead of their normal green or if the grass lays flat and won't spring back after being walked on, give your lawn a long, deep drink, to a depth of 6 to 8 in. Don't rewater until it's needed again.

- Mow often enough to remove no more than a third of the grass-blade height every time.

- A yearly or biannual lawn aeration is especially good for heavy soils.

Follow these suggestions and you should have a nice, thick, Texas lawn to enjoy in your "bare feet!"

If weeds insist on invading your lawn after you have followed the above program for 2 seasons, then other measures may be taken. The first of these involves a group of products called pre-emergents. Pre-emergents deny weeds the opportunity to become established in your lawn.

The two weed classifications are grassy and broadleaf. Rule of thumb: *If it walks, talks, and acts like a grass, it's a grassy weed—if it doesn't, it's a broadleaf weed.* Crabgrass, Johnsongrass, grass burs, and dallisgrass are all examples of grassy weeds commonly found in Texas. Dandelion, henbit, burclover, and dock are all broadleaf weeds.

Weeds are also classified as annual or perennial. Johnsongrass and dallisgrass are perennial "grassy" weeds while crabgrass and sand burs are both annuals. Dandelion and dock are examples of perennial broadleaf weeds found in Texas lawns. Henbit and burclover are annual broadleaf weeds.

Most weedy lawn pests are warm-season weeds, but henbit is a cool-season annual broadleaf weed, while annual bluegrass is a cool-season grassy pest.

Chapter Three

Selected pre-emergents will prevent label-listed annual broad-leaf as well as annual grassy weeds. Some types only prevent grassy weeds, while others prevent both types. Check the labels for effectiveness on perennials of either type.

Timing is important when using a pre-emergent to prevent weeds. If applied after weeds are up and growing, it is of little or no value. To prevent most warm-season weeds, apply approximately 2 weeks before the last average killing frost or freeze in your area. If spring comes early, you may need to apply the product early. To prevent fall and winter weeds, apply 6 weeks before the first average killing frost. Remember to always follow label directions when using any gardening aid.

If you follow the previously outlined program and the other suggestions, and you are still left with a few tough, pesky perennial lawn weeds, you may want to try another group of products classified as post-emergent. Most are liquids which can be spot applied on your troubled lawn areas. Again, always follow label directions.

Certainly, if you like the looks of some weeds in your lawn it's your choice whether to remove them or not. You may want to simply let the weeds grow, or hand dig them.

The table on page 97 lists some of the more common problems you may experience with your lawn.

For advice on how to combat these diseases and/or pests read the care and maintenance sections for each recommended lawn grass that follows.

And as always, consult garden center personnel for any additional help you may need.

Chapter Three

DAMAGE SYMPTOMS OF COMMON TURFGRASS PEST PROBLEMS AND POSSIBLE CAUSES

Symptom(s):   Possible causal agent(s):

A. Disruption of soil:
1. Hills, piles or structures of loose dirt on turf .... *ants*
   a. Mounds up to 18 inches tall with no visible entrance(s)
      or mound with ants emerging in mass when
      disturbed .... *red imported fire ant*
   b. Small mounds with rims around single central entrance
      holes and presence of small (³/₁₆ in.) grayish-black ants .... *pyramid ants*
   c. Many hills of coarse soil with central exit holes and
      presence of large (³/₈ in.) red-brown ant with spines
      on the thorax .... *Texas leafcutting ant*
   d. Flat cleared areas up to 3 ft. in diameter made of coarse
      soil particles with a single central exit hole and with the
      presence of large (³/₈ in.) reddish-brown ants with square
      heads .... *red harvester ant*
2. Trails of raised, loose dirt through turf roughly ¹/₂ inch wide in
   an "S" shaped pattern .... *mole crickets*
3. Small piles of dirt "pellets" (³/₁₆ in.) scattered through thatch ... *earth worms*
4. Earthen "chimneys" with central holes (about ¹/₂ inch diameter) ... *crawfish*
5. Small piles of loose dirt which are associated with exit
   holes .... *green June beetle larvae*
6. Round holes (up to ¹/₂ inch diameter) in soil .... *digger wasp nests or*
                                                          cicada exit holes
B. Direct damage to grass causing yellowing or plant death:
1. Grass blades chewed or missing .... *caterpillars*
   a. Presence of gray-brown caterpillars up to 1 in. long with an
      inverted cream-colored "Y" on the fronts of the head
      capsules .... *armyworms*
   b. Presence of gray-brown caterpillars up to 1 in. long that curl
      into a tight "C" position when disturbed .... *cutworms*
   c. Presence of translucent greenish caterpillars up to
      ³/₄ in. long with black raised spots on each
      body segment .... *tropical sod webworm*
2. Yellow or dead grass:
   a. Roots missing and presence of cream-colored "C" shaped
      grubs with three legs on body segments behind brown head
      capsule .... *white grubs*
   b. No tissue removed, with presence of pinkish-orange, white
      and black nymph and adult stages of bugs up to ³/₁₆ in. long . *chinch bugs*
   c. No tissue removed, but the "galls" or globular objects
      (scales) in the root zone .... *Rhodesgrass scale or*
                                                          ground pearls
   d. No tissue removed, but with shortened internodes producing a typical
      rosetting and tufted growth, or "witch broom" effect; grass may be
      very yellow or whitish in appearance with no insects visible to
      the naked eye .... *Bermudagrass (stunt) mites*
                                                or buffalograss (stunt) mites

Reprinted from:
The Texas Agricultural Extension Service publication #B-5083

Bermudagrass
Cynodon dactylon

EXPOSURE

Full Sun

COLD HARDINESS

All Texas

WATER USAGE

Semi-Arid/Semi-Mst.

GROWTH RATE

Fast

AVG. HT × WIDTH

Grass

SPACING

Sow 1½ lb./1000 sq.

Warm-season narrow-bladed grass; vigorous perennial. Spreads by above-ground runners and below-ground stems. Drought tolerant.

*B*ermudagrass grows best in full-sun areas—it will not tolerate heavy shade. It is considered the grass of Texas because it will grow in every area of the state. It is the grass used on all athletic turfs, and it is the grass of choice for commercial uses, for municipalities, and for schools. It has been used for lawns since the early 1800s.

WHEN TO PLANT
The earliest time to plant Bermudagrass is in spring when nighttime temperatures have been consistently above 70 degrees Fahrenheit for 2 weeks. Don't plant Bermudagrass seed if temperatures remain cool. Plant sod as soon as fresh green sod is available. Bermudagrass may be successfully planted spring, summer and early fall in Texas.

WHERE TO PLANT
Bermudagrass demands full sun. Use it in landscape areas where you wish to establish a warm-season turfgrass lawn that is tough and resistant to wear.

How to Plant

To plant from sod, follow these steps:

1. Measure the area to be planted in square yards.
2. Lightly till the soil, correct any drainage problems, rake, and remove any rocks, sticks, or other debris.
3. Apply a lawn-starter granular fertilizer, following label directions.

Lay the sod with edges flush, as if laying carpet or flooring. After the entire area is laid, water thoroughly. Maintain a moist condition, gradually reducing watering as your planting becomes established.

To plant from seed, follow these steps:

1. Measure the area to be planted in square feet. Purchase approximately 1 to $1^1/_2$ lb. per 1000 sq. ft. of hulled seed packaged for the current season. Till the area and correct any drainage problems.
2. To ensure even seed distribution, sow half the seed in one direction and half at a 90-degree angle to that. No mulching is normally necessary.
3. Irrigate the area with a lawn sprinkler system or hose sprinkler. Maintain moist soil throughout the critical establishment period.
4. After the grass becomes tall enough to mow it one time, begin a regular fertilizing program with 3-1-2 ratio lawn fertilizer.

Care and Maintenance

Bermudagrass may be attacked by brown patch, dollar spot, leaf spots, and other diseases, as well as by grubs, Bermuda mite, sod webworms, army worms, and other insects. If pests become a problem, be sure to visit your local retail garden center, which will offer several control possibilities. Remember, always read and follow label directions when using any lawn and garden aid. Normally mow common Bermudagrass to a height of one inch. You may wish to increase to $1^1/_2$ in. or taller in midsummer; by summer's end, try mowing as high as your mower will raise. My lawn is 95 percent coastal Bermudagrass, and that is what I do. Tip: Always mow with a sharp-bladed mower. Rotary mowers are quite acceptable when growing Bermuda. When watering Bermudagrass lawns, be sure to water to a minimum depth of 6 in. and 8 in. is even better. Begin fertilizing your lawn in the spring after you have seen new growth emerge. Mark your calendar and reapply premium-quality long-lasting slow-release 3:1:2 ratio fertilizers about every 10 weeks during the growing season, and once again in the fall. 3:1:2 ratios include 15-5-10, 18-6-12, 19-5-9, and 21-7-14. Apply according to label directions.

Additional Species, Cultivars, and Varieties

Hybrid Bermudagrasses include 'Hall's selection', 'Uganda', 'Bayshore', 'Royal Cape', 'U-3 Tiffine', 'Sun Turf', 'Tifflawn', 'Tiffgreen', 'Texturf 10', 'Tiffway', 'Toughcoat', 'Santa Ana', 'Midway', and 'Tiffwad'. I like 'Texture 10' because of the way it wears or stands up to lots of traffic. It is often used on athletic fields.

Buffalograss
Buchloe dactyloides

EXPOSURE

Full Sun

COLD HARDINESS

All Texas

WATER USAGE

Arid-Dry

GROWTH RATE

Medium

AVG. HT × WIDTH

Grass

SPACING

Sow 3/4–4 lb./1000 sq. '

Fine-bladed, slightly curly blue-green grass; native to Texas and much of the prairies. Established from seed or sod, spreads by seed or above-ground runners.

*B*uffalograss is a great grass of the plains that helped to nourish the tremendous buffalo herds. It was used by the settlers to build homes. Buffalograss is not for everyone, but for an extremely low maintenance lawn in full-sun locations, you should seriously consider this native grass. Buffalograss usually grows in the 4- to 6-in. range. It does not require mowing, but you may mow it if you wish to keep it at a 2- to 3-in. height. The lower height may require once a week mowing at the more active growing times of the year.

WHEN TO PLANT

Buffalograss is most successfully planted in the early spring, after soil and air temperatures warm to 70 degrees. Buffalograss sod is available in several selections that may be planted as soon as they are available.

WHERE TO PLANT

Plant buffalograss in clay soils, as it usually does poorly in sandy soils. It will not tolerate heavily shaded areas, but thrives in full sun. If you are looking for a grass to hold the soil on steep areas and don't want to mow, buffalograss is a top-notch candidate. If you wish to have turfgrass near entrances to your home or along a drive but are not interested in a lot of maintenance, buffalograss is a good choice for you. It works well when used in Xeriscapes of native Texas plants where the soil is conducive to successful long-term growth. If you have a vacation home or a home you seldom visit and would like to have grass that will survive without your presence, try planting buffalograss.

How to Plant
To establish a buffalograss from seed:

1. Measure the area to be planted in sq. feet.
2. Lightly till the area, correct any drainage problems, and rake to remove any rocks, sticks, or other debris.
3. Sow $3/4$ to 4 lb. of treated buffalograss per 1000 square ft. Sow one half of the seed in a north/south direction and the remaining half in an east/west direction. No mulching or coverage is required. Water thoroughly after planting. Maintain a moist soil for higher success of germination. As the seeds begin to germinate and the plants establish themselves, reduce frequency of watering.

Planting buffalograss from sod should be done in early spring when it is available fresh and green.

1. Prepare soil as for seed.
2. Lay the sod end-to-end and side-to-side in a solid mat for instant effect. As an option, it may be divided in strips no smaller then about 6 x 6 in. and plant in checkerboard style pattern, 12 to 16 in. apart. The lawn should be establish within one season. The closer the sod parts are planted, the faster you will realize total coverage.
3. Water as needed to prevent wilting.

Care and Maintenance
Buffalograss is free of pests. Mowing buffalograss lawns may be done if so desired, but it is not required. Water thoroughly and deeply, not frequently and lightly. Little to no fertilization is necessary, but if you do wish to fertilize, apply once in the spring a 3:1:2 ratio lawn fertilizer such as 21-7-14, 19-5-9, or 15-5-10 according to label directions. Be sure to use a premium-quality long-lasting slow-release fertilizer. If desired, apply once during the fall as well.

Additional Information
Buffalograss usually does best in areas that receive less that 30 in. of rain per year. Two main areas that buffalograss is not recommended for are East Texas and the Gulf Coast Prairie areas. Buffalograss will adapt to all other areas of Texas.

Additional Species, Cultivars, or Varieties
Selected varieties include: 'Prairie', 'Buffalawn', '609', 'Comanche', 'Texoka', 'Plains', 'Stampede', and 'Topgun'.

Centipedegrass
Eremochloa ophiuroide

EXPOSURE

Full Sun

COLD HARDINESS

East Texas

WATER USAGE

Semi-Moist

GROWTH RATE

Fast to Med.

AVG. HT × WIDTH

Grass

SPACING

Sow ¹/₂–2 lb./1000 sq.

Centipedegrass is a warm-season perennial grass that is spread by above-ground stolens and seed. It is bright green in color and well adapted to East Texas.

*W*hen looking for an alternative grass to plant in the acid soils of Texas, centipedegrass, a native of China and Southeast Asia, may work well for you. Centipede is not for alkaline soils and is best adapted to the eastern third of Texas. It isn't recommended for alkaline soils due to severe chronic iron chloris problems. In areas centipedegrass is well adapted to, it makes a gorgeous, thick, and relatively low-maintenance turf. If you do live in one of these areas, I strongly suggest that you investigate growing centipedegrass. I have seen absolutely gorgeous centipedegrass lawns in areas such as Longview, Tyler, Lufkin, Nacogdoches, and Beaumont. While centipedegrass needs less maintenance than St. Augustine or Bermuda, it does require some upkeep. Perhaps it should be called "reduced maintenance" rather than "low maintenance." Fertilizing and mowing can be less frequent, but sufficient water is required to maintain a good-looking turf through blazing July and August temperatures.

WHEN TO PLANT

Centipedegrass may be established from seed in the early spring after soil and air temperatures warm consistently to 70 degrees for a minimum of two weeks.

WHERE TO PLANT

Centipedegrass should be planted in full-sun locations for best long-term results, in areas of good soil drainage. Do not plant in low areas where the soil is poorly drained and water tends to stand. Centipedegrass will exist in lightly shaded areas, but don't plant in heavy shade. While it is considered more shade tolerant than Bermudagrass, it is less shade tolerant than St. Augustinegrass.

HOW TO PLANT

Centipedegrass is slow to establish from seed, but it can be done:

1. Till the area, correct drainage if needed, and rake to remove any rocks, sticks, or other debris.
2. Sow seeds at $^1/_2$ to 2 lb. per 1,000 sq. ft.

Maintain moisture at the soil level. After establishment and first mowing, watering may be gradually reduced to an as-needed frequency to prevent wilting.

From fresh green sod:

1. Prepare soil as for seed.
2. Lay sod end to end and side to side for an instant lawn. One option is to cut into 6 x 6 in. squares and plant in a 12-in. checkerboard pattern.
3. Maintain moisture to prevent wilting.

CARE AND MAINTENANCE

Centipedegrass is relatively free of pests, but if insects or disease such as brown patch happen to invade your lawn, visit your local retail garden center for control options. Remember to read and follow label directions when using any lawn and garden aid. It is usually not necessary to mow more than once per week to maintain a good-looking centipedegrass lawn. The height of mowing should be from 2 to 3 in. Irrigate as necessary to prevent wilting during the growing season. Water to a soil depth minimum of 6 to 8 in. Centipedegrass needs water from time to time during the winter more than any other turfgrass. Specialty centipedegrass lawn fertilizer is available, and is usually 15-0-15. Apply as growth begins in the spring, 12 weeks later, and once during the fall. If soil tests indicate a lack of phosphorous, in most cases 15-5-10 will also work well. Use all lawn products according to label directions. Do not apply a fertilizer with high levels of phosphorous unless a complete soil test indicates a shortage. Always use premium-quality long-lasting slow-release fertilizers on centipedegrass.

ADDITIONAL SPECIES, CULTIVARS, OR VARIETIES

No improved varieties of centipede are readily available to homeowners.

Ryegrass
Lolium multiflorum

EXPOSURE

F. Sun to Semi-

COLD HARDINESS

All Texas

WATER USAGE

Semi-Moist

GROWTH RATE

Fast

AVG. HT × WIDTH

Ann. Grass

SPACING

Sow 5–8 lb./1000 sq. '

Ryegrass is a medium- to dark-green bunch grass with no above- or below-ground runners. It spreads strictly by seed.

Ryegrass is typically used throughout Texas during the warm season. It is grown with lawngrasses such as St. Augustine, Bermuda, and centipede to maintain a year-round green appearance. An exception to this is the perennial ryegrass, *Lolium perenne*, which may be used successfully year-round in the Panhandle area when put under irrigation. Perennial ryegrass is usually used as an annual throughout the remaining portion of Texas. Both types of ryegrass tend to fizzle out as temperatures rise in the spring and summer.

WHEN TO PLANT
The best planting time is 6 to 8 weeks before the first killing frost in your area.

WHERE TO PLANT
Plant in full-sun to part sun/shade locations where any of our warm-season lawn grasses are grown.

How to Plant

Ryegrass establishes well in either acid or alkaline soils, clay, or sand. To help ensure that it will establish itself:

1. Mow your permanent grass low to the ground at the time of planting. Use 5 to 8 lb. of current-season seeds per 1000 sq. ft.
2. Sow the seeds in two directions, with the second direction at a 90-degree angle to the first.
3. Water frequently enough to maintain a moist soil at ground level. Ryegrass establishes quickly; as it becomes established, reduce frequency of watering.
4. If desired, a lawn-starting fertilizer may be applied at the time of seed sowing.

Care and Maintenance

Brown patch, leaf spot, and rust may appear on ryegrass. If these diseases become a problem, visit your local retail garden center, which will offer several control possibilities. Remember to read and follow label directions when using any product. In order to maintain a manicured lawn, mowing is required throughout the fall, winter, and spring. Annual ryegrass almost always requires more frequent mowing than does perennial ryegrass. If you desire a finer-bladed grass and a little less frequent mowing, perhaps the perennial ryegrass is for you. Keep in mind that perennial ryegrass is more costly to establish, but the difference in price may be worth it. Make sure that your lawn mower has a sharp blade. To prevent drying and wilting, water as necessary throughout the entire season. Fertilize at planting time with a starter fertilizer. Approximately 4 weeks after initial mowing from establishment, apply a 3-1-2 lawn fertilizer such as 15-5-10, 21-7-14, or 18-6-12. Make sure you use a long-lasting premium-quality lawn fertilizer according to the label directions. Three applications throughout the growing season—after establishment, mid-season, and then late winter/early spring—will aid in growing a beautiful dark-green ryegrass lawn.

Additional Information

To establish a lawn of ryegrass for the winter, it is very important that you plant early enough, while it is still warm. Ryegrass, while quite cold hardy once established, has difficulty in germinating and establishing itself after cold weather arrives.

Additional Species, Cultivars, or Varieties

There are two basic types of ryegrass: annual and perennial.

St. Augustine

Stenotaphrum secundatum

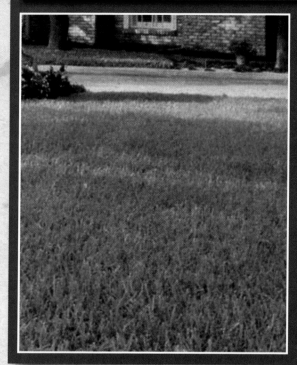

EXPOSURE	COLD HARDINESS
F. Sun to Semi-	All Texas

WATER USAGE	GROWTH RATE
Semi-Moist	Fast

AVG. HT × WIDTH	SPACING
Grass	Sod

St. Augustinegrass is a coarse, wide-bladed perennial grass that is widely grown in nearly all areas of Texas.

My Granddad Miller, a long-time dry land cotton and grain farmer from Indian Creek, Texas, said that once he got his St. Augustinegrass established after moving to Brownwood, it didn't need any more care than Bermudagrass. The turf traditionally made by St. Augustinegrass is so thick and lush that it usually does not require more frequent mowing than normal Bermudagrass. St. Augustinegrass has been used successfully in lawns since the 1700s. It is currently used in all areas of the Southeast and Southwest, in Bermuda, and as far south as New Zealand. It is a wonderful barefoot grass, and is great for lying on beneath a shade tree.

WHEN TO PLANT

The best time to plant St. Augustine is in the springtime after all danger of frost is past and fresh green sod is available.

WHERE TO PLANT

St. Augustine will grow in full-sun or shaded areas, but not complete shade. To do well, it needs a minimum of 4 hrs. of full sun per day, or 8 hrs. of mixed sun and shade.

How to Plant

St. Augustine must be planted from vegetative parts, either from plugs, blocks, or sprigs. My mother—with a little bit of help—sprigged an entire lawn at our home in Brownwood. It took a while to do it (more than a year), but St. Augustine still grows at the same address. Today, St. Augustine is often planted from blocks of sod. For an "instant" lawn, plant solid over the entire area. Or cut up in 6-in.-square blocks and plant in a checkerboard pattern, blocks approximately 6 in. apart. This method will establish a complete lawn in one growing season. Steps to follow:

1. Make sure the grade is proper so there will be no low areas with standing water. Where possible, lightly till the area and rake.
2. Place blocks solidly over the entire prepared area for an instant lawn, or plant plugs in a checkerboard pattern.
3. Water often during establishment to prevent wilting, then reduce watering frequency.

Care and Maintenance

St. Augustinegrass is susceptible to brown patch, leaf spot, and gray leaf spot, and it sometimes is visited by grubs, chinch bugs, and other unwanted visitors. Remember that a nice, thick, vigorously growing turfgrass will have fewer problems with insects and diseases. But if you have a problem, check for available methods of control. Remember to read and follow directions on any gardening aid that you use. If St. Augustine Decline (SAD) invades your lawn, replant with 'Raleigh', a variety that is resistant to this virus. For a thick, healthy lawn, St. Augustinegrass requires mowing at 2 in. or higher. Water frequently enough to ensure that the grass doesn't go into a prolonged and severe wilt. Fertilize in the springtime as new growth begins. The 3:1:2 ratio lawn fertilizers often recommended for warm-season grasses work well with St. Augustine. Among these fertilizers are 18-6-12, 19-5-9, 21-7-15, and 15-5-10. Use a premium-quality long-lasting type and read and follow label directions.

Additional Information

Because St. Augustinegrass doesn't have underground runners or rhizomes like Bermudagrass, it is relatively easy to keep from intrusion into gardens and flowerbeds.

Additional Species, Cultivars, or Varieties

In addition to common St. Augustinegrass, you may try 'Floratam' and 'Seville' (in South Texas only), and 'Raleigh', a variety resistant to SAD in all other areas where hardy.

Tall Fescue
Festuca arundinacea

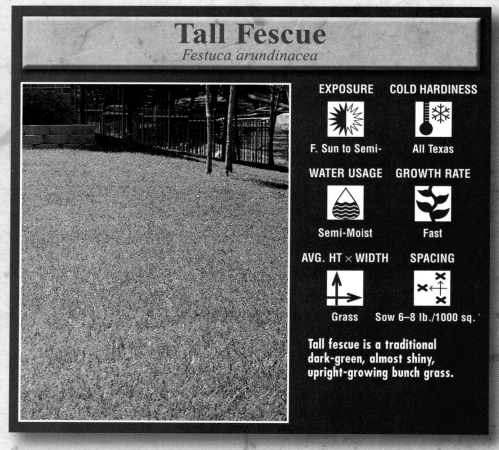

EXPOSURE
F. Sun to Semi-

COLD HARDINESS
All Texas

WATER USAGE
Semi-Moist

GROWTH RATE
Fast

AVG. HT × WIDTH
Grass

SPACING
Sow 6–8 lb./1000 sq.

Tall fescue is a traditional dark-green, almost shiny, upright-growing bunch grass.

*T*all fescue grass has been used successfully in the northern states for generations, and more recently in the "transitional zone" that includes the northern part of Texas. It is a good substitute for St. Augustine, and will adapt to heavier soils in northern Texas. Since their introduction, the tall fescue grasses have been the focus of a relatively active program to breed new varieties. It may sound a bit confusing, but now there are "dwarf" tall fescues on the market.

WHEN TO PLANT
The best time to plant tall fescue in Texas is in the fall. The second-best time is very early spring.

WHERE TO PLANT
Some gardeners think tall fescue will grow better than St. Augustine in areas of heavy shade. This is not true. In order for tall fescue to do well, it usually needs 4 hrs. of full sun or 8 hrs. of 50 percent sun, 50 percent shade, the same as St. Augustine. If all the trees in your yard are deciduous, after they have dropped their leaves in the fall there will be adequate sunlight for fescue, and it will continue to do well through the fall and early spring, before the trees put

out their leaves. After your trees put on their new set of leaves your fescue may begin to thin due to lack of sunlight. Make sure your area has adequate sunlight prior to planting.

How to Plant
Tall fescue is traditionally planted from seed in well-prepared seedbeds.

1. Rototill the area 3 to 4 in. deep. Hand-rake it, removing rocks, sticks, or any other debris.
2. Determine how many square feet will be planted. Use 6 to 8 lb. of fescue seed per 1000 sq. ft.
3. Sow half the seed in a north/south direction, the other half in an east/west direction. After planting, you may take a leaf rake, turn it upside-down, and drag it over the area.
4. Water thoroughly and maintain moist soil on the top level. After establishment, watering frequency may be reduced.

Care and Maintenance
Tall fescue lawns may have unwelcome visits from fusarium blight, leaf spot, or even brown patch. Insects such as army worms, cutworms, and white grubs may visit as well. Visit your local retail garden center for suggestions on ways to control fescue insects and diseases. Remember to read and follow label directions. Tall fescue lawns may thin out in the dry summer conditions common to Texas. To ensure a thicker lawn, apply extra seeds each fall. This is standard management practice for maintaining good thick stands of tall fescue lawns in Texas. Mow 2 to 3 in. tall on a regular basis in order to maintain a good, thick, healthy stand of tall fescue. Water frequently enough to prevent wilting. Fertilize tall fescue lawns approximately 3 times during the growing season: once in the early fall, once in late fall/early winter, and once again in late winter/early spring. Apply premium-quality, long-lasting slow-release fertilizer that meets the 3:1:2 ratio such as a 15-5-10, 19-5-9, 18-6-12, or 21-7-14. Remember to read and follow label directions, and water thoroughly after every application.

Additional Information
Tall fescue requires different management practices than St. Augustine and Bermudagrass. Do not fertilize during the summer, plant in early fall, and be prepared to sow additional seed each fall.

Additional Species, Cultivars, or Varieties
Available varieties of tall fescue grasses vary according to your part of the state and your wholesale supplier. Look for low-growing, heat- and drought-tolerant, disease-resistant, dwarf turf-type fescue grasses. Do not use pasture types of fescue for lawns.

Zoysiagrass
Zoysia japonica

EXPOSURE

F. Sun to Semi-

COLD HARDINESS

All Texas

WATER USAGE

Arid to Semi-Mst.

GROWTH RATE

Medium

AVG. HT × WIDTH

Grass

SPACING

Sod

A perennial turfgrass that spreads by both stolens above ground and rhizomes below ground.

Zoysia japonica is sometimes called Korean or Japanese lawn grass. It has been around since just before the turn of the century and is considered very cold tolerant, more so than other grass species normally grown in Texas. It is a beautiful grass that tolerates shade. It has a coarser texture than do some of the other zoysia varieties. 'Meyer' is an improved strain of the original parentage and has been grown in the United States since the 1940s. Both grasses are available in Texas and may be used in all areas of Texas. It may be zoysia's unusual name that makes it less popular than other grasses, but it is also very slow in establishing. For example, 2 × 2-in. zoysia plugs put into an existing fescue lawn may take as long as 5 years to overtake the fescue. Even if planted in a clean bed where no weeds and grass are growing, 2 × 2-in. plugs placed in a 12-in. checkerboard pattern may take as long as 2 years to cover the area. You may choose to put in solid sod on a clean prepared seedbed. The colors of zoysiagrass are very deep green. One variety is called 'Emerald'.

WHEN TO PLANT
The best time to plant zoysiagrass is in early spring after all danger of frost is past and the soil has warmed slightly.

WHERE TO PLANT

Plant in any area where you want a deep-green, rather lush lawn.
Do not plant in heavily shaded areas, locations that are difficult to
water, or poorly drained sites.

HOW TO PLANT

1. Till 3 to 4 in. deep and make sure the grade drains properly.
2. Rake to remove rocks, sticks, or other debris, and apply a starter
   fertilizer according to label directions.
3. Install 2 × 2-in. plugs set on 1-ft. centers in a checkerboard style
   pattern, or place solid sod area for an immediate lawn.
4. Water as needed to prevent wilting.

CARE AND MAINTENANCE

Zoysiagrass is considered relatively free of insects. One insect that
may become a problem is the old, common, white grub. Visit your
local retail garden center for the right types of products and in-
depth information on proper application. Brown patch, rust, and
leaf spot may visit zoysia, but the grass usually recovers very
quickly as soon as proper environmental conditions are established.
If these diseases tend to persist, ask your Lowe's customer service
associate about controls. Mow on a regular basis. While zoysiagrass
grows significantly slower than Bermudagrass, it is recommended
that it be mowed almost as often in order to maintain a nice even
turf and avoid the scalped look. Zoysia tends to have a good built-in
resistance to drought, but water often enough to prevent wilting.
Fertilize once in the springtime as new growth begins and once in
the fall, using a 15-5-10, 21-7-14, 19-5-9, 18-6-12, or other 3:1:2 ratio
lawn fertilizer. Be sure to choose long-lasting, slow-release, high-
quality brands, and always water thoroughly after each application.

ADDITIONAL INFORMATION

Before deciding to use zoysiagrass in your lawn, contact your
County Extension Agent for some facts or tip sheets on zoysia.

ADDITIONAL SPECIES, CULTIVARS, OR VARIETIES

Look for 'Meyer', 'El Toro', 'Omni', and 'Emerald'. New releases
from Texas A & M Research include 'Crowne', 'Palisades', and
Z. matrella 'Cavalier'.

Blue Fescue
Festica ovina

EXPOSURE

Full Sun

COLD HARDINESS

All Texas

WATER USAGE

Arid-Dry

GROWTH RATE

Medium

AVG. HT × WIDTH

10–12″ × 12–16″

SPACING

8–12″

Evergreen bunching grass, very drought tolerant.

*B*lue fescue, also known as clump fescue or ornamental fescue, makes a very interesting clump planting in a hot, dry location. It is also ideal for a border or mass effect, and is great as an edging plant. Blue fescue will take a small amount of shade, but it does prefer full sun. Poorly drained or wet soil is the worst problem for blue fescue. Do not put blue fescue in areas that have sprinkler systems and are watered frequently—it is a tough, durable plant that will take heat and drought.

WHEN TO PLANT
Plant blue fescue any time of the year. The best planting time is very early spring; the second-best time is very early fall.

WHERE TO PLANT
Plant in your full-sun, well-drained landscape locations. It even grows well in clay soils or sandy soils as long as they are properly drained. Do not plant in heavily shaded areas. Blue fescue is wonderful in rock gardens, and it will blend well with Xeriscape plantings where a naturalized look is desired. Not

only does it have a very interesting blue/gray color, but its buff-colored bloom stalks add extra interest to the landscape.

HOW TO PLANT
Blue fescue, clump fescue, or ornamental fescue will tolerate many different types of soils. In order to achieve maximum growth, improve the soil slightly. Till approximately 2 in. of organic matter into the top 6 in. of soil. Remove the plants from their containers and plant in individual planting holes no deeper than they were originally grown in the containers. Backfill with the loose soil mix, water thoroughly, apply root stimulator, and mulch with 3 in. of bark mulch.

CARE AND MAINTENANCE
Blue fescue has no serious insect or disease problems. No pruning is required. In fact, heavy pruning will damage, disturb, or destroy the ornamental shape. Water only as necessary to prevent total soil dryness. Fertilize a maximum of twice a year with a premium-quality long-lasting granular fertilizer in a 3:1:2 ratio. Examples of this analysis are 15-5-10, 21-7-14, and 18-6-12. Water thoroughly after each application. Fertilize no more than once in early spring and once in early fall at the maximum.

ADDITIONAL INFORMATION
Not only does blue fescue do well when planted in beds, it also works in large containers. When grown in containers, it is mobile and can be moved on decks or any other places where you want to create a special effect.

ADDITIONAL SPECIES, CULTIVARS, OR VARIETIES
In addition to the standard blue fescue, you may find 'Glauca' and 'Elijah Blue'.

Fountain Grass
Pennisetum alopecuroides

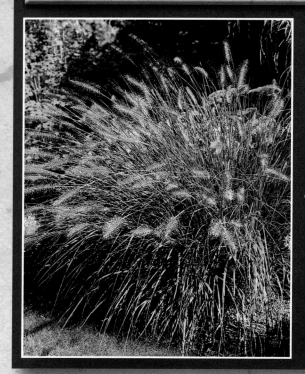

EXPOSURE	COLD HARDINESS
Full Sun	Varies

WATER USAGE	GROWTH RATE
Semi-Moist	Fast

AVG. HT × WIDTH	SPACING
10"–3' × 3–4'	3–4'

Clumping, bunch grass with foliage of purple to very dark green with foxtail plumage-like blooms.

Fountain grass is sometimes called crimson fountain grass or purple fountain grass. It is a very neat, upright, rounded, clump-type, grasslike foliage that has a reddish-brown coloring on its outside edge and red rose flower spikes. The spikes may grow as tall as 4 ft. and will decorate the plant through the entire summer—absolutely gorgeous for use in your landscape. I have used this grass along the sides of our deck. We enjoy the movement of the blooms or seedheads and the motion of the plants themselves. Do not plant in heavily shaded areas. These plants are quite drought tolerant and may be used in areas where you rarely have a chance to water, such as on banks or slopes.

WHEN TO PLANT
The best time to plant purple fountain grass is in the springtime, right after all danger of frost is past.

WHERE TO PLANT
In order to do its best, fountain grass needs to be planted in a full-sun location in improved soil. The grass may be used in smaller areas for spot or clump-

114

type plantings. It may create a large screen for dividing different areas of your color garden. I like to use it in large containers on the deck in full sun.

HOW TO PLANT

Till 3 to 4 in. of organic matter into the top 4 in. of your soil. Remove plants from containers, insert them into holes that are no deeper than rootball depth, and backfill with the improved soil mix. Water thoroughly and apply root stimulator according to label directions. After the planting is finished, mulch with about 3 in. of bark mulch. When planting in large containers, use a premium-quality light-weight potting soil.

CARE AND MAINTENANCE

No serious pests affect fountain grass, with the exception of an occasional grasshopper that may stop by to take a bite. Pruning is not necessary unless you wish to remove any wind- or storm-damaged parts or if you wish to use some plumage for indoor decoration. Water as necessary to prevent complete soil dryness. While this plant is quite drought tolerant, don't let it go "bone dry" for weeks in mid-July or August. Maintain a 3-in. depth of bark mulch through the entire growing season, especially in July and August. You may fertilize with water-soluble, liquid, or specialty granular fertilizer, or simply use your favorite lawn fertilizer. Those that work well are 15-5-10, 18-6-12, and 21-7-14 slow-release premium-quality types. Remember to read and follow label directions when applying fertilizers and water thoroughly after each application. Your first application can be 2 weeks after your initial planting, a second application 10 weeks later, and possibly a third early in the fall.

ADDITIONAL INFORMATION

Some of the best plantings I have seen have been at the great State Fair of Texas. If you are looking for something "different" to plant in your landscape, look at the varieties of fountain grass available.

ADDITIONAL SPECIES, CULTIVARS, OR VARIETIES

'Dwarf Fountain Grass' is hardy in all Texas zones. 'Little Bunny' is a dwarf variety that grows only about 12 in. high and is hardy in Zone 7 southward through Zone 9. Our normal fountain grass is considered hardy in Zones 8 and 9.

Maidengrass
Miscanthus sinensis

EXPOSURE

F. Sun to Semi-

COLD HARDINESS

All Texas

WATER USAGE

Moist to Arid (v.)

GROWTH RATE

Fast to Slow (v.)

AVG. HT × WIDTH

2–10′ × 2–4′

SPACING

Varies

Clump-forming, herbaceous grass. Green to silvery to white patterns of color in the upright, long, grass-type foliage.

Maidengrass is an ornamental clump-forming grass, with most of its cultivars in the 3- to 4-ft.-tall range. In the fall, the foliage may be golden bronze, and the leaves at that time may be fan-shaped. You might even notice the blossoms have changed to a silvery color. Frost or freeze on the foliage of miscanthus in wintertime can be quite lovely. I use miscanthus around the southwest end of the house and in our rock garden planting. Our prevailing southwesterly breezes create motion in the plumes of blooms as well as in the grass blades themselves. After the seed plumes have dried, you may want to use them in dried flower arrangements as my wife Judy does.

WHEN TO PLANT
The best time to plant maidengrass is in the early spring after all danger of frost is past in your area of Texas.

WHERE TO PLANT
For best results, maidengrass needs to be in full sun. Do not plant in heavily shaded areas or where soil drainage is poor. I enjoy planting it in pockets

among our existing landscape plants. Native Texas plants used in combination with miscanthus create interesting and desirable effects. Miscanthus can be outstanding specimens in the landscape and may be used in yardbeds. I would not use them near entryways or walkways, as they may be overpowering in these uses. Miscanthus also works well when planted in large containers.

HOW TO PLANT
Miscanthus does best in well-prepared soil. With a digging fork or shovel, till or blend approximately 4 to 6 in. of high-quality organic matter into the top 6 in. of soil. Remove plants from containers, dig individual planting holes no deeper than the top of the soilball, install plants in these new homes, and backfill with the loose soil mix. Water thoroughly, apply root stimulator, and mulch with about 3 in. of bark mulch. If planting in containers, use a premium-quality lightweight potting soil.

CARE AND MAINTENANCE
No insects or diseases are known to cause problems for miscanthus. Pruning once a year in the very early spring is desirable. Cut the top back to about 6 in. from the ground to remove all the dead aboveground parts. Water sufficiently to prevent soil dryness. Maintaining a thick layer of mulch through the entire growing season will greatly conserve your soil moisture, reducing the number of times you must water. Fertilize in the spring as new growth begins, again 10 weeks later, once again 10 weeks after that, and then again in the fall. Use a premium-quality 15-5-10, 18-6-12, or 21-7-14 according to label directions. Remember to water thoroughly after each fertilizer application.

ADDITIONAL INFORMATION
Miscanthus or maidengrass is a wonderful addition to the home landscape. It is very easy to grow and maintain, virtually trouble-free.

ADDITIONAL SPECIES, CULTIVARS, OR VARIETIES
In addition to the standard 'Gracillimus' maidengrass, try the following: *M. sinensis* 'Variegatus' (also known as variegated Japanese silver grass), *M. sinensis* 'Yakushima' (dwarf maidengrass), and *M. sinensis* 'Zebrinus' (zebra grass).

Mondo Grass
Ophiopogon japonicus

EXPOSURE

F. Shade to Semi-

COLD HARDINESS

All Texas

WATER USAGE

Semi-Arid/Semi-Mst.

GROWTH RATE

Fast

AVG. HT × WIDTH

3–10" × Spreading

SPACING

12"

Spreading evergreen, ornamental, grasslike groundcover; narrow blades.

*T*exas gardeners call mondo grass by several different names: lily turf, monkey grass, and ophiopogon. It is an evergreen plant that has multiple uses in our home landscape. It works well in shaded areas. It comes in a dwarf variety as well as standard varieties. Planting in a checkerboard pattern will eventually lead to a "grass" look. Keep in mind that mondo grass is not a turfgrass, so it is not one to be played on or to stand a lot of foot traffic. If you want a way to move through plantings of mondo grass, carefully place stepping-stones or walks. Do not expose mondo grass to daylong full sun or reflected heat. Morning sun with afternoon shade is desirable. You may want to try mondo grass in a hanging basket.

WHEN TO PLANT
The best time to plant mondo grass is very early spring; the second-best time is in the fall.

Where to Plant

Mondo grass may be used to line borders or walkways, or you may wish to create a groundcover in shade or partial-shade locations. In heavily shaded areas where turfgrass is not able to grow, mondo will thrive and acquire a deep-green color that looks like grass.

How to Plant

Mondo grass does best in well-prepared beds. Blend approximately 4 to 6 in. of high-quality organic matter into the top 6 in. of the existing soil. Remove the plants from their containers, dig individual planting holes no deeper than the top of the soilball, and place the plants into the planting holes. Backfill with a loose mix, water thoroughly, apply root stimulator, and mulch the finished planting with about 3 in. of bark mulch. When planting in containers, use premium-quality lightweight potting soil.

Care and Maintenance

Mondo grass is virtually insect- and disease-free when properly cared for. Shearing or mowing once a year is desirable for maintaining a more compact and uniform look. This is normally done in the spring after all danger of frost and freeze is over. Water as needed to prevent wilting. For optimum growth, fertilize in early spring with a 3:1:2 ratio, long-lasting, premium-quality lawn fertilizer such as 21-7-14, 18-6-12, or 15-5-10. Read and follow label instructions.

Additional Species, Cultivars, or Varieties

In addition to the standard or "normal" mondo grass, take a look at 'Nana' or dwarf mondo grass and/or 'Kigimafukiduma' or variegated dwarf mondo grass.

Monkey Grass
Liriope muscari

EXPOSURE

F. Sun to Shade

COLD HARDINESS

All Texas

WATER USAGE

Semi-Moist

GROWTH RATE

Fast

AVG. HT × WIDTH

8–30" × 8–30"

SPACING

12"

Clumping or spreading. Evergreen, grasslike plant with long narrow leaves. Blooms appear on stalks in lilac to purple to white.

*L*iriope muscari, commonly known as monkey grass or simply liriope, is often used to line walkways, pathways, or driveways. It also makes good ground-cover, growing in shady locations under trees where other groundcovers will not grow. Its main flush of growth is in the spring. It does not respond well to heavy foot traffic. Use carefully placed stepping-stones as walkways. Some lirope varieties stay rather low, while others get quite tall. Be sure you select the right variety to fit your specific application.

WHEN TO PLANT

The best time to plant is in early spring, after all danger of frost is past. The second-best time is early fall.

WHERE TO PLANT

Lirope can be used to line a formal walkway, breaking the harshness of those straight edges. It is also used to create natural-form pathways in the landscape and may be used in planter boxes or large pots. Try growing giant liriope (which can reach 30 in.) in a large hanging basket, allowing it to weep down the side.

How to Plant

Use a tiller, shovel, or digging fork to incorporate 4 in. of organic matter into the top 4 in. of the native soil. Remove your selections from their containers and install in the newly prepared bed to the same depth they grew originally. Backfill the soil around your plants, water thoroughly, apply root stimulator according to label directions, then mulch the entire bed with 3 to 4 in. of bark mulch. I usually use pine bark mulch for this operation. If you wish to plant in 15- to 20-gallon nursery containers or in a hanging basket, plant at the same depth they grew originally and follow the rest of the suggestions for planting in the ground.

Care and Maintenance

Usually there are no serious pests that bother liriope. Grasshoppers may occasionally visit. If grasshoppers become a problem, look for controls at your favorite nursery. Remember, always read and follow lable directions on any garden aid. Prune perhaps one time a year, cutting in early spring before new shoots emerge. You may cut liriope virtually to the ground after the winter to ensure that you remove all the growth that may have been damaged the previous year. Maintain a moist soil to ensure proper growth. Do not maintain a wet soil nor allow the soil to be continuously dry. Fertilize 2 weeks after the last average killing frost, then ten weeks later, again another ten weeks later, and then one time in the fall. Use a 3:1:2 ratio premium, long-lasting lawn fertilizer such as a 15-5-10, 19-5-9, or 21-7-14. Be sure that you read and follow label directions, and water thoroughly after each application.

Additional Information

Monkey grass sometimes gets confused with another plant that is often used in similar applications: *Ophiopogon japonicus* (mondo grass or lily turf). But the name monkey grass usually refers to liriope. The blades on liriope are generally wider than 1/4 in., sometimes 3/4 in. wide. The blades on lily turf never reach 1/4 in.; most of them are around 1/8 in. wide.

Additional Species, Cultivars, or Varieties

Try these varieties: 'Giant Liriope', 'Big Blue', 'Silver Dragon', 'Gold Banded', 'Christmas Tree', 'Lilac Beauty', 'Majestic', and 'Silver Sunproof'.

Pampas Grass
Cortaderia selloana

EXPOSURE

Full Sun

COLD HARDINESS

All Texas

WATER USAGE

Arid to Semi-Mst.

GROWTH RATE

Medium

AVG. HT × WIDTH

6–10′ × 6–12′

SPACING

8′

Large, fountain-like clump grass with white or pink plume-like blooms.

*P*ampas grass is the oldest, most frequently used ornamental grass in Texas. It has been used for decades in our gardens as well as for commercial applications. It makes a great privacy screen—but do not plant near the end of your driveway, because it may block your view—and do not plant in areas near your sidewalk where you move frequently, because the edge of the grass is rather sharp. Pampas makes interesting specimen plants and it is great for screening out noise and wind. It may be planted virtually anywhere in your landscape where you have full sun.

WHEN TO PLANT
The best time to plant pampas grass is early spring.

WHERE TO PLANT
Tough, drought-resistant pampas grass is a low-maintenance plant (it grows wild in Argentina). It tolerates all types of growing conditions except heavily shaded or damp areas, and it tolerates most soils except for those that are waterlogged or poorly drained. You may wish to create a secluded corner in

your landscape, and pampas grass will give you screening on any side you wish, giving you a private area in which to place a bench, table, and chairs; or use this large, clumping plant to screen an area in which you would like to enjoy a swing in complete privacy.

HOW TO PLANT

If you are going to plant pampas grass in beds, place the beds away from your home and make them at least 5 ft. wide. Improve the soil with about 5 in. of high-quality organic matter tilled into the soil. For spot plantings of individual plants, simply loosen the soil in an area about 3 times the width of the original container. Dig the hole only as deep as the soilball and set the plants in the soil no deeper than the soilball (this is true for pampas grass planted in beds as well). Backfill with loose soil or improved soil mix. Water thoroughly, apply root stimulator, and mulch heavily with about 4 in. of a bark mulch.

CARE AND MAINTENANCE

In most areas of Texas, pampas grass has no serious diseases or insect pests. Early in the spring or very late winter, just as new growth is beginning, cut your pampas grass rather short, about 12 in. in height. This may be done with a small hand pruner or a lopper—but I have seen some folks use a very small chain saw! Water sufficiently to prevent soil dryness. Moist soil will continue to encourage new growth which is attractive. If you wish to have an aggressive-growing pampas grass, fertilize with a premium-quality long-lasting lawn fertilizer like one used on Texas lawns. 3:1:2 ratios such as 19-5-9, 21-7-14, and 15-5-10 work very well. Remember, always read and follow label directions when applying fertilizers. Your first application should be in early spring as new growth begins; apply again 10 weeks later, and then apply again in another 10 weeks. Don't forget to fertilize one time in the fall.

ADDITIONAL INFORMATION

Pampas grass is quite ornamental in the landscape, but I would not encourage children to play near it because of the possibility of injury on the sharp grassblades.

ADDITIONAL SPECIES, CULTIVARS, OR VARIETIES

'Pumila', which is considered a dwarf pampas grass, generally grows to about 3 ft., but its plume may grow as tall as 6 ft. 'Movin' grows to only 4 ft. 'Rosea' is a pink pampas grass.

GROUNDCOVERS

GROUNDCOVERS MAY BE VINING PLANTS, EXTREMELY LOW-GROWING PLANTS, OR DWARF PLANTS that are grouped together to create a groundcover effect.

I frequently receive calls to my radio shows from home gardeners who are facing the fact that they can't grow turfgrass under their shade trees—not even St. Augustine or fescue. Most grasses that are considered shade tolerant actually need 4 hours of full sun per day or 8 hours of 50% mixed sun and shade. When I suggest that these gardeners remove some trees, I usually hear squeals of protest. I don't like to remove trees either. And there is another solution: groundcovers.

Groundcovers or "groundcover-type plants"—creepers, vines, prostrate shrubs, low-growing shrubs, and dwarf shrubs—allow home gardeners to have something green growing under their wonderful cooling shade trees. Keep in mind that these plants are not turfgrass, and they do not tolerate the foot traffic that is tolerated by turfgrass. But wonderful pathways can be made through groundcovers. Remember that not all groundcovers will grow in heavily shaded areas; some require full sun. Groundcovers are good for very steep areas or other "no mow" areas. Look for plants that can weep down the slopes, holding the soil together as they give an attractive appearance.

In this chapter are ten groundcovers, most of which are commonly used in Texas. Sedum, *Sedum* spp., and Santolina, *Santolina chamaecyparissus*, are a bit unusual and perhaps a little more difficult to locate than the rest, though they are wonderful in the home landscape and worth the effort to secure and utilize.

When buying groundcovers, first visit Lowe's and ask to see the selections. Find the ones whose looks you like and determine if they are suited for your landscape. Ask questions such as: *Will this grow in sun? Will it grow in full shade? Is it winter hardy in my area?*

Chapter Four

Once you have obtained all the information you can, determine which plants and how many plants you need for your home landscape.

Prepare the soil by tilling the area. If you have a poorly drained soil or one that lacks nutrition, you may need to add organic matter and some slow-release fertilizer. There are materials called erosion matte which can be placed on top of your prepared bed to hold the soil in place until your groundcover becomes established. Ground-covers and fertilizers can all be found at your local nurseries, along with the assistance required to make the best use of them.

If you have selected non-shrub groundcovers, you will achieve total coverage of an area in two seasons by planting from 4-in. containers on 12-in. centers. The more aggressive plants may accomplish total coverage in one season if planted early in the spring and provided with proper care.

Fertilization helps to encourage the spreading of groundcovers. Begin to apply 18-6-12 or any other premium-quality, long-lasting, slow-release 3:1:2 ratio lawn fertilizer approximately 6 weeks after planting, or as new growth begins. Apply at the same rate it is applied when used for fertilizing lawns. Always read and follow label directions, and water thoroughly after each application. You may apply fertilizer to established plantings as new spring growth begins, and reapply each time your lawn is fertilized.

Water your groundcover plantings deeply and thoroughly as needed. Don't water on a preset schedule.

Controlling weeds is also important to the successful establishment of groundcover plantings. This is especially true for recently planted areas. Mulching with bark will help, but hand-to-hand combat may be needed to remove persistent weedy pests. Selective pre-emergents for preventing weeds are available at local nurseries. Remember, always read and follow label directions.

Ajuga
Ajuga reptans

EXPOSURE

Shade to Semi-

COLD HARDINESS

All Texas

WATER USAGE

Semi-Moist

GROWTH RATE

Fast

AVG. HT × WIDTH

3–8" × Spreading

SPACING

6–12"

Spreading, with oval-shaped leaves, white, blue, and rose blooms, and green to purple and multicolor foliage. Habits similar to strawberries.

*A*juga is a groundcover that will grow in all Texas zones, but I suggest you try it in a small area to see how you like it before you plant large areas. It is excellent for rock gardens. It should receive morning sun and shade from the hot western afternoon sun in summer. Ajuga is also known as carpet bugle and bugle weed. An unusual use of ajuga is in hanging baskets. Ajuga is most attractive during its spring blooming period. If your ajuga begins to decline in July and August, don't worry; this is its worst time of the year. Make sure wherever you use it that the soil drains well.

WHEN TO PLANT

Container-grown ajuga may be planted 12 months out of the year. The best time to plant is early spring, but early fall is also a good time.

WHERE TO PLANT

Ajuga prefers loam or clay-type soils. Be sure to improve sandy soils with lots of organic matter. Ajuga is good to use in areas where you wish to have a groundcover-type effect but do not wish to grow something that will overtake the area. Ajuga is very easy to keep in bounds.

HOW TO PLANT

Plant ajuga in a well-prepared bed. In clay soil, add approximately 2 in. of high-quality organic matter and blend with the top 2 in. of the existing soil. Sandy soils may require a larger amount of organic matter. After beds are completed, insert your selection of ajuga into the soil at the same level it was grown in the containers. Water thoroughly, apply root stimulator according to label directions, and cover with approximately 2 in. of bark mulch. Calvin Finch, a horticulturist in Bexar County, says, "Ajuga has difficulty surviving in the San Antonio area, and it appears drainage is the problem." Make sure the soil in which you plant ajuga drains well.

CARE AND MAINTENANCE

Spider mites may visit your ajuga in hot, dry weather. If they become a problem, consult your Lowe's customer service associate about control possibilities. Remember to read and follow label directions on any garden product. Ajuga normally does not require pruning. Water as necessary to maintain a moist soil. Do not keep the soil wet nor allow it to go totally dry. Wet soils can induce rot and other diseases. Fertilize in the springtime with a premium-quality long-lasting slow-release rose food according to label directions. For maximum benefit, fertilize approximately 3 times during the growing season. Remember to read and follow label directions when using any type of fertilizer, and water thoroughly after every application.

ADDITIONAL INFORMATION

Ajuga is a plant that you may want to test in relatively small areas before adding to large areas. It is attractive, but it may not blend well with the other colors in your landscape.

ADDITIONAL SPECIES, CULTIVARS, OR VARIETIES

You may wish to try the following varieties of Ajuga: 'Alba' with white flowers; 'Rubra' with dark purple foliage; 'Atropurpurea' with blue flowers and bronze foliage; 'Burgundy Lace' with rose-white variegated foliage and rose flowers; 'Pink Silver' with silver-green foliage flushed with burgundy and an overall metallic-looking sheen; 'Silver Beauty' with a striking silver-green-and-white foliage and light blue flowers; and 'Pink Elf', which has pink flowers and short plants that spread rapidly.

Asian Jasmine
Trachelospermum asiaticum

EXPOSURE

F. Sun to Semi-

COLD HARDINESS

To 5° F.

WATER USAGE

Arid to Semi-Mst.

GROWTH RATE

Fast

AVG. HT × WIDTH

12–16″ × Vining

'SPACING

12–18″

Vining groundcover with shiny dark-green leaves.

*A*sian jasmine is the groundcover used most often in Texas. You will find it in many commercial applications as well as public gardens, and it is widely available. Asian jasmine is attractive in a bed by itself. It is also used to accent taller plants such as tall crape myrtles.

WHEN TO PLANT
Asian jasmine may be planted 12 months out of the year from 4-in., quart-sized, and larger containers. The best time to plant is early spring, though early fall is also a good time to plant. If planting during the winter, use quart-sized or larger plants.

WHERE TO PLANT
Asian jasmine may be grown in sandy soils or heavy clay soils. Do not plant in areas that are difficult to water or poorly drained. Asian jasmine works great in full-sun locations and will also do well in locations where it receives only 3 to 4 hours of sun per day. Do not plant in total-shade areas or you will most likely be disappointed.

HOW TO PLANT

Asian jasmine will tolerate less-than-desirable soil conditions. For best results, plant it in well-prepared beds. Add approximately 2 in. or more of organic matter to the top 2 to 3 in. of the existing soil. After the bed is completed, remove plants from containers, insert in the soil no deeper than they were originally grown in the containers, firm the soil, water thoroughly, and apply root stimulator according to label directions. Mulch with about 2 in. of bark mulch. If you plant Asian jasmine from 4-in. pots in early spring, arranging them 12 in. on center in a checkerboard pattern and watering and fertilizing properly, you will generally get full coverage at the end of the season.

CARE AND MAINTENANCE

Asian jasmine has no serious pests. Springtime pruning may be desired for removing winter-damaged top growth and evening out the planting beds. This may be done with a sharp-bladed power mower, one time only at the beginning of the season—or hedge shears or streamline trimmers may be used to accomplish this task. This pruning is not required; it is strictly optional. Water as necessary to maintain moist soil. Fertilize in the spring and every time you fertilize your lawn. Use the same fertilizer you use for your lawn, set at the same application rate. Good results are obtained by applying 3:1:2 ratio, premium-quality, long-lasting, slow-release fertilizers such as 19-5-9, 15-5-10, 21-7-14. Remember to read and follow label directions when using any fertilizer product, and water thoroughly after application.

ADDITIONAL INFORMATION

Do not plant Asian jasmine in beds with dwarf plants, as they will probably overpower the smaller plants. Asian jasmine is excellent in beds with standard landscape plants or in beds by themselves.

ADDITIONAL SPECIES, CULTIVARS, OR VARIETIES

Some varieties of Asian jasmine are 'Asia Minor', which is often considered a dwarf form; 'Variegata', a variegated form; and 'Northtex', a variety which has more spear-shaped or lance-shaped leaves than the *T. asiaticum*. *T. jasminoides* or star jasmine is a cousin to Asian jasmine, hardy in Zone 8 and southward, and may be grown on structures or trellises. It is similar in growth habit to Asian, but it has masses of small, star-shaped, lightly fragrant white blooms in the spring.

Gray and Green Santolina
Santolina chamaecyparissus and *virens*

EXPOSURE

Full Sun

COLD HARDINESS

To 0° F.

WATER USAGE

Arid-Dry

GROWTH RATE

Fast

AVG. HT × WIDTH
1–2′ × 2–5″ Spreading

SPACING
12–18″

Mounding, bushy in form, with very narrow gray or green leaves and yellow flowers.

*I*t is said that beauty is in the eye of the beholder, which is certainly true when it comes to deciding between gray and green santolina. I have grown and used both of these in my landscape and they both grow well well. Both are great when you need a bushy-type, low-growing, shrubby groundcover for a full-sun area that is hot, dry, and difficult to water. Such conditions are ideal for santolina. This is not a plant to be used in shady areas, where air drainage is poor, or where the soil is excessively moist. It grows equally well in sandy or clay soils. I have grown santolina for 20 years. I have discovered that if blooms begin to develop and you desire a compact plant, you need to keep the blooms snipped off. You may also wish to perform minimal shearing of branches that tend to grow out of the compact form—you may do this once or twice a year.

WHEN TO PLANT
Santolina is best planted in the early spring. Early fall is also acceptable.

WHERE TO PLANT
Santolina requires good soil drainage and sun in order to thrive.

How to Plant

If the soil in your location does not drain well, blend approximately 3 in. of ground bark into the top 3 in. of native soil to make a 6-in. raised bed. After bed preparation is complete, remove santolina from containers and install into pre-dug holes *no deeper* than the top of the soilball. Firm the soil around plants, water thoroughly, apply root stimulator according to label directions, and cover with 2 in. of bark mulch.

Care and Maintenance

Santolina has no pest problems. Prune as necessary to maintain desired shape and compactness. Water only as necessary to prevent soil dryness. Remember, do not overwater santolina. Fertilization is usually not required, but one application per year of a premium-quality slow-release 3:1:2 ratio fertilizer, such as 15-5-10 or 19-5-9, can be beneficial. Remember to read and follow label directions, and water thoroughly after fertilization.

Additional Information

If you are looking for different plants and ways to utilize them, try santolina weeping down a rock wall, concrete wall, or even over a bed edge raised with railroad ties or landscape timbers.

Additional Species, Cultivars, or Varieties

Look for: *S. neapolitana,* which is a white evergreen shrub reaching approximately 2$\frac{1}{2}$ ft. high and wide; *S. pinnata,* which is a globular green shrub about 2$\frac{1}{2}$ ft. high; and *S. rosmarinifolia.*

Groundcover Junipers
Juniperus spp.

EXPOSURE

Full Sun

COLD HARDINESS

All Texas

WATER USAGE

Arid to Semi-Mst.

GROWTH RATE

Fast to Slow

AVG. HT × WIDTH

1–1½ ′ × 3–5 ′

SPACING

Varies

Evergreen in colors from bright green and dark green to blue/gray.

*T*here are many varieties of groundcover-type junipers in Texas today. Some of the family groupings include *J. conferta*, *J. horizontalis*, and *J. procumbens*. No matter which species of juniper you like, the grouping is more important than the species. I strongly suggest that when looking for these plants you use the term "groundcover-type junipers." When you find the groundcover-type juniper that you like, remember to ask these questions: *How tall does this specific variety grow in my area? How wide does it spread? Will it take partial shade? What type of soil does it require?* After you receive this information, you will be able to determine which varieties you would like to plant. You may also wish to visit public gardens, theme parks, and botanical gardens to see how the junipers you are interested in look in a landscape after some time has passed.

WHEN TO PLANT
Groundcover-type junipers may be planted 12 months out of the year in Texas. Fall is an excellent planting time, but early spring is also good.

WHERE TO PLANT

Plant where you desire a small-leaved evergreen-type planting that is low growing and relatively easy to maintain. Do not plant in areas that have poorly drained soil or are difficult to water. I prefer to plant it in locations where that receive a minimum of 6 to 8 hours of sun per day and a little shade from the hot western afternoon sun.

HOW TO PLANT

Junipers will grow in practically any Texas soil, provided they receive good drainage. In order to receive maximum benefit from junipers, incorporate approximately 4 in. of organic matter into the top 4 in. of native soil. After the bed is prepared, remove plants from their containers and install no deeper than originally grown in the containers. It is important that you do not plant too deeply. Firm the soil thoroughly, apply root stimulator following label directions, and cover with approximately 2 in. of bark mulch. Spacing will depend on the variety selected. Ask your Lowe's customer service associate for suggestions.

CARE AND MAINTENANCE

Spider mites may visit your junipers during late summer in hot, dry locations. If this occurs, ask about the best control possibilities. Groundcover-type junipers normally do not require pruning. Water as necessary to maintain moist growing conditions and achieve maximum growth, but do not overwater. As new growth begins in the spring, fertilize with a premium-quality long-lasting slow-release lawn fertilizer with a 3:1:2 ratio. Reapply twice more during the growing season and once again in the fall. Remember to read and follow label directions, and water thoroughly after applying any fertilizer.

ADDITIONAL INFORMATION

Groundcover-type junipers look wonderful when allowed to weep over stone walls.

ADDITIONAL SPECIES, CULTIVARS, OR VARIETIES

Many varieties of groundcover-type juniper exist. The following varieties are among those suitable for groundcovers: 'Bar Harbor', 'Plumosa', 'Hughes', 'Youngs', 'Turquoise Spreader', 'Blue Rug', 'Emerald Sea', 'San Jose', and one of my favorites, 'Shore'.

Hardy Ferns
Ferns spp.

EXPOSURE

Shade to Semi-

COLD HARDINESS

All Texas

WATER USAGE

Moist to Semi-Mst.

GROWTH RATE

Fast

AVG. HT × WIDTH

1–3 ' (v.)

SPACING

12–24 ″ (v.)

Leaves are bright to dark green to multicolor.

*J*ust by their very presence, ferns seem to impart a cooling effect to a landscape. I have a wooded area on my property that has mixed hardwood trees, dogwoods, native hawthorns, redbuds, and other flowering plants, and we are fortunate enough to have a spring that flows through our property, nourishing a wide selection of ferns. Ferns sometimes sunburn in our Texas sun, and they are often found growing naturally in shaded areas along our creeks and streams. There are many different types of ferns available today. Many of these ferns make great groundcovers in heavily shaded areas where grass will no longer grow, and they can be planted in formal or informal beds.

WHEN TO PLANT
The best planting time for ferns is early spring, though they may be planted successfully in the summer and on into early fall.

WHERE TO PLANT
For best results, ferns need to be planted in shaded areas in soils with lots of organic matter. They may also be planted in large tubs or planters.

How to Plant

Incorporate as much organic matter as possible, up to 6 in., into the soil. One of the best sources of organic matter is brown sphagnum peat moss. After improving the soil, remove your selections from their containers and install into the beds no deeper than they were grown in the containers. Firm the soil, water thoroughly, apply root stimulator according to label directions, and mulch with about 3 in. of bark mulch.

Care and Maintenance

Ferns normally do not have pests. If pests happen to bother your planting, investigate control possibilities. Remember to read and follow label directions. Prune out dead parts every spring as new growth begins. No other pruning is normally necessary. Fronds or leaves make excellent indoor decorations throughout the growing season in arrangements with cut flowers. Maintain a moist soil at all times during the growing season. A thick layer of mulch will conserve moisture and enhance fern growth. Fertilize 3 times during the growing season with granular lawn, water-soluble, liquid, or encapsulated slow-release fertilizer. Read the directions, and always water after application.

Additional Information

Ferns may be used as background plantings with colorful shade-loving plants such as caladiums in front.

Additional Species, Cultivars, or Varieties

There are many varieties and several cultivars of hardy ferns available in the state of Texas. The term hardy simply means the plant will withstand the freezing temperatures in a particular zone. Some varieties are more evergreen than others, but most are deciduous. Make your purchasing decision based on the specific application, the desired look, and the plant's hardiness in your zone.

Hosta
Hosta spp.

EXPOSURE

Shade to Semi-

COLD HARDINESS

All Texas

WATER USAGE

Moist

GROWTH RATE

Fast to Med. (v.)

AVG. HT × WIDTH

12–18″ (v.)

SPACING

Varies

Arrowhead-, lance-, or heart-shaped leaves, green to multicolored. Deciduous.

I often get calls from listeners to my radio shows and readers of my newspaper columns who are seeking information on color plants for shaded areas. Hosta is a fine choice for this, and it can be grown singly or in masses to create groundcover effects. It gives great color from its foliage as well as from its blooms. I have seen gorgeous plantings of hosta in the heavy soils of Dallas, Fort Worth, Waco, and Houston, and also in the light, sandy soils of eastern Texas. It will grow in light shade or heavily shaded areas. Depending on the variety selected, you can have solid-green leaves, chartreuse-green leaves, leaves with cream colors in them, and various bloom colors. The best time to select hostas is in the spring.

WHEN TO PLANT
The best planting time for hosta is in early spring when the plants have recently become available. When making your selections, be sure to ask how tall and how wide specific varieties grow in your location.

WHERE TO PLANT

Plant hosta in well-prepared beds with lots of organic matter. Prepare the beds as you do for ferns: incorporate approximately 4 in. of organic matter into the top 4 in. of the soil.

HOW TO PLANT

After bed preparation is complete, remove your selections from their containers and install in the soil no deeper than they were originally grown. Spacing depends on the variety you have selected. After planting, be sure to water thoroughly, add root stimulator according to label directions, and mulch with approximately 3 in. of bark mulch.

CARE AND MAINTENANCE

Slugs or snails may visit your hosta plantings. If they become a problem, ask about the best control possibilities. Remember to read and follow label directions. If slugs and/or snails are already a major problem in your landscape, get the situation under control before you plant any hostas. Pruning is normally not necessary. Water as necessary to maintain a moist soil throughout the entire growing season. Fertilize as new growth begins in the spring with a premium-quality long-lasting, slow-release lawn fertilizer such as 18-6-12, 19-5-9, 21-7-14, or similar 3:1:2 ratio. Water-soluble, granular, encapsulated slow-release, or other types of fertilizer may also be used. Remember to read and follow label directions and water thoroughly after application.

ADDITIONAL INFORMATION

Hostas may be planted in the ground in shady locations, and they may also be planted in large tubs. Large-tub hosta plantings will give you portable color for shady areas.

ADDITIONAL SPECIES, CULTIVARS, OR VARIETIES

There are several varieties of hosta, including 'All Gold', 'Crown Jewel', 'Gold Standard', 'Francee', 'Golden Prayers', 'Green Elf', 'Krossa Regal', 'Royal Standard', 'Serendipity', 'Elegance', 'Halcyon', 'Wide Brim', and others.

Periwinkle
Vinca major/minor

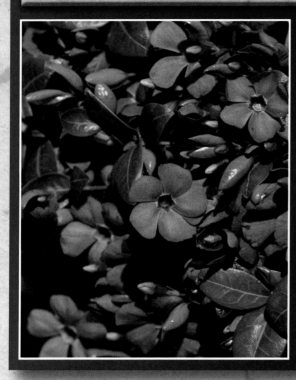

EXPOSURE	COLD HARDINESS
Shade to Semi-Sh.	All Texas

WATER USAGE	GROWTH RATE
Semi-Moist	Fast

AVG. HT × WIDTH	SPACING
4–18″ × 5′	1′

Has dark-green leaves, sometimes with white or creamy leaf markings. White to blue to purple blooms. Evergreen.

*A*s the two species names imply, vinca minor has smaller leaves and vinca major has larger leaves. Both types are ideal in woodland locations where dappled sunlight is available throughout the day and moist soil conditions exist. Both types will take full sun during the morning, but they must be shaded from the hot afternoon sun in order to do well. They will also grow in full-shade locations. Vinca, with its dark-green, almost waxy leaves and colorful blooms, is one of the best groundcovers we have in Texas. The variegated types provide color from both foliage and bloom. Periwinkle may also be grown in large tubs. Try one or both types in large hanging baskets or other containers.

WHEN TO PLANT
Either type of periwinkle may be planted 12 months out of the year in Texas. An ideal planting time is very early spring, but early fall is also good.

WHERE TO PLANT

Periwinkle does best in locations that drain properly. It will grow in sandy soil and in clay soil as long as adequate moisture is available. In order to achieve maximum benefits, incorporate approximately 2 in. of organic matter into the top 2 in. of the existing soil. Once the soil is improved, remove the plants from their container and install no deeper than they were originally grown in the containers. If you buy 4-in. pots in early spring and space the plants approximately 12 in. apart in a checkerboard pattern, you will have complete coverage by the end of one season as long as the plants are given proper maintenance.

CARE AND MAINTENANCE

In most locations, insects usually do not bother periwinkles. One type of pest that can be a problem, however, is caterpillars. In heavy infestations, caterpillars have the potential to strip all the leaves from vinca. If pests cause problems with your periwinkles, find out about the best control possibilities. Remember to read and follow label directions. Periwinkles normally do not require pruning. Water as necessary to maintain a moist soil especially through growing season. Do not overwater, especially in heavy clay soils. Fertilize in the spring, as new growth begins, with a long-lasting slow-release premium-quality lawn fertilizer. Use a 3:1:2 ratio such as 18-6-12, 19-5-9, and 15-5-10, and follow label directions. Always water after an application of any fertilizer product.

ADDITIONAL INFORMATION

Remember that periwinkle is a groundcover, not a turfgrass, and is not a plant for foot traffic. If passage is necessary through groundcover plantings, concrete walkways, stepping-stones, or other pathways can be installed.

ADDITIONAL SPECIES, CULTIVARS, OR VARIETIES

The following are some varieties you may wish to utilize in your periwinkle planting: *V. major* 'Variegata', with white or cream markings; *V. minor* 'Alba', with white flowers; and 'Variegata', with green-and-white leaves. 'Major Bowles' has flowers and deep-green leaves that are slightly larger than those of the parent plant.

Prostrate Rosemary
Rosmarinus officinalis 'Prostratus'

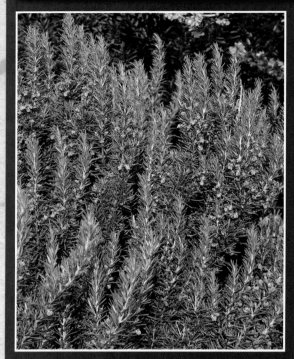

EXPOSURE
Full Sun

COLD HARDINESS
To 10° F.

WATER USAGE
Semi-Moist/Arid

GROWTH RATE
Medium

AVG. HT × WIDTH
2′ × 6′

SPACING
4–6′

Spreading, with aromatic gray-to blue-green needles.

*C*hicken and rosemary go together like love and marriage, and the rosemary most often used in cooking comes from a bush-type plant. Its low-growing cousin, however, works equally well for cooking, and it makes a gorgeous blooming groundcover in the landscape. Prostrate rosemay provides a multitude of benefits. It smells wonderful, it blooms, it is easy to dry, and it looks great in the landscape! Once you see a hot, dry, full-sun area of prostrate groundcover rosemary, you will wonder why you didn't plant it sooner.

WHEN TO PLANT
It is best planted in early spring after all danger of frost is past. Early fall is also a good planting time.

WHERE TO PLANT
Plant in sunny areas where the soil drains exceptionally well. A slightly alkaline soil is preferred. All types of rosemary may be grown in containers with great success. Weeping, creeping, or groundcover-type rosemary in large con-

tainers makes gorgeous plantings to use poolside and on decks, balconies, and patios. You may also wish to try it in large hanging baskets.

HOW TO PLANT
If you have a soil location that is less than ideal (in other words, that is poorly drained), raise the bed using several inches of 50 percent ground bark combined with the native soil. Install no deeper than the plants were grown in their containers, and firm the soil. Water thoroughly, apply root stimulator according to directions, and cover with approximately 2 in. of mulch.

CARE AND MAINTENANCE
Rosemary does not attract any serious pests. You may prune to obtain desired shape, but normally no other pruning is necessary. Water only when needed to prevent complete soil dryness. Be careful not to overwater. Fertilizing is usually not required.

ADDITIONAL INFORMATION
Retrieve rosemary selections at your leisure for use with your favorite chicken dish or for drying or other applications.

ADDITIONAL SPECIES, CULTIVARS, OR VARIETIES
In some catalogs and guides, you may see prostrate rosemary listed as creeping or groundcover form. Other worthwhile varieties of rosemary are 'Arp', 'Salem', 'Tuscan Blue', 'Benanden Blue', and 'Huntington Carpet'. *Great planting and good cooking!*

Sedum

Sedum spp.

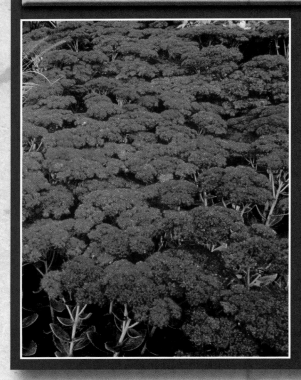

EXPOSURE	COLD HARDINESS
F. Sun to Semi-	All Texas
WATER USAGE	GROWTH RATE
Arid-Dry	Medium
AVG. HT × WIDTH	SPACING
4–18″ (v.)	6–10′

Leaves are fleshy and relatively light green. Flowers come in yellow, red, pink, pink-purple, and bronzy pink. Evergreen and deciduous.

*S*edum is a good choice as a groundcover for a sunny rock garden location. It is excellent in hot, dry Texas locations. Rock gardens are just one application—it may also be used for a groundcover effect elsewhere. Wherever you plant sedum, make sure that the soil drains well. Some varieties of sedum die out each year, while others remain evergreen. Ask about the types that interest you. Questions to ask include: *Is it evergreen or deciduous in our area? How tall does it grow?* What bloom colors are available? I am currently growing 'Gold Moss' sedum in a raised bed at the base of tall althea, allowing it to trail over the rock used to construct the raised bed. The soil is sandy with a good deal of organic matter in it.

WHEN TO PLANT

The best time to plant sedums is in early spring. Early fall is also a good time.

WHERE TO PLANT

Plant sedums in your landscape in any location where you want a succulent, fleshy-looking groundcover. Do not plant in shady locations or poorly drained soils. Try sedums in large pots, hanging baskets, or other containers.

How to Plant

Very little soil preparation is necessary, except in poorly drained soil. Plant transplants no deeper than they were grown in their containers—be very attentive to planting depth. Firm the soil around your transplant, water thoroughly, apply root stimulator according to label directions, and spread with 2 in. of bark mulch.

Care and Maintenance

Sedums are usually pest-free. If a problem with pests develops, ask about control possibilities. Remember to read and follow label directions. Sedum normally does not require pruning. Water as needed to prevent total soil dryness, but do not keep wet. Fertilize once in the spring, as new growth begins. Premium-quality long-lasting slow-release rose fertilizer works well.

Additional Information

There is a wide variety of sedums from which to choose—the reference *Hortus III* has over 6 pages of different sedum types.

Additional Species, Cultivars, or Varieties

Some varieties of sedum that are more readily available include: 'Gold Moss', 'Middendorf', 'Ruby Glow', 'Carmen', 'Red Carpet', and 'Autumn Joy'. If you happen to be a fan of butterflies, make sure you have at least some plantings of 'Autumn Joy'. The butterflies love it!

Wintercreeper

Euonymus fortunei

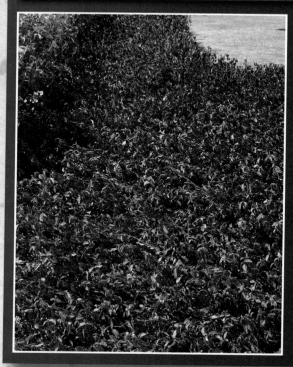

EXPOSURE	COLD HARDINESS
F. Sun to Semi-	All Texas

WATER USAGE	GROWTH RATE
Semi-Moist	Fast to Med.

AVG. HT × WIDTH	SPACING
6" to 2' × 2–8'	Varies

Rounded, waxy evergreen with green to variegated foliage.

I first came into contact with groundcover-type euonymus when I grew the variety 'Colorata' as production manager at a wholesale nursery in 1972. It is easy to propagate, easy to grow, and works beautifully in the landscape. If you have relatively large areas that need a winter-hardy groundcover, winter-creeper euonymus groundcover is an answer. Wherever you plant it, make sure it has plenty of room to grow and the soil drains well. Some varieties of wintercreeper euonymus, including 'Colorata', change color with the seasons. After a few hard frosts or freezes, its green leaves take on various shades of maroon, purple, and bronze. For something unusual or wild-looking, try euonymus in large hanging baskets.

WHEN TO PLANT

Container-grown euonymus may be planted in Texas 12 months of the year. The ideal time is early fall. Early spring is also a good planting time.

WHERE TO PLANT

Wintercreeper euonymus is extremely easy to grow, but do not locate it in hot, dry areas such as western locations that are difficult to water or areas with reflected heat. Neither should it be planted in heavily shaded areas or poorly drained soil.

HOW TO PLANT

Improve soil by incorporating 3 in. of organic matter into the top 3 in. of the soil. This will provide ideal growing conditions. After bed preparation is complete, remove individual plants from their containers and place in pre-dug holes. Plant no deeper than originally planted in the containers. Firm the soil around individual plants and water thoroughly. Add root stimulator according to label directions and spread with 2 in. of bark mulch.

CARE AND MAINTENANCE

Scale insects may visit euonymus. If this becomes a problem, apply a dormant oil during the winter season according to label directions. Pruning is usually not required. Water as necessary to maintain moist soil for ideal growing conditions. Do not keep wet, and do not allow the soil to become dry. Fertilize in spring, as new growth begins, with a premium-quality long-lasting slow-release 3:1:2 ratio lawn fertilizer. Examples include 15-5-10, 19-5-9, and 18-6-12. Remember to read and follow label directions, and water thoroughly after each application. Apply again around June 1, and once again in the fall.

ADDITIONAL INFORMATION

Wintercreeper euonymus grows particularly well in the Panhandle area where other groundcover-type plants may have difficulty surviving the harsh winters.

ADDITIONAL SPECIES, CULTIVARS, OR VARIETIES

Selections of wintercreeper euonymus include 'Argenteo Variegata', 'Creeping Variegated Euonymus', 'Corlutz', 'Emerald Surprise Euonymus', 'Colorata', and 'Purple Leaf Wintercreeper'.

CHAPTER FIVE

NATIVE TEXAS PLANTS

*T*HERE IS ABSOLUTELY NO PLACE LIKE TEXAS! And Texas has a wide selection of native trees, shrubs, vines, groundcovers, annuals, and perennials, many of which make outstanding landscape plants.

In this chapter I have assembled information on eight native annuals, ten native perennials, eight native shrubs, eight native trees, and five native vines. Certainly there are more native plants than the ones on my list, but those I have selected are outstanding.

Properly selected, placed, and maintained Texas natives are relatively low-maintenance plants. They have lived on their own in nature, and are tough. Many native plants live in hot locations, some live in damp locations, and others live in dry locations. Many of these native plants will grow in sand, clay, and a wide variety of our Texas soils. They are all considered adaptable to most landscape situations.

Just think about the diversity of our climate, from the cold Panhandle winters to the almost-tropical Rio Grande Valley, from Texarkana's 40-plus inches of rain per year to El Paso's 9. There is wide variation in soil types and growing zones as well.

The native annuals and perennials are commonly called wildflowers, and Texas is blessed with them in abundance as well as variety. Certainly everyone is familiar with our Native Texas Flower, the bluebonnet, *Lupinus texensis*—and take a look at black-eyed Susan, *Rudbeckia hirta* var. 'Angustifolia'. Both these plants provide wonderful color throughout their entire growing season. Clasping-leaf coneflower, *Rudbeckia amplexicaulis*, coreopsis, *Coreopsis lanceolata*, Indian blanket, *Gaillardia pulchella*, and Texas bluebells, *Eustoma grandiflorum*, are other wonderful native flowers available to us.

Some of the best and easiest-to-grow native Texas plants have become mainstream in the nursery industry and our home landscapes. Cenizo, or Texas sage, *Leucophyllum frutescens*, is a native plant that has become widely available across the state. Salvia

Chapter Five

greggii, *Salvia greggii,* is another native plant which does beautifully in well-drained Texas soils. The large native shrub wax myrtle, *Myrica cerifera,* has become a welcome addition to our landscapes.

I write garden columns for several publications in the state and do live call-in radio shows as well. Readers and listeners often ask me about fast-growing shade trees. I really don't recommend fast-growing shade trees—most of them, such as Arizona ash, *Fraxinus velutina,* tend to be loaded with problems. If you want to plant an ash, then look for the Texas ash, *Fraxinus texensis,* a very good-quality tree that is native to Texas. For outstanding fall color, plant a sweet gum, *Liquidambar styraciflua.* If you're a fan of elm trees—and most people who have seen some of the gorgeous specimen elms are fans—there is a native Texas elm that is wonderful in the landscape: the cedar elm, *Ulmus crassifolia.* All of these native Texas trees tend to have fewer problems than some imports.

A native vine with an exotic-looking blossom is maypop or passion vine, *Passiflora incarnata.* Doug Williams of the Mercer Arboretum and Botanic Garden in Humble says, "This vine is a good one. I don't know why it isn't used more often." If you like wisteria, but are concerned about it taking over your landscape, try Texas wisteria, *Wisteria macrostachya.* It has wonderful flowers and is much easier to manage than the imported wisterias.

Contact the Native Plant Society of Texas for recommendations on growing native Texas plants. Write to "Director" at this address:

N.P.S.O.T.
P.O. Box 891
Georgetown, TX 78627

Have fun with our native Texas plants in your landscape. Remember, there's absolutely no place like Texas—and no natives like Texas native plants!

Black-eyed Susan

Rudbeckia hirta 'Pulcherrima'

EXPOSURE

Full Sun

COLD HARDINESS

Annual

WATER USAGE

Arid to Semi-Mst.

GROWTH RATE

Fast

AVG. HT × WIDTH

1–3 ' × 24–30 "

SPACING

2 '

Rough, hairy plant. Flowers are single with yellow petals and dark-brown to blackish centers. Annual to very short-lived perennial.

*B*lack-eyed Susan (sometimes called brown-eyed Susan) is a member of the sunflower family and a very easy-to-grow Texas native flower. It should be used more often in our Texas landscapes. Some varieties are annuals, while others are short-lived perennials. Either type will work well in the home landscape in full-sun locations. Try black-eyed Susan in difficult-to-water areas that need great summertime color. Susan is found in East, South, and Central Texas, often in prairie areas or pinewoods.

WHEN TO PLANT

The best time to start Texas wildflowers, including Susan, is in the fall. If you decide to set out transplants, put them out in early spring after all danger of frost is past.

WHERE TO PLANT

Black-eyed Susan needs to be in well-drained locations that receive at least 8 hours of sunlight. Full sun is desirable.

How to Plant

If you are going to start from seed, prepare the soil by lightly tilling, removing sticks or other debris, and raking. Sow seeds according to package directions and water thoroughly. Maintain a moist soil until seeds germinate and establish themselves, then gradually reduce the watering. If planting in prepared beds from transplants in the spring, be sure to add a couple of inches of organic matter to the top 3 or 4 in. of the native soil. After soil improvement is complete, remove your transplants from their containers and install in the soil no deeper than they were growing in the containers. Firm the soil, water thoroughly, apply root stimulator according to label directions, and cover with 3 in. of bark mulch.

Care and Maintenance

There are no insects or diseases that plague black-eyed Susan, and no pruning should be necessary. Water sufficiently to prevent complete soil dryness, but do not overwater. Fertilize one time during the growing season with a premium-quality long-lasting rose food, following label directions.

Additional Information

While driving through the Texas byways, look for black-eyed or brown-eyed Susan (whichever name you wish to apply to *R. hirta*). You will find it readily available and easy to grow in the Texas landscape.

Additional Species, Cultivars, or Varieties

The two varieties of black-eyed Susan include *R. hirta* 'Pulcherrima', a true annual, and *R. hirta* 'Angustifolia', a short-lived perennial. Both varieties will work well in the home landscape.

Bluebonnet
Lupinus texensis

EXPOSURE

Full Sun

COLD HARDINESS

Annual

WATER USAGE

Arid to Semi-Mst.

GROWTH RATE

Fast

AVG. HT × WIDTH

15–24 " × 12–16 "

SPACING

12 "

Relatively soft 5-leaflet leaves with pointed tips. Bloom is generally on the top 2 to 6 in. of the flower bloom stem and is most often dark blue in color.

*W*hen the bluebonnet was originally designated the Texas state wildflower in 1901, the species of choice was the small *L. subcarnosa*, which is now considered a less showy species. In 1971, the state legislature decided to designate all bluebonnets the official state flower, from the short ones to the tall ones, including the extremely tall ones in the Big Bend area. All but two of our bluebonnets are considered true annuals. Bluebonnets are a member of the Lupine family. There are about 150 species in this family, found mostly throughout western North American but also in the Mediterranean area. We Texans are fortunate to have the best of the Lupines . . . the Texas bluebonnet.

WHEN TO PLANT
The best time to plant bluebonnet seed is in the early fall. Set out transplants in late January through February.

WHERE TO PLANT
Bluebonnets need to be planted in grass-free areas that drain well and have full sun. Do not plant in heavily shaded or poorly drained locations.

HOW TO PLANT

I have had many people call into my radio show or write to me, wanting to know if they can just throw bluebonnet seeds on the ground. The answer to that is, "Yes you can . . . if you want to waste your money, time, energy, and effort." In order to get a good stand of bluebonnets, vigorously rake the soil and make sure that you have removed grasses in the area. Even better is to lightly till the area and rake with a strong rake. Sow the seeds at a rate of approximately 12 seeds per sq. ft. Treated seeds, which are called scarified seeds, germinate very quickly and thrive with minimal irrigation. Some untreated seeds may take as long as 3 years to germinate. If you have not planted seeds in the fall but you decide in spring that you want some bluebonnets, plant transplants in tilled areas. Plant them no deeper than they were originally grown in their containers. Water thoroughly and apply a root stimulator.

CARE AND MAINTENANCE

Bluebonnets are considered insect- and disease-free by most gardeners. In landscape garden areas, there may be problems with pillbugs, doodle bugs, or sow bugs when plant concentrations are heavy. If this occurs in your plantings, seek help with controls. Remember, always follow label directions. Bluebonnets generally do not require pruning or fertilization. Water as necessary to prevent total soil dryness. The most crucial watering time is at initial plant establishment from seeds in the fall.

ADDITIONAL INFORMATION

You can find large beautiful shows of bluebonnets around the Austin area, Llano, and just about anywhere in Central Texas.

ADDITIONAL SPECIES, CULTIVARS, OR VARIETIES

L. subcarnosus is the original adopted Texas bluebonnet. It tends to grow in deep sands in South and Southeast Texas. The Big Bend bluebonnet, the largest blubonnet, is *L. havardii*. Some have been reported to grow as high as 3 ft. In addition to these annual bluebonnets, there are some perennial bluebonnets, including *L. perennis* and *L. plattensis*.

Clasping-Leaf Coneflower
Rudbeckia amplexicaulis syn. *Dracopis amplexicaulis*

EXPOSURE

Full to Semi-Shade

COLD HARDINESS

Annual

WATER USAGE

Arid to Semi-Mst.

GROWTH RATE

Fast

AVG. HT × WIDTH

12–30´× 12˝

SPACING

6–12˝

Has numerous blooms whose outer petals are yellow—often reddish-brown at the bases, with brown centers. Will adapt to all areas of Texas and grows in sand, loam, acid, and calcareous soils.

*T*here are several types of coneflowers growing in Texas. The name comes from their raised centers or "cones." Clasping-leaf coneflower will grow in moist or damp areas and even fairly poorly drained areas, though it will grow in well-drained areas as well. It is versatile and adaptable; use it in a low area of your landscape, up an incline, or even in a raised bed. It is possible to create large color drifts with this beauty. It works well in mass or mixed plantings, and as background plantings. Try some in tubs, pots, planters, or other large containers placed in sunny locations on your deck, patio, terrace, or balcony.

WHEN TO PLANT
As is true of nearly all Texas wildflowers, the best time to start seeds of clasping-leaf coneflower is in the late summer/early fall. If starting your own spring transplants, plant after all danger of frost is past and the soil is warm.

WHERE TO PLANT
Clasping-leaf coneflower is an ideal candidate for wildflower meadow plantings in clay, silt, sand, loam, and most other Texas soils. It will also grow in

areas that receive reflected heat, such as areas near driveways, hard-surfaced walks, and buildings.

How to Plant

If you are fortunate enough to find transplants, place them in a location where you have loosened the soil by lightly tilling and then raking it. Remove the plants from their containers and plant in the prepared bed no deeper than they were planted in the containers. Firm the soil, water thoroughly, apply root stimulator, and add about 3 in. of bark mulch.

Care and Maintenance

Clasping-leaf coneflower is considered insect- and disease-free, and usually requires no fertilization or pruning. You may wish to remove spent blossoms. Water as necessary to prevent soil dryness. Maintaining a thick layer of mulch will help conserve moisture.

Additional Information

The clasping-leaf coneflower gets its name from its interesting leaf structure, which wraps around the entire stem of the plant. It looks as if it is clasping the stem of the plant itself. It is one of the few native Texas wildflowers that will grow in moist areas such as ditches and other areas that are less-than-ideally drained.

Additional Species, Cultivars, or Varieties

Currently there are no known specific varieties of clasping-leaf coneflower.

Indian Blanket or Firewheel
Gaillardia pulchella

EXPOSURE

Full Sun

COLD HARDINESS

Annual

WATER USAGE

Arid-Dry/Semi-Mst.

GROWTH RATE

Medium

AVG. HT × WIDTH

1–2′ × 18–24″

SPACING

9–12″

Flowers have golden-yellow-tipped red petals and reddish-brown centers. Naturally occurs statewide, except in shaded forest areas and extremely dry locations.

Gaillardia, or Indian blanket or firewheel, happens to be one of my favorite native Texas wildflowers. It grows virtually everywhere in our state. If you think you can't grow any Texas wildflowers from seeds, I strongly suggest you try Indian blanket. This plant is one of the easiest ones to find, especially at a nursery that specializes in native Texas plants. In mass plantings in sunny locations, it provides breathtaking color. In addition to being a long-lasting color source in the home landscape, Indian blanket makes a wonderful cut flower because of its long vase life. If you are looking for an easy-to-grow, easy-to-care-for color source in your landscape that you can also use indoors, you can't go wrong with Indian blanket.

WHEN TO PLANT
The best time to plant Indian blanket from direct seeding is in late summer/early fall. Transplants are best set out in early spring after all danger of frost is past.

WHERE TO PLANT

Plant Indian blanket in any location in which you have gotten perennial grasses such as Bermudagrass under control. I have seen outstanding plantings of Indian blanket in Santa Fe, New Mexico, and in all areas of our state. Indian blanket requires at least 8 hours of full-sun to perform its best.

HOW TO PLANT

These plants will do best in a prepared bed. The best way to prepare a bed is to completely remove the vegetation from the area, lightly till, and rake. Seeds must be in contact with the soil in order to germinate properly. After sowing the seeds according to package directions, water thoroughly. Plant transplants in the same locations you would plant any other sun-loving annual, making sure that the soil drains well. Standard soil preparation for any landscape bed will be more than adequate for Indian blanket.

CARE AND MAINTENANCE

This plant has no serious diseases or insects. Remove spent blooms (called deadheading) to encourage more blooms and a longer blooming season. Water as necessary to prevent soil dryness. Fertilization is usually not necessary for overall care of Indian blanket. If you decide to fertilize, apply a premium-quality long-lasting rose food according to label directions. Water-solubles will also work well. Remember to follow label directions when using any fertilizer, and water thoroughly.

ADDITIONAL INFORMATION

Some Indian blanket flowers are more red with a slight tip of yellow on the edges. Other types have more yellow and less red. Some are completely red.

ADDITIONAL SPECIES, CULTIVARS, OR VARIETIES

There are several variations of *G. pulchella*. When selecting seeds, choose carefully so that you get the types you want. *G. aristata* is a perennial that is extremely drought hardy.

Indian Paintbrush
Castilleja indivisa

EXPOSURE

F. to Semi-Sun or Sh.

COLD HARDINESS

Annual

WATER USAGE

Semi-Moist

GROWTH RATE

Medium

AVG. HT × WIDTH

6–16″ × 3–6″

SPACING

8″

Actual blooms are white to slightly green. Bracts display intense color from red to red-orange. Usually found in nearly all areas of Texas except the Panhandle and far-west Texas.

C indivisa or Indian paintbrush is also known as Texas paintbrush and scarlet paintbrush. No matter what you call it, it brings outstanding color in masses to our roadsides and fields. It is wonderful in mixtures with Texas bluebonnets. Indian paintbrush will grow on its own root system until it intersects with the root system of another plant, and then it becomes partially parasitic. The plants may be used in clumps by themselves in landscape beds. Seeds of Indian paintbrush are extremely fine; it takes only about 1/4 lb. of seed to plant an entire acre.

WHEN TO PLANT
The best time to direct-seed Indian paintbrush is late summer/early fall in a prepared seedbed. If you find and purchase transplants, set them out very early in the spring.

WHERE TO PLANT
Indian paintbrush may be planted in and among existing vegetation with special seed-planting drills. If sowed on top of the ground, the vegetation needs to be cut extremely short. Sown seeds should be watered thoroughly. Keep soil

moist until well established then reduce. This beauty will grow in clay, loam, or sandy soil as long as it is well drained. It will tolerate a little shade.

CARE AND MAINTENANCE

There are no serious insect or disease problems with Indian paintbrush, and pruning is normally not required. If growing as a bedding or landscape-type planting, water as necessary to prevent soil dryness. Mulching the bed will help conserve soil moisture. If you fertilize grass during the growing season where plantings of Indian paintbrush will be planted, you will be providing adequate nutrition for the Indian paintbrush—no other fertilization is usually required.

ADDITIONAL INFORMATION

If you like to do some experimental gardening, try growing Indian paintbrush in very large tubs, pots, planters, or other containers. Use good-quality potting soil.

ADDITIONAL SPECIES, CULTIVARS, OR VARIETIES

Indian paintbrush is one of a widely distributed group of plants, some of which are annuals, some perennials. Most of those in the group have bracts, the specialized leafy structures that give us the color we enjoy. These are available in reds, purple, orange, yellow, or even the extremely rare white. *C. latebracteata* or western paintbrush is naturally found in West Texas and adjacent New Mexico. It is an erect, upright-growing perennial. Purple paintbrush or *C. purpurea* is naturally distributed in Arkansas through Texas and Arizona. It is also a perennial; its bracts are purple to reddish-purple, red-orange, or even brick red. In Central and West Texas, *C. sessiliflora* or downy paintbrush grows 6 to 10 in tall with yellow-green flowers and pink bracts. *C. integra* can also be found in Central and West Texas. It grows 6 to 16 in. tall and has bracts that come in cerise, scarlet, and occasionally yellow.

Phlox
Phlox drummondii

EXPOSURE

Full Sun

COLD HARDINESS

Annual

WATER USAGE

Semi-Moist

GROWTH RATE

Fast

AVG. HT × WIDTH

8–20" ' × 8–12 "

SPACING

6–10 "

Covered with sticky hair. Flowers grow in groups in colors of scarlet to dark velvet red. Due to hybridization, many other color combinations have become possible.

*T*his variety of phlox is named for Thomas Drummond, who harvested seeds in Texas in 1834. The seeds were transported to England, where plants were grown and named for him. When we buy varieties of *P. drummondii* seeds today, we are most likely buying hybridized types of this very colorful annual. The colors vary widely from violet to pink to white, and come in blends as well. You will find outstanding groupings of this wonderful Texas native plant on roadsides and in areas where the soil is sandy. Carry your camera with you and get some closeup colorful shots. This wildflower is a favorite with many Texas gardeners because of its bright colors and ease of growing. It will grow in good soils, but I've also seen it growing in some of the poorest soils in Texas. It is a true "blooming trooper."

WHEN TO PLANT

Seeds may be sown from Drummond phlox in late summer/early fall. Transplants should be set out in early spring.

WHERE TO PLANT

Whether planting from seed or from transplants, plant in sunny locations in well-drained soils for best results.

HOW TO PLANT

Plant seeds in well-prepared seedbeds using package directions. To set out transplants, plant in normally prepared bedding-plant soils that drain well. Plant no deeper than the plants were originally grown in the containers. Firm the soil well, water thoroughly, apply root stimulator, and cover with 2 in. of bark mulch.

CARE AND MAINTENANCE

Insects and diseases are normally not a problem for phlox. In enclosed areas of poor drainage and/or air movement, there is a possibility of powdery mildew. If this occurs, seek out the best controls. Remember to read and follow label directions. Phlox does not usually require fertilization or pruning. Water as necessary to prevent soil dryness. This helps to ensure better and prolonged bloom.

ADDITIONAL INFORMATION

Try some phlox in the spring, setting them out in large containers.

ADDITIONAL SPECIES, CULTIVARS, OR VARIETIES

If you wish to find the "true Drummond phlox," make sure you deal with reputable wildflower seed producers and tell them you are after the original plantings. If you are not interested in establishing a pure stand, purchase current-season seeds. Remember that these other seeds grow into plants that are just as colorful in the landscape as the original Drummond! To be able to see the color you are planting, you may wish to set out transplants in the spring. There are many types and varieties of phlox, but I know you will thoroughly enjoy the Drummond phlox.

Plains Coreopsis
Coreopsis tinctoria

EXPOSURE	COLD HARDINESS
Full Sun	Annual
WATER USAGE	GROWTH RATE
Arid to Semi-Mst.	Fast
AVG. HT × WIDTH	SPACING
Varies	12"

Upright to relatively open, rather delicate-looking plant. Covered with blooms that have yellow outside petals and maroonish to brown centers. Will grow in most soils in Texas and is adaptable.

*P*lains coreopsis is a member of the group of Texas wildflowers often referred to as golden wave, simply because a large field of them looks like a wave of gold. Other members of the Coreopsis family that are sometimes called golden wave are *C. grandiflora*, a perennial; *C. longipes*; *C. enuecensis*; *C. basalis*; and *C. cardaninaeforlia*. Another name for this group of plants is fig seed or fig weed. I truly enjoy *C. tinctoria* or plains coreopsis for its delicate look as well as its height. You can grow smaller native Texas flowers underneath it, all in sunny locations, for outstanding color combinations that will "knock your socks off." I like it in combination with Indian blanket (*Gaillardia pulchella*) and Texas bluebells (*Eustoma grandiflorum*).

WHEN TO PLANT
When direct-seeding, plains coreopsis is best planted in the late summer/early fall (this is true of most Texas wildflowers). If you are fortunate enough to find transplants in the spring, plant them at that time. Start your own spring transplants after all danger of frost is past.

WHERE TO PLANT

Plant coreopsis seeds in sunny locations where competition from perennial grasses such as Bermudagrass has been reduced.

HOW TO PLANT

Follow package directions. Water thoroughly. If planting from transplants in landscaped beds, place in prepared flower beds as background plantings in early spring. Plant no deeper than they were growing in their containers. Firm the soil, water thoroughly, apply a root stimulator, and mulch.

CARE AND MAINTENANCE

Plains coreopsis is free of diseases and insects. It usually requires no fertilization or pruning. You may wish to remove spent blossoms (deadhead) to tidy the plants and expand their bloom period. For continued blooms throughout the season, water to prevent soil dryness. Maintaining a nice 3-in. layer of mulch will help conserve soil moisture.

ADDITIONAL INFORMATION

If there is a slight breeze, you will see the outstanding waving motion of coreopsis when in bloom throughout the state. Always carry a camera or something to write with when you visit our Texas highways and byways. Do the same when visiting our botanical gardens, where you will find many wildflowers as well as other labeled plants. Write down the names of the ones you like. That will make it easy to secure the same plants when you select seeds or transplants.

ADDITIONAL SPECIES, CULTIVARS, OR VARIETIES

Lance-leafed coreopsis, *C. lanceolata*, has a normal height of approximately 3 ft. and takes about 2 years to establish well. *C. lanceolata* is also available in a dwarf form called dwarf lance-leafed coreopsis. This is a very hardy, drought-tolerant perennial that reaches a height of about 16 to 20 in. It is a prolific reseeder and blooms all summer. There is also a dwarf red plains coreopsis.

Texas Bluebells
Eustoma grandiflorum

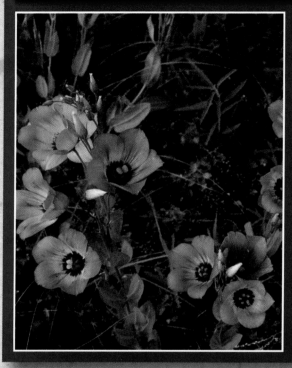

EXPOSURE	COLD HARDINESS
F. Sun to Semi-Sh.	Annual

WATER USAGE	GROWTH RATE
Arid to Semi-Mst.	Medium

AVG. HT × WIDTH	SPACING
24–30″ × 5–7″	12–16″

Covered with an unusual whitish coating. Colors range from white, blue, purple, even off-white, mixed with purple or yellow.

*M*any consider bluebells the most beautiful wildflowers in the state of Texas. These plants also do exceptionally well under cultivation. Bluebells are available in many retail garden centers throughout the state. Their flowers have been known to last for more than a week in cutflower arrangements, and this is one of the reasons that bluebells have been overharvested. Do your part: don't harvest bluebells in the wild. Let them produce for us so we can all enjoy their beauty. If you wish to plant them, purchase seeds or transplants.

WHEN TO PLANT
Bluebell is probably best planted from transplants in early spring after all danger of frost is past.

WHERE TO PLANT
Plant bluebells as if you were going to plant marigolds, petunias, or any other bedding plant, in well-prepared beds in sunny, well-drained locations. This is one native Texas plant that responds well to fertilizers, mulching, and supple-

mental irrigation. Though it can stand some shade from the hot western afternoon sun, it needs a minimum of 6 hours of full sun every day.

HOW TO PLANT
Plant in well-prepared beds. Plant no deeper than the plants were originally grown in their containers. Firm the soil, water thoroughly, apply root stimulator according to label directions, and cover with 3 in. of bark mulch.

CARE AND MAINTENANCE
Texas bluebells normally have no problems with insects or diseases. Remove spent blooms in order to encourage more blooms through-out the season. No other pruning is usually required. Water as necessary to maintain a moist soil for maximum production, growth, and beauty. Maintain a 3-in. layer of mulch throughout the growing season to conserve soil moisture. Fertilize in spring as new growth begins, in mid-season, and then once again in the fall. Premium-quality long-lasting slow-release granular rose fertilizers work well. Other fertilizers such as liquids and water-solubles may be used. Remember to read and follow label directions, and water thoroughly after applying fertilizers.

ADDITIONAL INFORMATION
Texas bluebells may be grown in large tubs.

ADDITIONAL SPECIES, CULTIVARS, OR VARIETIES
Texas bluebells are a member of the Gentian family, which includes meadow-pink, *Sabatia campestris*, and mountain-pink, *Erythraea beyrichii*. A blue-flowered first cousin, *Exaltatum*, is often found in the southern half of the state.

Black-eyed Susan

Rudbeckia hirta var. 'Angustifolia'

EXPOSURE

F. Sun to Semi-Sh.

COLD HARDINESS

All Texas

WATER USAGE

Arid to Semi-Mst.

GROWTH RATE

Fast

AVG. HT × WIDTH

1–3 ′ × 24–30 ″

SPACING

2 ′

Upright and stiff, growing to a somewhat open form. Leaves are hairy. Flowers are yellow (or yellow with brown at the base of the leaves) with brown centers.

'Angustifolia' is a perennial cousin of the annual *R. hirta* 'Pulcherrima'. Both types are often seen growing in vast numbers in Texas. They will grow in prairie soils, sandy soils, loam, or clay soils, as long as the soil drains well. They will grow in full sun, but they tend to bloom longer and better if they receive some shade from the hot west afternoon sun or are grown in dappled sun and shade throughout the entire day. Doug Williams says that at the Mercer Arboretum and Botanical Garden in Humble, Texas, "'Angustifolia' tolerates damp soil and grows 7 feet tall." Don't be surprised if these plants remind you of a sunflower, for they are members of the sunflower family. You may wish to grow them at the bases of tall-growing sunflowers, and let the sunflowers provide their afternoon shade. This is a native Texas plant that you can let your little one plant in the spring with complete assurance that there will be outstanding blooms throughout the season.

WHEN TO PLANT

Seeds may be sown in very early spring as soon as the soil is warm, or in early fall. Transplants are best set out in the spring after all danger of frost is past.

WHERE TO PLANT

Plant in any location in your landscape where you desire a relatively tall, upright-growing, easy-to-maintain, flowering native Texas plant. Do not plant in poorly drained locations or in full shade.

HOW TO PLANT

If you plan to start from seed, prepare a seedbed and sow seeds according to seed packet directions. Firm the soil and water thoroughly. When setting out from transplants, set in soil that you have improved with the addition of organic matter. Approximately 3 in. of soil blended 3 in. deep into the native soil will be excellent for black-eyed Susan. Remove plants from their containers and install in the soil no deeper than they were growing in the containers. Firm the soil, water thoroughly, apply root stimulator according to label directions, and cover with 3 in. of bark mulch.

CARE AND MAINTENANCE

There are no serious insects or diseases of black-eyed Susan. Remove spent blooms to encourage additional blooming through the season and to tidy up the plants. Water as necessary to maintain moist soil, but do not overwater. Maintaining a 3-in. layer of bark mulch will conserve water. Fertilize as necessary throughout the growing season with your favorite type of fertilizer. Usually a one-time application of a granular, premium-quality long-lasting, slow-release rose food in the spring is sufficient. Remember to read label directions, and always water thoroughly after each application of any fertilizer.

ADDITIONAL INFORMATION

Rudbeckia hirta is one of the plants you have probably seen growing everywhere. You may have enjoyed it and wondered if it is easy to grow. The fact is, it is extremely easy to grow—you won't find a plant any easier.

ADDITIONAL SPECIES, CULTIVARS, OR VARIETIES

Rudbeckia hirta is available as an annual form; 'Angustifolia' is the perennial form. The variety name for the annual is *R. hirta* 'Pulcherrima'. There are several species of rudbeckia you may wish to try, including *R. grandiflora* or rough coneflower, *R. missouriensis* or marsh coneflower, *R. laciniata* or cutleaf coneflower, and *R. nitida* or skinny coneflower.

Evening Primrose
Oenothera spp.

EXPOSURE

Full Sun

COLD HARDINESS

All Texas

WATER USAGE

Arid-Dry/Semi-Mst.

GROWTH RATE

Fast to Med.

AVG. HT × WIDTH

6–25"× 10–12"

SPACING

8"

Has many branches. Blooms are "buttercup" in shape and almost-white to rose to yellow in color.

*P*rimrose grows in all areas of our state, though different common names are used, depending on the species. For example, *O. speciosa* is known as the showy-primrose, while *O. missouriensis* is known as the Missouri primrose. Our fellow Texas gardeners along the coast may be most familiar with the beach-evening-primrose, or *O. drummondii*. These are all perennial primroses, but there is an annual primrose called stemless-evening-primrose, *O. triloba*, and *O. lamarckiana* is an outstanding annual that is naturalized across the United States. A biannual or short-lived perennial is *O. hookeri*, often call yellow-evening-primrose. Either Missouri-primrose or showy-primrose is ideal for a perennial bed in a nice sunny location. If you prefer yellow, by all means go with the Missouri, but if you prefer light pink, choose the showy-primrose.

WHEN TO PLANT

Primroses may be direct-seeded in late summer/early fall. If you are fortunate enough to find some transplants, plant them as soon as you get them. You may start your own transplants in early spring after all danger of frost has passed and temperatures are warm.

WHERE TO PLANT
Whether starting from seed or from transplants, plant in sunny, well-drained locations.

HOW TO PLANT
Plant seeds in late summer/early fall the same way all Texas wild-flowers are planted—in well-prepared beds, according to package instructions. Place transplants in prepared beds no deeper than the top of the soilball, firm, water throughly, apply root stimulator according to label directions, and cover with 2 in. of bark mulch.

CARE AND MAINTENANCE
Evening primrose has few insect and disease problems. If chewing insects become a problem, look for the best control possibilities. Remember to read and follow label directions when using any lawn and garden aid. Pruning is usually not required with any of the evening primroses. If you wish to tidy up the plant, remove spent blossoms and damaged parts. Water as necessary to prevent soil dryness, but do not keep wet. Maintaining a nice 2-in. layer of bark mulch will help to conserve soil moisture. Fertilize as new growth begins in the spring. Apply a premium-quality long-lasting slow-release granular rose food, or you may prefer to use water-soluble, liquid, or slow-release granular fertilizers. All will work when applied according to label directions.

ADDITIONAL INFORMATION
Primroses are sometimes called buttercups because of their cupped petals—and because of that buttery yellow pollen, of course.

ADDITIONAL SPECIES, CULTIVARS, OR VARIETIES
Certain varieties, cultivars, and species of evening-primrose, showy-primrose, and other types of primrose are adaptive in all parts of Texas.

Lanceleaf Coreopsis

Coreopsis lanceolata syn. *grandiflora*

EXPOSURE	COLD HARDINESS
Full Sun	All Texas

WATER USAGE	GROWTH RATE
Arid to Semi-Mst.	Fast

AVG. HT × WIDTH	SPACING
18–36″ × 12–24″	12″

Long, narrow leaves. Numerous flowers with yellow petals and yellow centers. Known also as Golden Wave.

*L*anceleaf coreopsis is a very good drought-tolerant perennial which can grow in full-sun locations in all Texas soils. The dwarf variety and a taller variety are both available. Coreopsis is easy to start from seeds. Enjoy this plant's blooms and enjoy its ability to reseed itself, giving you more coreopsis to enjoy in years to come.

WHEN TO PLANT

Seeds may be sown in the early spring or early fall. Seedlings are easy to transplant; transplants purchased at local garden centers should be set out in early spring after all danger of frost is past.

WHERE TO PLANT

Plant your coreopsis transplants in full-sun locations for best results. They will grow in a partially shaded area as long as they receive a minimum of 6 hours of sun per day. Never plant in heavily shaded locations, or growth and bloom will be greatly curtailed.

HOW TO PLANT

Transplants should be planted in the early spring in beds that are adequate for growing marigolds, petunias, or any other bedding plant. To create these beds, incorporate approximately 3 in. of organic matter into the top 3 in. of the existing soil. After improvement is complete, remove transplants from their containers and install them in the planting bed, placing them no deeper than they were grown in their original containers. Space them about a foot apart in a checkerboard pattern if you want a solid bed. Firm the soil well, water thoroughly, apply root stimulator according to label directions, and spread with 2 in. of bark mulch. If you prefer to start from seeds sown directly in the beds after bed preparation is complete, first rake the improved bed to a nice smooth level with your garden rake, then sow seeds according to seed package directions. Lightly firm the media with your hand and water thoroughly with a seedling nozzle. Keep the bed moist until the seeds germinate, then gradually reduce watering frequency.

CARE AND MAINTENANCE

Lanceleaf coreopsis has no serious pest or disease problems. You may wish to prune out spent blooms to encourage additional blooming, but no other pruning is usually required. Water as necessary to prevent dryness and encourage additional buds and blooms. Fertilize in the spring as new growth begins. Apply premium-quality long-lasting, slow-release, granular rose food according to label directions. You may also try water-soluble, liquid, or encapsulated slow-release fertilizers. Be sure to follow label directions and water thoroughly after application.

ADDITIONAL INFORMATION

Coreopsis is one of the easiest plants for children to grow. After they set out their transplants in the spring, show them how to fertilize the plants. Allow the children to water the plants, mulch them, and if they are old enough, let them be responsible for taking care of them. They will enjoy the blooms and you will enjoy the children's responses to them.

ADDITIONAL SPECIES, CULTIVARS, OR VARIETIES

Lanceleaf coreopsis does have a dwarf variety that is simply called dwarf lanceleaf coreopsis. Its normal height range is 16 to 20 in., while the standard lanceleaf coreopsis may reach 3 ft. or more.

Mealy Blue Sage
Salvia farinacea

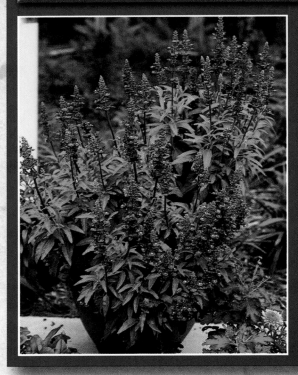

EXPOSURE	COLD HARDINESS
F. Sun to Semi-	All Texas
WATER USAGE	**GROWTH RATE**
Arid to Semi-Mst.	Fast
AVG. HT × WIDTH	**SPACING**
2–3′ × 12–18″	12–18″

Has clusters of small purple to blue flowers. Leaves are lance-shaped.

*O*ur daughter Ashley planted some mealy blue sage together with some dusty miller to create a silver-and-blue combination. It was installed in a bed on the west side of our home in full sun, in deep sandy soil. The combination was striking. These plants are easy to plant, easy to grow, and easy to maintain, and they offer interesting color. I highly recommend mealy blue sage for the gardener who would like to use a native perennial plant for blue and purple in the landscape. The sage family has over 500 species; about 20 of these occur wild in Texas. The one most widely distributed across the state is the mealy blue sage, and it is probably the most widely available plant in our retail garden centers.

WHEN TO PLANT
Mealy blue sage is best planted from transplants set out in the spring.

WHERE TO PLANT
We have had good results planting mealy blue sage in well-drained beds in full sun. They need a minimum of 6 hours of sun every day—do not plant them in heavily shaded areas.

How to Plant

It is best to plant mealy blue sage in well-prepared beds. If the beds at your place have not been improved and you wish to add mealy blue sage to your landscape, blend approximately 3 in. of organic matter (compost, brown peat moss, or ground bark) into the top 3 in. of the soil. Remove individual plants from their containers, and space them 1 to 2 ft. apart in the bed. Plant in checkerboard style if you wish to create a mass effect. After planting no deeper than they were originally grown in the containers, firm the soil, water thoroughly, apply root stimulator according to label directions, and cover with 3 in. of bark mulch.

Care and Maintenance

Mealy blue sage has no serious insect or disease problems, and normally no pruning is required, though more branching and bloom will occur after some tip pinching or light pruning. Water as necessary to prevent soil dryness and to encourage more growth and blooms. Maintaining a 2- to 3-in. layer of bark mulch will help conserve soil moisture. Fertilize one time in the spring as new growth begins. A premium-quality long-lasting rose fertilizer is a good choice. You may also use water-soluble, liquid, or encapsulated fertilizers according to label directions. Remember to water thoroughly after applying any fertilizer.

Additional Information

If you like the purple or blue color of mealy blue sage, try some in pots out on your sunny deck, balcony, patio or other full-sun spots.

Additional Species, Cultivars, or Varieties

Some other types of salvia you may wish to try are 'Cedar Sage', *S. roemeriana*, Texas sage, *S. texana*, and two of my favorites, 'Scarlet Sage', *S. coccinea*, which I have in abundance in a full-sun location around our deck, and salvia greggii, *S. greggii*.

Mexican Hat
Ratibida columnaris

EXPOSURE	COLD HARDINESS
F. Sun to Semi-	All Texas

WATER USAGE	GROWTH RATE
Arid to Semi-Mst.	Fast

AVG. HT × WIDTH	SPACING
2–3′ × 12″	10″

Flowers are yellow to reddish-brown or mixed.

*M*exican hat is a wildflower with a unique look. Its leaves are very long and narrow and it is often seen in large masses that can be seen from a long distance away. It can be found in all types of Texas soils and all kinds of habitats throughout our great wildflower state. It is naturally found in fairly large areas such as ungrazed fields or prairies. It is also outstanding in garden plantings. It is very easily grown in the garden and will last for a long time as a cut flower as well.

WHEN TO PLANT
An ideal time to plant Mexican hat from seed is late summer/early fall. If you are fortunate enough to find transplants, set those out in early spring.

WHERE TO PLANT
Plant Mexican hat in sunny locations that receive at least 6 hours of sun. For long-term blooming, they will benefit from some protection from our hot afternoon sun, but do not plant in heavily shaded locations or in poorly drained soils.

How to Plant

In order to have the best chance at success, prepare a seedbed before sowing the seeds of Mexican hat. Remove any existing vegetation that might provide competition and lightly till the soil. If the soil drains well, no additional improvement will be necessary. If the soil is a poorly drained type, blend approximately 3 in. of organic matter into the top 3 in. of the existing soil. Sow the seeds according to directions on the package. When using transplants, install them in prepared beds no deeper than they were originally growing in their containers. Firm the soil, water thoroughly, apply root stimulator, and cover with 3 in. of bark mulch.

Care and Maintenance

Mexican hat has few to no problems with insects and diseases. But if the planting in your garden does at some time attract unwanted pests, look for the best control possibilities. Remember to read and follow label directions on any pest- control products. To encourage extra blooms and a longer bloom season, prune out spent bloom heads. No other pruning is usually required for maintenance of Mexican hat. Water as necessary throughout the growing season to prevent soil dryness. In landscape beds, maintaining a soil that is moist but not wet will encourage profuse season-long blooming. To conserve moisture, maintain a 3-in. layer of bark mulch. Fertilize with your favorite type of fertilizer as new growth begins in the spring. Long-lasting slow-release premium-quality granular rose food works well. You may also wish to use water-soluble or encapsulated slow-release forms. Remember to read and follow label directions and water thoroughly after applying any fertilizer.

Additional Information

If you wish to try some Mexican hats in sunny locations, perhaps in pots on your deck or patio, make sure that the soil drains thoroughly. Do not allow the plants to stand in water-filled saucers.

Additional Species, Cultivars, or Varieties

At this time there are no named species or varieties of Mexican hat. Enjoy this great native Texas perennial.

Phlox
Phlox spp.

EXPOSURE

F. Sun to Semi-

COLD HARDINESS

All Texas

WATER USAGE

Arid to Semi-Mst.

GROWTH RATE

Fast to Med.

AVG. HT × WIDTH

6–20" × Mat

SPACING

12–16"

A low-growing mat with bloom colors of pink, rose, lavender, or purple.

*I*n addition to the outstanding annual phlox grown in our state, you may wish to try some perennial phloxes. *P. pilosa*, for example, imparts a wonderful fragrance to the landscape. It is often called fragrant phlox, or prairie phlox. *P. divaricata*, or Louisiana phlox, will grow in East Texas locations where soil conditions are moist. Phloxes have the ability to slowly creep. They are not overpowering, and they present an interesting-looking groundcover when used in small areas. The bloom color is anywhere from white, pink, or lavender to blue, and blooms are about an inch across. *P. nana*, which is also known as dwarf phlox, is an unusual white/pink color. It is somewhat woody around its base, and it has bright pink flowers.

WHEN TO PLANT

The best time to start perennial phlox from seeds is very early fall. Louisiana phlox is often available as transplants in the spring, which is the ideal time to set them out.

WHERE TO PLANT

All these perennial phlox will grown in limestone, loam, or clay soils, as long as the soils are well drained. Louisiana phlox needs at least 6 in. of good soil and at least 6 hours of full sun per day. Do not plant in poorly drained locations or heavily shaded spots, though the plants will benefit from a little shady protection from the hot western afternoon sun. It may be grown as a bedding plant in a landscape bed, or add it to your perennial plantings.

HOW TO PLANT

If planting from seeds, prepare the seedbed as you do when starting any bedding plants—at the minimum, lightly till the soil. In locations that need more preparation, blend 3 in. of organic matter with the top 3 in. of the existing soil. After bed preparation is complete, sow the seeds according to label directions. Water thoroughly. If planting from transplants, install them in prepared locations no deeper than they were originally grown in their containers and firm the soil well. Water thoroughly, apply root stimulator according to label directions, and cover with 3 in. of bark mulch.

CARE AND MAINTENANCE

Perennial phlox has very few insects or diseases. If pests do visit your planting, find out about the best control possibilities. Remember to read andfollow label directions when using any lawn and garden aid. Removing spent bloom masses is recommended for encouraging additional bloom throughout the season. No other pruning is normally required for perennial phlox. Water as necessary to prevent soil dryness, but do not keep the soil wet. Fertilize in the spring as new growth begins. A premium-quality long-lasting slow-release granular rose fertilizer works well but you may wish to try water-soluble, liquid, or encapsulated slow-release fertilizer. Remember to read and follow label directions, and water thoroughly after applying any type of fertilizer.

ADDITIONAL INFORMATION

If you enjoy fragrant phlox, try it in some large tubs or beds near your entryway. You will be able to enjoy the fragrance as you go in and out of your home.

ADDITIONAL SPECIES, CULTIVARS, OR VARIETIES

Perennial phlox in Texas include *P. divaricata* (Louisiana phlox); *P. pilosa* (fragrant phlox or prairie phlox); *P. nana* (dwarf phlox); and *P. nivalis* (trailing phlox).

NATIVE PERENNIALS

Prairie Verbena
Verbena bipinnatifida

EXPOSURE

F. Sun to Semi-

COLD HARDINESS

All Texas

WATER USAGE

Semi-Moist

GROWTH RATE

Fast

AVG. HT × WIDTH

6–16" × Creeping

SPACING

Varies

Creeping form. Many small flowers, in purple/lavender to pink, in round to flat-topped groups.

*P*rairie verbena is one of the perennial verbenas that belongs to the Vervain family. We have at least ten of these verbenas in Texas, but prairie verbena may be the one most commonly seen. When grown in masses, it is an absolutely breathtaking native wildflower. I have seen it growing successfully in Central Texas and in East Texas, in road ditches and fields of deep sandy soil. It is extremely easy to grow in the home landscape. It can be enjoyed in specialized locations, too, such as in a rock garden or semi-trailing over the edge of a flower bed.

WHEN TO PLANT
For direct-seeding prairie verbena, sow the seeds in late summer/early fall. If you are fortunate enough to find transplants, set them out in early spring.

WHERE TO PLANT
Plant in sunny locations in well-drained soil. The plants will grow in cliché, clay, limestone, and sand as long as the soil is well drained. They do best in full sun, but they will tolerate a little shade from the late afternoon sun. You

may plant a pure stand of them in a landscape bed, or plant them with other wildflowers.

HOW TO PLANT

Prepare a seedbed by removing any existing vegetation or debris, then tilling the soil and raking. Sow the seeds according to label directions. If planting from transplants, you may wish to first incorporate 3 in. of organic matter into the top 3 in. of the existing soil. After bed preparation is complete, remove transplants from their containers and install in the soil no deeper than they were growing in their containers. Firm the soil around the new transplants, water thoroughly, apply root stimulator according to label directions, and cover with 3 in. of bark mulch.

CARE AND MAINTENANCE

Prairie verbena has no serious insects or diseases. Pruning is usually not required, though you may wish to remove spent blooms to encourage extra blooming throughout the season. Water as necessary to prevent soil dryness, especially when planted in the landscape. Maintaining a thick layer of bark mulch will help conserve soil moisture. Using your favorite type of fertilizer, fertilize in the spring as new growth begins; premium-quality long-lasting slow-release rose fertilizers work well. Remember, read and follow label directions and water thoroughly after application.

ADDITIONAL INFORMATION

Prairie verbena offers striking color and will accent virtually any location.

ADDITIONAL SPECIES, CULTIVARS, OR VARIETIES

The following plants are listed as vervaines instead of verbenas: *V. rigida* (tubor vervaine), *V. brisiliensis* (Brazilian vervaine), *V. halei* (Texas vervaine), and *V. canadensis* (rose vervaine).

Purple Coneflower
Echinacea augustifolia

EXPOSURE

F. Sun to Semi-

COLD HARDINESS

All Texas

WATER USAGE

Semi-Moist

GROWTH RATE

Fast

AVG. HT × WIDTH

1½–3' × 8–12"

SPACING

12"

Bloom colors range from white to light pink to deep rose.

I am often asked, "Why is purple coneflower called purple coneflower when most of its flowers are pink?" I really don't have a good answer for that question, except that quite a few of the blooms have a little bit of purple in them when they first start to form. Purple coneflower comes in a variety of colors. Some are white, some are pale pink, some rose pink . . . and some are even pale purple. Even the forms of the blooms vary quite a bit. Some petals tend to hang down and some tend to stand out straight. The central parts of the blooms come in different shapes. Purple coneflower can be hybridized, and you will be able to find different varieties. Not long ago a caller to my radio show asked if purple coneflower could be planted in full sun. It has been my experience that these plants grow best in dappled shade, or at least where they get some shade from the hot Texas afternoon sun. I think they do best when you install them as mass plantings spaced about 1 ft. apart in a checkerboard pattern. This mass effect looks wonderful in the home landscape.

When to Plant

Seeds may be sown in spring after the soil warms up, or in very early fall. Transplants should be set out as soon as they become available.

Where to Plant

Purple coneflower is known to grow in clay, loam, or sandy soils, as long as the soils are well drained. For best results, plant where they will get dappled sun throughout the day or where they will get 6 hours of morning sun and shade from the hot western afternoon sun. Do not plant in heavily shaded locations, poorly drained areas, or areas that are difficult to water.

How to Plant

If you are going to start purple coneflower from seeds, first prepare a bed. Remove vegetation and debris, till the top 3 in. of soil, and blend about 3 in. of organic matter into the soil. After the bed is completed, rake thoroughly, sow seeds according to package directions, and water deeply. If setting out transplants, remove them from their containers and install them in the soil no deeper than they were growing in the containers—about 1 ft. apart in a checkerboard pattern. If you are planting in rows, do a double or triple row for an outstanding look. After planting is complete, firm the soil well, water thoroughly, apply root stimulator according to label directions, and cover with 3 in. of bark mulch.

Care and Maintenance

Purple coneflower has no serious insects or diseases. Remove spent blooms and stems; no other pruning is necessary. Water as necessary to prevent soil dryness. To conserve moisture, maintain a 3-in. layer of mulch throughout the growing season. Fertilize as new growth begins in the spring with a premium-quality long-lasting slow-release rose fertilizer, applied according to label directions. Remember to water thoroughly after every application.

Additional Information

You may wish to try some purple coneflowers in large tubs or planters on a porch where they will receive at least 6 hours of sun.

Additional Species, Cultivars, or Varieties:

Other species of coneflower are *E. purpurea*, *E. pallida*, and *E. sanguinea*.

Texas Lantana
Lantana horrida

EXPOSURE

Full Sun

COLD HARDINESS
To 0° F.

WATER USAGE

Arid/Semi-Mst.

GROWTH RATE
Fast

AVG. HT × WIDTH
3–5′ × 4–8′

SPACING

2′

Blooms are on dense heads; their colors are yellow, orange, red, and combinations.

I have grown and enjoyed Texas lantana for decades. It is a low-maintenance plant that will thrive even in areas that are difficult to water, blooming the first year and for many years thereafter. Texas lantana makes an outstanding planting in any full-sun location with soil that drains well. It may be used alone or in combination with other plants. It's a very easy plant for first-time gardeners, including the little ones, to grow.

WHEN TO PLANT

You may start Texas lantana from freshly gathered mature seeds any time you can find them during the growing season, or make tip cuttings and root them for a start. It is best to set transplants out in early spring after all danger of frost is past.

WHERE TO PLANT

Plant lantana in any location that has a minimum of 6 hours of full sun, and preferably full sun all day long. Due to lantana's large size, make sure you have adequate space available, or it may overpower the location. Lantana does have some prickly leaves and stems, so this is not a plant to place in areas where people brush by.

HOW TO PLANT

Prepare seedbeds by improving the soil with organic matter and raking finely. Plant fresh, mature seeds in the prepared seedbeds during the growing season, no later than the end of August. To set out transplants in the spring, dig individual planting holes no deeper than the plants were originally grown in their containers. Because of lantana's wide spread, you can space the plants as far as 3 ft. apart and still have a solid mass planting if that is your desire.

CARE AND MAINTENANCE

Spider mites may visit your lantana during the hot, dry times of the year, though I have grown lantana for over 20 years and never had this problem. But if they do visit your planting, consult with your Lowe's customer service associate for the best control. Remember to read and follow label directions. To encourage new growth beginning at the base, I prune Texas lantana very severely just as new growth begins in the spring. This practice also gives me control of the plant's ultimate size. No other pruning is usually required, but if the plants become too large for your area, they may be pruned successfully throughout the entire growing season. Water as necessary to prevent soil dryness—this will help enhance the blooms. Maintaining a thick mulch around the entire root system will help to conserve soil moisture. Fertilize in the spring as new growth begins. Use one application of a premium-quality long-lasting slow-release granular rose food, applied according to label directions. Remember to water thoroughly after applying the fertilizer.

ADDITIONAL INFORMATION

I suggest you try growing lantana at a seldom-visited location such as a vacation home where your landscape maintenance must be kept to a minimum. I live in Texas Zone 7B, and my lantanas have continued to return year after year for more than 16 years—this means that these plantings are truly perennial!

ADDITIONAL SPECIES, CULTIVARS, OR VARIETIES

Other lantanas worth trying are *L. camara; L. montevidensis*, a trailing form; and *L. macropoda*, a very aromatic shrub somewhat less than 3 ft. tall with white, pink, or even yellow flowers.

Wild Petunia
Ruellia spp.

EXPOSURE

F. Sun to Semi-

COLD HARDINESS

All Texas

WATER USAGE

Arid to Semi-Mst.

GROWTH RATE

Fast to Med.

AVG. HT × WIDTH

12–30" × Creeping

SPACING

12"

Long, narrow, dark-green leaves. "Petunia-shaped" blooms are light lavender to deep purple.

*M*y family has enjoyed ruellia for several years. It is planted in beds with a southwestern exposure, right out the back door of our home. Ruellia seems to thrive in this location, receiving lots of morning sun and shaded from the hot western afternoon sun. Unlike many of the petunias that are grown in our gardens today, ruellia will bloom throughout the entire season. It is in fact not related to the true petunia family at all, though it is often called a petunia or wild petunia or even Mexican petunia. The true petunia is a member of the solanaceae family, and has tomatoes, peppers, and eggplants as cousins; ruellia is a member of the Acanthus family.

WHEN TO PLANT
I suggest that ruellia be started from root divisions that you have received from a friend, relative, or fellow gardener; or start it from transplants purchased in early spring.

WHERE TO PLANT
Plant ruellia in any well-drained location in the landscape. It will grow in sand, clay, or loam-type soils. I prefer placing it where it will have dappled

shade throughout the day, or at least shade from the hot western afternoon sun. As long as it doesn't receive heat reflected off your home or other structures, it should do well in a location that receives morning sun.

How to Plant
Plant in prepared bedding soils whose top 3 in. have been blended with approximately 3 in. of organic matter. After bed preparation is complete, set your new transplants in individual planting holes no deeper than they were originally growing in their containers, spacing them approximately 2 ft. apart. Planting in a checkerboard pattern will give you a mass effect the first year. After planting is complete, water thoroughly, apply root stimulator according to label directions, and cover with 3 in. of bark mulch.

Care and Maintenance
We have had no insect or disease problems with ruellia. Usually no pruning is required. For continuous bloom through the season, water as necessary to maintain a moist growing environment. Fertilize in the spring as new growth begins, using a premium-quality long-lasting slow-release granular rose food. You may use other fertilizers if you like, including water-soluble and encapsulated slow-release forms. Remember to read and follow label directions, and water thoroughly after application.

Additional Information
Ruellia is easily multiplied from new transplants taken from divisions of parent plants or from the root system.

Additional Species, Cultivars, or Varieties
Several ruellias, or "Summer Petunias," may be found at Lowe's: *R. nudiflora* (often called violet ruelia), *R. humilis* (low ruellia), *R. caroliniensis*, *R. occidentalis*, *R. pedunculata*, *R. metzae*, and *R. malacosperma*. 'Bonita' blooms in pink. In the Houston area, non-native *R. brittoniana* 'Katie's Compact' also does well in local landscapes. Try one or all of these ruellias in the home landscape. I know you will enjoy them.

Agarito
Berberis trifoliolata

EXPOSURE

Semi-Shade

COLD HARDINESS

All Texas

WATER USAGE

Arid-Dry

GROWTH RATE

Slow to Med.

AVG. HT × WIDTH

3–6´ × 2–3´

SPACING

2´

Green to grayish-green leaves are holly-like, each with 3 short spines or points. Fragrant yellow blooms. Produces bright-red edible berries. Evergreen.

*A*garito grew in the mesquite woods of Brownwood, my hometown and the county seat of Brown County. We called these interesting native shrubs "agarito berries" because of their edible berries. Yes, the berries were a bit difficult to harvest, due to the spiny leaves, but they had a nice red, tart juice, and we enjoyed them. We also looked for agarito berries when visiting my grandparents in the Keys Crossing area at Indian Creek, about 19 miles south of Brownwood along the Colorado River. Even today, in certain Texas stores you will find jelly made from agarito berries. If you like birds, plant agarito in your Texas landscape; it will provide both food and cover for them—and you will enjoy the fragrance of the plant's bright-yellow blooms.

WHEN TO PLANT
Agarito may be planted in early fall; early spring is also a good planting time.

WHERE TO PLANT
Plant agarito in a well-drained location that receives full sun, or at least 6 hours of full sun. It will grow in sand or clay soils. Do not plant in heavily shaded areas or in soils that tend to stay damp.

HOW TO PLANT

To use agarito as a landscape shrub in beds, a thorough tilling of the soil is all the preparation that is necessary. If you wish to plant in a poorly drained location, plant the shrubs in raised beds to which you have added lots of organic matter and other drainage materials. Remove your agaritos from their containers and plant in the soil no deeper than they were growing in their original containers. *It is very important that you plant agarito no deeper than this.* Firm the soil well around the root system, water thoroughly, apply root stimulator, and spread with about 3 in. of bark mulch.

CARE AND MAINTENANCE

Agarito is considered pest-free. If at any time insects do visit your planting, investigate appropriate control possibilities. Remember to read and follow label directions when using any lawn and garden aid. Agarito may be pruned if desired, but it is much better to allow it to grow to its natural shape. Water only as necessary to prevent complete soil dryness. It is important not to overwater. Fertilize no more than one time per year with a premium-quality long-lasting slow-release rose fertilizer applied according to label directions. Remember to water thoroughly after applying any fertilizer.

ADDITIONAL INFORMATION

There are several different agarito selections. Ask about each agarito you are shown: *How tall and how wide will that particular selection grow in my area?*

ADDITIONAL SPECIES, CULTIVARS, OR VARIETIES

B. swaseyi is the Texas berberis. One of its unique features is that its leaves can turn reddish or yellow in the fall and remain that way till new growth begins in the spring. Note: The common name algerita is also used.

American Beautyberry
Callicarpa americana

EXPOSURE

F. Sun to Semi-

COLD HARDINESS

All Texas

WATER USAGE

Arid to Semi-Mst.

GROWTH RATE

Medium

AVG. HT × WIDTH
4–6' × 4–6'

SPACING

3'

Large deciduous shrub. Inconspicuous flowers, masses of very colorful purple berries.

*A*h, American beautyberry. Judy and I get more compliments and comments on our American beautyberry than on any other plant we have in the large bed near our back entry. It is growing in a rocky location in and among other native plants and imported plants, and it is spectacular. It receives plenty of morning sun, and some shade from the hot western afternoon sun. We allow it to grow as it should be grown, reaching a relatively large size with weeping, arching branches and clusters of bright purple berries. Plant an American beautyberry for the birds. Beautyberry also comes in white, but I prefer the purple one.

WHEN TO PLANT
American beautyberry is best planted in early spring, but will also grow well when planted in fall.

WHERE TO PLANT
Plant your American beautyberry in a spot where it will have plenty of room to grow. It can grow as tall as 10 ft., though it usually grows around 4 ft. in our

landscape. To help make it more compact, cut it back very severely at the beginning of each season. If you wish to plant two or more, space them about 5 to 7 ft. apart. American beautyberry has the ability to grow in various types of soils. It will grow in sand, loam, and clay, as well as in soils that are rather acid, alkaline, or calcareous. It will also grow in fairly moist areas.

HOW TO PLANT

American beautyberry will grow quite well in our native soil, but if you decide to do some soil preparation, do it as if you were making up a bed for any other landscape plant. Loosen the soil in an area several times wider and no deeper than the soilball. Remove the plant from its container, place into its individual planting hole, backfill, and firm the soil. Water it thoroughly, apply root stimulator according to label directions, and cover with about 3 in. of bark mulch.

CARE AND MAINTENANCE

We have had no insect or disease problems in the 16 years we have been growing American beautyberry. You may prune quite severely every year to encourage a thicker plant with more branches. Heavy pruning is best done just before spring growth. This pruning is not required; it is simply a matter of taste and choice. Water as necessary to prevent soil dryness, especially during the months of July and August. The most important time to have moist soil is during the blooming and fruiting stage. Fertilize one time as new growth begins in the spring and once again in the fall with a premium-quality long-lasting slow-release granular rose food. Remember to read and follow label directions, and water thoroughly after application.

ADDITIONAL INFORMATION

American beautyberry is known in some quarters as French mulberry.

ADDITIONAL SPECIES, CULTIVARS, OR VARIETIES

The white variety of American beautyberry is *C. americana* cv. *Lactea*, and has abundant creamy white berries. It grows under the same conditions as the standard American beautyberry.

Salvia Greggii

Salvia greggii

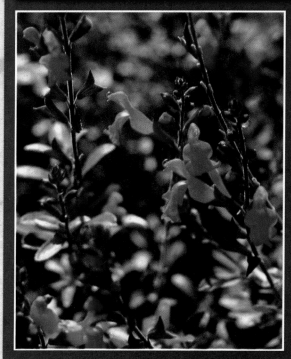

EXPOSURE

Full Sun

COLD HARDINESS

To 10° F.

WATER USAGE

Arid-Dry

GROWTH RATE

Fast

AVG. HT × WIDTH

2–3´ × 24–30˝

SPACING

2–3´

Leaves are small and green. Flowers are white to pink to purple and red.

*S*alvia greggii is a true member of the sage family. It has wonderful foliage whose fragrance becomes obvious when you simply brush by the plant. It is available in several outstanding colors. When put together in masses, it makes a spectacular planting in the landscape. We use it in a large landscape bed at the southwestern corner of our home next to our deck, a full-sun location in which salvia greggii thrives. It will grow in cliché soils, limestone, clay, and sandy soils, as long as they are well drained. The flowers are only about 1 in. in size, but they are extremely colorful in the landscape. If you like Texas landscape plants but your space is limited, try salvia greggii in large containers. You will also find it growing in commercial establishments; when we visit our son, Aaron, in Austin, we see mass plantings in that area. Note: Salvia greggii may grow into a relatively woody plant, become more shrublike, and reach 3 ft. in height. Under these conditions it is often used as and called a shrub. Cut radically to approximately 4 in. and allowed to regrow, it is called a native flowering perennial. However you classify it, salvia greggii is a great native flowering plant. I use it as a flowering shrub.

When to Plant

The best time to plant salvia greggii is early spring. The second-best time is early fall.

Where to Plant

Plant in any well-drained location that receives a minimum of 6 hours of full sun. Salvia greggii prefers full sun all day long, but if it must be in shade part of the day, make sure it receives shade from the hot west afternoon sun. It gives outstanding color when placed along walkways going into your home. It is quite appealing when planted in masses to create a tall groundcover-type effect.

How to Plant

Salvia greggii requires no special soil preparation other than making sure the soil drains well. For planting in native soil, dig the hole several times wider than the plant soilball, but no deeper (very important). Remove your plants from their containers, set in the planting holes, and backfill with the loosened soil. Water thoroughly, apply root stimulator according to label directions, and cover with 2 in. of bark mulch. Remember: do not plant too deeply.

Care and Maintenance

There are no serious insects or disease problems for salvia greggii except for those that arise from poorly drained soils. Prune rather severely in early spring to encourage new growth and to maximize bloom possibilities. To encourage even more blooms, the plants may be pinched, trimmed, or cut back periodically throughout the growing season. Water as necessary to prevent soil dryness, but do not overwater or keep wet. You may fertilize one time per year. Use a premium-quality long-lasting slow-release granular rose fertilizer, applied according to label directions. Remember to water thoroughly after applying any fertilizer.

Additional Information

Salvia greggii is a great plant for those little gardeners at your home. It is a good size for them to handle, it is easy for them to maintain, and they will enjoy its small blooms.

Additional Species, Cultivars, or Varieties

Various selections come in orange, pink, red, white, and purple.

Texas Sage or Cenizo
Leucophyllum frutescens

EXPOSURE
Full Sun

COLD HARDINESS
To 5° F.

WATER USAGE
Arid-Dry

GROWTH RATE
Slow to Med.

AVG. HT × WIDTH
4–8′ × 4–8′

SPACING
3–5′

Leaves are small and silvery white to silvery gray. Flowers cover the entire shrub and may range from white to pink to shades of purple. Will grow in all types of Texas soil.

I love our plantings of Texas sage. We have the standard gray type and we also have the green. There are various sizes as well. *L. frutescens* is the variety normally thought of as Texas sage. It is also known as cenizo, and in some quarters it is called purple sage or silver leaf. Texas sage will grow in areas that have very little rainfall. If you live in an area that has a minimal amount of water, just wait until we have one of our nice drenching rains. After the rain, stand back and watch the blooms on Texas sage—they will be absolutely outstanding. I've seen this magic occur in municipal landscapes as well as along mediums and highways where the reflected heat is tremendous. Texas sage always stands up to the task. After a rain, there are blooms everywhere—people stop to look and point at the beauty.

WHEN TO PLANT
Cenizo may be planted in the spring or in the fall. Both times of year work well.

WHERE TO PLANT

Plant Texas sage anywhere in the landscape that has a minimum of 6 hours of full sun. It does extremely well in full sun, all day long. It can take a little bit of shade, but not a large amount.

HOW TO PLANT

Cenizo will grow in any of our native Texas soils as long as they are well drained. Dig the planting hole several times wider than the plant soilball, but no deeper. (Be very careful about not planting any deeper than the plant's original soilball.) Remove the plants from their containers, place in the holes, backfill, and firm the soil well. Water thoroughly. After watering, apply root stimulator according to label directions and cover with 2 in. of bark mulch.

CARE AND MAINTENANCE

Texas sage is a relatively pest-free plant. In the 5 years we have been growing it, we have encountered no insects or diseases. Water as necessary throughout the growing season to prevent complete soil dryness. Remember, do not overwater. You may fertilize if desired. If you do, I suggest a premium-quality long-lasting slow-release rose food applied according to label directions.

ADDITIONAL INFORMATION

If you are going to grow only one native Texas plant, choose Texas sage.

ADDITIONAL SPECIES, CULTIVARS, OR VARIETIES

Noted Texas plant hunter Benny Simpson spent many years on the trail of Texas sage, seeking out different types. Because of his efforts and those of the Texas nursery industry, we can now find several varieties of cenizo. These include 'Silver Cloud', which has a very regal purple-colored flower; 'Thunder Cloud', a heavy-blooming dwarf plant; a cold-hardy variety called 'Bend'; 'Rain Cloud'; 'Green Cloud'; 'White Cloud'; and 'Compacta'. 'Green Leaf' and 'Silverado' are two other varieties on the market. When you are looking at cenizo, be sure to ask, "How tall and how wide does that variety of cenizo grow in my area?"

Turk's Cap

Malvaviscus arboreus var. *drummondii*

EXPOSURE

Full to Shade

COLD HARDINESS

All Texas

WATER USAGE

Arid to Semi-Mst.

GROWTH RATE

Fast

AVG. HT × WIDTH

2–6′ × 3–4′

SPACING

3′

Large bright-green leaves. Blooms are bright red and twisted. Fruits are apple-shaped and red. Known also as Bleeding Heart.

*T*urk's cap is a rather large, spreading herbaceous shrub. In South Texas it is more woody than it is in North Texas, where it dies down to the ground and comes back every year. It is one native Texas plant that will grow in shaded areas. At my house we grow it near the back porch in a bed that was raised with natural stone and receives morning sun and afternoon shade. Hummingbirds just love Turk's cap. We are able to enjoy the beauty of the plant itself, its blooms, its fruits, hummingbirds . . . and butterflies!

WHEN TO PLANT

Plant Turk's cap in early spring after the soil is warm.

WHERE TO PLANT

Turk's cap will grow in sunny locations as long as they have adequate soil moisture. They tend to do best in areas that get morning sun and afternoon shade, though they will also do well in dappled shade and even in relatively heavy shade. They work well planted in and among other landscape plants.

We have planted ruellia at the base of our Turk's cap, and bouncing Bet and other easy-to-grow perennial plants around it.

HOW TO PLANT

Turk's cap will grow in clay, loam, sand, or any mixture of these three types as long as the soil is moist and well drained. To enhance overall growth, you may wish to improve the soil by incorporating 3 in. of organic matter into the top 3 in. Dig planting holes no deeper than the soilball and insert the plants in the holes. Firm the soil, water thoroughly, apply root stimulator according to label directions, and mulch with a bark mulch.

CARE AND MAINTENANCE

Turk's cap is usually not bothered by serious insect or disease problems. Once new growth begins in the spring, remove any growth that was killed by winter freezes. No other pruning is required. For maximum growth, water as necessary to maintain a moist soil. Turk's cap benefits from having a well-mulched root system. Fertilize 2 or 3 times throughout the growing season to maximize blooms. I fertilize with a long-lasting slow-release rose food, but you may have another preference. Whatever type of fertilizer you use, be sure to read and follow label directions, and water thoroughly after each application.

ADDITIONAL INFORMATION

Turk's cap is easy to start with transplants or from seed. I got my transplants from my Granny Miller several years ago in Brownwood, where it was growing in heavy clay soil. I am growing the same plant in a light soil, but it has adapted quite well. Unlike most shrubs, Turk's cap is classified as a herbaceous perennial shrub, and usually has a woody to semi-woody base. Most herbaceous plants die to or near the ground each year and regrow the following growing season; Turk's cap follows this pattern in all areas of Texas which receive killing frosts and freezes.

ADDITIONAL SPECIES, CULTIVARS, OR VARIETIES

M. arboreus var. *drummondii* is the Turk's cap grown most often in Texas. *M. arboreus* is larger-leaved and has larger blooms and overall size. Thanks to horticulturist Calvin Finch and the San Antonio Master Gardener program for the information which distinguishes these two plants. If you want to create a backyard habitat to attract hummingbirds, butterflies, and other wildlife to your area, be sure to include a significant planting of Turk's cap.

Wax Myrtle
Myrica cerifera

EXPOSURE

F. Sun to Semi-

COLD HARDINESS

All Texas

WATER USAGE

Moist to Arid

GROWTH RATE

Fast

AVG. HT × WIDTH

2–20' × 2–10'

SPACING

6–10'

Leaves are light to yellowish green, evergreen, and aromatic. Flowers are inconspicuous, but the plant produces a very small, dark-purple to very blackish fruit.

Wax myrtle generally prefers a moist soil when grown in its native habitat in woodlands and other locations. If you are looking for a moist area in the woods, perhaps an underground spring, a sign that you may have found one is the sight of a wax myrtle. Wax myrtle often grows on top of a moist area or spring. But it also thrives in hot mediums, in our multi-lane highways, and in urban applications. I am growing some wax myrtle on the west side of my well house. The well house is painted solid white, so there is reflected heat in this location, but the wax myrtle is flourishing. If you have enjoyed a tall-growing Yapon holly and want to try something else that has similar characteristics, be sure to take a look at the tall-growing wax myrtle.

WHEN TO PLANT

Wax myrtle may be planted 12 months of the year in Texas. The best time to plant it is early fall; the second-best time is early spring.

WHERE TO PLANT

Adaptable wax myrtle may be planted in any type of Texas soil, whether it be sand or loam or clay, and it will even grow in relatively poorly drained areas. Wax myrtle will grow in sunny or shady spots—provided that it receives dappled not heavy shade. It is a good plant to grow over under-plantings such as groundcovers. And if you want an extremely tall, thick, dense, low-maintenance screening plant in an area you seldom visit, such as a vacation home, wax myrtle will fill the bill.

HOW TO PLANT

Wax myrtle needs no special soil preparation. Dig the planting hole several times wider than the soilball, and loosen the soil and the plant soilball. After digging the hole to soilball depth, insert wax myrtle, approximately 3 ft. apart in mass plantings. Backfill with loose soil, water thoroughly, apply root stimulator according to label directions, and cover with 3 in. of bark mulch. Wax myrtle may also be grown as a specimen plant.

CARE AND MAINTENANCE

This plant has no serious insects or diseases. Prune if you would like to maintain or create a desired shape, but no pruning is really required. For best growth, maintain a moist soil. Fertilize 2 or 3 times during the growing season, once as new growth begins in the spring, once in the fall, and possibly once in mid-season. Use a premium-quality long-lasting slow-release 3:1:2 lawn fertilizer. Read and follow label directions, and be sure to water thoroughly after each application. 21-7-14, 18-6-12 and 15-5-10 are all 3:1:2 ratio lawn fertilizers.

ADDITIONAL INFORMATION

I cannot overemphasize how easy it is to grow wax myrtle—and how much I think you will enjoy it in your home landscape. Next time you go to your retail garden center, take a look at the wax myrtle and consider it for home use.

ADDITIONAL SPECIES, CULTIVARS, OR VARIETIES

In addition to the tall-growing wax myrtle or *M. cerifera*, there is a variety called *M. pussila* which is often called dwarf wax myrtle. Keep in mind that the term dwarf is relative. Dwarf wax myrtle may reach as high as 6 ft., though it can be easily maintained in the 3-ft. height range. When planted and allowed to run, it will form a very thick, dense mat. It is easy to maintain when kept inside borders, and it will create a very dense, thick, wonderful, usable shrub—without any stickers on it. Other cultivars are 'Sima Alba', 'Rosa', 'Royal Purple', 'Texas Purple', and 'Violaca Plena'.

Wooly Butterfly Bush

Buddleia spp.

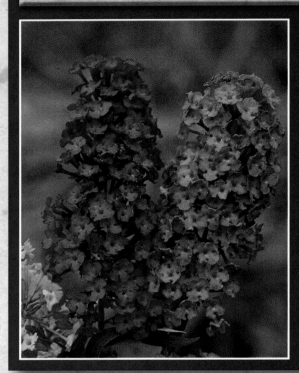

EXPOSURE	COLD HARDINESS
Full to Semi-	-20°

WATER USAGE	GROWTH RATE
Arid to Semi-Mst.	Fast

AVG. HT × WIDTH	SPACING
2–4' × 4–6'	2–3'

Leaves are pale green and covered with white pubescence, or fuzz. Semievergreen.

*T*he wooly butterfly bush belongs to a larger group (or family) called Logania. In this family is a wide assortment of plants often referred to as butterfly bush, many of which are fragrant and attract lots of butterflies. The wooly butterfly bush is native to Texas. It does not bloom as profusely as many of it cousins, but its blooms are interesting, and it is excellent for large border plantings. It works well when part of a design around courtyards, patios, or pools, and it grows especially well in large tubs or containers. Its appearance is striking, and it can be combined with other native plants, such as Texas mountain laurel, yapon holly, and wax myrtle, as well as with imported plants. Just make sure the soil drains well and the plant receives good air movement and lots of sun.

WHEN TO PLANT

The best time to plant your wooly butterfly bush is in early spring; the second-best time is early fall.

Where to Plant

Plant in your landscape where it will receive full sun, or a minimum of 6 hours of sun per day. It is fine to provide it with some shade from the hot afternoon sun. It will grow in sand or nice loam, as well as limestone-type soils as long as they are well drained

How to Plant

Wooly butterfly bush is quite drought tolerant. It will survive harsh conditions, growing in parts of Texas that receive only 12 in. of rain per year. But to get best results from the plant, grow it in the type of beds where you would plant hollies and other landscape plants: incorporate approximately 4 in. of organic matter into the top 4 in. of the soil. After the soil is improved (or at least thoroughly loosened in an area several times wider than the plant soilball), dig holes no deeper than the depth of the soilball and plant. Backfill with soil, firm, and water thoroughly. Apply root stimulator according to label directions and cover with 3 in. of bark mulch.

Care and Maintenance

Wooly butterfly bush has no serious insects or diseases. Prune as necessary if you wish to maintain a desired shape, though it is best to allow the wooly butterfly bush to grow to its normal shape. You may wish to prune severely one time as spring begins for compactness. Water as necessary to prevent soil dryness; to maximize growth, maintain a moist but not wet soil. Fertilize 2 times throughout the growing season with a premium-quality long-lasting slow-release rose fertilizer. Follow label directions and always water thoroughly after application.

Additional Information

Butterfly bush is easy to start from seed. Gather your seeds in late spring and plant as soon as possible in warm soil. About 2 times the depth of the seed is the proper planting depth. Keep the soil moist and transplant after 2 sets of true leaves have emerged.

Additional Species, Cultivars, or Varieties

This large family has several cultivated plants. Ask to see selections of butterfly bush. If you want to see the wooly butterfly bush, you need to be specific: ask for it by name.

Cedar Elm

Ulmus crassifolia

EXPOSURE

Full Sun

COLD HARDINESS

All Texas

WATER USAGE

Arid to Semi-Mst.

GROWTH RATE

Medium

AVG. HT × WIDTH

60–80 ′ × 40–50 ′

SPACING

50 ′

Leaves are dark green, almost shiny, somewhat hairy, and very stiff. Some slight yellowing with fall colors.

If you like elm trees but want to stay away from elm diseases, cedar elm is the tree for you. It is found growing naturally in some of the central areas of Texas, but it is adaptive to all areas of Texas. I've seen it growing quite well in heavy clay soil as well as in very light sandy soils. It is an absolutely gorgeous tree. Because of its spread of 40 to 50 ft. and its oval upright crown, it can be used in a landscape yard that is relatively small. It is a very strong tree, with built-in wind resistance. It will even stand some compaction of the soil it grows in.

WHEN TO PLANT

Cedar elm may be planted from containers any time of the year, but the ideal planting time is in the fall. The second-best time to plant is very early spring.

WHERE TO PLANT

Plant anywhere in your landscape that you wish to have a top-quality shade tree. A prime location is on the west side of your home. Because the tree is deciduous, it can help lower your energy bills by providing shade in summer and allowing the sun to strike your home during the winter after it has lost its leaves.

How to Plant

Cedar elm is often sold balled in burlap, but you can also find it in containers. If you want to plant from a container, buy one no larger than the 20-gallon size. If you buy a tree in a larger-sized container or in a very large ball, I strongly suggest you have a landscape contractor plant it for you. When you do plant, dig the hole no deeper than the depth of the soilball, but you may dig it significantly wider and loosen up that soil. Remove the plant from its container and set in the planting hole. Backfill with your loosened material and water thoroughly. Construct a berm in order to hold water. If necessary, stake temporarily to prevent top movement. Cover with 3 in. of bark mulch after watering thoroughly and applying a root stimulator according to label directions.

Care and Maintenance

Elm leaf beetles may visit your cedar elm, but in most cases they are not a big problem. If they do become a problem, visit your retail garden center for control possibilities. Remember to read and follow label directions. The best time to prune is very early spring as new growth begins to shape the cedar elm. Water as necessary, especially during the two-year establishment period, to prevent soil dryness. After the tree has been in your landscape one year, fertilize it 3 times a year. Try a premium-quality long-lasting slow-release lawn fertilizer with a 3:1:2 ratio. Apply once in the spring when new growth begins, once in the fall, and once in mid-season. Always follow directions, and remember to water thoroughly after applying any fertilizer product. 15-5-10, 18-6-12 and 21-7-14 are all 3:1:2 ratio lawn fertilizers.

Additional Information

Several years ago our country's American elm trees were hit by a disease called Dutch elm disease. Cedar elm is resistant to Dutch elm disease—plant it without worrying about this common disease.

Additional Species, Cultivars, or Varieties

Some Texas gardeners may confuse the cedar elm with the lower-quality winged elm, *U. alata*. A high-quality cousin of cedar elm is *U. parvifolia*; I particularly like the cultivar 'Drake'.

Flowering Dogwood

Cornus florida

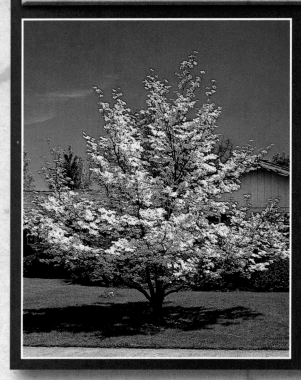

EXPOSURE	COLD HARDINESS
Semi-Shade	All Texas
WATER USAGE	GROWTH RATE
Semi-Moist	Medium
AVG. HT × WIDTH	SPACING
20–30′ × 25′	20′

Bright-green color throughout the growing season and red to red/ orange fall color, very showy.

*I*f you ever have the opportunity to visit the eastern half of our state in the spring when the native dogwoods are in bloom, you are in for a treat. In the rural area in which I live, native dogwoods bloom in and among mixed hardwoods, along with redbuds and native hawthorns. It is quite a sight. Not only will dogwoods grow naturally in the soils of East Texas, they will grow throughout our great state if given well-prepared soil and proper care. You don't have to have a large yard to group several dogwoods together in a multiple planting. There's nothing more showy in a home landscape than a group of dogwoods as an understory planting, perhaps beneath some tall-growing oak trees or elms. Dogwoods relish the dappled shade in these locations.

WHEN TO PLANT

Dogwood is best planted in early fall; early spring is the second-best time.

WHERE TO PLANT

Dogwood may be used several different ways. The best planting locations are beneath the canopies of larger trees where they can receive shade from the hot western afternoon sun. Plant dogwood in a patio area near your home, near garden structures, or on the border of your landscape.

How to Plant

Soil drainage is important to overall health and long-term growth of dogwood, so make sure the soil drains well, wherever you plant the tree. Dig the planting hole no deeper than the depth of the tree soil-ball, but you may dig it several times wider. Loosen the soil, install the tree in the planting hole, and backfill. Water thoroughly, apply root stimulator according to label directions, and mulch with about 3 in. of bark mulch.

Care and Maintenance

Leaf spot may visit your planting of dogwood, especially in areas of high humidity and poor air circulation and drainage. Sometimes bores will attack dogwood if the tree is under stress. Leaf spot can be reduced by making sure your trees are planted in areas with good air movement. Bore attack can be reduced by making sure the tree is kept in a good state of health. Should insects or disease become a problem, ask about control possibilities. Remember to read and follow label directions when using any gardening aid. Prune as necessary to maintain a desired shape; early-spring pruning after blooming is recommended. Water as necessary to prevent soil dry-ness. Dogwoods do not like waterlogged soils, but because of their shallow root system, they will not tolerate soils that are dry for pro-longed periods of time. Maintaining a layer of mulch is a good way to help keep the root system in good health. If you decide to fertilize your dogwood, fertilize no more than twice a year, once in the spring as new growth begins and once in the fall. Use a premium-quality long-lasting slow-release azalea/camellia-type fertilizer. Apply according to label directions and water thoroughly. Never overfertilize these trees.

Additional Information

Gardeners have been successfully using dogwoods in gardens since the 1700s, so don't be intimidated by this beautiful tree. Try one or more in your home landscape. Note: There is an exception: along our Gulf Coast, growing a flowering dogwood tree may be a bit of a challenge in the home landscape.

Additional Species, Cultivars, or Varieties

There are other varieties besides the traditional white flowering dogwood or *C. florida*. Among them are 'Cherokee Chief', which has dark-pink flowers; 'Cloud Nine', a heavy-blooming white variety; 'White Cloud', a well-established, heavy-blooming variety; 'Spring Song', a rose-red blooming variety; 'First Lady', which has varie-gated foliage; 'Rubra', with pink flowers; and 'Welch Junior Miss', a pink-flowered variety.

Oak

Quercus spp.

EXPOSURE

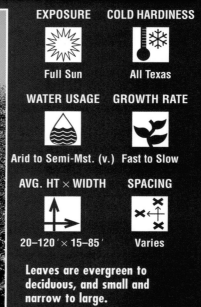

Full Sun

COLD HARDINESS

All Texas

WATER USAGE

Arid to Semi-Mst. (v.)

GROWTH RATE

Fast to Slow

AVG. HT × WIDTH

20–120' × 15–85'

SPACING

Varies

Leaves are evergreen to deciduous, and small and narrow to large.

There is no group of trees more proper for Texas landscapes than those in the oak family. They come in many different sizes, types, shapes, and colors. When you want to determine the varieties that are best adapted to your location, ask your Lowe's customer service associate for in-depth information. Be prepared to tell them your soil type, soil pH, natural rainfall, drainage, heat, and winter temperatures. I like several oak varieties, but if I had to pick a favorite, it would be the live oak, *Q. virginiana*. Where I grew up in Brownwood, our yard had 73 small live oak trees, and I continue to enjoy live oaks today.

WHEN TO PLANT

The best time to plant oaks in our landscapes is in the early fall. The second-best time is very early spring.

WHERE TO PLANT

Plant oak trees where they will be of benefit in the landscape. You may wish to try planting a deciduous variety, such as shumardii or burr oak, on the west side of your home. It will provide shade during the hot time of year, and after the leaves fall off, the sun will strike your home to warm it in the winter.

HOW TO PLANT

Dig the planting hole several times wider than the soilball, though the hole should not be deeper than the depth of the soilball. Loosen the soil; no other soil improvement is necessary. Backfill with the loosened soil, water thoroughly, apply root stimulator according to label directions, and cover with about 3 in. of bark mulch. Stake temporarily if necessary.

CARE AND MAINTENANCE

Some oak trees may have insect and disease problems, but if your trees are kept healthy and vigorous, these will be kept to a minimum. If insects or diseases do become a problem, visit your local retail garden centers for the best control possibilities. Remember to follow label directions when you use any lawn or garden aid. Prune as necessary to maintain the natural shape of your oak tree. The preferred time for pruning is in early spring as new growth is beginning, though the tree may be pruned 12 months out of the year. Water as necessary, especially during early establishment to prevent soil dryness. Fertilize throughout the growing season with premium-quality long-lasting slow-release 3:1:2 lawn fertilizer. Apply according to label directions and water thoroughly. I like to fertilize once in the spring as new growth begins, perhaps once during mid-season, and once again in the fall. 21-7-14, 19-5-9, 15-5-10 are all 3:1:2 ratio lawn fertilizers.

ADDITIONAL INFORMATION

Oaks have the ability to hybridize naturally, and you may find some available at your local retail garden centers. Ask your customer service associate where a tree came from and to give you the tree's exact identity. This is especially important when selecting certain live oaks. Live oaks that were selected, grown, and produced in the Texas Gulf Coast area, for example, may not survive at all in the High Plains area because of the difference in temperatures.

ADDITIONAL SPECIES, CULTIVARS, OR VARIETIES

Trees in the Quercus family: *Q. virginiana* or live oak, which is considered an evergreen and whose height is from 40 to 65 ft., with a spread of 50 to 80 ft.; Texas red oak or *Q. texana*, whose height is 30 to 50 ft. with a 30 to 40 ft. width; shumard or *Q. shumardii* grows 50 to 80 ft. tall and spreads about 50 to 65 ft. East Texas gardeners should take a look at willow oak or *Q. phellos* and chinquapin oak or *Q. muehlenbergii*. The height of both of these ranges from 40 to 60 ft., and their spreads are 30 to 40 ft. Burr oak, *Q. macrocarpa*, ranges in height from 60 to 80 ft. and has a spread of 35 to 50 ft.

Pecan
Carya illinoensis

EXPOSURE

Full Sun

COLD HARDINESS

All Texas

WATER USAGE

Semi-Moist

GROWTH RATE

Medium

AVG. HT × WIDTH

40–80´ × 35–100´

SPACING

35–50´

Leaves are compound. Light green to dark green during growing season, turning to dull yellow in the fall.

I just love pecan pie, and I also enjoy pecan shade trees. If you love "Texana," you ought to have at least one pecan tree on your property, for it is the Texas State Tree. I grew up in Brown County where a lot of pecans are grown. The United States Department of Agriculture has had a research facility there for many years, and you'll find large pecan orchards in that area. Across the Colorado River south of Brownwood in the San Saba area, you will find tremendous pecan orchards; there is even a pecan variety called San Saba. There are other great pecan-producing areas in our state, and there are over a hundred varieties of pecans on the market today. If you want to grow pecan trees for shade and pecans for pies, make sure you get the best locally adapted varieties.

WHEN TO PLANT

Container-grown pecan trees are best planted in the fall, but early spring is also a good planting time. Bareroot or packaged selections should only be planted during your zone's dormant season.

WHERE TO PLANT

Plant pecan trees in your landscape where they will have sufficient room to grow. Visit your local retail garden center and ask about the varieties you have selected. Ask questions such as *How wide and tall do they normally get?* This will give you the information you need to space your tree properly away from driveways, pools, your home, and other structures.

HOW TO PLANT

No special soil preparation is necessary to plant pecan trees success-fully in Texas. Make sure you dig the planting hole no deeper than the depth of the plant's soilball, but you may dig it several times wider. After installing your plant in the soil, backfill with loosened soil, water thoroughly, apply root stimulator according to label directions, and cover with 3 in. of bark mulch. Stake temporarily if necessary.

CARE AND MAINTENANCE

There are several insects and diseases that may visit your pecan trees. You may wish to pick up a pecan spray schedule from the local Texas Agricultural Extension Service office, typically called the County Agent's Office. Prune as necessary to maintain strong branching and to remove dead wood. Water as necessary to prevent soil dryness; in orchards, drip irrigation is often employed for this task. Maintaining a thick layer of mulch around the root system will conserve soil moisture. Fertilize throughout the growing season. You may use premium-quality long-lasting, slow-release 3:1:2 lawn fertil-izer such as 21-7-14, 19-5-9 and 15-5-10, and there are specialty fertilizers for pecan trees available as well. In certain areas of the state and highly alkaline soils, supplemental spraying of the foliage with zinc may be necessary. Tip and fact sheets on proper fertiliza-tion of pecan trees are available at your County Agent's Office.

ADDITIONAL INFORMATION

You'll find that pecan trees grow satisfactorily in clay soils as long as the soil is deep. Don't plant in shallow or rocky soil.

ADDITIONAL SPECIES, CULTIVARS, OR VARIETIES

There are many cultivars of pecans trees available. These include 'Choctaw', 'Desirable', 'Cheyenne', 'Caddo', 'Mohawk', 'Shawnee', 'Kiowa', 'San Saba', 'Western', 'Stewart', and 'Sioux'. Remember to check with your County Agent's Office for the best locally adapted varieties. Enjoy the shade of your pecan tree, and enjoy your pecan pie with ice cream.

Pine

Pinus spp.

EXPOSURE

Full Sun

COLD HARDINESS

All Texas

WATER USAGE

Arid to Semi-Mst.

GROWTH RATE

Fast

AVG. HT × WIDTH

20–125′ × 15–70′

SPACING

10–50′ (v.)

Evergreen, short to long needle-like leaves.

When many of us think of naturally-occurring pine trees, the East Texas pine automatically comes to mind. It is true that our heaviest pine tree forests are in East Texas, but pines also grow in West Texas, at Big Bend, and in the Panhandle. Certain pine trees will grow in all areas of the state. Perhaps you favor a clump or group planting of them in your landscape simply because you like the look and the smell of pine. Other gardeners like the sound of wind blowing through the trees. Some tall-growing pines can create a wind break when planted in multiple rows, or you may wish to use a small variety for a patio tree.

WHEN TO PLANT
Pine trees are best planted in early fall, though early spring is also a good time.

WHERE TO PLANT
Planting location depends on the desired application as well as the ultimate height and width of the tree. Smaller pine trees, such as pinon, may be planted very close to your home. Some of the larger-growing varieties may need to be

spaced farther away. Depending on the variety selected, pine trees will grow in light and sandy soils to heavy clay soils.

HOW TO PLANT

No special soil preparation is necessary for planting pine. Dig individual planting holes wider than the soilball of the transplant, but not deeper, and loosen the soil. Install plants, backfill with the soil, and water thoroughly. Apply root stimulator according to label directions, spread 2 in. or more of bark mulch around the planting area, and stake temporarily if necessary.

CARE AND MAINTENANCE

Insects and diseases may visit your pine trees. If these pests become a problem, ask about the best control possibilities. Remember to read and follow label directions when using any lawn and garden aid. You may wish to contact the local Texas Agricultural Extension Service office in your county (typically called the County Agent's Office) to get tip or fact sheets on pine trees used in the home landscape. Keep in mind that healthy pine trees have few or no problems with insects and diseases. Prune as necessary to remove dead wood and maintain desired shape. Don't prune all the branches off a pine tree or you will permanently change its natural shape, losing some of its appealing characteristics. Water as necessary, especially during establishment. Fertilize approximately 3 times throughout the growing season with your favorite granular fertilizer. Long-lasting slow-release 3:1:2 ratio lawn fertilizers work well. Remember, follow label directions and water thoroughly after each application of fertilizer. 15-5-10, 18-6-12, 19-5-9 are all 3:1:2 ratio lawn fertlizers.

ADDITIONAL INFORMATION

Some pine trees grow relatively fast while others are slower. Make sure you understand the growth habit and characteristics of selected pine trees before purchasing.

ADDITIONAL SPECIES, CULTIVARS, OR VARIETIES

Other varieties are short-leafed pine, or *P. echinata*, which has a growth range of 80 to 100 ft. tall and 50 to 70 ft. wide; pinon pine or *P. cembroides*, which has a growth habit of 20 to 30 ft tall and 15 to 20 ft. wide; long-leafed pine, or *P. palustris*, which grows 80 to 100 ft. tall and 40 to 55 ft wide; ponderosa pine or *P. ponderosa* var. *Scopulorum*, which has a growth habit of 100 ft. plus and 40 to 55 ft. wide; and loblolly pine, or *P. taeda*. There are many imported pine trees that adapt well to Texas landscapes. Seek information from your Local County Agent's office for some of the best-adapted varieties.

Southern Magnolia
Magnolia grandiflora

EXPOSURE

Full Sun

COLD HARDINESS

To 0° F.

WATER USAGE

Semi-Moist

GROWTH RATE

Slow

AVG. HT × WIDTH

30–60 ' × 30–50 '

SPACING

35–50 '

Evergreen, large. Coarse, shiny, durable leaves. Very fragrant blossoms. Very colorful red fruits.

Nothing speaks to Southern gardeners like *Magnolia grandiflora*, or the southern magnolia. It is one of the oldest ornamental trees used in our landscapes. It is native to acid soils, but it does well in deep clay soils if moisture is adequate. Because southern grandiflora puts out such dense shade, it is difficult to grow anything beneath it. I have had several requests from callers to my radio shows and readers of my garden columns about what to grow under magnolias. The best solution is to not plant anything under magnolias, and allow the branches to reach the ground. Magnolias can be dominant in the landscape, and they will be a focal point. Keep this in mind when deciding to purchase one. It can become a wonderful feature in your landscape when placed properly, but part of its root system is very near the soil surface, and I would not suggest planting it close to a house. This is the type of tree to place to one side of a landscape and allow to grow to its full potential, limbs all the way to the ground. It will be an outstanding pyramidal-shaped long-lived quality tree.

When to Plant
Southern magnolia is best planted in the fall. Early spring is also a good time for planting.

Where to Plant
Plant southern magnolia in deep soils. It will grow in sandy soils and clay soils as long as adequate moisture is present, and it prefers a relatively fertile soil. Do not plant near existing trees or structures or in very shallow soils, especially if it would be difficult to apply supplemental irrigation.

How to Plant
Southern magnolia requires no special soil preparation as long as the soil is deep and fertile, and adequate moisture is available. Dig the planting hole no deeper than the tree soilball, but dig it as wide as you like. After loosening the soil and digging it to its proper depth, remove your selection from the container and install it in the planting hole. Backfill with loose soil, water thoroughly, apply root stimulator according to label directions, and cover with 3 in. of bark mulch. Stake temporarily if necessary.

Care and Maintenance
There are no serious pests attracted to southern magnolia. Prune only dead or damaged limbs and leaves. Do not prune off lower limbs, as this would change the entire growth habit of the tree; allow the limbs to reach the ground. Water as necessary to prevent soil dryness. If you have a location that is difficult to water, do some plumbing and set up a drip irrigation system, a good solution for southern magnolia. Fertilize approximately 3 times during the year with the same type of granular fertilizer used on azaleas, camellias, or gardenias, following label directions. Apply in the spring as new growth begins, mid-season, and once in the fall. Always water thoroughly after application.

Additional Information
Southern magnolia is pleasing to the eye, provides a pleasant fragrance, and makes large flowers that can be cut and brought indoors. Parts of the plant may be preserved to last for a long time in dried arrangements.

Additional Species, Cultivars, or Varieties
There are several different magnolia species and varieties. Southern magnolia has some cultivars of its own, including 'D. D. Blanchard', 'Majestic Beauty', 'St. Mary', 'Little Gem', 'Samuel Sommers', and 'Southern Pride'. Visit Lowe's to get specific information on the heights and widths of the named varieties. You will enjoy southern magnolia if you make the right selection, plant it in deep soil, and allow it to grow to maturity.

Sweet Gum
Liquidambar styraciflua

EXPOSURE

Semi-Sh. to F. Sun

COLD HARDINESS

All Texas

WATER USAGE

Arid to Semi-Mst.

GROWTH RATE

Medium

AVG. HT × WIDTH

45–50' × 40–60'

SPACING

80–100'

Leaves are star-shaped; dark green during the growing season, turning yellow to red to reddish orange and burgundy in the fall.

*T*he highways of East Texas display fall color with naturally occurring plantings of sweet gum. One highway section with excellent fall color is Highway 19 between Athens and Canton. My listeners and readers often want to know about good-quality shade trees that are long lived and fast growing. Sweet gum meets all of these requirements. It grows not only in East Texas soil, but in heavy clay soil, as long as the soil is deep and the trees do not hit limestone. It is best used away from the home, out in the landscape where the sharp sweet gum balls that fall after leaves drop will not be a problem when you (or children) are walking barefoot across the lawn.

WHEN TO PLANT

Sweet gum trees are best selected and planted in the fall. Spring planting is fine, but fall selection will allow you to determine the leaf color before you plant.

Where to Plant

Sweet gum will grow in loam or clay soils as long as the soil is deep and moist. Because there will be falling debris, and the tree will be large, do not plant it next to existing structures, walkways, or patios. Do not plant in shallow soil or in areas that are difficult to water.

How to Plant

Sweet gum trees require no special soil preparation, other than making sure the soil is deep; it is also a good idea to make sure the soil is relatively fertile and has sufficient moisture. Dig the planting hole no deeper than the tree soilball, though you may dig it several times wider. After the soil is loosened, remove your selection from its container and install in the planting hole. Backfill and water thoroughly. Apply root stimulator according to label directions and cover with 3 in. of bark mulch. Stake temporarily if necessary.

Care and Maintenance

Tent caterpillars and occasional aphids may visit your tree. In hot dry seasons, spider mites may become a problem as well. If any of these pests invade your planting of sweet gum, ask about the best control possibilities. It has been my experience that if sweet gums are kept in good health, there are few to no insect problems. Prune as necessary to remove dead branches; no other pruning is usually needed. Water as needed to prevent soil dryness. Sweet gum is a tree for moist growing conditions, so plant where you can easily supply moisture. This is especially true in July and August Texas heat waves. Fertilize once in the early spring as new growth begins, once mid-season, and once again in the fall. A premium-quality long-lasting slow-release 3:1:2 ratio lawn fertilizer will work well. Remember to follow label directions and water thoroughly after applying any fertilizer. 19-5-9, 18-6-12, 21-7-14 are all 3:1:2 ratio lawn fertilizers.

Additional Information

People contact me from time to time wanting to know if there is any product or technique that prevents the sweet gum balls from forming. The answer is: "No, there is not."

Additional Species, Cultivars, or Varieties

Some named varieties of sweet gum are 'Palo Alto', 'Festival', 'Autumn Glow', and 'Burgundy'.

Texas Ash
Fraxinus texensis

EXPOSURE

Full Sun

COLD HARDINESS

All Texas

WATER USAGE

Arid-Dry/Semi-Mst.

GROWTH RATE

Fast to Med.

AVG. HT × WIDTH

35–50' × 25–35'

SPACING

25–30'

Compound leaves, dark green during the growing season, changing to various colors of yellow, copper, tangerine, rose, and lime in the fall.

White ash will grow in Texas, but the best ash selection for use in our state is Texas ash. Arizona ash is often used in some developments and it is widely available, but it has nothing like the drought tolerance of Texas ash. Texas ash is a relatively fast-growing tree, strong, of good quality, and long lasting. There are male and female ash trees. If you are concerned about fruit drop and seeds germinating, make sure your customer service associate knows that you want only male selections. Texas ash works well in urban lots that are rather small.

WHEN TO PLANT

Texas ash may be planted 12 months out of the year in our state. Fall is an excellent time of year to plant any tree in Texas, including Texas ash, though early spring is also a good time.

WHERE TO PLANT

Plant Texas ash anywhere there is sufficient room for it to grow into its normal shape. Make sure the soil is deep for best overall growth. While Texas ash will grow in rather harsh conditions, such as restricted root zone areas and even compacted soil, for best results plant in locations that have better soil. You may wish to plant Texas ash where its fall colors may be easily viewed from the home, and where its dense shade will benefit the home through the summertime. Its leaves will fall off when the weather turns cold, allowing the sun to strike your home during the winter, thus conserving energy.

How to Plant

Texas ash needs no special soil preparation. Simply dig the hole the same depth as the soilball and no deeper, though you may dig it several times wider. After the planting hole is complete, remove your selection from the container and install in the planting hole. Backfill with the loosened soil, water thoroughly, apply root stimulator according to label directions, and cover with 3 in. of bark mulch. Stake temporarily if needed.

Care and Maintenance

Aphids have been known to visit ash trees. If they become a problem, ask for advice on control possibilities. Remember to read and follow label directions. Prune only as required to remove dead or damaged limbs and correct growth habit. Water as necessary, especially during initial establishment, to prevent soil dryness. After establishment, Texas ash is extremely tough, durable, and drought resistant. Fertilize once in spring and once in fall. Premium-quality long-lasting slow-release granular fertilizer with a ratio of 3:1:2 will work well. Remember to follow label directions and water thoroughly after each application. 15-5-10, 18-6-12 and 21-7-14 are all examples of 3:1:2 ratio granular fertilizers.

Additional Information

If you are looking for a small- to medium-sized tree that is tough and durable and provides outstanding shade as well as great fall colors, I highly recommend Texas ash.

Additional Species, Cultivars, or Varieties

At this time there are no known named selections or cultivated varieties of Texas ash. Other ash trees are White Ash, *F. americana*, and Green Ash, *F. pennsylvanica*. When shopping for Texas ash, be sure you are not persuaded to purchase Arizona ash trees instead. Don't plant Arizona ash even if someone gave you one!

Carolina Jasmine/Jessamine
Gelsemium sempervirens

EXPOSURE

Full Sun

COLD HARDINESS

To 10° F.

WATER USAGE

Semi-Mst., D.T.

GROWTH RATE

Fast

AVG. HT × WIDTH

As Trained

SPACING

3'

Semi-evergreen to evergreen vine with tapered pointed leaves and yellow blooms that are trumpet-shaped. Showy and fragrant.

*G*elsemium sempervirens, called Carolina jasmine in some circles, may also be called Carolina jessamine. Whichever name you choose, it is an excellent native vine for Texas gardeners. It the most widely used native vine in our landscapes, and perhaps the most widely used vine of any type, imported or native. I have it growing on two large trellises on the west side of our home. The trellises go from the ground up to the eve of the house, are fastened directly to the wall, and are covered with Carolina jasmine. It is a beautiful show and it also helps conserve energy for us by acting as a barrier to heat during the summer.

WHEN TO PLANT
Carolina jasmine grows best when planted in spring or fall.

WHERE TO PLANT
Carolina jasmine will grow in full-sun and shady areas, though blooming is reduced in the shady areas. For best bloom and overall growth, plant in loca-

tions that receive 6 to 8 hours of full sun. It will grow in sandy, loamy, and clay soils, will tolerate damp conditions, and has moderate drought resistance.

HOW TO PLANT

Carolina jasmine will tolerate various types of soils throughout Texas, but to achieve maximum growth, it is best to improve the native soil. If you have very light, sandy soil or clay soil, incorporate organic matter into the planting area, combining approximately 3 in. with the top 3 in. of your soil. This will make a well-prepared bed approximately 6 in. deep. I prefer to plant Carolina jasmine from gallon-size containers so I can start low on the vine as I train it. Set your containers approximately 4 ft. apart if you are going to cover a solid wall, and insert plants no deeper than they were grown in their containers. Firm the soil well around them, water thoroughly, apply root stimulator, and cover with about 3 in. of bark mulch.

CARE AND MAINTENANCE

Carolina jasmine has no serious pests. Prune and train as necessary to meet specific goals. Keep in mind that Carolina jasmine tends to grow rapidly, especially in early spring after bloom is complete, so pay close attention to directing and training. Elastic stretch tie is wonderful for tying Carolina jasmine to any structure. Water sufficiently to prevent soil dryness; this is especially important in July and August. Maintain a 3-in. layer of bark mulch around the root system year-round. Fertilize after blooming has completed in the spring with premium-quality long-lasting slow-release granular rose food. Reapply mid-season and again in the fall. Remember, follow directions and water thoroughly after each application.

ADDITIONAL INFORMATION

You may grow Carolina jasmine on trellises or other structures in large tubs or planters on your deck or balcony. You may train it in specific patterns if you desire.

ADDITIONAL SPECIES, CULTIVARS, OR VARIETIES

I know two named varieties (though there may be more now). One is called 'Pale Yellow'; the other is 'Pride of Augusta', which is double flowered and early blooming.

Coral Honeysuckle
Lonicera sempervirens

EXPOSURE

F. Sun to Shade

COLD HARDINESS

All Texas

WATER USAGE

Arid to Semi-Mst.

GROWTH RATE

Fast

AVG. HT × WIDTH

As Trained

SPACING

12–36"

Vine with interestingly shaped, bluish green leaves jointed at their bases. Blooms are coral and trumpet-shaped.

*I*f you love the excitement hummingbirds bring to the home landscape, you should plant coral honeysuckle. Not only does coral honeysuckle attract hummingbirds, it also attracts many admirers. It is easy to grow on any type of gardening structure. We currently have a planting growing on a structure that I built on a wall from 1-in. chicken wire on the east side of our home. Planted with gallon-sized containers of coral honeysuckle 4 ft. apart, in 2 years it was solid from top to bottom and remains absolutely loaded with blossoms. Coral honeysuckle is easy to find, but make sure that you specify this native plant; it is less rambunctious than imported types.

WHEN TO PLANT

Coral honeysuckle is best planted in early spring so it can have the entire growing season to establish itself. Fall planting is also acceptable.

WHERE TO PLANT

A preferred planting area for coral honeysuckle is with eastern exposure and shade from the hot west afternoon sun. While it will grow in full sun, it will need supplemental irrigation in order to maintain the looks of its foliage. I have seen it successfully grown in commercial establishments as well as in home gardens. On certain walls of the Crescent Hotel near downtown Dallas, you will see large trellis structures covered with coral honeysuckle. Not only does it work well on structures, it also does well when allowed to weep over rock walls. It will grow in sandy, loam, or clay soils, and will even grow in some areas where drainage is poor. It has relatively good drought resistance.

HOW TO PLANT
Coral honeysuckle will grow in many of our native Texas soils, but if you wish to help its establishment and maintain a more luxurious growth habit, prepare your soil well. The addition of several inches of organic matter to the top 6 in. of the native soil will greatly improve growing conditions. You may use compost, brown sphagnum peat moss, ground-bark mulch, or some of each. After bed preparation is complete, dig individual planting holes no deeper than the plant soilball, install the plants in their new homes, firm the soil well, and water thoroughly. Apply root stimulator according to label directions and spread with 3 in. of bark mulch.

CARE AND MAINTENANCE
There are no serious pests. Prune and train as necessary to reach desired goals. Tie to growing structure with elastic stretch ties. To prevent soil dryness, water as necessary throughout the growing and blooming season. The most critical time is during rain-parched July and August. Maintaining a thick bark mulch will greatly conserve soil moisture. Fertilization may be necessary during the early establishment period and any time extra nourishment is needed. If planted in rich, deep soils, fertilization is seldom necessary.

ADDITIONAL INFORMATION
If you like to have blooming plants that require minimal care, but you do not have a lot of square footage, try coral honeysuckle on wires or other upright structures.

ADDITIONAL SPECIES, CULTIVARS, OR VARIETIES
At this time there are no named varieties of coral honeysuckle.

Passion Vine
Passiflora incarnata

EXPOSURE

Semi-Shade

COLD HARDINESS

To 0° F.

WATER USAGE

Arid to Semi-Mst.

GROWTH RATE

Fast

AVG. HT × WIDTH

Vine 20´

SPACING

1–3´

Dark-green leaves with 3 to 5 points. Exotic, intricate blooms from pale to pinkish lavender. Fruits approximately 3 in. in diameter.

*P*assiflora incarnata is known by several names to Texas gardeners, including passionflower, passion vine, and maypop. In most Texas zones it will die down each year, then spring up easily the following spring and grow to its normal size, producing the blossoms that so many people admire. In good-quality soils it branches readily and gives outstanding regrowth, with more vines and blooms every year. It will grow up walls with some assistance and will also run along the ground. Its long tentacles act as holdfasts to attach the stems to whatever structures they are growing on. Chicken wire makes an ideal structure, and it also grows well on chain link fences, or a grid pattern on a solid wall that was built with smooth small-diameter galvanized wire. Passion vine is wonderful near an outdoor seating area where you wish to enjoy its blooms. It is also especially good because of its adaptability, allowing it to grow in full sun or dappled shade. It will grow in virtually any type of soil as long as it is well drained, though it prefers sandy and loam soils.

WHEN TO PLANT
Plant passion vine in spring after all danger of frost has passed.

WHERE TO PLANT

Plant in any location where the soil drains well. If your soil is heavy or poorly drained clay, raise your bed several inches with a good organic mix as if preparing a bed for bedding plants. Do not plant in poorly drained areas, full shade, or areas that are difficult to water.

HOW TO PLANT

Special soil preparation is not necessary. In poorly drained areas, or if you wish to have a raised bed, add several inches of organic matter, such as compost, brown sphagnum, peat moss, ground-bark mulch, or a combination of these. Four in. of these materials blended with the top 4 in. of your soil is a good mix for growing any flowering or vining plant. Plant in individual holes no deeper than they were growing in their containers. Firm the soil well, water thoroughly, apply root stimulator, and cover with 3 in. of bark mulch to complete the planting.

CARE AND MAINTENANCE

Normally pests and diseases are not a problem with passion flower. If you happen to have problems with them, ask for advice on the best control possibilities. Prune only as needed to achieve your training goal. Water as necessary to prevent soil dryness and maintain a moist soil. Fertilize as new growth begins in the spring with your favorite type of fertilizer that is high in the middle ratio number. Remember to read and follow label directions when using any product, and water thoroughly after fertilizer application.

ADDITIONAL INFORMATION

Passion vine may be used with other vining plants, or at the back of screening-type shrubs that will allow the vine to grow up and above them.

ADDITIONAL SPECIES, CULTIVARS, OR VARIETIES

P. lutea, a small yellow variety, is also available. I first collected it in 1970 while attending Stephen F. Austin State University. It is a bit more difficult to locate than *Passiflora incarnata*, but if you prefer a smaller version and like yellow, this is the one to ask for.

Texas Wisteria
Wisteria macrostachya

EXPOSURE

F. Sun to Shade

COLD HARDINESS

All Texas

WATER USAGE

Arid to Semi-Mst.

GROWTH RATE

Fast

AVG. HT × WIDTH

20–35´ As Trained

SPACING

10–12´

Robust, vigorous, high-climbing deciduous vine. Blooms sweetly fragrant and grow in a "grape cluster" shape; range in colors from lilac to bluish purple.

You may like the looks and fragrance of wisteria, but you may be a bit worried that imported varieties will get out of hand and take over the entire yard. Your fears are not unfounded. Sometimes wisteria can turn into Frankenstein, though Texas wisteria can be managed much better than the imported wisterias. The blooms are smaller on our Texas wisteria than they are on the imported types, but it has nice, dark-green, glossy foliage. The combination of blooms and leaves make this quite a showy plant. When traveling through East and Southeast Texas areas, you may find Texas wisteria growing in the wild, though it may be a bit difficult to find. For best results in locating it, shop at nurseries that specialize in native plant material, for it is worth the effort.

WHEN TO PLANT

The ideal planting time is during the spring when you can find it in bloom; fall planting is also acceptable. And because of its hardiness, Texas wisteria may be planted 12 months out of the year if desired.

WHERE TO PLANT

Plant Texas wisteria in any location you wish to have a good-look
ing, easy-to-grow vine with fragrant blossoms. I think it works
especially well on arbors. Pergolas, gazebos, arches, and entries are
all likely candidates for Texas wisteria.

HOW TO PLANT

Till or otherwise loosen the soil in beds or other planting locations
where your selection of Texas wisteria will be planted. Dig planting
holes the same depth as the plant's rootball. After planting, backfill,
firm the soil, water thoroughly, apply root stimulator according to
label directions, and cover with 3 in. of bark mulch.

CARE AND MAINTENANCE

There are no insects or diseases associated with Texas wisteria.
Prune and train as necessary to reach your desired goal, and water
as necessary to prevent complete soil dryness. Fertilization is usu
ally not required.

ADDITIONAL INFORMATION

If you have a full-sun area on the west side of your home and you
wish to create a lattice shaded area, cover that structure with Texas
wisteria.

ADDITIONAL SPECIES, CULTIVARS, OR VARIETIES

There are no selected cultivars or named varieties of Texas wisteria.
Simply ask for Texas wisteria or *Wisteria macrostachya*. It may be
more easily found at retail nurseries which specialize in native
Texas plants. There are several Japanese and Chinese selections of
wisteria, but be aware that they are quite rambunctious and can
become invasive.

Virginia Creeper
Parthenocissus quinquefolia

EXPOSURE

F. Sun to Shade

COLD HARDINESS

All Texas

WATER USAGE

Semi-Moist

GROWTH RATE

Fast

AVG. HT × WIDTH

As Trained

SPACING

12–18″

Climbing vine. Leaves have 5 parts; they are dark green during the growing season, turning brilliant red in early fall.

*C*onsider Virginia creeper if you need a vine to give complete coverage of a cottage. It is also excellent for use on walls or structures—it will help save money on air-conditioning when it is planted on the full-sun west side of your home. It may be used as a thick groundcover that requires mowing only once a year. When used as a vine on large garden structures, it will provide complete shade in the summer and gorgeous color in the fall, and it will allow sunlight in during the winter. It requires no spraying, no fertilization, and little watering after establishment. You may wish to do some pruning, training or directing its growth. Though it has 5-part leaves, it is sometimes mistaken for poison ivy, which has 3-part leaves. Virginia creeper has no known toxic effects and is a wonderful native vine.

WHEN TO PLANT

Ideal planting times are spring or early fall, but you can plant Virginia creeper any time of the year, as it is extremely hardy.

WHERE TO PLANT

Virginia creeper will grow in virtually any type of Texas soil, including clay and sand, as long as the soil is well drained. It will also grow in heavily shaded areas, dappled shade, part shade, or full sun. I think the best application for Virginia creeper is on large garden structures, but it can also be used in expansive areas, used underneath trees, and allowed to weep over stone walls with great effect. When growing underneath groups of trees, it helps to create a "woodland" effect. Because it is adaptable to heavily shaded areas where St. Augustine won't grow, it can come to the rescue and provide needed vegetation cover.

HOW TO PLANT

Simply loosen the native soil. If you are going to plant a large bed, you will need a tiller. After soil is prepared, plant Virginia creeper at the same depth it was growing in the container. Firm the soil, water thoroughly, apply root stimulator, and cover with 3 in. of bark mulch.

CARE AND MAINTENANCE

This plant has no pests. Prune as required to maintain desired shape and size; water as necessary during establishment. After establishment, occasional watering to prevent soil dryness is advisable. Fertilization is usually not required.

ADDITIONAL INFORMATION

If you wish to enhance or speed the growth of Virginia creeper, be aware that it does grow vigorously in response to fertilization. It also responds well to a moist soil condition.

ADDITIONAL SPECIES, CULTIVARS, OR VARIETIES

There are no known named varieties at this time. A first cousin, Boston ivy *P. tricuspidata*, covers the campuses of many Ivy League Colleges.

CHAPTER SIX

PERENNIALS

*I*F YOU LIKE TO SEE THE SAME FLOWERS BLOOM YEAR AFTER YEAR, be sure to include perennials in your landscape. Annuals complete their life cycle in one season and biennials in two seasons, but perennials grow and bloom for three years or more.

Perennials can bloom in almost every season, as there are varieties for spring, summer, and fall. Some bloom for a very short time, then rest for many months; some bloom repeatedly during a season; still others bloom continuously. When selecting a perennial, find out its bloom season, bloom colors, height, and cultural requirements. For example, it is useful to know that even though a single daylily bloom will last but a day, each daylily plant will produce a daily profusion of blooms for an extended period.

Texas has a wide range of soils and several hardiness zones. Are the perennials that interest you hardy in the zone where you live? If you live in Zone 6 and plant perennials that are hardy in Zones 8 and above, there is a definite danger the plants will freeze. Select plants that flourish and are hardy in your zone.

Some perennials will do extremely well in your area but may not in a fellow gardener's planting across the state—and vice versa. Zones, winds, soils, drainage, sun, care, and individual types and varieties will determine whether or not a perennial planting will be successful. Before purchasing, be sure to ask about the plant's ability to withstand the summer heat in your area. Some winter-hardy cool-season perennials will not do well at all in the Texas heat.

Some perennials are nearly maintenance-free, while others require a little more attention. Care requirements are among the criteria for selection of perennials for the home landscape.

Some perennials are grown for their colorful foliage, not for their blooms. Among these are dusty miller, *Centaurea cineraria*, and artemisia, *Artemisia abrotanum*, also known as wormwood or southernwood. Both these plants provide interesting foliage color and tex-

texture that accents other perennials or annuals in the home land-scape. Four-o-clock, *Mirabilis jalapa*, is an old-fashioned perennial that's easily started from seed and will grow all over Texas. These plants are tough, durable, low maintenance, and fragrant. Ruellia, *Ruellia brittoniana*, is easy to start from divisions and will bloom during its first season. Members of this very tough and easy-to-grow family may also be started from seed. And don't forget perennials like garden mums, *Dendranthema* cultivars, which are grown for their outstanding fall color. Some plant people suggest growing them as annuals, but in most of Texas we can enjoy them year after year. I've enjoyed our planting for more than 10 years, which makes our bed of "mums" truly perennial.

Some perennials are native plants that have been selected and cultivated for the home landscape. See the Native Plants chapter for more information on these.

I have selected an even dozen perennials for you to try in your home landscape. In each family group you will find many varieties.

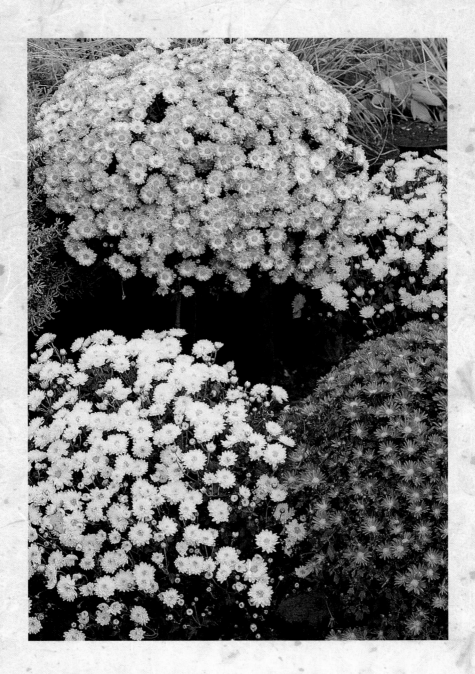

Astilbe
Astilbe spp.

EXPOSURE

Shade to Semi-

COLD HARDINESS

All Texas

WATER USAGE

Moist

GROWTH RATE

Fast to Med.

AVG. HT × WIDTH

15″–5′ (v.)

SPACING

Varies

Foliage is dark green, almost fern-like. Blooms are held high above foliage, with large quantities of very small flowers in white, pink, lavender, or red or erect plume-like bloom stalks.

*A*stilbe may be a relatively new perennial to many Texas gardeners, but has been used for quite a few years across the South. It works especially well in shady, moist locations. This is not a perennial to put out in full Texas sun, especially in areas that are hard to water. Astilbe needs a deep, very rich, moist growing condition and dappled shade throughout the entire day. Because of the diversity in their height, different types of astilbe may be grouped together, the shorter ones forming a groundcover effect in shaded areas, or working equally well as border plants. The taller varieties make great background cover for an outstanding garden in lightly or dappled shaded areas. Some varieties bloom early-, mid-, and late-season, providing an extended bloom period. If you would like some color in a lightly or dappled shaded area where other plants have failed, you need to give astilbe a try.

WHEN TO PLANT
The best time to plant astilbe is in the spring after all danger of frost has passed in your area. The second-best time is early fall.

WHERE TO PLANT

Astilbe is a perennial that is well adapted to the Texas soils that are rich in organic matter. They will not do well in waterlogged or boggy soils, but they do require a moist growing condition. Astilbe performs best with a mix of dappled sunlight and light shade. Do not plant in full-sun or total shade locations.

HOW TO PLANT

Add lots of organic matter to your soil. This may require more bed preparation than is normal for most flowering plants. I suggest the incorporation of 4 in. of brown sphagnum peat moss into the top 4 in. of your existing soil to obtain a mixture of about 50 percent organic matter and 50 percent native soil. After the bed is complete, move your astilbe from their containers and insert into the newly prepared bed. Plant no deeper than they were originally grown in the containers and backfill with the soil mix. Firm the soil around the rootball, water thoroughly, apply root stimulator according to label directions, and mulch with 3 to 4 in. of bark mulch. I normally use pine bark mulch.

CARE AND MAINTENANCE

Slugs, snails, and powdery mildew can be a problem. Ask about control possibilities. Remember to read and follow label directions for any gardening aid. Deadheading may be done to enhance the look of astilbe during its blooming stages. If blooming seems to be reduced, it may indicate that your astilbe needs to be divided. After 3 to 5 years, most astilbe should be lifted from the soil, divided, and replanted. Maintaining a moist soil is critical to successful long-term growth of astilbe in the state of Texas. This is a perennial that definitely benefits from a drip irrigation system to maintain moist soil. Be sure to maintain a season-long mulch 3 to 4 in. deep around the entire planting. Fertilization of astilbe may be accomplished by water-soluble, liquid, or granular fertilizers applied according to label directions. Make your first application in the early spring, and reapply as necessary according to label directions.

ADDITIONAL INFORMATION

When selecting astilbe, ask which varieties have performed best in your specific area. Butterflies like astilbe.

ADDITIONAL SPECIES, CULTIVARS, OR VARIETIES

Look for some of these at your next visit to Lowe's: 'Europa', 'Gladstone', 'Bridal Veil', 'Fanal', 'Peach Blossom', 'Amethyst', 'Intermezzo', and 'Red Sentinel'. Other species groups to try are *A. chinensis* var. 'Pumila', 'Superba', 'Hennie Graafland', and 'Ostrich Plume'.

Coral Vine
Antigonon leptopus

EXPOSURE

F. Sun to Semi-

COLD HARDINESS

To 10° F.

WATER USAGE

Semi-Moist

GROWTH RATE

Fast

AVG. HT × WIDTH

10–15' Vine

SPACING

18"

A vining, flowering perennial with heart-shaped leaves and lacy pink or white blooms.

My first sight of coral vine was in Brownwood on Granny Miller's fence. Granny Miller never grew a flowering plant that was difficult to care for, and coral vine worked wonderfully on her chain link fence. You may know it as queen's wreath or Mexican love vine. But whatever the common name, if you are looking for an easy-to-grow flowering perennial vine that will thrive where hardy in Texas, take a look at this vine. It puts out a sufficient amount of leaves to make nice shade in the summertime on a trellis or other structure. Try it on a gazebo or other upright structure where you wish to have a great blooming plant. In Zones 8 and 9, it comes back year after year, but it is "iffy" in Zone 7. Heavy mulching may ensure its reemergence in succeeding years.

WHEN TO PLANT
The best time to plant coral vine is early in the spring after all danger of frost has passed.

WHERE TO PLANT

Coral vine is relatively easy to grow and drought tolerant, which makes it a great plant to try in a Texas landscape. You can find it in pink or white, and it puts on a great display of flowers in summer, on into the fall. It needs to be in a location where the soil drains well and it requires sun in order to grow and bloom.

HOW TO PLANT

For best results, improve the native soil where coral vine is to grow. This is accomplished with the incorporation of 3 in. of organic matter into the top 3 in. of native soil. Remove transplants from their containers and insert them into the soil at soilball depth. Firm the soil, water thoroughly, apply root stimulator according to label directions, and mulch. When planting seeds, make sure the soil temperature is above 70 degrees Fahrenheit. Plant in the improved bed according to seed package directions.

CARE AND MAINTENANCE

Coral vine is considered pest-free. Prune as necessary to train and direct its growth. Water as necessary to prevent soil dryness. Remember, while coral vine is quite drought tolerant, it will appreciate an occasional long, deep drink of water. Maintain a layer of 3 to 4 in. of bark mulch to aid in soil moisture retention. Coral vine will benefit from applications of fertilizer throughout the growing season. You may use specialty granular, water-soluble, or liquid fertilizers of your choice. Remember to read and follow label directions when applying any fertilizer. Make your first application in the spring as new growth begins. Follow with an additional application approximately 12 weeks later, and one early in the fall.

ADDITIONAL INFORMATION

You may tie coral vine to a structure to get it established in the way you wish it to grow.

ADDITIONAL SPECIES, CULTIVARS, OR VARIETIES

Currently there are only two known colors of coral vine, the standard pink, and a white variety called 'Album'.

Dusty Miller

Centaurea cineraria spp. *cineraria*

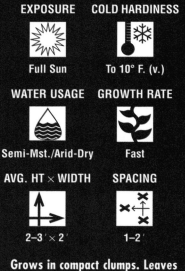

EXPOSURE
Full Sun

COLD HARDINESS
To 10° F. (v.)

WATER USAGE
Semi-Mst./Arid-Dry

GROWTH RATE
Fast

AVG. HT × WIDTH
2–3′ × 2′

SPACING
1–2′

Grows in compact clumps. Leaves are velvety white to silver.

*A*shley, my young home gardener, likes the looks of dusty miller in a landscape bed with colors. It works wonderfully when combined with blue. Dusty miller is grown for its foliage, not its flowers. While it does produce some flowers, they are not a part of the striking effect created in the home landscape by dusty miller. It is excellent in sunny locations. When planting in borders, use a dwarf variety such as 'Frosty' or 'Silver Queen'. At this time, our planting of dusty miller is 3 years old, definitely a perennial. Our soil is well-drained, sandy soil. Whether your soil is sandy or a clay-type soil, dusty miller requires a well-drained location.

WHEN TO PLANT

The best time to plant dusty miller is in the spring after all danger of frost has passed.

WHERE TO PLANT

Dusty miller may be used in several different locations, but make sure the soil drains well and receives a lot of sun. Do not plant in poorly drained or damp soil, or in shady locations. The shorter varieties may be used in masses to create a groundcover effect. Taller ones are excellent background plants and help to accentuate the color of shorter plants used in front of them. We are currently growing dusty miller in front of broadleaf evergreens. The combination is outstanding.

HOW TO PLANT

Improve the soil before you plant dusty miller by incorporating 3 to 4 in. of organic matter into it. Organic matter may be brown peat moss, compost, or ground bark. After improvement of the bed is complete, remove your transplants from their containers, insert them into the prepared soil no deeper than they were originally grown in the containers, and firm the soil. Water thoroughly, apply root stimulator according to label directions, and mulch with 3 in. of bark mulch.

CARE AND MAINTENANCE

Dusty miller is considered virtually insect- and disease-free. If any insects or diseases become a problem with your dusty miller, ask about control possibilities. Always read and follow label directions on any garden product. Be sure to remove blooms in order to help maintain a more compact growth habit for this plant. I prefer not to allow it to bloom, which helps it stay more compact. It may need to be pruned throughout the growing season in order to maintain a more compact and uniform habit. Water as necessary to prevent soil dryness. While this is considered a relatively tough plant, do not allow the soil to become dry for a prolonged period of time. Fertilize dusty miller in the springtime as new growth begins. Specialty granular, water-solubles, or liquid fertilizers work equally well. Be sure to read and follow label directions.

ADDITIONAL INFORMATION

The name dusty miller is a common name applied to more than one group of plants. The artemisia genus is often called dusty miller in Texas. Be sure to ask to which group your selection of dusty miller belongs. Check with local retail nurseries to determine the hardiness of the dusty miller you select for planting in your landscape.

ADDITIONAL SPECIES, CULTIVARS, OR VARIETIES

Other varieties of *cineraria* are 'Diamond', 'Silver Queen', and 'Frosty'. *C. gymnocarpa* may reach a height of 3 ft.

Four-o-Clocks
Mirabilis jalapa

EXPOSURE

F. Sun to Semi-

COLD HARDINESS

To 0° F.

WATER USAGE

Arid to Semi-Mst.

GROWTH RATE

FAST

AVG. HT × WIDTH

3–4´ × 3´

SPACING

2´

Dense, dark-green foliage with a large amount of lightly fragrant trumpet-shaped flowers in colors of white, pink, salmon, lavender, yellow, and blends.

*T*hough many gardeners don't think of them as perennials, four-o-clocks are truly old-fashioned Texas perennials. They are loaded with many beautiful, scented flowers that begin opening in the afternoon and remain open through the evening and night. Because they are open late and remain open during the evening and night, they can add a wonderful fragrance to our gardens during these hours. Four-o-clocks are so tough and durable they can grow in full sun in all parts of Texas, though they would like a bit of shade from the really hot afternoon sun. They may be seen in areas where old, abandoned homesteads have been. This is just another indication of how tough and durable these plants are, even when on their own.

WHERE TO PLANT

Four-o-clocks will grow in sandy soils or heavy clay soils, if given sufficient light and moisture. They do best in 6 to 8 hours of full sun, with shade from the hot afternoon sun. They may be used as tall background plants. The dwarf variety, which reaches only 20 in. high, may be used as filler plants, border plants, or in mass plantings. Four-o-clocks also work well in large containers.

How to Plant

Four-o-clocks will grow in many different types of soil conditions, but they prefer moist, loamy soils. In order to obtain best results from four-o-clocks, make sure your soil is improved. Incorporate 3 to 4 in. of organic matter into the top 4 in. of the existing soil with a tiller, spading fork, or shovel. Remove transplants from the containers and insert them into the prepared seedbed at the same level they were growing in their containers. Firm the soil around the root-ball, water thoroughly, add root stimulator, and mulch with 3 in. of bark mulch. When planting seeds, plant them approximately 1/2 in. deep in a well-prepared bed.

Care and Maintenance

Four-o-clocks are virtually insect- and disease- free. If they become too large for an area, you may prune them as necessary through the summer season. If you carefully select the location for your four-o-clocks, you will reduce the need for future pruning. If your space is limited, look at the dwarf varieties. Water as necessary to maintain a moist soil and to reap maximum bloom benefit. Maintaining a thick 3- to 4-in. mulch layer will greatly aid in moisture retention and reduce the frequency of watering. Fertilize four-o-clocks in the spring as growth emerges, using a granular rose food or any other form of fertilizer, including water-soluble and liquid. Remember to read and follow label directions.

Additional Information

I have grown four-o-clocks for many years, as have my parents and grandparents. If they start taking over an area, begin removing germinated seedlings as soon as possible in the spring. In severe cases of "takeover," you may wish to rework the entire planting.

Additional Species, Cultivars, or Varieties

Four-o-clocks generally come in seed mixtures. One mixture that includes the 20-in. height is 'Pygmy Mixture'. A taller-growing mixture is called 'Four-o-clock Special'.

Garden Mum
Dendranthema cultivars

EXPOSURE

Full to Semi-

COLD HARDINESS

All Texas

WATER USAGE
Semi-Mst.

GROWTH RATE
Fast to Med.

AVG. HT × WIDTH
12–20″ (v.)

SPACING
1–2′

Bushy with dark-green leaves and a wide range of bloom types and colors.

Garden mums belong to a family that includes florist's chrysanthemums, "Football Mums", and feverfew. Because of the variation in height and form, garden mums may be used as border plants, mass plantings, or a single planting. When clustered in baskets or other containers, they may be grown into cascade form, hanging basket, or miniature tree form specimens. Garden mums are relatively easy to grow in Texas. They need a deep, rich, well-drained soil with adequate moisture. They require a sunny location that receives approximately 6 hours of full sun, but shade from the hot afternoon sun.

WHEN TO PLANT
Many garden mums are planted in the fall in full bud or full bloom. Planting is also acceptable in the spring. When planting in the spring, make sure all danger of frost has passed.

WHERE TO PLANT
Garden mums may be used in many different locations in your landscape. They can be planted along various walkways, around garden structures such

as decks, gazebos, benches, ornamental pools, water fountains, or other structures. They also work well in large containers. Don't plant them in heavily shaded areas that are difficult to water or in poorly prepared or poorly drained soil.

HOW TO PLANT

Garden mums are best planted from container-grown stock. They are normally available in 4-, 5-, or 6-in. pots as well as in larger nursery containers. Plant in well-prepared beds. Improve the soil by incorporating 4 in. of organic matter, including brown peat moss and compost, into the top 4 in. of the existing native soil. Remove your mum selections from their containers and plant no deeper than they were originally grown in the containers. Firm the soil around each individual plant, water the plants thoroughly, apply root stimulator according to label directions, and mulch thoroughly with 3 in. of bark mulch. When planting in containers of any size, use premium-quality lightweight potting soil.

CARE AND MAINTENANCE

Garden mums may be susceptible to a relatively wide range of insects as well as many diseases. I have had virtually no problems with insects and none with diseases. You can prevent insect and disease problems with your mums by selecting the best locally adapted varieties for your area. If insects or diseases do attack your chrysanthemums, ask about control possibilities. Remember to read and follow label directions. Pinching is important if you wish to have a good show of blooms in the fall. Begin pinching in the springtime after growth reaches 6 in., pinching back to approximately 4 in. This is a pruning activity that goes on till mid-July for most growers of garden mums. Water as necessary to maintain a moist soil, and do not allow chrysanthemums to become totally dry. Fertilize as new growth begins in the spring with a premium-quality long-lasting slow-release granular rose food or a water-soluble, liquid, or encapsulated fertilizer of your choice. Remember to read and follow label directions. Apply approximately every 8 weeks throughout the growing season.

ADDITIONAL INFORMATION

Visit botanical gardens through the state of Texas in the fall and you will see magnificent sweeps of color created by chrysanthemums.

ADDITIONAL SPECIES, CULTIVARS, OR VARIETIES

There are many different types of chrysanthemums, including pompom, singles (which have flowers that look similar to daisies), cushion, spoon (with Anemone-type blossoms), and buttons. Colors run the range of the rainbow except for blue. Some varieties to look for are 'Bull Finch', 'Chiquita', 'Classic', 'Cloud Nine', 'Joy Bringer', 'Mischief', 'Rustic', 'Yellow Jacket', 'Daphane', 'Ginger Ale', 'Texas Hombre', 'Adorn', 'Frolic', 'Lancer', 'Ruby Mound', 'Target', 'Tinkerbell', 'Clara Curtis', 'Ryan's Pink', and 'Zest'.

Lantana
Lantana montevidensis

EXPOSURE

Full Sun

COLD HARDINESS

To 5° F.

WATER USAGE

Arid to Semi-Mst.

GROWTH RATE

Fast

AVG. HT × WIDTH

12–30″ × 30–48″

SPACING

2–4′

Lantana does well throughout the entire state of Texas.

*T*his group of lantanas is often referred to as trailing lantana. The trailing forms of lantana are excellent for use in beds to create a groundcover effect, to weep over walls, or in large containers. They work wonderfully in an area that is difficult to water as long as it is a sunny location and the soil drains well. Lantanas not only lend themselves to excellent season-long color in Texas, including July and August, but butterflies love to gather around. If you'd like a multi-purpose plant grouping in your home landscape, add some of the different varieties of lantana. You will enjoy them, and be ready to enjoy butterflies as well. I live in a 7b zone and have grown the same lantanas for 16 years which makes them a true perennial in my beds.

WHEN TO PLANT
Lantana, a tough and durable plant, may be planted in early spring through the fall in Texas. The ideal planting time is very early spring.

WHERE TO PLANT
Use lantana anywhere in your landscape where you wish to have extremely tough and durable color the entire season with minimum maintenance. It

needs a location where the soil drains well and receives a minimum of 6 hours of full sun. Do not plant in heavily shaded locations or poorly drained soils, though it will grow in heavy clay or light, sandy soils. Lantanas may be used in large nursery containers. The trailing forms are especially useful in hanging baskets. The different varieties of lantana add great color with minimal care to areas around garden structures such as decks, gazebos, or swimming pools.

HOW TO PLANT

While lantana will tolerate rather difficult locations, in order to obtain maximum growth and benefit, plant in well-prepared beds. Incorporate 3 in. of organic matter into the top 3 in. or more of the existing soil. Quality organic matter includes brown sphagnum peat moss, compost, and ground bark mulch. After your bed is complete, remove the transplants from their containers and set in individual planting holes no deeper than they were originally grown in the containers. Firm the soil well around the plants, water thoroughly, apply root stimulator according to label directions, and mulch with 3 to 4 in. of bark mulch. If you plant in large containers, be sure to use premium-quality lightweight potting soils.

CARE AND MAINTENANCE

I've never had any pest problems with lantanas, but they are subject to white fly, lacebugs, and red spider mites. If pests become a problem with your planting of lantana, ask about control possibilities. Remember to read and follow label directions. Prune as necessary to maintain the shape you desire for your lantana, and water as necessary to prevent soil dryness. Fertilize lantana in the spring with a premium-quality long-lasting slow-release granular rose food, or a water-soluble, liquid, or encapsulated season-long fertilizer. Reapply every 10 to 12 weeks throughout the growing season.

ADDITIONAL INFORMATION

I find lantana in old abandoned homesites, on roadways, and on highway medians that receive minimal to no care. You or that little one may plant lantana and be assured of great bloom throughout the entire growing season. Check with local nurseries for individual variety hardiness.

ADDITIONAL SPECIES, CULTIVARS, OR VARIETIES

Look for some of these varieties and give them a try: 'Lavender Swirl', 'White Lightning', and 'Patriot Rainbow'. Also look for *L. camara*, a native of Texas in bicolor mixtures of red, yellow, pink, orange, and white, and *L. horrida*, whose colors are yellow to orange.

Mexican Petunia
Ruellia brittoniana

EXPOSURE

F. Sun to Semi-

COLD HARDINESS

To 0° F.

WATER USAGE

Arid to Semi-Mst.

GROWTH RATE

Fast

AVG. HT × WIDTH

10–36 " × Creeping

SPACING

18–24 "

Groundcover or upright shrub. Blooms are lavender to purple with a petunia shape. Foliage is dark-green or purple-tinted.

Mexican petunia is also known as summer petunia or, simply, ruellia. This is an extremely tough, durable, virtually care-free perennial. We are currently growing it in a bed at the southwest corner of our home, and it has consistently bloomed for us for the past 5 years. We have both the standard varieties, which may reach as tall as 3 ft., as well as the dwarf variety, 'Katie', which generally grows around 8 to 10 in. The taller-growing variety of ruellia can be used in and among other perennials, including some Texas native plants. It lends itself well to all types of cultures. It will grow in light, sandy soil and will also grow in heavy clay soils. It will tolerate damp conditions and will also tolerate dry conditions. What more could you ask of a plant?

WHEN TO PLANT
Ruellia may be planted virtually any time of the year in the areas where it is hardy in Texas. The preferred planting time is very early spring, which will give the plant time to put on its foliage growth and produce blooms during its first season. Planting in early fall is also quite acceptable.

WHERE TO PLANT

Plant anywhere in your home landscape that receives at least 6 hours of sun. The color is accentuated when planted with some dusty miller. If you have an area in your landscape where other perennials have not survived, plant some ruellia and enjoy its color throughout the season. Do not plant ruellia in heavily shaded areas; it will perform poorly.

HOW TO PLANT

While ruellia will grow under adverse conditions, for good results, plant in well-prepared beds. Incorporate 3 to 4 in. of high-quality organic matter into the native soil by tilling or blending with a fork or shovel. After the bed is prepared, remove your selections of ruellia from their containers and install them in the soil no deeper than they were originally grown in the containers. Firm the soil well around the plant's rootball, water thoroughly, apply root stimulator according to label directions, and mulch with 3 in. of bark mulch. Ruellia may also be planted in large nursery containers—be sure to use premium-quality lightweight potting soil.

CARE AND MAINTENANCE

Ruellia has no insect or disease problems. Pruning is rarely necessary unless you wish to remove some bloom stalks. Water as necessary to prevent soil dryness and to encourage great growth, vigor, and bloom. Maintaining mulch through the entire growing season will reduce the frequency of watering and conserve soil moisture. Fertilizing may be done if desired, but it is not necessary.

ADDITIONAL INFORMATION

Ruellia is very easy to propagate from divisions or seeds. See native perennials for more ruellias.

ADDITIONAL SPECIES, CULTIVARS, OR VARIETIES

R. brittoniana is a tall purple variety. A pink variety is named 'Chi Chi' and a dwarf purple is 'Katie'. *R. malacosperma* comes in purple and white. They're all great!

Phlox
Phlox paniculata

EXPOSURE

Semi-Shade

COLD HARDINESS

All Texas

WATER USAGE

Semi-Moist

GROWTH RATE

Fast

AVG. HT × WIDTH

24–48" × 14–18"

SPACING
15–18"

Dark-green leaves; rounded, ball-shaped, multi-bloom heads of small flowers in lilac, pink, rose, and white.

P. paniculata is also known as summer phlox, border phlox, standing phlox, and hardy phlox. Whatever you call it, it will add interest and excitement to your summer garden planting. It works equally well in mass plantings, along borders, or as background plantings. The taller varieties, with their colorful heads held high, can be staked to prevent them from falling. The shorter varieties of phlox, annual as well as perennial, can be used in the foreground to cover tall stems. These gorgeous blossoms can be enjoyed through our Texas summers. Summer phlox does best where it receives approximately 6 hours of sun per day and shade from the hot afternoon sun. It is also desirable to keep its root system mulched throughout the growing season.

WHEN TO PLANT
The best time to plant border phlox is in the spring after all danger of frost has passed. The second-best planting time is early fall.

WHERE TO PLANT
Summer phlox may be used in deep, wide borders, along fence lines, on the back of a property, or in any other area in the home landscape where the

height and large, rounded bloomheads of phlox are desired. Do not plant in poorly drained locations or in areas that are difficult to water.

HOW TO PLANT

In order to do its best, summer phlox needs to be planted in beds that are thoroughly improved. Add approximately 4 in. of high-quality organic matter into the top 4 in. of the native soil. After the beds are completed, remove the individual plants from their containers and place in planting holes to the same depth they were growing in the containers. Firm the soil around each plant, water thoroughly, apply root stimulator according to label directions, and mulch with approximately 3 in. of bark mulch.

CARE AND MAINTENANCE

In hot, dry weather, spider mites may pay a visit to your planting. In cloudy, damp, humid weather, rust or powdery mildew may become a problem. If any of these problems arise, ask for information on the best controls. Remember to read and follow label directions. Prune out individual bloom heads shortly after the completion of the blooming period. Water as necessary to maintain a moist soil, especially during droughts. Drip irrigation is highly suggested for long-term culture of border phlox, and maintain a thick layer of mulch, approximately 3 to 4 in., all around its root system. Fertilize in the spring as new growth begins, using a premium-quality long-lasting slow-release granular rose food—or you may elect to use a water-soluble, liquid, or season-long encapsulated fertilizer. Remember, read and follow label directions.

ADDITIONAL INFORMATION

There are several garden phlox to try in your home landscape. Some are more available in some areas of Texas than in others.

ADDITIONAL SPECIES, CULTIVARS, OR VARIETIES

Phlox are available in red, pink, salmon, magenta, purple, bicolor, lavender, and white. Seek out the colors you believe will work best in your local landscape. The old-fashioned magenta color is considered the most widely adapted summer phlox in Texas. See Native Annuals and Perennials for more phloxes.

Pinks
Dianthus spp.

EXPOSURE

Full Sun

COLD HARDINESS

All Texas

WATER USAGE

Semi-Moist

GROWTH RATE

Fast

AVG. HT × WIDTH

4–15" × 12–16"

SPACING

Varies

Upright stems, covered with blue-gray narrow-leaf foliage. Blossoms of rose, salmon, pink, and white.

Pinks are an old-time favorite of Texas gardeners. They are excellent for use in areas where you wish to create a mass effect for early-season bloom. The taller varieties make nice background plantings. The varieties and colors available today are vast when compared with those availabe in past decades. Ask to see the selections of pinks or dianthus. You are in for a treat. While dianthus in Texas is commonly called pinks because of the outstanding pink flowers, they are now available in other colors including white, reds, and lavenders, and they have single and double flowers.

WHEN TO PLANT
The best time to plant dianthus, or pinks, is in early spring after all danger of frost has passed in your area. They can also be planted in early fall.

WHERE TO PLANT
Dianthus need to be planted in areas in your landscape where they receive plenty of morning sun but are shaded from hot afternoon sun. They tend to bloom best under cooler conditions—difficult to achieve in Texas in the sum-

mertime. Shade is very important. Do not plant in areas that are difficult to water, poorly drained, or in heavily shaded areas. According to *Hortus III*, there are over 300 species of dianthus available, so be sure to ask about the type of dianthus you are looking at before deciding to buy. Seek additional information at local nurseries on where to use specific varieties you've selected for your landscape.

HOW TO PLANT

Plant dianthus in well-prepared beds where you have improved the soil by adding 3 to 4 in. of brown sphagnum peat moss or compost to the native soil. You may rototill or blend with your favorite shovel or digging fork. After the beds are improved, remove your selections from their containers and set in individual planting holes dug no deeper than the depth of the plant soilball. Backfill with the soil mix, water thoroughly, apply root stimulator according to label directions, and mulch with 3 to 4 in. of bark mulch.

CARE AND MAINTENANCE

Leaf spot may visit your planting during cloudy, humid, muggy days. This is generally corrected when the sun comes out, humidity decreases, and good air movement occurs. If leaf spot becomes a concern, ask about appropriate controls. Remember to read and follow label directions on any gardening aid you decide to purchase. Remove spent blooms to encourage additional blooming and to tidy up the overall look of your plantings of dianthus. Water as needed to maintain a moist soil, but do not overwater. Maintaining a thick layer of 3 to 4 in. of mulch around your planting will greatly conserve soil moisture and reduce the frequency of watering. Fertilize in the spring as new growth begins. Reapply fertilizer as needed through the entire growing season.

ADDITIONAL INFORMATION

When selecting dianthus, look for dark-green foliage on relatively compact plants loaded with buds, in 4- or 6-in. containers. In addition to the beauty that dianthus gives us, it is a treat for the nose. Plant them where you can enjoy their fragrance. Pinks do best in the cooler Texas months.

ADDITIONAL SPECIES, CULTIVARS, OR VARIETIES

Pinks are available in clumping or clump-forming types, as well as low-growing groundcover selections. Just a few of the varieties are 'Queen of Hearts', 'Magic Charms', 'Snowfire', and 'Snowflake'.

Shasta Daisy

Leucanthemum × superbum

EXPOSURE

F. Sun to Semi-

COLD HARDINESS

All Texas

WATER USAGE

Semi-Moist

GROWTH RATE

Fast to Med.

AVG. HT × WIDTH

12–30″ × 8–12″

SPACING

12–24″

Dark-green, narrow foliage held relatively close to the plant; covered with white flowers that have yellow to gold centers.

*T*exans have successfully grown Shasta daisies for many years. This is a plant that is relatively easy to grow, but it does have some care needs. For example, it needs to be used in areas where it receives approximately 6 hours of full sun, with some shade from the hot afternoon sun. It may be used along walkways, around garden structures, and even in large nursery containers. It is a versatile perennial plant whose simple white with yellow centers blends well in many locations.

WHEN TO PLANT
The best planting time for Shasta is in the early fall. The second-best time to plant is very early spring.

WHERE TO PLANT
Plant Shasta daisies in areas of your landscape where you can enjoy these classy-looking sources of outstanding color. They have a relatively compact growth habit. We currently grow Shasta in a raised perennial bed at the southwest corner and back entrance to our home. They receive plenty of morning

sun and are shaded from the hot afternoon sun. Do not plant Shasta daisies in areas that are difficult to water or in areas where the soil tends to remain wet throughout the entire year, heavily shaded or in unimproved heavy clay.

HOW TO PLANT

Shasta daisies do best in soils that you have improved with the addition of 3 to 4 in. of high-quality organic matter. After the bed is completed, dig individual planting holes no deeper than the depth of the plant's soilball. Slide the individual plants into their new homes and firm the soil around them. Water thoroughly, apply root stimulator according to label directions, and mulch with 3 to 4 in. of bark mulch. I normally use pine bark mulch.

CARE AND MAINTENANCE

Leaf spot may visit your planting of Shasta in areas that are too wet or poorly drained. Root rot may also be a problem. To prevent root rot, plant in areas where the soil drains thoroughly, and never overwater. If diseases become a problem with your planting, get information on control possibilities. Generally these problems will self-correct once growing conditions improve. Prune out spent blossoms to encourage additional blossoms and to help dress up your plantings of Shasta. Shasta daisies benefit from annual or biannual digging, dividing, and re-transplanting in the fall. This will allow your planting to multiply, spread, and renew for outstanding blooms the following season. To have prolonged success with Shasta, this digging, dividing, and replanting is necessary. Water as needed, especially during the bloom and growing season, to maintain a moist soil. Do not allow the soil to become dry and never overwater. Maintaining a thick layer of bark mulch year-round will greatly aid in moisture retention and moderating soil temperatures. Fertilize in the spring as new growth begins, using granular premium-quality long-lasting slow-release rose food, or a water-soluble or liquid fertilizer of your choice. Remember to follow label directions.

ADDITIONAL INFORMATION

If your Shasta daisies, even with the best of care, tend to look a little bit ragged toward the end of the summer, don't despair. As the cooling rains and temperatures arrive in the fall, they will be rejuvenated.

ADDITIONAL SPECIES, CULTIVARS, OR VARIETIES

Some varieties you may ask for are 'Little Miss Muffet', 'Alaska', 'Aglaia', 'Snow Lady', 'Marconi', and 'Cobham Gold'.

Southernwood

Artemisia abrotanum

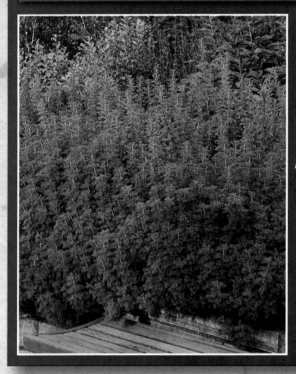

EXPOSURE	COLD HARDINESS
Full Sun	Varies

WATER USAGE	GROWTH RATE
Arid/Semi-Mst. (v.)	Fast to Med. (v.)

AVG. HT × WIDTH	SPACING
12–24 " × Spreading	12–30 ' (v.)

Feathery, green, fragrant foliage.

Southernwood is an unusual type of artemisia. Instead of having gray or silvery foliage, its foliage is green. The finely divided feathery foliage lends itself well to dispensing wonderful fragrances. This is a relatively compact grower that needs good drainage. It has small whitish to yellow, nearly round flowers that hang loosely. You will find varieties of southernwood that smell like tangerine or lemon as well as camphor. This is an interesting plant to use in home landscapes for appearance as well as fragrance. This plant has multiple year-round uses. It is popular for its appearance, fragrance, feel, and its many uses when cut and dried. Potpourris, table arrangements, bouquets and wreaths extend its value.

WHEN TO PLANT
Plant artemisia or southernwood in early spring or early fall.

WHERE TO PLANT
Well-drained soil is important to growing artemisia in Texas. If you have heavy clay soil, improve it thoroughly before attempting to grow any varieties

of artemisia, including southernwood. It needs a sunny location with sandy, deep, well-drained soil. They need to be in a sunny location where they receive a minimum of 6 hours full-sun and can be grown in locations where it is sunny all day.

HOW TO PLANT
If planting in heavy clay soil, add 2 in. of coarse, washed sand, 1 in. of perlite, and 2 in. of pine bark mulch to the top 4 to 5 in. of existing soil. In sandy soil, the incorporation of some ground bark mulch, approximately 2 in. deep, blended with the top 4 in. of existing soil, will be sufficient. Make sure all soil drains well. Dig individual planting holes the depth of the plant's soilball. Remove from existing containers and plant in the holes no deeper than they were in the original container. Firm the soil around the rootball, water thoroughly, apply root stimulator according to label directions, and mulch with 2 in. of bark mulch.

CARE AND MAINTENANCE
Artemisia has no serious insect pests. Prune it to maintain more compact growth, and remove spent blooms as necessary. Water only when soil becomes dry. Do not allow prolonged or extended periods of drought, but do not overwater. Overwatering can cause root rot and a decline. Fertilization is minimal; perhaps apply one time in the spring with a premium-quality long-lasting slow-release granular rose food according to label directions.

ADDITIONAL INFORMATION
My long-time friend and fellow gardener, Patsy Tindell in Woodway, introduced me to artemisia. Patsy and other Texas gardeners must deal with heavy black clay soils, and Patsy has been successful in growing artemisia. You can too. Follow the suggestions for improving the soil for good drainage. It is worth it.

ADDITIONAL SPECIES, CULTIVARS, OR VARIETIES
Additional species of artemisia include *A. absinthium*, known as common wormwood; *A. dracunculus*, which is the true French Tarragon and is best grown in containers; *A. ludoviciana*, which is probably the common artemisia; *A. schmidtiana* 'Nana', also known as 'Silver Mound'; and *A. vulgaris*, known as 'Mugwort'. Give one or all a try.

Yarrow
Achillea cultivars

EXPOSURE

F. Sun to Semi-

COLD HARDINESS

All Texas

WATER USAGE

Semi-Mst. to Arid

GROWTH RATE

Fast

AVG. HT × WIDTH

3–6 ′ (v.)

SPACING

1–2 ′ (v.)

Feathery fern-like green to gray-green foliage. Blooms are very small in masses and normally flat-topped with colors of white, yellow, or red.

*L*et this be the season or year for you to plant some yarrow. It is so easy to grow, and it gives us great color all season long, especially in the hot times in Texas. There are several different sizes and types available. Ask retail salespeople how large the various varieties will grow that are particularly interesting to you. Once yarrow is established, it is relatively drought tolerant and will thrive in difficult-to-water areas. It should be free of competition from shrubs and trees, but it will exist if adequate sunlight is available, a minimum of 6 hours of full sun per day—never plant in heavily shaded areas.

WHEN TO PLANT
Yarrow may be successfully planted in the early spring after all danger of frost has passed. If you are not familiar with the average killing frost date in your area, contact your local County Agent or nursery. Either will be able to supply you with accurate information on these dates.

WHERE TO PLANT
Plant in any location in your landscape that receives at least 6 hours of sun-light and the soil drains well. Don't plant in poorly drained locations, damp

areas, or areas with heavy shade. The taller-growing varieties make excellent background plantings for the smaller varieties, which can be used in mass plantings or in border plantings. They will also grow well in containers. Yarrow is excellent as a cut flower.

HOW TO PLANT
If your soil is heavy and poorly drained, you may need to blend 2 or more in. of coarse washed sand, perhaps some perlite, and 2 in. of ground bark into the top 4 in. of your existing soil. This will create a well-drained area for growing yarrow. Once the bed is complete, remove the yarrow from their existing containers and place them in the new bed no deeper than they were growing in the containers. Firm the soil well around the root system, water thoroughly, apply root stimulator according to label directions, and mulch with 2 in. of bark mulch.

CARE AND MAINTENANCE
No insects cause serious problems for yarrow. Prune as necessary to maintain a desired shape. When making selections for dried flowers, be sure to make the cuttings before blooms open. Water as needed to prevent soil dryness, but never overwater.

ADDITIONAL INFORMATION
Yarrow, especially before it puts on blooms, reminds many gardeners of ferns. It is sometimes called a sun-loving fern until the blooms come out. This is a great plant for the little gardeners. It will give them 100 percent success.

ADDITIONAL SPECIES, CULTIVARS, OR VARIETIES
Try some of these varieties: 'Coronation Gold', 'Moonshine', 'Gold Plate', 'Cerise Queen', 'Paprika', 'Summer Pastels', and 'Parker's Variety'.

CHAPTER SEVEN

ROSES

*T*HERE IS NOTHING THAT SPEAKS TO A TEXAN'S HEART the way roses do. We Texans take pride in our roses, and there are many selections from which to choose.

The area of Northeast Texas around Tyler is often rightly considered the "Rose Capitol of the World." Many of our nation's rosebushes are produced there. Texas roses are available to us in a rainbow of colors, forms, types, and growth habits. They come packaged or container grown.

As you investigate rose classification, you will find they can be grouped in several ways. The American Rose Society (ARS) lists over 50 categories. This can be a bit confusing, even intimidating.

Some of these groups have sub-groups. For example, old garden roses may include teas, climbers, ramblers, and several other different types. The cutoff date set by the American Rose Society (ARS) for old garden roses is 1867—all roses introduced after this date are supposed to be "Modern Roses." The date seems inappropriate to some gardeners. They say, "Roses that are 75 or 80 years old and have all the characteristics of old garden roses introduced before 1867 should also be called old garden roses." It is an interesting debate, but for you and me, it is probably sufficient to know that there are roses which have been in cultivation for a long, long time. We can leave the debate to others.

You will find rose aficionados who are very serious about classification. I think growing roses should be much like other gardening activities: fun! I have tried to keep it fun as I supply you with information that you can use while selecting roses to enjoy in your home landscape. In this chapter I've simplified classification into nine groups: climbers (which includes ramblers), floribundas, grandifloras, hybrid tea roses, miniatures, old garden roses, polyanthas, shrub roses, and species roses.

Some varieties of shrub roses can be used as groundcovers, while other varieties will grow to 6 ft. tall. Species roses are those

Chapter Seven

that occur naturally, but keep in mind that roses may hybridize in nature. You may come across a hybrid species rose, which makes it more difficult to identify.

If you have the opportunity to visit public rose gardens around the state, carry a camera, paper, and something to write with. You may find just the variety you want, and if you record its name, you will be able to ask for it when you want to purchase roses. Like the Dallas Botanic Gardens, the Fort Worth Botanic Garden has a planting of roses—and don't forget to visit the free rose garden in the City of Tyler, where you will find 14 acres with thousands of rosebushes, all for viewing by the general public. And just east of Texas, right off I-20 headed towards Shreveport, is the National Headquarters for the American Rose Society (ARS). This is also a great place for rose-growers to visit—even if it isn't in Texas.

I hope you enjoy your rose plantings as much as we do ours. Don't be intimidated by growing roses. Go out and have some fun with them.

Eldon Lyle, PhD, world-renowned plant pathologist, retired Executive Director of the Texas Rose Research Foundation, ARS Judge, and all-around encyclopedia of rose information, told me: "Roses don't need a lot of care, just a little care on a regular basis." If you will tend your roses on a regular basis, the results will be most satisfying.

Here are some suggestions to help you enjoy your roses:

- Purchase and plant only top-grade healthy specimens. An under-sized or diseased "bargain" plant that has shrunken canes or dead limbs is truly not a good buy. You will receive much more value for your investment by purchasing top-quality plants. I prefer to use 2-gal. or larger container-grown plants.

- Select the best locally adapted varieties for *your* area. The varieties I've selected for each of the 9 categories are some of the best for Texas gardens.

- Plant in soils that drain well and receive a minimum of 6 hours of full sun. Professional rose producers grow in full sun, and most successful home rose gardeners do, too. Shade from our hot afternoon sun is fine.

- In sandy soils, try a planting mixture of 50 percent native soil and 50 percent organic matter. A 25 percent native soil to 75 percent organic matter mixture is advised for heavy clay soils. Raising beds 12 in. or more above heavy clay soils is also advised. It's not uncommon to have 18-in. raised beds built on top of heavy clay soils.

- Disease control is very important in rose culture. More than one rose producer has told me that if he or she doesn't have insect-controlling products and fertilizers, but does have disease-controlling products, he or she can outproduce competitors who don't have such products, even if the competition has insect-controlling products and fertilizers. Diseases are better prevented than controlled. Here are some suggestions for a program that will help prevent diseases. Note: You don't do just one of these activities; combining them is most effective in preventing rose diseases.

  1. Purchase disease-resistant varieties.
  2. Plant in sunny locations with good air movement.
  3. Don't water the foliage. Drip irrigation works well.
  4. Apply recommended fungicides according to label directions. During the spring and fall when humidity is higher, there are usually more cloudy, rainy days. At these times a weekly preventive application is often recommended. In summer, application every 14 days is usually sufficient. Note: Many successful rose gardeners begin applying fungicides shortly after initial spring pruning and cleanup of debris. Check with your local retail nurseries, ARS Consulting Rosarians, or your County Agent's office for the best fungicides to prevent or stop rose diseases.

- Control pests such as insects and mites. Identify pests and check with your expert sources to determine the best means of control, or ask these sources to aid in pest and disease identification.

- Roses are considered relatively heavy "feeders"—fertilize them, but don't overfertilize. Always read and follow label directions, and water thoroughly after each application. Use the type of fertilizer you prefer, though premium-quality long-lasting slow-release granular rose fertilizers work well. Begin fertilizing as new leaves emerge, and discontinue about 6 weeks before the first average killing frost/freeze date in your area.

- Roses derive great benefit from a 3- to 4-in. layer of organic mulch covering their entire root system year-round. Pine bark, clean hay, hardwood bark, cypress bark, pecan shells, peanut hulls, aged wood shavings, shredded tree trimmings, pine needles, and other plant parts and products are often used as organic mulches in Texas.

- Water sufficiently to maintain a moist soil. Do not allow the root system to become dry any time of the year, even in winter. Roses like a moist soil, especially during their growing and blooming times, but they will not tolerate prolonged wet soil. "Moist" is the key word. Poorly drained or wet soils are detrimental to rose health and vigor. If such a problem is not corrected, roses will decline and terminate. And do not set a watering system to apply water by the clock! Instead, be observant, check the soil moisture, and water as needed. When irrigating, water deeply and thoroughly. Drip irrigation systems are great for watering roses, and they will save 50 percent or more on your water bill.

- Initial pruning is best done in later winter or early spring, 3 to 5 weeks before the last average killing frost/freeze date. Prune to shape and train, and remove spent blooms and dead branches during the growing and blooming season. Note: Spent bloom removal is often referred to as "deadheading."

Climbing Rose
Rosa

EXPOSURE

Full Sun

COLD HARDINESS

Protect @ 15° F.

WATER USAGE

Semi-Moist

GROWTH RATE

Fast

AVG. HT × WIDTH

10'–20' As Trained

SPACING

Varies

Available in a variety of colors, including white, pink, yellow, and red. Length of bloom period varies according to type; some bloom continuously, others bloom only once or twice a season.

"Climber" is really a misnomer for this plant. Climbing roses don't climb—they lean or must be tied to structures. They tend to have rather long, stiff branches that grow 10 to 15 ft. tall. Their blooms are carried in clusters, come in a wide range of flower forms, and usually bloom twice during the year, though some may rightly be called "continuous bloomers." Pillar is a sub-group of climbing roses that tend to reach only about 10 ft. in height and have strong stems that can be leaned against or tied to pillars or posts—hence the name pillar roses. Another sub-group is called ramblers. Ramblers tend to have very long and slender canes whose usual height is 10 to 20 ft. Their blooms are thick and small, generally about 2 in. across, and they bloom only once a year. They are extremely hardy. I get questions on climbing roses from time to time. They are an interesting group of roses to grow. I like to see them on some sort of structure, be it an entryway to a garden, a gazebo, or other gardening structure. They are often grown on fences as well, though fences often do not provide the height that is usually required. Tall walls work quite well. Climbing roses (including pillar, large-flowered climbing, and rambling roses) may be the answer if you are looking for tall, blooming plants that can help camouflage or break some areas in your landscape.

WHEN TO PLANT

Plant in very early spring.

WHERE TO PLANT

Full-sun locations that provide at least 6 hours of sunlight per day are best, in soils that have been prepared with plenty of organic matter.

HOW TO PLANT

Bareroot plants should be planted in prepared locations no deeper than they were growing in the nursery row. Container-grown selections should be planted no deeper than the top of the plant's soilball.

CARE AND MAINTENANCE

These roses require only minimal trimming, and this should be done after they finish blooming. Train your climbers to grow horizontally, and you will see an increase in blooming. Water as necessary to maintain a moist soil. Ask about control possibilities, and prevent diseases and control pests as needed. There are lots of different ways to fertilize roses. Premium-quality long-lasting granular rose food is a good choice, but you may choose any one you like. Read and follow label directions, and water throughly after applying any kind of fertilizer.

ADDITIONAL INFORMATION

Various types of climbers are often used to frame entrances to homes or to frame other structures, including gardening structures.

ADDITIONAL SPECIES, CULTIVARS, OR VARIETIES

Try some of these varieties: 'America', 'Blaze', 'Chrysler Imperial, Cl.', 'Don Juan', 'Dortmund', 'Golden Showers', 'Handel', 'New Dawn', 'Red Fountain', 'Queen Elizabeth, Cl.', 'Tempo', 'High Noon', 'Peace, Cl.', 'Royal Sunset', 'Joseph Coat', 'Sun Flare, Cl.', 'Altissimo', 'Sombrevil', and 'Iceberg, Cl.'. (Note: Cl. = Climbing.)

Floribunda
Rosa

EXPOSURE

Full Sun

COLD HARDINESS

Protect @ 15° F.

WATER USAGE

Semi-Moist

GROWTH RATE

Fast

AVG. HT × WIDTH

2–3 ' × 30 "

SPACING

2–5 '

Low-growing. Bloom color is like that of hybrid teas. Continuous bloom late spring through autumn.

The parent roses that were crossed to create the wonderful group floribunda are hybrid tea and polyantha. Floribunda's blooms are reminiscent of hybrid tea, while its foliage resembles that of polyantha, resulting in a plant that is hardier than the hybrid tea. It is a low-growing plant in the 2- to 3-ft. range and produces an extensive amount of continuous bloom in late spring through autumn. The flowers actually come in clusters—growers say, "I can cut an instant bouquet from my floribunda." There are many cultivars, and they come in every color of the hybrid teas. Some people say, "Roses don't have a strong scent today," but take a look at floribundas. Not only do they have delightful fragrance, they are among the easiest roses to grow. They are excellent for use in landscaping, work wonderfully when used in beds, and may be planted in masses for an outstanding effect. Floribundas may be used to edge walkways or borders, surround garden structures, or create a low hedge. Try planting floribundas in groups of the same color and variety. This will allow you to create a drift of color throughout your landscape. Don't plant them in squares or rectangles; plant them in free-form masses.

WHEN TO PLANT
Plant very early in spring.

WHERE TO PLANT
These roses will grow in 6 hours of full sun, but full sun all day long is best. They work well in large tubs on sunny decks, balconies, patios, or other areas where you have limited space.

HOW TO PLANT
Plant in soil that has been prepared well.

CARE AND MAINTENANCE
Prevent or control diseases and pests as necessary. Remember, always read and follow label directions when using any garden aid. Prune severely just before early spring growth. Maintain a moist soil throughout the growing season. Fertilize according to label directions. Premium-quality long-lasting slow-release rose fertilizer works well. Follow label directions and water thoroughly after any fertilizer application.

ADDITIONAL INFORMATION
This is a good rose to allow your little one to plant and care for. It doesn't grow too large, and it provides a wonderful show.

ADDITIONAL SPECIES, CULTIVARS, OR VARIETIES
Varieties include 'Angel Face', 'Bonbon', 'Apricot Nectar', 'Cathedral', 'Charisma', 'Cherish', 'Europeana', 'Evening Star', 'First Edition', 'French Lace', 'Iceberg', 'Impatient', 'Intrigue', 'Ivory Fashion', 'Little Darling', 'Marina', 'Orangeade', 'Sunfire', 'Vogue', 'Sea Pearl', 'Spartan', 'Sun Flare', 'Baby Talk', 'Columbus', 'Sweet Inspiration', 'Sun Bonnet', 'Fashion', 'Blast Off', 'Brass Band', 'Playboy', 'Sweet Vivien', 'Hot 'n' Spicy', 'Amber Queen', 'Scentimental', 'Summer Fashion', 'Pillow Talk', and 'Smooth Talk'.

Grandiflora
Rosa

EXPOSURE

Full Sun

COLD HARDINESS

Protect @ 15° F.

WATER USAGE

Semi-Moist

GROWTH RATE

Fast to Med.

AVG. HT × WIDTH

5–7′ × 3–5′

SPACING

3–5′

Colors may be white, pink, orange, red, yellow, blends, and outstanding bicolors. Continuous bloom from late spring through autumn.

Grandifloras are among the most recent classifications in rose groups; they are a cross between hybrid tea and floribunda. They exhibit positive characteristics of both of their parents, but they grow taller than either one of the two, ranging in height from 5 to 7 ft., and even taller in some cases. The flower form and the long stems are reminiscent of the hybrid tea parent, while the increased hardiness and continuous, abundant blooming come from the floribunda parent. Bloom sizes tend to be between the sizes of the two parents, and the flower may be single or multiple, though they are double in most cases. Because of their continuous bloom, the amount of bloom, and the size of the plants, majestic grandifloras may work best as background plants. Fragrance, when present, is relatively mild. Grandiflora makes a nice, tall screen for hiding certain areas. For an absolutely breathtaking planting, try tall grandifloras with the next-size-down rose group in front, and another next-size-down rose group in front of that. Grandifloras, hybrid teas, floribundas, and miniatures are all good for use in such a planting. Be sure to select the best varieties and pay attention to proper spacing, planting, and overall care.

WHEN TO PLANT

Plant in very early spring.

WHERE TO PLANT

Plant in prepared soil that receives at least 6 hours of full sun per day. Daylong full sun is best.

HOW TO PLANT

When planting container-grown grandifloras, plant no deeper than the top of the soilball. Bareroot roses should be planted no deeper than they were grown in a nursery row.

CARE AND MAINTENANCE

Prevent diseases and control insects if they become a problem. Ask about prevention and control possibilities. Remember, always read and follow label directions. Prune severely just before new spring growth. Maintain a moist soil, especially during the growing and blooming season. Fertilize as needed. Premium-quality long-lasting slow-release rose fertilizers work well. Follow label directions and water thoroughly after applying any fertilizer.

ADDITIONAL INFORMATION

If you want something different in your landscape, train one or more grandifloras into specimen types.

ADDITIONAL SPECIES, CULTIVARS, OR VARIETIES

Varieties of grandiflora include 'Arizona', 'Aquarius', 'Carrousel', 'Candy Apple', 'Ole', 'San Antonio', 'Love', 'Montezuma', 'Queen Elizabeth', 'Gold Medal', 'Buckaneer', 'Tournament of Roses', 'Mount Shasta', 'Pink Parfait', 'Camelot', 'Sonia', 'Caribbean', 'New Year', 'Shreveport', 'Prominent', 'Sundowner', 'White Lightnin', and 'Solitude'.

Hybrid Tea
Rosa

EXPOSURE

Full Sun

COLD HARDINESS

Protect @ 15° F.

WATER USAGE

Semi-Moist

GROWTH RATE

Fast

AVG. HT × WIDTH

3–6' × 3–4'

SPACING

3–4'

Color ranges from reds, oranges, and yellows to mixtures, blends, and almost everything in between. Bloom is continuous throughout the growing season, late spring through autumn.

*H*ybrid tea is parented by hybrid perpetuals and tea roses. This is a hybrid that came from lots of effort and decades of crossbreeding. Hybrid tea roses gain their fragrance and delicate look from the tea roses, and their hardiness and vigor from the hybrid perpetuals. Most blooms are fragrant and double, and they generally bloom throughout the entire growing season. Because they have a long, sturdy stem with one relatively large, fragrant, double blossom, these blooms are often sold in flower shops and on street corners. Hybrid tea roses are the rose group of choice for rose show enthusiasts.

WHEN TO PLANT
Plant bareroot selections in late winter/very early spring before they break dormancy. Container-grown plants may be planted in spring, summer, or fall, though early spring is best.

WHERE TO PLANT
Daylong full-sun locations are usually best, though you may plant in any moist, well-drained, fertile location that receives a minimum of 6 hours of sun per day.

How to Plant

Plant bareroot selections no deeper than they were growing in the nursery row. Container-grown roses should not be planted any deeper than the top of the individual plant's soilball. Make sure the soil is well prepared before planting.

Care and Maintenance

Control insects when needed, and prevent diseases. Ask about prevention and control possibilities. Read and follow label directions. Prune severely just before new growth in the spring. Many Texas home gardeners like to have all rose pruning completed by February 14, and some may start and finish on the same day. Experience has shown this late winter date to be a good "time-frame" choice for pruning these beauties. Water as needed to maintain a moist soil, especially during the growing and blooming season.

Additional Information

I have seen hybrid tea roses grown coast to coast and all over Texas. If you would like to have a show-type rose for your own personal use, try one, two, or more hybrid teas. They are worth the effort.

Additional Species, Cultivars, or Varieties

Varieties include 'Swathmore', 'Sweet Surrender', 'Toro', 'Touch of Class', 'Tropicana', 'Voodoo', 'White Masterpiece', 'Alabama', 'Alec's Red', 'Big Ben', 'Blue Moon', 'Bobby Charlton', 'Brandy', 'Broadway', 'Century II', 'Chicago', 'Christian Dior', 'Chrysler Imperial', 'Color Magic', 'Confidence', 'Dainty Bess', 'Die Welt', and 'Dolly Parton'. I saw Dolly Parton's pretty namesake rose at Dolly's theme park in Tennessee called Dollywood. Other varieties are 'Double Delight', 'Electron', 'Fascination', 'First Prize', 'Flaming Beauty', 'Folk Lore', 'Fragrant Cloud', 'Friendship', 'Party Time', 'Granada', 'Grand Masterpiece', 'Ivory Tower', 'Keepsake', 'Lady X', 'King's Ransom', 'Medallion', 'Milestone', 'Miss All-American Beauty', 'Mr. Lincoln', 'Mon Cheri', 'Olympiad', 'Orgeold', 'Paradise', 'Pascali', 'Peace', 'Perfume Delight', 'Peter Frankenfeld', 'Princesse de Maraco', 'Pristine', 'Red Lion', 'Red Masterpiece', 'Red Queen', 'Sea Shell', and 'Sun Bright'.

Lady Bank's Rose
Rosea banksiae

EXPOSURE

Full Sun

COLD HARDINESS

Protect @ 15° F.

WATER USAGE

Semi-Moist

GROWTH RATE

Fast

AVG. HT × WIDTH

20´ As Trained

SPACING

As Trained

Very narrow leaf petals and yellow or white fragrant blossoms.

While Lady Bank's is technically classified as a type of species rose, its growth habit makes it act much more like a vine. Bank's rose is one of the oldest roses that we use in our landscapes, dating back to the early 1800s. If your grandmother or your great-grandmother planted it, it is probably still growing in its original location. Bank's rose is predominantly light yellow in color and loaded with lots of blossoms in the early spring. A white variety is also available; it may be a bit more difficult to find, but it will reward you with a stronger fragrance. While the yellow is completely thornless, you may find an occasional thorn or two on the white. Bank's roses are excellent for a large arbor; they will cover it very densely and create a spectacular spot in the landscape. Bank's does not require support; it will stand on its own. It is excellent when used as a vine to cover any sort of relatively large garden structure you may have in your home landscape, or try letting it spill down a tall retaining wall.

WHEN TO PLANT
Bank's rose does well planted in the fall, but spring is also great for planting.

WHERE TO PLANT

Bank's roses need a minimum of 6 hours of full sun in order to do their very best for you, though they have been grown in less sunlight. They need a location where the soil drains well, and they prefer a location where the soil is deep, loose, and relatively fertile.

HOW TO PLANT

Bank's is a species rose, and will grow in less-than-ideal conditions. To achieve maximum growth from your Bank's rose, plant in a well-prepared bed. Incorporate approximately 3 in. of organic matter into the top 3 in. of the native soil. Remove plants from their containers and install them in your newly prepared location no deeper than they were grown in the containers. Firm the mixed soil well around the rootball. Water thoroughly, apply root stimulator according to label directions, and cover with 3 in. of bark mulch.

CARE AND MAINTENANCE

Bank's roses are generally free of pests and diseases, but if insects or diseases do become a problem with your planting, ask about the best control possibilities. Remember to read and follow label directions. Prune as necessary after spring bloom. These roses can be trained on any sort of structure—wood, steel, or a combination with wire. Whatever the structure, Lady Bank's will adapt well as long as you do the necessary training, which means pruning and tying. Water as necessary to prevent soil dryness, but do not overwater. Maintaining a thick layer of mulch is desirable. Fertilize in the spring as new growth begins with a premium-quality long-lasting slow-release rose food according to label directions. Reapply twice more throughout the growing season. Remember to water thoroughly after each application.

ADDITIONAL INFORMATION

Give your Lady Bank's adequate space to grow, for it can reach a substantial size. If you do not train it properly, it will virtually take over an area.

ADDITIONAL SPECIES, CULTIVARS, OR VARIETIES

Bank's yellow rose variety is *Lutea*. The white variety is 'Alba Plena'. The yellow variety is considered slightly more winter hardy than the white.

Miniatures
Rosa

EXPOSURE

Full Sun

COLD HARDINESS

Protect @ 15° F.

WATER USAGE

Semi-Moist

GROWTH RATE

Fast to Med.

AVG. HT × WIDTH

8"–2' × 12–24" (v.)

SPACING

12–18"

Miniature roses are available in a wide variety of colors. Continuous bloom.

*M*iniatures are the smallest of all roses, yet they have all of the characteristics of many of the larger roses. Scale of bloom, leaf size, and stem size are all reduced. Bloom sizes generally range from $1/2$ to $1^1/2$ in. across. Bloom colors are as wide and variable as the many colors available in other roses today. Miniatures are perfect for the gardener who loves roses but has limited space. People sometimes call in to my radio shows to ask about growing miniatures indoors. They can be grown indoors if you have a very sunny location, but they will be difficult to grow because of the reduced humidity. It is probably better to grow them outside, where they will be as hardy as their larger cousins. They may be planted in the ground or grown in containers outdoors. When temperatures drop below 20 degrees Fahrenheit, be sure to give them some protection, especially if temperatures will be in the mid-twenties or lower for an extended period. Miniature roses are excellent when used as borders around landscape shrubs, in front of perennials, or in front of their taller rose cousins. You may create a complete miniaturized rose garden using the various types of miniature roses available today. The gardener who has a zero-lot line or a townhome with limited space may happily plant an entire bed of the many mini roses.

WHEN TO PLANT

Plant in spring.

WHERE TO PLANT

Plant in full-sun locations or in areas that receive a minimum of 6 hours of full sun. If planting in large containers, you will be able to locate them in sunny spots to receive adequate amounts of sun. Never plant in heavily shaded locations.

HOW TO PLANT

For best results, plant in prepared full-sun beds. Container-grown selections should be planted soilball-deep. Bareroot plants should be planted at the same depth they were growing in the nursery.

CARE AND MAINTENANCE

Control insects and diseases as needed. Ask about control and prevention possibilities. Always read and follow label directions. Prune rather severely as new spring growth begins on all except the running forms. Prune the running forms after the bloom cycle is complete. Maintain a moist soil, especially during the growing and bloom season.

ADDITIONAL INFORMATION

Because of their small leaf, stem, and flower size, many Texas gardeners mistakenly think miniature roses are delicate roses, and they may decide not to grow them. In fact, miniature roses are as easy, if not easier to grow than many of their larger cousins.

ADDITIONAL SPECIES, CULTIVARS, OR VARIETIES

Climbing miniature roses include 'Merry Marshall, Cl.', 'Jackie, Cl.', 'Golden Song', 'Jazz Time', and 'Touch o' Midas'. Hanging container miniature roses include 'Sweet Chariot', 'Royal Carpet', 'Red Pendant', 'Red Cascade', 'Green Ice', and 'Pink Carpet'. Micro-minis are 'Trinket', 'Bo Peep', 'Cinderella', 'Lynne Gold', and 'Red Imp'. Bush varieties include 'Starina', 'Acey Deucy', 'Anne's Delight', 'Baby Katie', 'Beautyglo', 'Beauty Secret', 'Big John', 'Black Jack', 'Black Jade', 'Center Gold', 'Charmglow', 'Cupcake', 'Hula Girl', 'Little Jackie', 'Loveglo', 'Minnie Pearl', 'Loving Touch', 'Olympic Gold', 'Pacesetter', 'Peaches 'n' Cream', 'Rainbow's End', 'Simplex', 'Red Beauty', 'Red Love', 'Starglo', and 'Toy Clown'. Note: Cl. = climbing variety.

Old Garden
Rosa

EXPOSURE

Full Sun

COLD HARDINESS

Protect @ 15° F.

WATER USAGE

Semi-Moist

GROWTH RATE

Fast

AVG. HT × WIDTH

Varies

SPACING

Varies

Tend to be rather large bushes. They come in a variety of colors that are usually of a softer hue than modern roses. Many are available in white, pink, or red. Some bloom continuously.

*G*ardeners can become totally confused by rose classification, to a point where they are not really sure what they are planting. The definition and classification of roses is often subjective—it just depends on who is providing the information. Old garden roses are sometimes called heritage roses. Some believe that any roses found or introduced after 1867 cannot be considered old garden roses. Others feel that roses close to 80 years old and exhibiting the characteristics of old garden roses should be classified as old garden roses. One of those old garden characteristics is petal color: it tends to be less intense than that of many modern roses. Yet the outstanding fragrance is indisputable, and many of these roses have the large hips that can be harvested to make tea and even jellies. Unlike some of the modern roses, most old garden roses will do well on their own without regular pruning. They tend to be relatively low-maintenance roses. If you have seen roses in bloom in a long-abandoned homesite where no foundation remains, the garden was probably at one time planted with old garden roses. They do need room to grow and spread, so take that into consideration when selecting your planting sites. Among the sub-classifications in this group are alba, centifolia, damask, gallica, moss, tea, China, bourbon, Portland, noisette, and hybrid perpetual.

WHEN TO PLANT
Very early spring is the best time to plant.

WHERE TO PLANT
Plant in full-sun locations for best results, making sure they receive a minimum of 6 hours of sun per day. They will perform best if planted in improved soils, but they will survive in almost any Texas soil as long as it is well drained.

HOW TO PLANT
Plant container-grown selections no deeper than soilball depth. Bareroot selections should be planted no deeper than they were grown at the nursery.

CARE AND MAINTENANCE
Old garden roses require a minimum of pest and disease control and prevention. If you have running- or rambling-type old garden roses, prune after bloom as necessary. Bush-type roses require no special pruning unless you wish to shape or form them. If so, prune in early spring just before new growth. Water as needed to prevent soil dryness.

ADDITIONAL INFORMATION
Many things in the plant world are subjective. I think gardening should be for personal fun and enjoyment, including growing roses, so please don't become burdened with worrying about classifications. Plant the type of rose whose look and characteristics you enjoy. If you see a rose you want to purchase, ask these questions: *How tall does this plant get? How wide does this plant get? Does it have fragrance? Is it an old garden rose?* Ask before purchasing so you can enjoy the rose for many years.

ADDITIONAL SPECIES, CULTIVARS, OR VARIETIES
Try some of these varieties: 'Archduke Charles', 'Buff Beauty', 'Jacques Cartier', 'Maiden's Blush', 'Paul Neyron', 'Rose du Rui', 'Salet', Sombreuil', 'Belinda', 'Old Blush', 'Sparrieshoop', 'Yellow Lady Banks', 'Seven Sisters', 'Chestnut Rose', 'Prairie Rose', 'Safrano', 'Devonienis', 'Mary Van Houtte', 'Lady Hillingdon', 'Red Radiance', 'Radiance', 'Crimson Glory', 'Louise Odier', and 'Baroness Rothschild'.

Polyantha
Rosa

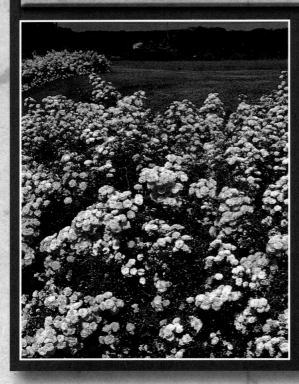

EXPOSURE

Full Sun

COLD HARDINESS

Protect @ 15° F.

WATER USAGE

Semi-Moist

GROWTH RATE

Fast to Med.

AVG. HT × WIDTH

2–5 ′ × 3–4 ′ (v.)

SPACING

2–4 ′

They come in wonderful pastel shades of orange, pink, and yellow, as well as white and red. Continuous bloom from spring through autumn.

*P*olyanthas are usually low-growing roses. Because of this low growth, they are ideal candidates for mass plantings, hedges, and borders, though some varieties such as 'La Marne' may reach 4 to 6 ft. in height. These roses have been in existence for many years. Their parentage is a combination of multiflora rosa and hybrid teas. "Polyantha" means "many flowers." Polyantha does produce many small flowers in great quantities, from spring till the first hard freeze hits in the fall. They are much hardier than their hybrid tea parent. They have very small, narrow leaves that are delicate-looking and finely textured; the leaves come from their multiflora parentage. The plants tend to be dwarf or compact, a quality that makes them good for container growing as well as for mass planting and use in borders. They have perfectly formed buds, which look wonderful in small bud vases. Their blooms are single, double, or semi-double, and come in colors that are less intense than those that characterize other modern roses such as their parent hybrid tea. Sometimes they are scented, sometimes not.

When to Plant
Plant in early spring for best results.

Where to Plant
Plant in well-prepared soil in full-sun locations; a minimum of 6 hrs. of full sun is needed. Polyantha roses are spectacular when planted where space is reduced yet a profusion of bloom is desired through the entire season. When planted in masses of single-variety colors, this is a show-stopping group of roses.

How to Plant
Plant container-grown varieties at soilball depth. Bareroot selections should be planted no deeper than they were grown at the nursery.

Care and Maintenance
Prevent disease and control insects as needed. Visit local nurseries for control and prevention possibilities. Always read and follow label directions. Prune severely just before new spring growth. Water as needed to maintain a moist soil, especially during the growing and blooming periods, and fertilize throughout this time. Premium-quality long-lasting slow-release rose fertilizer works well. Remember, read and follow label directions and water thoroughly after application of any fertilizer.

Additional Information
Certain selections of polyantha may need to be special-ordered.

Additional Species, Cultivars, or Varieties
The number of polyantha selections is smaller than that of many other roses, but the ones that are available make nice plantings. The varieties include 'China Doll', 'Cecile Brunner', 'Margo Koster', 'Pearl d' Or', 'The Fairy', 'Climbing Cecile Brunner', 'La Marne', 'Jean Mermoz', 'Garnette', 'Mother's Day', and 'Marie Pavie'.

Shrub
Rosa

EXPOSURE

Full Sun

COLD HARDINESS

Protect @ 15° F.

WATER USAGE

Semi-Moist

GROWTH RATE

Fast to Med.

AVG. HT × WIDTH

1-6 ′ × 4 ′

SPACING

3-4 ′

Blooms come in a variety of colors, including red, pink, and orange. Some bloom continuously, others bloom only once a year.

Shrub roses may serve as groundcovers, background plants, or mass plantings. Depending on the type and variety selected, they may be low-growing and used as a groundcover or may grow all the way up to 6 ft. Most have a large number of canes and extremely thick foliage. They have the same blooming characteristics as other types of roses. The flowers may be double, semi-double, or single; the blooms are often red, orange, or other typical rose colors. Some of the shrubs bloom only once, while others will bloom throughout the entire growing season. They tend to produce seedpods or hips after flowering. These rose hips, beloved by birds, are high in vitamin C and are often used to make rose tea. Shrub roses are wonderful, especially the lower-growing type, when allowed to grow over rock or brick walls; they are a good shrub for dividing areas; and the lower-growing type when planted in masses is quite eye-catching.

WHEN TO PLANT
Early spring is a great time to plant shrub roses.

WHERE TO PLANT

Plant in any location that receives a minimum of 6 hours of full sun, in well-prepared soil. Do not plant in heavily shaded areas or growth will be inferior. Screening hedges for privacy, direction, or any other purpose are easily created with shrub roses.

HOW TO PLANT

Plant bareroot plants no deeper than they were grown at the nursery. Container-grown selections should be planted at soilball depth.

CARE AND MAINTENANCE

Prevent diseases and control insects as needed. Ask about the best prevention and control possibilities. Remember, always read and follow label directions when using any garden aid. Prune as necessary to maintain desired shape, form, and size. Severe pruning is best done in early spring. Water to maintain a moist soil, especially during the growing and blooming season, and fertilize as desired throughout the season. Premium-quality long-lasting slow-release rose fertilizer works well. Follow label directions and water thoroughly after application. Generally speaking, shrub roses require minimal care.

ADDITIONAL INFORMATION

Certain varieties of shrub roses may be rooted directly on their own rootstock. Others may be budded or grafted onto another rootstock.

ADDITIONAL SPECIES, CULTIVARS, OR VARIETIES

The following are shrub roses you may wish to try: 'Othello', 'The Pilgrim', 'China Doll', Cl.', 'Orange 'N Lemons', 'Carefree Wonder', 'All That Jazz', 'Bonica', 'Carefree Beauty', 'Pink Meidiland', 'Blanc Double de Coubert', 'Red Meidiland', 'Seafoam', 'Belinda', 'Golden Wings', 'Blank Double', 'Decourbert', 'Hansa', 'F. J. Grootendorst', 'Pink Grootendorst', 'Sir Thomas Lipton', 'Teresa Bugnet', and 'Sparrieshoop'. Note: Cl. = climbing variety.

Species
Rosa

EXPOSURE

Full Sun

COLD HARDINESS

Protect @ 15° F.

WATER USAGE

Semi-Moist

GROWTH RATE

Fast

AVG. HT × WIDTH

4–20" × Varies

SPACING

3–8'

Species roses are the oldest rose group. They may be difficult to find, but they are worth searching for.

There are over 100 different species of roses all over the world. Some are shrubs, others are climbing or trailing. Species roses are basically roses that grow naturally in the wild, or are indigenous to particular areas. They may grow as low as 4 ft. or as high as 20 ft. Be sure to allow them plenty of room to grow to their maximum size. Most species roses are very fragrant, but not all are. They require a minimum of overall care and maintenance, which is one of the reasons they grow so well in their native habitats. The species rose most commonly used in Texas home landscapes may be *Rosa banksia* 'Lutea', commonly known as the "Yellow Lady Banks" rose. Remember that roses can hybridize while being grown in the wild. If you would like to make sure your rose is a definite species, it is worthwhile to visit members of a local Rose Society, or consult with rose enthusiasts in your area, especially those who are interested in heritage, old garden, or species roses. They should be able to help you with identification. Species roses are grown, in most cases, by specialized growers, and most of these reputable growers will also make sure that you are purchasing a true species rose.

WHEN TO PLANT

Early spring is a great planting time.

WHERE TO PLANT

Plant in full-sun locations for best results. Species roses should receive a minimum of 6 hours of full sun in order to do their best. While they will grow in virtually any native Texas soil, they benefit from improved soil preparation.

HOW TO PLANT

Plant container-grown selections at soilball depth. Bareroot plants should be planted at the same depth they were growing while being produced.

CARE AND MAINTENANCE

Minimum care is usually necessary for species roses. In order to enhance the overall vigor and blooming period of species roses, they benefit from watering, mulching, and fertilizing as other roses do. Normally no pruning is necessary. However, pruning may be performed if desired. Insects and diseases are usually not a problem for species roses.

ADDITIONAL INFORMATION

Species roses may be more difficult to find than other rose types. If you are a fan of roses in general and you'd like to be a plant hunter, species roses are worth the hunt.

ADDITIONAL SPECIES, CULTIVARS, OR VARIETIES

The following are some of the many (over 100) species roses you may wish to try: *R. banksiae* vars. 'Alba Plena' and 'Lutea'; *R. centifolia* or Cabbage Rose cvs. 'Cristata', 'Muscosa', 'Parvifolia' and 'Alba'; *R. eglanteria* or Eglantine or Sweetbriar, cv. 'Duplex'; *R. foetida* or Austrian Rose vars. 'Bicolor', 'Austrian Copper', 'Austrian Yellow', and 'Persiana', *R. gallica* or French Rose, cvs. 'Conditiorum', Pumila', and 'Complacata'; *R. laevigata* or Cherokee Rose; *R. moschata* or Musk Rose; *R. multiflora* including the cvs. 'Carnea', 'Platyphylla' or 'Seven Sisters', 'Japonica', and 'Nana'; *R. palustris* or Swamp Rose; *R. roxburghii* or Chinkapin Rose or Chestnut Rose; and *R. setigera* or Prairie Rose.

CHAPTER EIGHT

SHRUBS

SHRUBS CAN BE THOUGHT OF AS THE FURNITURE IN OUR HOME LANDSCAPES. We can move them around, arrange them, and dress up our foundations with them. They range from a dwarf height of only 12 in. up to tall shrubs that grow to 20 ft. or more.

It is strongly recommended that you ask the following questions when selecting shrubs.

- How tall and wide does this shrub grow in my area?

- Does it require full sun or will it grow in shaded areas? Morning sun/afternoon shade, daylong dappled sun/shade? What specific sun/shade conditions are best?

- Does it have blooms, and if so, what are the bloom colors? When does it bloom and for how long?

- Does it have any special soil requirements? Acid or alkaline soil, well-drained soil, deep soil, moist soil?

- Does it require special bed preparation? (For example, azalea nearly always requires special beds in Texas gardens.)

  If it is deciduous, ask these two additional questions:

- Does it have fall leaf color? If so, what are the colors?

- Are there any special conditions necessary to obtain these colors? (Special conditions might be a gradually cooling fall, sun/shade, relatively mild or harsh summers, or overall care.)

This information will help you decide whether to purchase or not and where to place a shrub in your landscape or outdoor room. If you are not interested in doing much pruning, select shrubs that will grow to desired height and width without requiring pruning.

When laying out your landscape beds at home, be sure to make them at least 5 ft. wide, wider in many cases. Improve the soil thoroughly before planting.

Chapter Eight

Once you have your bed laid out and the soil is prepared, determine where you wish to plant your shrubs by using the accurate information you have obtained as well as your own personal taste. You may find it helpful to draw a diagram of your home on 1/4-in. grid drafting paper. (One-quarter in. on paper will equal 1 ft. of your property). Draw your house on the paper, marking the windows, doors, and any existing plants and structures. You will be able to see the places that are suitable for planting new shrubs. If you don't feel comfortable putting together a plan, pay a visit to a landscape designer or landscape architect.

If you are purchasing a home with an existing landscape, it does not have to remain the same. We remodel our homes, repainting, recarpeting, rearranging furniture, adding rooms, and moving walls. You can do the same thing with the home landscape—if you don't like its looks, change it!

Some blooming shrubs bloom in the spring, some in the fall, and others bloom almost continuously. Two of the best blooming shrubs in Texas are abelia, *Abelia × grandiflora,* and crape myrtle, *Lagerstromeia indica.* If you are not sure how to determine a good-quality shrub and do not know a lot about shrub varieties, consult with your Lowe's customer service associate.

I have included 36 shrub families in this chapter; there's something for every Texas gardener's taste.

Abelia
Abelia × grandiflora

EXPOSURE

F. Sun to Semi-

COLD HARDINESS

All Texas

WATER USAGE

Semi-Moist

GROWTH RATE

Medium

AVG. HT × WIDTH

3–8′

SPACING

3–5′

Fountain and mounding forms. Blooms are white to a pinkish tint. Leaves are waxy and deep green to green, with a purplish tint that may change to bronze during the winter.

I'm just a kid at heart, and I enjoy the butterflies and birds that abelia attracts. This is an easy-to-grow family of flowering shrubs that add interest to landscapes with their foliage and blooms. Abelias are durable, often found in former homesites. Plants that survive this way in our Texas climate must have something desirable going for them. These are what my granny called "thrifty" plants: they go a long way on a little water. This was especially important to Granny because she had to carry all the water she applied to her Indian Creek garden. Thrifty also means tough, requiring minimum care.

WHEN TO PLANT
In Zones 7A, 7B, 8A, 8B, 9A, and 9B, plant any time of the year. In Zones 6A and 6B, plant early spring through early fall.

WHERE TO PLANT
Abelias grow in light sandy soils or heavy clay when located in full sun. Do not plant in wet, poorly drained, or shady locations.

How to Plant

For foundation plantings, install in beds 5 ft. wide tilled with 4 to 6 in. of organic matter. Individual planting holes may be dug as wide as desired, but no deeper than the soilball. After placement in the hole, backfill, water thoroughly, apply a root stimulator, and cover with 3 to 4 in. of an organic mulch such as pine, fir, or hardwood bark.

Care and Maintenance

This plant has no serious pests. Disease is not a problem in full-sun locations that have good air movement. If you live in an area with high humidity and plant abelia against a solid fence, leaf spot or powdery mildew may occur, though I lived in Tyler for a decade and never experienced disease problems with abelia. If you experience such problems, they will probably be minor and easily controlled with widely available fungicides. Remember, always read and follow label directions. Prune as desired to maintain the shape you want, but please don't make a boxed hedge out of this shrub. Abelias will take rather severe pruning and come back with more blooms on the new growth. Early spring is best for radical pruning, and selective pruning may be done throughout the growing season. Don't prune after September. Water as needed to maintain soil moisture; deep and infrequent irrigation is preferred over light, frequent applications. Drip irrigation works very well, and maintaining a thick mulch will conserve soil moisture. I use 3 to 4 in. of pine bark mulch. I fertilize with premium-quality slow-release rose or lawn granular fertilizers according to label directions. The amount to apply will depend on the analysis used: read the label. If you live along the Gulf Coast, first apply around March 15; in Central Texas, March 21; and in North Texas, including the High Plains, April 1. Reapply twice during the growing season for optimum growth and once again in the fall. For a less aggressive fertilizer plan, apply only in spring and early fall.

Additional Information

Abelia is great as tall, wide-blooming shrubs. Do not plant in front of porches, low windows, narrow beds, or in limited spaces, because they will soon outgrow these areas.

Additional Species, Cultivars, or Varieties

Abelia grandiflora, or glossy abelia, is the tallest-growing and oldest abelia we commonly use. 'Compacta' is a favorite of ours. Our 15-year-old planting is 4 ft. by 4 ft. 'Frances Mason' is a variegated cultivar. 'Edward Goucher' is semievergreen in some areas, has small clear-pink blooms, and grows 3 to 5 ft. tall. White-flowered 'Prostrata' is the lowest, with a height and width of 3 ft. 'Sunrise' is a recently patented variety with cream-and-pink variegated foliage, which is small and mounding in form.

Althea
Hibiscus syriacus

EXPOSURE

Full Sun

COLD HARDINESS

All Texas

WATER USAGE

Arid to Semi-Mst.

GROWTH RATE

Fast

AVG. HT × WIDTH

8–12′ × 3–6′

SPACING

6–12′

Bright-green serrated leaves. Upright deciduous shrub. Blooms are white, pink, red, purple, and blends in singles and doubles.

Althea, also known as rose of Sharon, is another of the old-fashioned landscape plants that have been around as long as I can remember in my parents' and grandparents' landscapes. Altheas are great summer color plants which can be used as tree forms, accomplished by selective pruning. In this form they are excellent patio trees. Unpruned, they tend to grow into tall, upright, bushy shrubs.

WHEN TO PLANT
Althea is hardy in Zone 6. From Baily to Wheeler County in the Panhandle, plant in very early spring. In the rest of Texas, plant any time you desire. Fall is a great time.

WHERE TO PLANT
Plant in a location with a minimum of 6 hours of full sun, though they do best in daylong full-sun locations. Do not plant in full-shade locations or where soil drainage is poor. They will grow in the soils of Amarillo, Lubbock, Abilene, El Paso, San Antonio, Houston, Austin, Tyler, Dallas/Ft.Worth, and others that drain well.

How to Plant

If you intend to use althea as a summer-blooming screening planting, plant in a well-prepared bed. Here's how: measure the area in length and calculate at least one plant for every 6 ft. Make your bed at least 5 ft. wide. Remove any rocks, sticks, and weeds, and till the area. Add 4 to 6 in. of organic matter and till again. Plant in the center of the bed: dig the planting holes as deep as the plant's soilball and no deeper. Install the plants, backfill, and water thoroughly. Apply a root stimulator and 3 to 4 inches of an organic mulch. I use pine bark mulch.

Care and Maintenance

Aphids may occasionally visit tender new leaf growth, but this usually isn't much of a problem. During July and August when the humidity is usually very low, spider mites may become a problem. There are products available to control aphids and spider mites. Remember to read and follow label directions. These summer bloomers respond very positively to good fertilization programs. I prefer a premium-quality slow-release granular rose food. In Zone 9, make the first application around March 1; Zone 8, mid-March to April 1; Zone 7, April 1; and Zone 6, April 1 to mid-April. Reapply approximately every 6 to 8 weeks through early fall. For a less aggressive program, fertilize only in spring and fall. Remember to water plants thoroughly after fertilizers are applied. Maintaining a 3- to 4-in. mulch blanket is beneficial to your altheas.

Additional Information

As tropical hibiscus *Hibiscus rosa-sinensis* is often used for summer color, altheas trained as tree forms may be used in large containers.

Additional Species, Cultivars, or Varieties

'Diana', my favorite, is a beautiful single variety that is large and pure-white. This is a United States National Arboretum release. Some other U.S.N.A. selected releases are 'Aphrodite', which is deep rose-pink with a showy deep-red center; 'Helene', pure white with a deep reddish purple center; and 'Minerva', a lavender-pink variety with a reddish purple center. Non-U.S.N.A. releases include: 'Blushing Bride' (a double pink), 'Collie Mullens' (a double purple-lavender), 'Blue Bird' (a single blue), 'Admiral Dewy' (a single pure white), 'Rubis' (a single red), and 'Hamabo' (a pale pink single with red stripes).

Aralia
Fatsia japonica

EXPOSURE

Shade to Semi-

COLD HARDINESS

To 10° F.

WATER USAGE

Semi-Moist

GROWTH RATE

Fast

AVG. HT × WIDTH

4–5' × 4–5'

SPACING

3–4'

Leaves are large, deep green, waxy, deeply cut, and very showy. Lends a tropical effect. Grown for foliage.

*W*e Texas gardeners love shade, but if an entire property is shaded, the selection of landscape planting materials is limited. If I suggest, even in jest, that a caller to my live call-in radio show cut down trees to get more light, I usually hear a moan, sigh, or some other response that lets me know that the suggestion is unacceptable. Aralia, or fatsia, is known by several names in catalogs, advertisements, books, and nurseries. The scientific names are usually *Fatsia japonica* or *Aralia seboldi*, sometimes *Aralia japonica*. All of these names will lead you to the same plant.

WHEN TO PLANT
In Zone 8A, plant in early spring through early fall. In Zones 8B, 9A, and 9B, plant anytime; fall is a great time to plant.

WHERE TO PLANT
These outstanding shrubs do best in shady areas. They will not grow well in western full sun or hot, dry, windy locations. An eastern exposure with sun until 10 a.m., or daylong dappled sun, should be fine. Aralia works well as a

corner foundation planting. Use as a mass background planting in shady bed locations with ferns to create a pleasing effect under trees.

HOW TO PLANT

Unlike most shrubs, aralia will tolerate a relatively poorly drained clay or sandy soil. This does not mean this type of soil is a preferred growing condition, but aralia will put up with it. To maximize growth, invest the time, energy, and funds necessary to improve your soil before planting. The addition of compost, brown sphagnum peat moss, ground bark, and similar organic materials to the native soil is highly recommended. If you decide to develop beds around trees, don't add soil to these beds; just blend organic matter with the native soil between the roots. Don't destroy or damage roots with a tiller; handwork is best to help you achieve your goal. Plant no deeper than the plant's rootball, backfill with loose soil, and apply root stimulator. Water thoroughly and cover with 3 to 4 in. of your favorite bark mulch.

CARE AND MAINTENANCE

Keep moist but not wet. This plant has no serious pests. Aralia responds with vigor to a good fertilization program. Use a 3:1:2 ratio premium-quality long-lasting lawn fertilizer such as 15-5-10, 19-5-9, and 18-6-12. Note: These are the fertilizers often recommended for our Bermuda and St. Augustine lawns in Texas. Don't use agricultural-grade fertilizers or any with herbicides. In Zones 9A and 9B, make your first application around mid-March; in Zones 8A and 8B, around April 1. Apply approximately every 6 to 8 weeks through early fall. For a less aggressive fertilization program, fertilize in spring and early fall only. Remember to water thoroughly after fertilizing.

ADDITIONAL INFORMATION

If you are looking for an unusual plant for shady areas in your landscape, give aralia a try. It works well with ferns and aucuba to create interesting tropical effects. You may also use aralia singularly or in combination with aucuba and ferns in large containers.

ADDITIONAL SPECIES, CULTIVARS, OR VARIETIES

'Moseri' is a more compact form, and 'Variegata' has creamy white leaf margins. 'Fatshedera' is a similarly used plant. It is a hybrid of English ivy, or *Hedera helix*, and *Fatsia japonica*.

Arborvitae

Thuja orientalis and *Thuja occidentalis*

EXPOSURE

Full Sun

COLD HARDINESS

All Texas

WATER USAGE

Semi-Moist

GROWTH RATE

Slow to Med.

AVG. HT × WIDTH

Varies

SPACING

Varies

T. orientalis: Upright, dense, more oval-shaped than cone-shaped. Bright-green leaves.
T. occidentalis: Upright growth is loosely arranged and open. Medium- to dark-green leaves.

*O*riental arborvitae, Chinese arborvitae, and eastern arborvitae are all common names for the different types of this plant. If you have seen arborvitae plants in abandoned homesites or nurseries, these are most likely Chinese arborvitae. They are exceptionally tough and will grow just about anywhere. The eastern arborvitae grows best in Texas in an area from Wichita County along the Red River south-southeast to Blanco County in Central Texas and northeast to Sabine County along the border.

WHEN TO PLANT

Fall is a great time to plant, but plant any time of the year you desire.

WHERE TO PLANT

Arborvitae is best used as tall screening, windbreak, or specimen plantings. I would not use it as foundation plantings. It grows in all Texas soils, including loose blow sand and compact clay. The eastern arborvitaes do better when protected from drying southwestern summer winds. Chinese arborvitaes will take any exposure, including drying winds. Both types prefer rich, moist, fertile soils.

How to Plant

When planting in beds, first till 4 to 6 in. of organic matter into the soil. For the larger-growing specimens or tall screen plantings, pick the best location and plant individually in the loosened native soil. Whether planting in beds or individually, dig the plant's hole no deeper than the soilball, but loosen the soil as wide as desired. After setting the plants into their new homes, backfill, water thoroughly, apply root stimulator, and cover with 3 to 4 in. of a bark mulch. I use pine bark mulch.

Care and Maintenance

Juniper blight, spider mites, and bagworms are more of a problem on Oriental than on eastern varieties. The gardening aid industry has products to help control these. An unusual positive attribute of arborvitaes is that they may be sheared into all sorts of shapes, including animals. So if you are interested in some clipped plantings, either very formal or "unusual," try arborvitae! Fertilize in early spring: in Zones 9A and 9B around March 1; Zones 8A and 8B in mid-March; Zones 7A and 7B on April 1; and Zones 6A and 6B in mid-April. Use favorite brands of premium-quality slow-release lawn fertilizer that have the 3:1:2 ratio recommended for St. Augustine and Bermuda lawns (such as 21-7-14 and 15-5-10). Be sure to water thoroughly after each application. After a spring application of fertilizer, reapply in mid-growing season, and in the fall. Make sure there are no herbicides in the fertilizer you use. Water as needed to maintain sufficient moisture for growth: to maximize growth and water usage, install a drip water system. Maintain a 3- to 4-in. layer of bark mulch year-round to help conserve moisture and control weed competition as well as moderate soil temperatures.

Additional Information

Be sure you know an arborvitae's ultimate height and width before placing in your landscape. Some varieties can quickly overgrow their locations.

Additional Species, Cultivars, or Varieties

T. occidentalis 'Golden Globe' is 4 ft. tall and wide; 'Holstrup' is 5 to 7 ft. tall and 2 to 3 ft. wide; 'Little Giant' is 6 ft. high and wide; 'Dark American' is 20 to 30 ft. tall and 5 to 10 ft. high. *T. orientalis* 'Aurea Nana' is 4 to 6 ft. high and 3 to 5 ft. wide; 'Blue Cone' is 8 ft. high and 4 ft. wide; 'Westmont' is 3 ft. high and 2 ft. wide; 'Minima Glauca' is 3 to 4 ft. high and wide.

Aucuba or Gold Dust Plant
Aucuba japonica

EXPOSURE

Shade

COLD HARDINESS

To 0° F. (v.)

WATER USAGE

Moist to Semi-Mst.

GROWTH RATE

Medium

AVG. HT × WIDTH

4–8' × 4–6'

SPACING

6–10'

Tropical-looking evergreen. Upright and oval in form. Leaves are waxy, dense, relatively coarse, and usually deep green with various patterns of yellow-gold.

*I*currently have two 20-gal. containers of aucuba, which I use for seasonal shady color. Diversity is easily accomplished by using different colors in containers each season, or anytime during the season you want a change. Aucuba cannot build up the ability to take direct sun, and it sunburns badly: the color drains out of the leaves, which eventually turn black. If your aucubas get sunburned, do not try to nurse them through the problem—move them! Either relocate them or construct a shade.

WHEN TO PLANT
Plant any time of the year you are in the mood for some color in shady situations. Fall is a great time to plant.

WHERE TO PLANT
Plant on any side of your property as long as it's shady. Aucubas make wonderful tall foundation plantings. Don't place in front of a low window, porch, or entry unless you want them covered up. Try planting on the inside of a protected courtyard, atrium, or solarium. They also lend themselves well to containerized culture.

How to Plant

Aucubas will grow in heavy clay or sandy soils. They prefer a moist growing condition but will not tolerate constantly wet soil. Do not plant in a poorly drained area. When I plant these shade-loving jewels, I make sure the soil is thoroughly improved. Remove rocks, sticks, and weeds before adding any organic matter. Till the area to be planted, add 4 to 6 in. of high-quality organic matter such as compost, ground bark, brown sphagnum peat moss, and/or similar materials, and till again. I prefer to add approximately 2 in. of compost, peat, and bark, blending them thoroughly with the existing native soil. Be sure to make beds at least 5 ft. wide. Planting holes should be no deeper than the plant's soilball. After setting plants in their new homes, backfill with planting mix, water thoroughly, apply a root stimulator, and mulch.

Care and Maintenance

This plant has no serious pests. Maintain a moist but not wet soil throughout the growing season. Keep a mulch of 3 to 4 in. in the beds year-round. Aucubas respond to light applications of a 15-5-10 or 21-7-14 premium-quality slow-release lawn fertilizer. In Zones 9A and 9B, fertilize around March 1; in Zones 8A and 8B, mid-March; in Zone 7A, April 1. Be sure to water thoroughly after each fertilizer application.

Additional Information

Prune selectively—pruning scars remain visible longer on aucuba than on most landscape plants.

Additional Species, Cultivars, or Varieties

'Mr. Goldspike' has dark-green leaves splashed with gold. 'Picturata' has lots of bright gold-yellow centers on its leaves. 'Sulfur' has wide golden leaf edges. 'Variegata' is dark glossy green with specks of gold, and compact. 'Serratifolia' has serrated solid-green leaves with showy red fall berries.

Azalea

Rhododendron spp.

EXPOSURE

F. Sun to Semi-

COLD HARDINESS

All Texas (v.)

WATER USAGE

Semi-Moist

GROWTH RATE

Medium

AVG. HT × WIDTH

3–10' × 3–8'

SPACING

Varies

Mounded irregular semievergreen to evergreen spring-blooming shrubs. Dull, hairy, medium- to dark-green leaves, often changing to unusual winter colors.

*F*or outstanding spring color, these beauties are hard to beat. They require more effort than many shrubs, but the rewards often exceed the requirements. Azaleas are members of the rhododendron family, and have some of its typical characteristics. There are several types of azalea that do well in Texas. The kurumes, which include 'Coral Bells', 'Hino-Crimson', and 'Flame', are hardy into the Panhandle's Zone 6B. They will also grow in all other Texas zones. The southern indicas are hardy in Zones 8A, 8B, 9A, and 9B. These include 'George L. Tabor', 'Fielder's White', and 'Formosa'. The satsukis are hardy in Texas Zones 7A, 7B, 8A, 8B, 9A, and 9B. These include 'Higasa', 'Macrantha', and 'Pink Gumpo'.

WHEN TO PLANT

Plant in early spring through fall in Zones 6A, 6B, and 7A. In Zones 7B, 8A, 8B, 9A, and 9B, plant any time.

WHERE TO PLANT

Depending on the type, azaleas may be planted under low windows or used as tall specimens. The kurumes and satsukis benefit from shade. Southern indicas will grow well in full sun. Azaleas need an acid soil that drains well. Don't plant in heavy clay soils, poorly drained soils, or those with a high-alkaline pH.

HOW TO PLANT

These beauties perform best in naturally occurring sandy acid soils amended with organic matter. In heavy clay soils, remove 12 in. of soil, backfill with a 50/50 mixture of brown peat moss and pine bark mulch, and raise the bed an additional 6 in. above the grade. Azaleas are shallow fibrous-rooted plants that require moist soil but will not tolerate "wet feet" or poorly drained soils. Organic matter like brown sphagnum peat moss and pine bark mulch help improve moisture-holding capacity, acidify the soil, and improve drainage, so don't forget to add plenty. Plant azaleas in thoroughly prepared, raised, 5-ft.-wide beds. Dig planting holes the depth of the plant's soilball and install. Backfill with planting mix, apply root stimulator, water thoroughly, and cover with 3 to 4 in. of pine bark mulch.

CARE AND MAINTENANCE

Mites, lace bugs, and scale are potential pests. Leaf gall, leaf spots, and flower or petal blight are potential diseases. Chlorosis is also possible. Keeping plants in a healthy state will prevent most pests and diseases. If any of these do become a problem, the gardening aid industry has specific products available to arrest them. Contact your County Agent's office to identify problems and obtain recommendations for treatments. Keep soil moist but not wet. Fertilize after bloom drop, mid-season, and early fall with granular azalea fertilizer according to label directions, and water thoroughly.

ADDITIONAL INFORMATION

These are great spring color plants, but don't plant unless you plan to spend time, energy, and funds to take care of them for a long time.

ADDITIONAL SPECIES, CULTIVARS, OR VARIETIES

You may want to try the following, along with many other cultivated varieties. Kurume: 'Hershey Red', 'Hino Crimson', 'Lavender Queen', 'Mildred', 'Orange Cup', 'Pink Pearl', 'Salmon Beauty', 'Sherwood Red', and 'Snow'. Southern indica: 'Daphne Salmon', 'Fisher Pink', 'Judge Solomon', 'President Clay', 'Pride of Mobile', and 'Mrs. G. G. Gerbin'. Satsuki: 'White Gumpo', 'Pink Gumpo', 'Keisetsu', 'Myogi', and 'Pink Macrantha'. The 'Encore Series' blooms in spring and fall.

Barberry
Berberis thunbergii

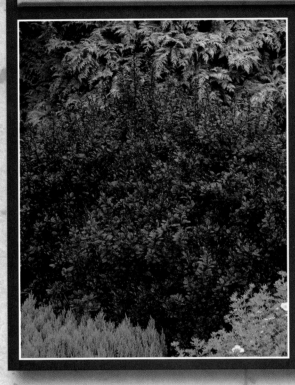

EXPOSURE	COLD HARDINESS
F. Sun to Semi-	To -30° F. (v.)
WATER USAGE	**GROWTH RATE**
Moist to Arid-Dry	Medium
AVG. HT × WIDTH	**SPACING**
1½–6′ × 2–7′	3–8′

Showy evergreen, semiever-green, and deciduous shrubs that are dense and rounded. Leaves are green to maroon to purple-black, changing to red and amber to crimson in the fall.

Most barberry shrubs are in the *B. thunbergii* group. The ones I am most familiar with are all deciduous. However, there are some interesting ever-green varieties. These are tough, durable, low-care plants that add interesting spots of color to the landscape. They can take both Texas heat and cold (what a deal!), though they will not do well in prolonged dry spells. They do best in moist, fertile beds that are neither too wet nor poorly drained. They are especially useful in color accent beds.

WHEN TO PLANT
Plant any time you like. Fall is a great time.

WHERE TO PLANT
All species and cultivars do best in full sun for growth and color. Don't plant in any location that is poorly drained or that receives less that 6 hours of full sun. For the best effect, mass planting is recommended. Multiple off-set rows also work well in specific applications.

How to Plant

Remove sticks, rocks, weeds, and turfgrass from a sunny location. Till the area to be planted, add 6 in. of organic matter, and blend thoroughly by tilling again with the native soil. Make beds a minimum of 5 ft. wide, larger if possible. Determine the number of plants needed based on the area to be covered and the ultimate width of the selection. Dig planting holes as deep as the plant's soil-ball (no deeper) and set the plants into their new homes. Backfill, water thoroughly, apply root stimulator, and mulch with your favorite bark mulch or similar material. I usually use pine bark.

Care and Maintenance

Aphids may visit the new growth, but they usually aren't much of a problem. Should they become one, there is a wide assortment of products available to help you. Remember to read and follow label directions on any product. Root rot may be a problem in wet locations. The best solution is to simply not plant in those areas. A drip irrigation system is ideal for maintaining a moist, but not wet, soil. It may also save 50 percent on your water bill. Fertilize during the spring approximately 2 weeks after your last killing frost. Fertilize twice more during the growing season, and once in the fall. A premium-quality slow-release lawn fertilizer such as 21-7-14, 15-5-10, or any other that meets the 3:1:2 ratio analysis, works well. Be sure to read and follow label directions and water thoroughly after each application. Prune as desired during the growing season.

Additional Information

Barberry is best used as special plantings in color beds. There are exceptions, however: a couple of good varities to be used as foundation plantings are *B. buxifolia* 'Nana', a 1½- by 2-ft. evergreen, and *B. × gladwynensis* 'William Penn', a 4- by 4- to 5-ft. evergreen.

Additional Species, Cultivars, or Varieties

You may wish to try *B. × mentorensis*, or mentor barberry, which is semievergreen. *B. thunbergii*, 'Atropurpurea', 'Aurea', 'Monomb', 'Crimson Pygmy', 'Kobold', 'Rose Glow', and 'Sparkle' are others worth trying.

Boxwood
Buxus microphylla

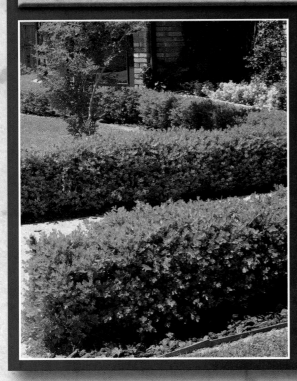

EXPOSURE	COLD HARDINESS
Full to Semi-	0° to -10° (v.)

WATER USAGE	GROWTH RATE
Semi-Moist	Medium

AVG. HT × WIDTH	SPACING
1–20 ′ × 1¹/₂–6 ′ (v.)	3–10 ′ (v.)

Upright, oval, evergreen shrub. Leaves are medium to dark green.

*B*oxwood is the shrub of choice for training into formal clipped hedges. *B. microphylla* is the largest shrub group and contains the popular bright-green Japanese boxwood, which is hardy in both Zones 7A and 7B, but does better in Zones 8A, 8B, 9A, and 9B. The other varieties of *B. microphylla* are hardy anywhere in our state. *B. microphylla* 'Winter Gem' has dark-green foliage year-round with small, oval-shaped leaves. I've planted it in two full-sun locations, one southeast and the other due west.

WHEN TO PLANT
The American Association of Nurserymen (AAN) says, "Fall is for planting," and I agree that fall is a good time for planting boxwood— but you may actually plant it any time of the year.

WHERE TO PLANT
Some boxwoods such as *B. microphylla* 'Koreana' are great dwarf shrubs, while others are relatively tall. *B. sempervirens* 'Arborescens' may reach 10 to 12 ft. in height. Be sure you ask how high and wide the selections of boxwood you are

interested in normally grow in your area. There are usually one or more boxwoods that will fit specific spots in your landscape. Do not plant in poorly drained soils or where the shrubs will receive reflected heat from a driveway or west walls in full sun. Boxwoods are good choices for shady locations; most prefer shade from the hot western sun.

HOW TO PLANT

The versatile boxwood may be used as foundation plantings, screens, or specimens. For foundation or other "bed" plantings, remove all sticks, rocks, weeds, and turfgrass from the area to be planted and till the area. I find a rear tine tiller works best. Such tillers are available at most tool rental dealers across the state. After the initial tilling, add 2 in. each of brown sphagnum peat moss, compost, and ground pine bark. Thoroughly till these materials into the native soil, and you are ready to plant. Remember to make all your foundation beds a minimum of 5 ft. wide, and dig planting holes no deeper that the plant's soilball. After setting the plants in their new homes, backfill, water thoroughly, apply root stimulator, and cover with 2 to 3 in. of your favorite bark mulch. I usually use pine bark mulch.

CARE AND MAINTENANCE

If your soil has root knot nematodes, don't plant boxwood; dwarf yaupon holly is a better choice. You may have your soil tested for these pests by the Texas Agricultural Extension Service. Leaf miners and spider mites may visit, but they usually don't cause problems for healthy plants. Control products and help are available. Your County Agent may assist you if pest or disease problems are suspected. Keep soil moist but not wet. Boxwood must drain well or root rot may occur. Fertilize 2 weeks after your last killing frost, twice more during the growing season, and once again in the fall. I use a premium-quality slow-release 15-5-10, 21-7-14, or similar 3:1:2 ratio lawn fertilizer. Water thoroughly after each application.

ADDITIONAL INFORMATION

'Green Velvet', 'Winter Gem', Japanese, and 'Green Mountain' are the better selections for shady locations.

ADDITIONAL SPECIES, CULTIVARS, OR VARIETIES

B. harlandii is harlandi or Korean boxwood; *B. sempervirens* is English boxwood, the boxwood of old England and France.

Burning Bush

Euonymus alata

EXPOSURE

F. Sun to Semi-

COLD HARDINESS

All Texas

WATER USAGE

Semi-Moist

GROWTH RATE

Slow to Med. (v.)

AVG. HT × WIDTH

6–10 ′ × 4–12 ′ (v.)

SPACING

5–20 ′ (v.)

This densely-branched deciduous plant has deep-green leaves that may take on a flat-topped appearance.

*B*urning bush is a show-stopper. If you want fall color in your landscape this tough, durable, and easy-to-grow shrub is for you. Their growth rate is moderate to slow, so these shrubs require minimal pruning. Try them as background plantings in that color bed you have been thinking about developing near your mailbox. They also work well as plantings in sunny locations for viewing from inside your home.

WHEN TO PLANT

Burning bush is hardy in Zone 3, which is along the Canadian border. Because of this hardiness it may be planted anytime. Fall is a good planting time.

WHERE TO PLANT

Burning bush is suitable for use as a screening hedge. For a super look, plant in front of dark-green broadleaf evergreen shrubs, such as tall-growing holly. They also lend themselves well to large tubs or containerized culture. Burning bush may be trained into a multiple-stemmed small tree suitable for sunny patios and other limited-space applications. It will grow in almost any soil condition, including moderately moist to moderately dry. It does best in moist, well-drained, fertile soils and full-sun locations. For best growth and fall color, don't plant in areas with less than 6 hours of full sun.

HOW TO PLANT

If you want success the first time you plant or transplant a shrub, then burning bush is for you. Remove any turfgrass, weeds, rocks, and sticks from the area to be planted and till the native soil. This will probably be sufficient soil preparation, but I'd add around 4 in. of organic matter and till again. In heavy clay soils I might even add 6 in. After the soil is prepared you will be ready to plant. If you plan to use burning bush as a foundation planting, background planting, or hedge, or in front of other landscape shrubs, make the beds at least 5 ft. wide. A spacing of 3 to 4 ft. should work well in most bed applications. After digging the hole no deeper than the soilball, set the plant in its new home and backfill. Water thoroughly, apply a root stimulator, and cover with 3 to 4 in. of a bark mulch.

CARE AND MAINTENANCE

Burning bush has no serious pests or diseases. Water as needed to prevent soil from drying out. Prune as desired; spring is best for radical pruning. Fertilize with a 15-5-10 or similar 3:1:2 ratio pre-mium-quality slow-release lawn fertilizer according to label directions. Administer spring applications 2 weeks after the last killing frost date, twice more during the growing season, and once in the fall. Water thoroughly after each application

ADDITION INFORMATION

You won't find a more winter hardy or colorful shrub for Texas landscapes.

ADDITIONAL SPECIES, CULTIVARS, OR VARIETIES

E. alta 'Compacta' is slow growing and compact, sometimes called dwarf. Occasionally this dwarf may grow 5 to 6 ft. tall.

Butterfly Bush
Buddleia davidii

EXPOSURE

Full Sun

COLD HARDINESS

To -20° F.

WATER USAGE

Semi-Mst.

GROWTH RATE

Fast

AVG. HT × WIDTH

3–10 ′ × 4–6 ′

SPACING

6–10 ′

A many-branched deciduous shrub with long, slender, dark-green leaves and fragrant flowers on long spikes.

As the name implies, butterflies like this shrub. If you are looking for a shrub family that has wonderful summer color and fragrance and attracts Mother Nature's flying living color, buddleia is for you! Its bloom colors range from pure white to bright pink to deep purple-black. All those that I've had the pleasure of visiting up close and personal have been fragrant. For summer blooms in a perennial bed, large border plantings, or use in masses, you'd have a hard time finding a better choice.

WHEN TO PLANT
Buddleia is hardy even in Zone 5, so it is definitely "Texas-hardy." This means you can plant any time you wish, though I find early spring to be the best planting time.

WHERE TO PLANT
I do not endorse the use of butterfly bush as a foundation planting. I highly recommend its use as mass bed plantings and in combination with perennials or relatively large blooming specimens. I have buddleia among perennials and

blooming natives adjacent to our deck, and they are great! Make sure the location you select is in full sun, well drained, and fertile for best growth and bloom. Don't plant in areas that are poorly drained or receive less than 6 hours of full sun.

HOW TO PLANT

Remove any weeds, turfgrass, rocks, and sticks. Till the area and add 4 to 6 in. of organic matter such as compost, brown peat moss, or ground pine bark, then till again. After the second tilling, you should be ready to plant. Ask how wide your selected variety normally grows. This will determine your spacing as well as the number of plants. Remember to make your bed a minimum of 5 ft. wide, larger if possible. Dig planting holes no deeper than the soilball, but as wide as desired. Plug in plant, backfill, and water thoroughly. Apply root stimulator and cover with 3 to 4 in. of your favorite bark mulch (I usually use pine).

CARE AND MAINTENANCE

Butterfly bush has no serious disease or insect problems. Water as needed to keep the soil from drying out. More frequent watering is needed during the first year, less in the following years. Never allow the plant's rootball to dry out. A premium-quality slow-release granular rose fertilizer is an ideal choice to nourish buddleia. Apply according to label directions when new growth begins in the spring, twice during the growing season, and once again in the fall. Water thoroughly after each fertilizer application. You may prune to shape during the growing season, and it may be radically pruned just before new spring growth if desired.

ADDITIONAL INFORMATION

No matter where you live in our great gardening state, you owe yourself the treat of growing one or more buddleia. At least give one a trial for a couple of years.

ADDITIONAL SPECIES, CULTIVARS, OR VARIETIES

Any of the following varieties of B. davidii are worth trying: 'Black Knight', 'Ile De France', 'Pink Delight', 'Royal Red', 'White Bouquet', 'White Profusion', and 'Harlequin'. You may also want to try these varieties of B. nanhoensis, or compact butterfly bush: 'Nano Blue', 'Nano Purple', 'Monum', and 'Mongo'. For more buddleias check out wooly butterfly bush under Native Shrubs.

Camellia
Camellia japonica

EXPOSURE

Semi-Shade

COLD HARDINESS

To 0° F. (v.)

WATER USAGE

Moist/Semi-Mst.

GROWTH RATE

Medium

AVG. HT × WIDTH

Varies

SPACING

Varies

Shape is generally pyramidal with relatively loose, many-branched, upright to arching stems. Evergreen.

*G*reat blooming shrubs from Texarkana to Presidio, and points southeast of this line, camellias offer outstanding, beautiful blooms. These shrubs are favorites of Casey Kasem, Bob Hope, General George Patton, and Elizabeth Arden, to name a few. With proper care, camellias are very long lived, so not only are you planting for enjoyment today, but perhaps for generations to come. Blooms come in very showy reds, pinks, whites, roses, and blends. Bloom shapes are labeled as single, semidouble, formal double, peony form, anemone form, and rose form. Sizes range from 2½ to over 5 in. across. Super! Camellias are to some Texas gardeners as rhododendrons are to other areas of the country—outstanding landscape color shrubs. Unless your home is exceptionally tall or you plan to keep *Camellia japonica* pruned, don't install camellias as foundation plantings.

WHEN TO PLANT

I prefer spring or fall plantings. They may be planted in the summer in northern parts of Zone 8A, and in winter through Zones 9A and 9B, but for most of us spring and fall are the best planting times.

Where to Plant

In Texas, camellias may not grow or bloom well in full sun. Heavy shade is not recommended either. Dappled sun throughout the day is ideal. If used in beds, most northern locations work well. Eastern locations that have sun until 10 a.m., with dappled shade for the remainder of the day, will work well also. Don't plant in full-sun locations on the west side. Camellias are great when used in large containers or trained into patio trees, screens, hedges, or color beds. I believe the *Camellia sansanqua* group lends itself better to foundation plantings than nearly all varieties of *C. japonica*.

How to Plant

Camellias require a soil that has an acid pH and drains well but is moist and fertile. In areas where the climate is conducive to growing camellias, but the natural soil isn't, it may be best to grow in totally raised beds. An option is to remove the existing soil approximately 12 in. deep, fill with a 50/50 mixture of ground bark mulch and brown sphagnum peat moss, then raise this 6 in. above the existing grade. In sandy soils add 6 in. of high-quality organic matter and till, after removing rocks, sticks, weeds, and turfgrass. After beds are prepared you will be ready to plug in the plants. Dig the planting hole no deeper that the plant soilball. Make sure when you backfill that you cover the plant's soilball. After backfilling is complete, water thoroughly, apply a root stimulator, and cover with 4 in. of pine bark mulch.

Care and Maintenance

Tea scale is usually the camellia's only pest problem, and a once-a-year application of dormant oil according to label directions will take care of it. Some diseases such as leaf spot may create a problem. Camellias in good health usually don't have pest or insect problems. Should you suspect such a problem, carry samples into your local nursery or County Agent for identification and controls. Fertilize with a granular azalea/camellia fertilizer according to label directions after bloom, 2 weeks after the last killing frost in spring, once in mid-season, and once again in the fall. Water thoroughly after each application.

Additional Information

The most spectacular camellias are usually found in beds underneath the canopies of large shade trees.

Additional Species, Cultivars, or Varieties

Varieties of *C. japonica* include 'Kramer's Supreme', 'Professor Sargent', 'Snow Queen', and 'Anita'. The *C. sasanqua* family boasts 'Hana Jiman', 'Yuletide', 'Shishi Gashira', 'Setsugekka', and others. *C. oleifera* is a great fall bloomer.

Cherry Laurel or English Laurel
Prunus laurocerasus

EXPOSURE

F. Sun to Semi-

COLD HARDINESS

To 5° F.

WATER USAGE

Semi-Moist

GROWTH RATE

Fast to Med.

AVG. HT × WIDTH

8″–25′ × 3–16′ (v.)

SPACING

6–30′ (v.)

Evergreen. Dark-green glossy leaves, relatively long and narrow. Blooms are white, fragrant, and in clusters. Fruit is green, turning dark purple. Low spreading to relatively oval and upright.

*D*ue to its many varieties, cherry laurel may be a low foundation planting, a large specimen, or many applications in between. 'Mount Vernon' reaches 18 to 20 in. in height but spreads 7 to 8 ft., making it an interesting choice for wide, low shrub plantings or a tall groundcover effect. Other cherry laurels reach 12 ft. or more in height with a width of 8 ft. or more, making excellent screens when placed in rows. Because of their ability to grow in almost any type of Texas soil and in partial shade or full sun, along with their extensive size ranges, they should find spots in many Texas landscapes.

WHEN TO PLANT
In the zones in which cherry laurel is hardy, plant any time you desire. I prefer fall planting; early spring also works well.

WHERE TO PLANT
The tall-growing *P. laurocerasus* is best used as individual specimens, screen plantings, or trained into patio trees. Don't plant near walkways or driveways, as foundation plantings, or in front of entrances or windows. It will quickly

outgrow these areas. The variety 'Nana' makes an excellent 4- to 6-ft.-high and -wide hedge or tall foundation planting. For a 4- to 6-ft.-tall and 6- to 8-ft.-wide hedge, 'Schipkaensis' fills the bill. Cherry laurel tolerates a wide range of soils, including light sandy soil and heavy clay. It prefers well-drained locations in moist, fertile soils. Do not plant in wet areas.

HOW TO PLANT

Where individual plants will be used as specimen plantings, remove any weeds, turfgrass, rocks, and sticks from the area, as you do when preparing beds. Do not add any soil amendments, however—simply loosen the native soil thoroughly with a shovel, digging fork, or tiller to the soilball's depth and as wide as desired. When planting in beds, as in foundation plantings or mass bed plantings, add 4 to 6 in. of organic matter such as brown sphagnum peat moss, compost, or ground pine bark mulch, and till. For all types of plantings, after the plants are set inside their new homes, backfill, water thoroughly, apply a root stimulator, and cover with 3 to 4 in. of your favorite bark.

CARE AND MAINTENANCE

Grasshoppers may visit during the summer. Leaf spots may be seen in areas where air movement is poor and humidity is very high. Planting in sunny locations with good air movement will usually prevent this problem. Grasshoppers can be controlled with a wide range of control possibilities. Water as needed to prevent the soil from drying out. Fertilize in the spring 2 weeks after your last killing frost. Premium-quality slow-release 3:1:2 lawn fertilizers such as 21-7-14 and 15-5-10 work well. Apply according to label directions again twice during the growing season and once again during the fall. Water thoroughly after each application.

ADDITIONAL INFORMATION

Cherry laurel is a relatively uncommon group of small to tree-like shrubs that make excellent hedges, screens, and borders as well as foundation, specimen, and mass plantings, all in one family.

ADDITIONAL SPECIES, CULTIVARS, OR VARIETIES

Prunus caroliniana or Carolina cherry laurel is a Texas native. 'Bright'n'Tight' is a compact variety of *P. caroliniana*. Varieties of *P. laurocerasus* include 'Mount Vernon', 'Nana', 'Schipkaensis', 'Otto Luyken', and 'Zabeliana'.

Cleyera
Ternstroemia japonica

EXPOSURE

Shade to Semi-

COLD HARDINESS

To 5° F.

WATER USAGE

Semi-Moist

GROWTH RATE

Slow

AVG. HT × WIDTH

6–10′ × 6–8′

SPACING

3–4′

Upright-growing evergreen shrub. Leaves are leathery, and a beautiful deep green.

I first became familiar with cleyera in 1969 while pursuing a horticulture degree at Stephen F. Austin State University in Nacogdoches, Texas. My wife Judy and I lived in married housing on campus where I kept noticing this interesting-looking plant, as well as at off-campus locations. Since then I've seen it in many landscape applications. I also propagated thousands of them as a nursery production manager. You might say I've had the opportunity to know these shrubs from the seed up. Cleyera is a candidate for areas that do not get the hot direct western sun.

WHEN TO PLANT
In the zones in which cleyera is hardy, you may plant at any time, though I don't recommend planting in July, August, or the middle of winter. Fall is best, with early spring a close second.

WHERE TO PLANT
Cleyeras are great when planted in groups. These groups may be applied to corners, alcoves, and other areas that need an unusual shrub that is interesting

to view. I would not use them as hedges; their rate of growth is slow to moderate under average conditions. Because of their growth rate and form, they are not the best candidates for screens either. If you are patient, cleyera will grow to make interesting specimens in shady areas. Don't plant in daylong full-sun locations, western exposures, or where radiant heat is received. An eastern exposure with sun until 10 a.m. is acceptable in most cases. Cleyera prefers daylong dappled shade. It also makes interesting plantings in beds under tall trees. Because of its texture, growth pattern, form, and leaf color, it is a good companion for dwarf hollies.

HOW TO PLANT

While cleyera has some tolerance to various soil conditions, don't expect great results if you plant in poor locations. Hard, compact soils or poorly drained areas are not desirable. For plantings around the foundation, or out in the landscape, make the beds at least 5 ft. wide. Once an acceptable location is established, remove any turf-grass, weeds, rocks, or sticks from the area, till, and add 6 in. of high-quality organic matter such as compost, brown sphagnum peat moss, or ground pine bark mulch. Approximately 2 in. of each is good. Till the area again, and you will be ready to plant. Dig the individual planting hole no deeper than the plant's soilball, install, and backfill. Water thoroughly, apply a root stimulator, and cover with 4 in. of pine bark mulch.

CARE AND MAINTENANCE

Cleyera has no serious pests or diseases. Water as necessary to maintain a moist soil during the growing season, and to prevent soil from drying in the winter. Fertilize in the spring 2 weeks after the last killing frost, twice during the growing season, and once again in the fall. Light applications of a 3:1:2 ratio premium-quality slow-release lawn fertilizer should work well. Follow label directions, and water thoroughly after each application.

ADDITIONAL INFORMATION

After the first hard freeze in the fall, cleyera often takes on various shades of bronze. This makes it a valuable plant for adding color to winter landscapes.

ADDITIONAL SPECIES, CULTIVARS, OR VARIETIES

The *T. japonica* 'Variegata' and 'Burnished Gold' varieties have colorful creamy to yellow to yellow-gold foliage in various patterns.

Cotoneaster

Cotoneaster spp.

EXPOSURE

F. Sun to Semi-

COLD HARDINESS

All Texas

WATER USAGE

Arid/Semi-Mst.

GROWTH RATE

Slow to Med. (v.)

AVG. HT × WIDTH

1–8 ' × 3–10 ' (v.)

SPACING

Varies

Low groundcover to shrub. Bright to dark green leaves, or green leaves with a gray cast. Single and clustered blooms are white or pink; plant produces bright- to dark-red berries. Semievergreen.

*T*his member of the rose family adds interest to many landscape applications. *C. salicifolius* 'Repens', *C. dammeri* 'Coral Beauty' or 'Royal Beauty', and *C. dammeri* 'Moner', all 6 to 18 in. tall, may be used as groundcovers. In the cotoneaster group there should be a plant size for any application in your landscape. For rock gardens I suggest 'Moner', *C. horizontalis* 'Perpusilla', and *C. dammeri* 'Eichholz'.

WHEN TO PLANT

Plant these interesting landscape additions at any time—fall is great, spring is good, but they may be planted whenever you are ready.

WHERE TO PLANT

Install in locations with good air movement and well-prepared soils that are moist and fertile. I would not plant in a full-sun location that receives more than 6 hours of full sunlight, next to a solid fence, or in an area where there is reflected heat (full sun is fine if there is good air movement and no reflected heat). Some varieties of cotoneaster, such as *C. apiculatus* or cranberry cotoneaster, which reaches 3 ft. tall and 3 to 6 ft. wide, make very interesting foundation plantings in Texas. Cranberry cotoneaster grows in a spreading vase form. The larger-growing varieties of cotoneaster may also be trained into interesting tree-type forms and other horticulturally manipulated shapes. Such training may be done in large containers or planting beds.

HOW TO PLANT

For any plantings, make the beds a minimum of 5 ft. wide. Remove rocks, sticks, weeds, and turfgrass, then till or hand dig. Add 4 to 6 in. of organic matter such as ground bark mulch, brown sphagnum peat moss, and compost, and till a second time. The soil is now ready to plant. The same preparations should be made when planting cotoneaster in rock gardens and groundcover beds, but it's not necessary to make these areas 5 ft. wide. For all applications, dig the planting holes no deeper than the plant's soilball, install, and backfill. Water thoroughly, apply a root stimulator, and mulch with your favorite bark.

CARE AND MAINTENANCE

Cotoneaster is susceptible to a bacterial disease known as fire blight. Installing the plants in ideal locations and keeping them healthy are the best prevention measures, though there are products available for fire blight control. The Texas Agricultural Extension Service also has a fact sheet on fire blight control for landscape plants. Your local contact is the County Agent's Office. Water to prevent soil from drying. Apply spring fertilizer 2 weeks after the last killing frost in your area. Reapply 1 time during the growing season, and once in the fall. Use a premium-quality slow-release granular rose fertilizer according to label directions, and water thoroughly after each application.

ADDITIONAL INFORMATION

The next time you visit the nurseries in your area, ask to see their selections of cotoneaster. They are an interesting group of plants, though I wouldn't advise planting a substantial portion of your landscape with them. Try a bed or a grouping first to see how you like them.

ADDITIONAL SPECIES, CULTIVARS, OR VARIETIES

There are many species and even more cultivars. The selections vary in Texas from region to region. Here are a few: *C. acutifolius* or Peking cotoneaster; *C. adpressus* 'Praecox' and 'Tom Thumb'; *C. congestus* or Pyrenees cotoneaster; *C. divaricatus* or spreading cotoneaster; *C. glaucophyllus* or gray-leaved cotoneaster; and *C. horizontalis* 'Variegatus' and 'Robusta'.

Crape Myrtle
Lagerstroemia indica

EXPOSURE

Full Sun

COLD HARDINESS

To 0° F.

WATER USAGE

Arid/Semi-Mst.

GROWTH RATE

Fast to Med.

AVG. HT × WIDTH

Varies

SPACING

Varies

Leaves are medium green and not showy. Bloom colors range from white, pink, red, and lavender, to various other shades, and are very showy. Deciduous.

Crape myrtle has been used successfully for decades in Texas landscapes. These plants may be found in old homesites and roadways, growing and blooming their beautiful heads off. It is as tough as any imported blooming shrub, and as durable as many natives. Crape myrtles are without a doubt my favorite blooming landscape shrubs. They are easy to grow, come in a wide range of sizes, and provide outstanding summer bloom color. What more could we ask for? You owe it to yourself, your family, and your area to select the varieties and bloom colors that work best in your landscape—and plant them this year. They will yield rewards for a long time.

WHEN TO PLANT
Plant any time of the year in most Texas zones, although I prefer fall planting. Early spring planting is my second choice. Crape myrtle can also be planted in midsummer, as well as during the winter.

WHERE TO PLANT
Plant in full sun. Do not plant in shady areas! In order for crape myrtles to perform in growth and bloom, they must be in full-sun locations receiving at

least 8 hours of full sunlight. They are very drought tolerant once established, but plant in a location where they can be easily watered. Don't plant in a poorly drained location. Crape myrtles will grow i n sandy or heavy clay soils, but they prefer a moist, but not wet, fertile loam soil. Under these growing conditions, the plants will provide great shows of growth and bloom. They work well as specimens, in mass plantings, in large containers, as plant features, as extended foundation beds, and as stand-alone beds developed in sunny locations.

How to Plant

Remove sticks, weeds, turfgrass, and rocks from the planting area and till. Add 4 to 6 in. of high-quality organic matter such as brown sphagnum peat moss, compost, or ground bark. Till again and the area will be ready to plant. Dig the planting hole no deeper than the rootball and set in plant. Backfill, water thoroughly, apply a root stimulator, and cover with 3 to 4 in. of whatever bark you like.

Care and Maintenance

Powdery mildew may pay an unwelcome visit to your crape myrtle under very humid conditions with poor air movement. I've grown these outstanding shrubs for over 25 years and have had *almost* no problem with powdery mildew. Aphids, also known as plant lice, may visit as well. If you have either of these problems, there are several control possibilities. Remember to follow label directions on any product. Water as needed to maintain a moist soil—while these plants will tolerate dry conditions, they don't like it. Best bloom occurs on new growth that is stimulated by moist, fertile growing conditions and pruning. Apply 21-7-14, 15-5-10, or a similar 3:1:2 ratio premium-quality slow-release lawn fertilizer in the spring 2 weeks after the last killing frost in your area. Reapply twice more during the growing season and once again in the fall. Water thoroughly after each application. When pruning is desired for shaping, late winter is best. Prune selectively and do not make a flat-top out of your plants.

Additional Information

We really enjoy our dwarf varieties planted in masses at the bases of tall-growing varieties, all planted in an L shape on the northwest corner of our property in full sun. I'm sure you'd enjoy something similar in your garden.

Additional Species, Cultivars, or Varieties

'Natchez', 'Near East', 'Pink Lace', 'Potomac', 'Firebird', and many more are available for your enjoyment. Note: Write me for a list of mildew resistant varieties. Be sure to include a long stamped self-addressed envelope with your request.

SHRUBS

Elaeagnus
Elaeagnus pungens

EXPOSURE

F. Sun to Semi-

COLD HARDINESS

To 0° F.

WATER USAGE

Semi-Moist

GROWTH RATE

Fast

AVG. HT × WIDTH

8–12 ′ × 8–10 ′

SPACING

6–10 ′

Leaves are covered with tiny silver-gray scales. A semi-upright spreading-form shrub that is large and irregular. Evergreen.

*E*laeagnus is a moderate- to rapid-growing shrub that is large and dense, and makes excellent screens and natural hedges. It may also be used in wind-breaks. It needs plenty of room to grow and regrowth from pruning is rapid. Both old and new growth have sharp spurs, so be sure to wear protective gloves when pruning. Elaeagnus is tough and grows rather well in difficult locations. High heat, drought, and a wide range of soil conditions will all be tolerated, and it grows in full sun or partial shade.

WHEN TO PLANT
Plant any time you wish. Fall is best; early spring is also good.

WHERE TO PLANT
Excellent for large screening plantings. With training, could make a large spec-imen in sunny locations. Not recommended as a home foundation planting. While *E. pungens* will tolerate relatively undesirable conditions, it prefers a moist, loamy, fertile soil.

HOW TO PLANT

When planning beds of screening plants or other applications, remove any weeds, rocks, turfgrass, or sticks from the area to be planted. Till the area and add 4 in. of organic matter such as brown sphagnum peat moss, ground pine bark mulch, or compost (home-made or commercial). After the organic matter has been added, till again. The beds are now ready for planting. Because of their wide spread, *E. pungens* could be planted on 8-ft. centers if desired. For a quicker impact, plant on 6-ft. centers. Dig individual planting holes where the plants are to be located, install them, and backfill. Water thoroughly, apply a root stimulator, and cover with 3 to 4 in. of your favorite bark mulch. I usually use pine bark mulch.

CARE AND MAINTENANCE

Spider mites may occasionally visit elaeagnus plantings. If this occurs, ask about control solutions. Remember to follow label direc-tions on any gardening aid. There are no other pest problems. Water as needed to prevent soil from drying out. Fertilize with a premium-quality slow-release product—once in the spring, 2 weeks after the last killing frost in your area, and once during the fall. Fertilizer ratios of 3:1:2 work well on our warm-season lawns and elaeagnus. 21-7-14, 18-6-12, 19-5-9 and 15-5-10 are all 3:1:2 ratios. Apply accord-ing to label directions and water thoroughly after each application. Prune as desired for shape. Pruning can be a frequent chore if you try to maintain a relatively short and narrow elaeagnus. Allowed to grow to its natural shape and size; very little pruning is necessary.

ADDITIONAL INFORMATION

If you are looking for a large-growing plant that requires minimum maintenance and will add a silvery color to your landscape, try elaeagnus. Birds enjoy elaeagnus fruit, and use the branching foliage for nesting.

ADDITIONAL SPECIES, CULTIVARS, OR VARIETIES

E. macrophylla is a more compact grower than *E. pungens*. *E. × ebbengi* has larger leaves and no spines, flowers in the fall, and is usually considered an overall better choice than *E. pungens*. *E. pungens* 'Fruitlandii' has leaves that are more rounded and a deeper green than its parent, and the leaf margins are wavy. 'Aurea' has leaves with yellow to yellow-gold margins. 'Nana' is a dwarf form, and 'Maculata' has leaves with yellow to golden-yellow centers.

Euonymus
Euonymus japonica

EXPOSURE

Full Sun

COLD HARDINESS

To 0° F.

WATER USAGE

Semi-Moist

GROWTH RATE

Medium

AVG. HT × WIDTH

1–10' × 1–6'

SPACING

2–10'

Compact upright-growing evergreen shrub. Leaves are leathery and medium to deep green, with various color patterns of creamy white to silver and yellow to yellow-gold.

*E*uonymus is a durable, easy-to-grow shrub that will grow in nearly all Texas conditions. If you have a little one who wants to pick out some colorful shrubs to plant and take care of, *E. japonica* is a good one to start. The same is true for you first-time gardeners. There are many varieties to choose from.

WHEN TO PLANT
Plant anytime, though fall is best and early spring is also good.

WHERE TO PLANT
E. japonica has the desirable ability to grow in dense shade or full sun. It will tolerate difficult and dry soils, but it prefers moist, fertile soils. In soils with adequate moisture, a well-nourished euonymus can burst forth with great flushes of new growth. Don't plant in poorly drained locations. Because of their leaf colors and ability to regrow, euonymus plants make good candidates for screens, hedges (formal and natural), foundation plantings, mass plantings, and specimens. They may also be used in large pots, planters, and other containers. *E. japonica* may be planted on any side of your landscape, in sun or

shade. I believe 6 to 8 hours of full sun, along with shade from the hot west afternoon sun, is most desirable.

HOW TO PLANT

Soils are the foundation for all our successful gardening experiences . . . so build a good foundation before you start planting. Remove turf-grass, rocks, sticks, and weeds from the area to be planted, and till (in small areas you may hand dig). Tillers with tines in the rear work best. If you don't own one, you can rent one. After the initial tilling, add compost, brown sphagnum peat moss, and ground bark. Till again and the area will be ready to plant. I prefer beds at least 5 ft. wide, much wider in some applications. After creating new homes no deeper than their soilballs, install plants. Backfill, water thoroughly, apply root stimulator, and cover with 3 in. of your favorite bark or similar material.

CARE AND MAINTENANCE

E. japonica sometimes attracts a major insect pest known as scale. An application of dormant oil once a year will usually control scale and should be done without fail. In areas where air movement is poor, powdery mildew may also visit. New growth is more prone to such a problem. If this occurs, there are several products that will control it. Remember to read and follow label directions on any product. Water as needed to prevent the soil from drying; maintaining a heavy mulch year-round will aid in moisture conservation. Pruning usually isn't required if a natural shape is desired. Euonymus lends itself well to shearing and may be trained into various shapes. It responds with vigor and growth to a good fertilization program. Fertilize 2 weeks after the last killing frost in your area, 2 times during the growing season, and once in the fall. The same 3:1:2 ratio fertilizers often recommended for use on our lawns will work well. Be sure to use only premium-quality slow-release fertilizers according to label directions, and water thoroughly after each application.

ADDITIONAL INFORMATION

Euonymus is available in several sizes.

ADDITIONAL SPECIES, CULTIVARS, OR VARIETIES

There are many cultivars, and here are a few to choose from: 'Aureo-marginata', 'Aureo-variegata', 'Microphylla', 'Microphylla Variegata', 'Silver King', 'Grandifolia', and 'Silver Princess'. Additional species are *E. alata*, *E. fortunei*, and *E. kiautschovica*.

Flowering Quince
Chaenomeles japonica

EXPOSURE

Full Sun

COLD HARDINESS

All Texas

WATER USAGE

Arid to Semi-Mst.

GROWTH RATE

Medium

AVG. HT × WIDTH

4' × 6'

SPACING

4'

Deep-green glossy leaves. Blooms are similar to apple blossoms in appearance, and come in white, red, pink, and coral. Deciduous.

Many mature Texas gardeners call flowering quince "japonica." If you are speaking of flowering quince and the other gardeners mention their beautiful japonica, you are probably talking about the same plant. Japonica actually denotes that the plant's original home is Japan. We Texans have been using flowering quince in our home and commercial landscapes for decades. Flowering quince grows in almost any soil type in Texas, and it is sometimes found in old homesites and abandoned areas.

WHEN TO PLANT
Japonica may be planted at any time—fall is ideal, early spring is good.

WHERE TO PLANT
Plant in full-sun locations where there is adequate moisture and fertile soil. I like them for mass plantings, in which they are very striking. In sunny areas where azaleas are very difficult to grow, flowering quince works well. It may be clipped, if desired, to form an interesting hedge or other arrangements. Flowering quince also works well in color beds. Its blooms are a standout

when used in wide beds in front of tall-growing broadleaf evergreens like holly. Flowering quince may also be used in extended foundation planting beds, though I wouldn't use them as primary foundation plantings.

HOW TO PLANT

I like to welcome new plants with proper homes. Select good locations and prepare the soil thoroughly. Remove any debris, including sticks, rocks, weeds, and turfgrass, from the planting area. Till or hand dig the area, add 4 to 6 in of your favorite organic matter. Till or dig again until the materials are evenly blended and your bed will be ready to plant. I usually make beds at least 5 ft. wide and use compost, ground pine bark, and brown sphagnum peat moss. Dig planting holes no deeper that the plant's soilball, install, and backfill. Water thoroughly, apply a root stimulator, and cover with 3 to 4 in. of bark mulch.

CARE AND MAINTENANCE

Aphids may visit new top growth, but they usually aren't a long-term problem. There are several ways to control aphids. Remember to read and follow label directions on any product. Water as needed to prevent soil dryness. Prune as desired, although it is not required. Severe pruning is best done in the spring, just after blooming is complete. Fertilize in the spring 2 weeks after the last killing frost, in mid-growing-season, and in the fall, with a premium-quality slow-release granular rose fertilizer according to label directions. Water thoroughly after each application.

ADDITIONAL INFORMATION

If you are interested in the Oriental horticultural art form called bonsai, flowering quince works well. It can be cultured using containers, or directly in the ground.

ADDITIONAL SPECIES, CULTIVARS, OR VARIETIES

There are several varieties and here are some to try: 'Cameo' is a soft apricot-pink double flower; 'Super Red' or 'Monred' has extra-bright large blooms; 'Texas Scarlet' has fiery-scarlet blooms; and 'Jet Trails' has white blooms. C. speciosa grows considerably larger than C. japonica, in blooms, height, and leaf size. If you want an enlarged version of flowering quince, take a look at: 'Snow', which has white blooms; 'Crimson Beauty', with single red flowers; and 'Apple Blossom', with pink blooms. Please note: Varieties of C. speciosa may be a bit difficult to find. The named variety of flowering quince that is easiest to find is C. japonica 'Texas Scarlet'. And understandably so in Texas!

Forsythia
Forsythia × intermedia

EXPOSURE

Full Sun

COLD HARDINESS

All Texas

WATER USAGE

Semi-Moist

GROWTH RATE

Fast

AVG. HT × WIDTH

6–8' × 6–10'

SPACING

10–18'

This deciduous shrub's form is irregular, upright to weeping, and spreading. Foliage is medium green and blooms are shades of gold and yellow.

*F*orsythia originally came from Japan, but it adapts well to Texas landscapes. Indeed, it is a spring-blooming shrub that has been used for generations in Texas gardens, both in home and commercial applications. This is an "easy plant" to transplant, propagate, grow, and enjoy where adapted. It is one of the earliest bloomers in the landscape and is very dependable about putting on its show. The sunny bloom colors are a welcome harbinger of spring. It will grow in almost any soil as long as the soil is not dry.

WHEN TO PLANT
Fall is best for planting forsythia, early spring second best, midwinter third, and midsummer fourth. Unless you are going to be home to take care of July/ August watering needs, simply skip this planting time.

WHERE TO PLANT
Forsythia makes a wonderful show of color in large beds with early spring-blooming bulbs planted outside its driplines. It requires sun in order to put on its best show: after 6 hours of sun, it may be shaded for the rest of the day.

Morning sun with afternoon shade is best. Never plant in total-shade locations. The best soils are those that drain well but hold adequate moisture for good growth. Don't plant in low wet or other poorly drained locations, or in areas where the soil tends to dry rapidly and is difficult to irrigate.

How to Plant

Clay or sandy soils should be improved with organic matter. After removing all debris, weeds, and turfgrass and tilling the soil, add 4 to 6 in. of compost, brown sphagnum peat moss, and/or ground pine bark to the planting area. Then till again and the area will be ready for planting. Don't dig the planting holes any deeper than the plants' soilballs. Set the plants in their planting holes, backfill, water thoroughly, apply root stimulator, and mulch with 4 in. of bark or 6 in. of clean hay, straw, pine needles, or similar materials.

Care and Maintenance

There aren't any serious pests or diseases that bother forsythia. Soil moisture is important even during our winters—though it is winter hardy, forsythia isn't fond of dry conditions at any time. Especially during the growing season, it prefers a moist soil. In winter, it requires sufficient moisture to prevent the soil from drying around the root system. A heavy mulch is quite beneficial year-round, as it will help to conserve soil moisture. Prune to shape in the spring after blooming is complete. Don't prune in late summer, fall, or winter or you will find you have cut off the bloom buds. Fertilize 3 times a year with your favorite brand of premium-quality slow-release granular rose fertilizer. Follow label directions and water thoroughly after each application. Make the first application 2 weeks after the last killing frost in your area or when new leaves are appearing, whichever comes first. Make the second application approximately 10 weeks later, and make the last one in the fall.

Additional Information

Because of forsythia's size, the plants may be trained into specimens or hedges.

Additional Species, Cultivars, or Varieties

'Lynwood Gold', with yellow-gold blooms, is the variety that is easiest to find. 'Beatrix Farrand' has golden-yellow blooms. 'Spring Glory' flowers are primrose yellow.

Gardenia
Gardenia jasminoides

EXPOSURE	COLD HARDINESS
Semi-Shade	To 20° F.

WATER USAGE	GROWTH RATE
Moist	Medium

AVG. HT × WIDTH	SPACING
6″–6′ × 3–6′ (v.)	5–10′

Dark glossy green leaves of various sizes. Blooms are white to creamy with very heavy fragrance. Spreading to upright growth form. Evergreen.

According to Bailey's *Hortus Third*, gardenias are among 200 species of shrubs and small trees native to the tropical and subtropical regions of the world. In our slice of the world, an old-time Texas and Southern favorite, Cape Jasmine, is a member of *Gardenia jasminodies*. There is friendly discussion at times about which variety of *G. jasminodies* is the true Cape Jasmine. Some say the variety 'Mystery' is the true Cape Jasmine, while others believe it is 'August Beauty'. I suggest both of these plants as well as others may be called Cape Jasmine, and we can enjoy them all. Gardenias can be as much of a challenge to grow as roses, but if you want an extremely fragrant bloomer, they are hard to beat—and if you can grow roses, you can grow gardenias.

WHEN TO PLANT

Plant gardenias in the very early spring, or as a second choice, in the very early fall. Summer planting is acceptable if you are able to maintain a moist soil condition. Winter planting is acceptable in Zone 9.

WHERE TO PLANT

Plant in a location that has sun all morning and shade from the direct hot afternoon sun. Dappled daylong sun/shade also works well. Don't plant in locations that receive reflected heat, or in soils that tend to be dry or poorly drained. Gardenias do best in moist, sandy, acidic soils. The taller-growing varieties make interesting foundation plantings. Other varieties are good as mass plantings, specimens, hedges, groundcovers, and container plants.

HOW TO PLANT

Because of this plant's pH requirements, if the soil in which you plan to install it is heavy clay, you will have to do some serious growing-media preparation. The beds should be a minimum of 5 ft. wide. Remove at least 6 in. of the soil, 1 ft. if possible. After this is done, blend brown sphagnum peat moss and pine bark mulch 50/50 with the removed soil, and backfill the excavated area to 6 in. above the natural grade. Water thoroughly and allow to drain overnight before planting. Install the plants in this mixture no deeper than their soil-balls, firm the mix, water thoroughly, and apply a root stimulator. Place 4 in. of pine bark mulch on top of the finished planting.

CARE AND MAINTENANCE

Aphids, white flies, nematodes, mites, scale, sooty mold, and leaf spots can all plague gardenias. It's like growing roses—you must want to grow them and be willing to take care of all their cultural requirements, including insect control and disease prevention and control. There is a wide assortment of aids and methods available. Always read and follow label directions. Drip irrigation is good for keeping the growing media moist, and will save 50 percent on your water bill. Fertilize with a granular azalea fertilizer after their spring bloom flush, once in mid-season, and again in the fall according to label directions. Water thoroughly after each application. Gardenias like a soil pH in the 5 to 6 range. Sometimes this is difficult to maintain over a long time, even with good soil/media preparation. An inexpensive test available through the Texas Agricultural Extension Service can give you an accurate reading and, if needed, treatment recommendations.

ADDITIONAL INFORMATION

You may want to try a couple of gardenias in the ground for a trial run before investing in an entire bed planting. If you want to grow gardenias but don't have much room, try one of the smaller varieties such as 'Radicans' as an indoor/outdoor container planting.

ADDITIONAL SPECIES, CULTIVARS, OR VARIETIES

Try these varieties or cultivars of *G. jasminoides*: 'August Beauty', 'Candle Light', 'Variegated', 'Mystery', 'Veitchii', 'Radicans', 'Radicans Variegata', and 'First Love' or 'Aimee'.

Hardy Hibiscus
Hibiscus moscheutos

EXPOSURE

Full to Semi-

COLD HARDINESS

All Texas

WATER USAGE

Semi-Moist

GROWTH RATE

Fast

AVG. HT × WIDTH

2–6′ × 3–6′

SPACING

4′

Large dark-green foliage on rather upright and open branchings. Blooms are extremely large in white, pink, purple, and red. Herbaceous deciduous shrub.

*I*f you like the beauty of tropical hibiscus blooms but want one that doesn't freeze, you're in luck: hardy hibiscus is great for adding color to any landscape. Texas gardeners who have seen cotton grow and bloom may believe that hardy hibiscus looks as if it is in the same family—and it is! Hardy hibiscus is a wonderful large-leaved, large-bloomed plant that adds color to beds, nook and corner plantings, mass plantings, or planters. They work in several kinds of locations, are easy to plant and maintain, and are rewarding to grow. Parents who help a little gardener plant hardy hibiscus will be doubly rewarded when they see the excitement in the children's eyes during the spring.

WHEN TO PLANT

Early spring to early summer is the best planting time, summer is second best, and fall third. I do not recommend planting during the winter except along our coast and the Rio Grande valley.

WHERE TO PLANT

The best locations provide shade from our hot afternoon summer suns. Try locations that receive morning to midday full sun with afternoon shade, or dappled sun/shade all day long. These plants tend to do better away from reflected heat sources such as bright walls and concrete, and good air movement is advised. Don't plant in difficult-to-water areas, as they do best in moist soils. They will even grow in sand or clay soils as long as adequate moisture is present. I do not recommend them for primary foundation plantings, though they work in front of broadleaf evergreen foundation plantings in extended beds.

HOW TO PLANT

Because hardy hibiscus prefers moist soils, be sure adequate organic matter is incorporated into the planting area. Brown sphagnum peat moss holds over 20 times its weight in water and is highly recommended. Remove any debris, weeds, and turfgrass, and till the planting area. Add 4 in. of peat and 2 in. of compost, or 6 in. of peat only, and till again. The planting area is now ready. After digging the planting hole soilball deep, insert the plant, backfill, water thoroughly, apply a root stimulator, and mulch with 4 in. of pine bark mulch. When developing hardy hibiscus beds, make them at least 5 ft. wide. If spot planting, it is not necessary to make the planting area that wide.

CARE AND MAINTENANCE

Pests and diseases are usually not problems for this plant. Fertilize in early spring 2 weeks after the last killing frost in your area, or when you see new buds arising from the ground, whichever comes first. Apply slow-release premium-quality granular rose fertilizer according to label directions. Apply again approximately 10 weeks later, then once in the fall. Water thoroughly after each fertilizer application, and water as needed to maintain a moist soil. Maintaining a mulch of 4 to 6 in. of clean hay, straw, or pine needles will greatly help in soil moisture retention. Prune very low or to the ground by the end of the winter. I usually prune to approximately 1 ft. after hard fall freezes, then to the ground in late winter.

ADDITIONAL INFORMATION

Don't use these plants indoors because they will go dormant and drop leaves, even inside. They are great outside.

ADDITIONAL SPECIES, CULTIVARS, OR VARIETIES

H. moscheutos 'Disco Belle' is red, purple, pink and white; 'Frisbee' is deep crimson to white and blends. There is a separate variety called 'Pink' or pink rose mallow that has very large, pink blooms. '*H. coccineus* 'Lord Baltimore' has leaves with red edges and red flowers, while 'Texas Star' has red blooms with white throats. Both are marginal bog plants. *H. mutabilis* 'Rubra' produces single, showy, large red blooms. *H. mutabilis* 'Raspberry Rose' produces extremely large, showy, single raspberry-colored blooms, and 'May Grande' has 12-in. hot-pink blooms.

Holly
Ilex spp.

EXPOSURE

F. Sun to Semi-

COLD HARDINESS

All Texas

WATER USAGE

Semi-Mst. to D.T.

GROWTH RATE

Fast to Slow "v.)

AVG. HT × WIDTH

3–50 ' × 3–20 ' (v.)

SPACING

Varies

Shiny, dark-green, dense foliage; some have many spines. Some berry heavily while others are void. Low mounding to upright forms. Evergreen.

The holly family is without a doubt my favorite landscape shrub group. These shrubs are versatile, available in many varieties, easy to grow, reliable, and found statewide. You will find these tough, durable shrubs growing at old homes, schools, churches, and other buildings. Look in the older parts of your town and you'll be sure to find them.

WHEN TO PLANT
Plant any time the mood strikes you, though fall is the best planting time.

WHERE TO PLANT
Most varieties grow in full-sun or partly shady locations. Some produce a denser and more robust planting in full sun than when grown in the shade. Others prefer some protection from the hot afternoon sun. The dwarfs work well in front of low windows and porches and along walkways. Holly prefers a moist soil; don't plant in hard, compact, or poorly drained soils. All varieties will grow in acidic soils; several grow well in alkaline soils.

HOW TO PLANT

To improve the soil, add 4 to 6 in. of organic matter to the planting area. Do this after all debris, weeds, and turfgrass have been removed and the native soil tilled. After the brown sphagnum peat moss, compost, ground pine bark, or similar materials have been spread, till again and the soil will be ready to plant. In prepared beds at least 5 ft. wide, dig planting holes no deeper than the plant's soil-ball, set the plants, backfill, water thoroughly, apply a root stimulator, and cover with 3 to 4 in. of your favorite bark mulch.

CARE AND MAINTENANCE

Tea scale could become a problem on some varieties in relatively shady areas; this is usually not a problem in sunny locations. Grasshoppers may visit in rural areas, and there are several solutions for control. Read and follow label directions, of course. Irrigate as needed to prevent drying of the soil, and maintain a thick mulch blanket year-round to aid in conserving soil moisture. Holly responds well to a good seasonal fertilizer program. Make your first application 2 weeks after the last spring frost in your area, reapply 2 times during the growing season, and once in the fall. Premium-quality slow-release 3:1:2-ratio lawn fertilizers work well (examples: 19-5-9, 15-5-10, 21-7-14). Always apply according to label directions and water thoroughly after each application. Prune as desired almost any time the urge hits you. For severe pruning, early spring is best. I don't recommend substantial to severe late-fall pruning. Hollies that produce fruit/berries usually do so on second-year wood.

ADDITIONAL INFORMATION

Many different types of holly are available to Texas gardeners, in sizes ranging from 1 gal. to large ready-to-plant specimens.

ADDITIONAL SPECIES, CULTIVARS, OR VARIETIES

Several species and many varieties include *I. cornuta* 'Bufordii', 'Dwarf Bufordii', 'Carissa', 'Nellie R. Stevens', 'Rotunda', 'Needle Point', and 'Dazzler'; *I.* × 'Nellie R. Stevens'; *I. vomitoria* 'Nana', 'Stoke's Dwarf', 'Pendula', 'Pride of Houston', dwarf 'First Lady' and 'Will Fleming'; *I. crenata* 'Compacta', 'Green Lustre', 'Helleri', and 'Hetzi'.

Hydrangea

Hydrangea macrophylla

EXPOSURE

Semi-Shade

COLD HARDINESS

All Texas

WATER USAGE

Moist to Semi-Mst.

GROWTH RATE

Medium

AVG. HT × WIDTH

5–7 ' × 6–8 '

SPACING

10–16 '

Very large-leaved deciduous round-form shrub. Blooms are white, red, pink, and blue, in clusters.

Many Moms in Texas got their hydrangea starts as gifts on Mother's Day. This has been a tradition for generations. The first hydrangea I remember seeing was in Nacogdoches, Texas, when my wife and I were attending Stephan F. Austin State University—it was an outstanding blue color. The naturally acidic soils of the area lend themselves to producing blue colors in ydrangeas, and the shrub I saw was a "beaut." These are colorful, low-maintenance, showy plants, and they should be used more often.

WHEN TO PLANT

Anytime is hydrangea-planting time in Texas, though very early spring is probably best and early fall is second best.

WHERE TO PLANT

While hydrangea will adapt to a relatively broad range of locations, they do best in fertile, deep, moist soils that drain well. Eastern or northern locations are often preferred. Southern and western locations will work if shaded from the hot sun from midday on. Dappled daylong sun/shade also works well, but don't plant in daylong full sun. Many hydrangeas do very well as understory plantings beneath shade trees with tall canopies. In Central Texas, I've seen them under oaks; in East Texas, under pines. Some homeowners use them as foundation plantings. I believe they are more of a standout when used in wide beds with a tall-growing broadleaf evergreen such as holly growing behind them. They are also great as accent or background shrubs in shady color beds. Hydrangea may be grown in large containers on a shady deck; they may be used in masses or as a single specimen.

HOW TO PLANT

Remove any weeds, turfgrass, and debris from the area to be planted, and then till it. Blend in 6 in. of organic matter such as brown sphagnum peat moss, compost, and ground pine bark, and till again; the bed is now ready to plant. Dig the planting holes no deeper than the plant's soilball, set the plant(s), backfill, water thoroughly, apply a root stimulator, and mulch with 4 in. of your favorite bark mulch. Because of its size, hydrangea needs plenty of room to grow, so please don't crowd it.

CARE AND MAINTENANCE

This plant has no serious pests. Maintain a moist soil throughout the growing season, especially during bud-forming and blooming periods. Prevent the soil from drying out during the dormant season. A mulch layer of 3 to 4 in. will greatly aid in moisture conservation. To create pink blooms, the soil needs to be alkaline, above 7 pH. Blue blooms are formed by plants grown in an acid soil below 7 pH. Soil pH tests will tell you about your soil, and a good way to get this done is by contacting your County Agent's office. They can supply everything needed to test your soil. Lime is usually used to increase soil alkalinity, resulting in pink blooms, while sulfur, iron, and/or aluminum sulphate are used to make the soil more acid for blue blooms. Fertilize with granular rose fertilizer if pink blooms are desired, and granular azalea fertilizer if you want blue. It may be necessary to add lime, iron, sulfur, and/or aluminum sulphate to supplement these fertilizers and enhance bloom color. Apply in spring just as new growth begins, 10 weeks later, and once in the fall according to label directions. Water thoroughly after each application. Prune if needed to shape after peak bloom, but before September.

ADDITIONAL INFORMATION

Don't be shy about trying hydrangea. They will reward you with great landscape color.

ADDITIONAL SPECIES, CULTIVARS, OR VARIETIES

Try one or more of the following in your landscape: *H. macrophylla* 'Kuhnert', 'Mariesii Variegata', 'Merritt's Pride', 'Nikko Blue', 'Sister Teresa', 'Monred', 'Lanarth White', and 'Bluebird'; *H. paniculata* 'Grandiflora' or peegee hydrangea; *H. quercifolia* or oak leaf hydrangea.

Indian Hawthorne
Raphiolepis indica

EXPOSURE

F. Sun to Semi-

COLD HARDINESS

To 5° F.

WATER USAGE

Semi-Moist

GROWTH RATE

Medium

AVG. HT × WIDTH

3–8 ′ × 3–6 ′ (v.)

SPACING

2–6 ′ (v.)

Medium- to dark-green, shiny, broad-leaved evergreen. Blooms are white to shades of pink to rose-red, and showy.

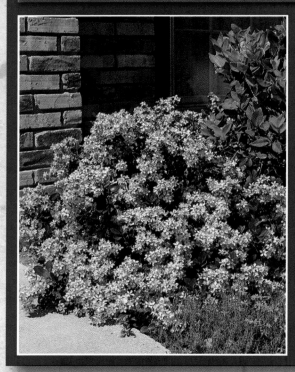

*I*ndian hawthorne is a very showy evergreen shrub that does well in a large portion of our state. It is a good shrub to try if you have had difficulty growing azaleas but continue to want spring-blooming broadleaf evergreen shrubs. It has many application possibilities in the landscape. With good soil preparation, Indian hawthorne should provide you with a good show year after year.

WHEN TO PLANT
In zones where Indian hawthorne is hardy, it can be planted anytime, though fall is probably best and very early spring is second best.

WHERE TO PLANT
Plant almost any place except in total shade, poorly drained soils, or a location with reflected heat. Some of the taller varieties make top-notch foundation plantings against relatively tall walls. Other varieties work equally well in mass plantings or under rather low windows or other structures. Indian hawthorne usually looks best when allowed to grow into natural forms, but it can be trained as hedges. The taller varieties may also be trained into "tree

forms" which have several applications, including large containers. They do well in full-sun to partial-shade locations. I suggest a minimum of 6 to 8 hours of full sun without reflected heat.

HOW TO PLANT

Indian hawthornes do best in deep, fertile, moist, well-drained soils. Remove weeds, turfgrass, and debris from the planting area, till it, then add 4 to 6 in. of compost, brown peat moss, and/or ground bark. Till a second time and the bed will be ready to plant. Dig the planting holes soilball deep and no deeper, install plants, backfill, water thoroughly, apply root stimulator, and cover with 3 to 4 in. of bark mulch. Your beds should be at least 5 ft. wide. Our southside bed is 7 ft. wide. Give your Indian hawthornes plenty of room to grow for best results.

CARE AND MAINTENANCE

This plant has no serious pests. Leaf spot may appear, but in full-sun locations it is usually not a problem. If leaf spot does visit your planting, you will find various controls are available. Remember, always read and follow label directions when using any garden aid. Maintain a moist soil; a thick mulch year-round will help. Drip irrigation works very well with Indian hawthorne. First fertilize in the spring 2 weeks after the last killing frost, again 10 weeks later, and once again in the fall. I find a premium-quality slow-release granular rose food works well. Remember to read and follow label directions, and water thoroughly after each application. Do any severe pruning during the spring after bloom is finished. Selective pruning may usually be done as needed. Don't prune mid- to late fall.

ADDITIONAL INFORMATION

I've grown Indian hawthornes for over 20 years and continue to enjoy them. Ask for suggestions on some of the best varieties available.

ADDITIONAL SPECIES, CULTIVARS, OR VARIETIES

Try one or more of these: *R. indica* 'Moness', 'Monto', 'Monrey', 'Monme', 'Monant', 'Pink Dancer', 'Baybreeze', 'Clara', 'Harbinger of Spring', 'Pinkie', 'Ponto's Pink Clara', 'Majestic Beauty', 'Ballerina, 'Dwarf Pink', 'Pink Lady', and 'Snow White'; and *R. umbellata* 'Minor'.

Japanese Yew
Podocarpus macrophyllus

EXPOSURE

F. Sun to Semi-

COLD HARDINESS

To 10° F.

WATER USAGE

Semi-Moist

GROWTH RATE

Slow to Med.

AVG. HT × WIDTH

8–12' × 3–10'

SPACING

6–10'

Upright to columnar, dense ever-green shrub. Leaves are dark green, long, and narrow.

Japanese yew is also known as podocarpus. It will grow in most soils unless they are wet or poorly drained. It tolerates considerable shade, but the density of the foliage is decreased with an increase in heavy shade. I believe they do best in deep, loose, moist soils where at least 6 to 8 hours of full sun is available daily. Japanese yew makes striking specimens in the landscape. These shrubs may be clipped into interesting shapes using proper pruning techniques. The Oriental horticultural art of bonsai works well when applied to Japanese yew.

WHEN TO PLANT
Plant anytime in the zones in which it is hardy, though fall is tops and very early spring is good.

WHERE TO PLANT
Plant in almost any well-drained place you desire tall, dense, upright shrubs. Japanese yew does not tolerate "wet feet" (a root system in wet soils) for prolonged periods of time. When planted relatively close together, these shrubs

will make very tall screens and/or hedges. They are not recommended in most applications as foundation plantings, but they are great for use as specimens and accents. Make sure there is room for the plants to grow to their usual height.

HOW TO PLANT

Remove debris, weeds, and turfgrass, and till the planting area. Blend in 4 to 6 in of brown sphagnum peat moss, compost, and/or ground bark mulch. Till again and the soil will be ready to plant. Dig individual planting holes no deeper than the plants' soilballs, set the plants in them, backfill with soil mix, water thoroughly, apply root stimulator, and cover with 3 to 4 in. of bark mulch.

CARE AND MAINTENANCE

This plant has no serious pests. In poorly drained areas, root rot is a possibility, so make sure the soil is not kept wet. Japanese yew lends itself to shearing almost anytime, though early spring is best for severe pruning, if needed. Fertilize in the spring 2 weeks after the last killing frost in your area, 2 times during the spring/summer growing season, and once in the fall. A granular 3:1:2 ratio 21-7-14, 19-5-9, 15-5-10, or similar premium-quality slow-release granular lawn fertilizer works well. Follow label directions and water thoroughly after each application. Irrigate as needed to maintain a moist soil. Maintain a 3- to 4-in. layer of bark mulch year-round.

ADDITIONAL INFORMATION

If you decide to try Japanese yew in Zone 7B, be aware that it may suffer freeze damage. It will suffer freeze damage without a doubt in Zone 7A. Japanese yew is also known as yew podocarpus. CAUTION: Don't get the true yew or *Taxus* fruits or seeds confused with *Podocarpus* or Japanese yew because *Taxus* plant parts are poisonous.

ADDITIONAL SPECIES, CULTIVARS, OR VARIETIES

Unlike most shrubs in this book, there are only limited choices of Japanese yew. The parent is *P. macrophyllus*, and there is one variety, 'Maki', which is hardy in Zone 7B. Plants are grown from seeds, so variation may occur.

Juniper
Juniperus chinensis

EXPOSURE

Full Sun

COLD HARDINESS

All Texas

WATER USAGE

Arid to Semi-Mst.

GROWTH RATE

Fast to Slow

AVG. HT × WIDTH
1–20´ × 3–15´ (v.)

SPACING
5–25´

Thick foliage with scale-like leaves that are usually green to blue-green, but sometimes golden yellow and gray. Groundcover to upright shrub in form. Evergreen.

J. chinensis or Chinese junipers—or simply junipers—offer a wide range of possibilities for use in our landscapes. They range from very low-spreading groundcover applications to tall, upright shrubs. All are sun loving and will not do well in shady areas. As a family, Chinese juniper offers colors and forms that are hard to beat. Among them are light green, deep rich blue-green, golden-yellow, bright green, frosty blue, bluish green, mint green, gray-green, silvery-blue, brilliant green, sage green, and emerald green. Before purchasing, ask at your local retail nursery about the ultimate height and width of specific junipers when used locally.

WHEN TO PLANT
Plant anytime in Texas, though early fall is best and very early spring is second best.

WHERE TO PLANT
Chinese junipers will grow on most soils as long as they drain well. They prefer full-sun locations, but they will tolerate a few hours of shade. If they need to be in shade some time during the day, try to let it be shade from the very

intense afternoon sun, and no more than 4 hours of shade. They may be used as hedges, around foundations, as corner plantings, with other varieties used in the same bed, as groundcovers and screens, and in formal or natural arrangements. Chinese junipers also work well in horticulturally manipulated forms such as bonsai, twists, spirals, and pom poms, and they work in confined areas such as planters and large containers.

HOW TO PLANT

Chinese junipers will tolerate nearly any type of Texas soil if it isn't poorly drained or wet, but they prefer a relatively moist, well-drained, fertile soil for best growth and performance. First improve the soil. Remove any debris, weeds, and turfgrass from the area to be planted, then till it. Add 4 to 6 in. of organic matter such as compost, brown sphagnum peat moss, and ground bark, then till a second time. The bed is now ready for its new occupants. After digging the holes no deeper than the plants' rootballs, install the plants, backfill with the soil mix, water thoroughly, apply root stimulator, and cover with 3 in. of your favorite bark.

CARE AND MAINTENANCE

Spider mites could be a problem in hot, dry locations with poor air movement. Plant in areas where they will not receive reflected heat, and irrigate as needed to prevent dry soil. If spider mites do become a problem, there are several possible solutions for control. Remember, read and follow label directions. Prune lightly to shape as new spring growth appears. Do not perform radical pruning on older stems without foliage, or they may not regrow new foliage. Soil fertility, new growth, and overall health and vigor can all be improved by fertilizing. Two weeks after the last spring frost in your area, fertilize with your favorite 3:1:2 ratio premium-grade slow-release lawn fertilizer according to label directions. Reapply 10 weeks later and again in the fall. 19-5-9, 21-7-14, 15-5-10 are all 3:1:2 ratio lawn fertilizers.

ADDITIONAL INFORMATION

When you visit a theme park, take a look at the landscape—chances are, you will see one or more Chinese junipers trained into interesting shapes.

ADDITIONAL SPECIES, CULTIVARS, OR VARIETIES

Some varieties you may wish to try: 'Torulosa'/'Kaizuka' or "Hollywood", 'Wintergreen', 'Densa Spartan', 'Glauca' or "Blue Sargent's", and 'Blue Point'. Other species are *J. conferta*, *J. horizontalis*, *J. procumbens*, *J. sabina*, *J. scopulorum*, *J. squamata*, and *J. virginiana*.

Loquat
Eriobotrya japonica

EXPOSURE

Full Sun

COLD HARDINESS

Varies

WATER USAGE

Semi-Moist

GROWTH RATE

Fast to Med.

AVG. HT × WIDTH

25' × 25'

SPACING

15–25'

Very large, dark-green leaves. Large open shrub to small tree. White to light-yellow fragrant fall flowers producing yellow-orange edible spring fruit. Evergreen.

I've seen this plant grown in the Zone 7B areas of Brown, Van Zandt, Smith, Tarrant, and Henderson Counties, but it does sometimes "winter burn" (parts including leaves and stems freeze). In very severe winters, the entire plant may freeze. Because of its unusually large leaves, loquat tends to impart a tropical effect wherever it is used. This is a very coarse-textured plant. The fruit is small, edible, and interesting to the taste buds—but I still prefer a peach. In Zones 7B and the upper parts of Zone 8A, its ultimate height and width will most likely not be reached due to winter burn. In Zones 8B, 9A, and 9B, expect full growth of this interesting landscape addition.

WHEN TO PLANT

In Zones 8B, 9A, and 9B, any time is an acceptable planting time, but spring is the best. In Zones 7B and 8A, spring is the best planting time.

WHERE TO PLANT

In Zones 8A, 9A, and 9B, large containers of loquat work well in locations such as pools, decks, or other outdoor entertainment areas. A loquat will complement banana trees, tropical hibiscus, mandevilla, and other tropical or tropical-looking plants in these areas. Loquats are interesting specimens or accent plants because of their leaf size and color and umbrella-like crowns. Don't use as foundation plantings. They may be used in very tall full-sun screen plantings. Loquat will grow in sandy or clay soils or poorly drained locations, but it prefers relatively moist and fertile soils.

HOW TO PLANT

When installing individual plants, select a location where the soil drains well and is easily irrigated. Remove sticks, rocks, turfgrass, and weeds from the planting area. Dig the planting hole as deep as the soilball and no deeper, but twice the width of the ball. Install the plant, backfill, water thoroughly, apply root stimulator, and cover with 3 to 4 in. of your favorite bark mulch. I usually use pine bark. For bed plantings, first till the area, then add 4 to 6 in. of organic matter such as brown sphagnum peat moss, compost, and/or ground bark. Till a second time, and plant.

CARE AND MAINTENANCE

Loquat has no serious insect problems, but the bacterial disease fire blight may be an unwelcome visitor. Don't overfertilize your loquats or place in areas with poor air movement, because fire blight has a better chance of invading under these circumstances. Products for fire blight control are available. Remember, read and follow label directions. Fertilize twice a year with a premium-quality long-lasting slow-release granular rose food according to label directions. Apply 2 weeks after the last killing frost in your area and again in the middle of the growing season. Water thoroughly after each application. Prune as needed to shape the plant's natural form in the spring. Water as needed to maintain a relatively moist soil.

ADDITIONAL INFORMATION

Gardeners often try one or more plants for the "fun" of it. Loquat may be one of these plants for you.

ADDITIONAL SPECIES, CULTIVARS, OR VARIETIES

The only other loquat variety I'm familiar with is the hybrid 'Coppertone', which is more leathery in appearance and has smaller leaves. 'Coppertone' retains its coppery-color foliage most of the year. It works as a specimen, screen, or background plant. Additional cultivars most likely exist.

Mahonia
Mahonia bealei

EXPOSURE

Semi-Shade

COLD HARDINESS

All Texas

WATER USAGE

Semi-Moist

GROWTH RATE

Slow

AVG. HT × WIDTH

4–6 ′ × 3–5 ′

SPACING

3–4 ′

Medium multiple-stemmed shrub. Foliage is stiff, broad, holly-like, dark deep green, and leathery in appearance. Clusters of yellow flowers produce dark-blue berries. Evergreen.

*P*atsy Tindell, a longtime friend, lives in Woodway, a suburb of Waco, and has lots of shade in her backyard. Her soil is typical of the area: heavy black clay. *Mahonia bealei* is also known as leatherleaf mahonia—any plant that grows with relatively heavy shade in black clay soil like Patsy's must be "leathery" tough. Mahonia actually does prefer shady locations, and does not do well in daylong full sun or reflected heat. Eastern sun till midmorning is acceptable, but mahonia prefers shade for the remainder of the day. Dappled daylong conditions are also acceptable.

WHEN TO PLANT

Due to its winter hardiness, leatherleaf mahonia may be planted any time of the year—though midwinter in the Panhandle may be a bit brisk for most gardeners! Fall is really the best planting time, and spring is second best.

WHERE TO PLANT

Plant in shady locations. Leatherleaf mahonia will grow in light to heavy Texas soils as long as they aren't wet or poorly drained, but it does best in moist, improved, fertile locations. It may be used as foundation plantings in 2 or more rows, in masses under trees, or in containers. When used as multiple-row foundation plantings, alternate in a "checkerboard" pattern for a very interesting planting. Use the same technique when planting in masses, adding as many rows as needed to fill your designed area. It works well in shaded areas along with aucuba, aralia, English ivy, and ferns.

HOW TO PLANT

Improve your planting area with 4 to 6 in. of organic matter such as compost, brown sphagnum peat moss, and/or ground bark mulch. First remove turfgrass, weeds, rocks, sticks, and other debris, and till. Spread the organic matter and till again. Be careful about damaging the root systems if you are planting near trees. It may be necessary to try a mini-tiller or the old shovel-and-fork method to incorporate organic matter in your soil. Spend the time, effort, and energy necessary to do the best job possible. After the soil improvements are complete, dig planting holes as deep as the plant's soilballs and no deeper. Install plants, backfill, water thoroughly, apply a root stimulator, and cover with 3 to 4 in. of bark mulch.

CARE AND MAINTENANCE

Leatherleaf has no serious pests. For a great look, prune back one or more stems of each plant at different levels in very early spring. Water as needed to maintain a moist soil. A 3- to 4-in. layer of bark mulch will greatly aid in soil moisture retention. Leatherleaf mahonia will respond with vigor to a fertile soil. Here's one plan to accomplish this goal: apply 15-5-10, 21-7-14, 19-5-9, or a similar 3:1:2 ratio premium-quality long-lasting slow-release lawn fertilizer 4 times a year according to label directions; apply 2 weeks after the last spring frost in your area, twice more during the growing season, and once during the fall. Remember to water thoroughly after each application.

ADDITIONAL INFORMATION

Several leatherleaf mahonia placed in a group in a shady area gives an attractive effect.

ADDITIONAL SPECIES, CULTIVARS, OR VARIETIES

Mahonia bealei has no known cultivars, but it does have some relatives you may wish to try: *M. aquifolium* or Oregon grape holly and 'Compacta'; *M. fortunei* or Chinese mahonia; and *M. repens* or creeping mahonia.

Nandina
Nandina domestica

EXPOSURE

F. Sun to Semi-

COLD HARDINESS

All Texas

WATER USAGE

Arid to Moist

GROWTH RATE

Medium

AVG. HT × WIDTH

5–7′ × 3–6′

SPACING

3′

Erect multiple-stemmed evergreen shrub with whorls of compound lacy leaves held high. Clusters of tiny white summer flowers followed by red berries.

Nandina domestica or, simply, nandina is also known as heavenly bamboo. It may be heavenly, but it is not a bamboo. It is an extremely easy-to-grow multi-trunk or -stemmed shrub. It is medium to dark to metallic green during the growing season, and has outstanding fall and winter foliage colors of red, bronze, and purple tints when grown in full sun. Sunny spots are indeed the best location for nandina. My first experience in relocating *N. domestica* was in 1973 when we purchased our first home 2 1/2 miles south of downtown Canton on Texas State Highway 19. We were certainly proud of that place. The nandinas were scattered throughout the landscape. I dug them all up in early winter after preparing a rather large bed on the northwest side of our home. I mass planted them in the bed, and the planting turned out great! It's still thriving today, and I continue to enjoy group plantings of nandina.

WHEN TO PLANT
Plant anytime, though early spring and early fall are the best planting times. If you are going to relocate or transplant existing plantings, wait until after a hard

freeze in the fall, then dig and relocate any time during the dormant season. I prefer the earlier part of the dormant season.

WHERE TO PLANT

Plant in sunny locations without reflected heat. Nandina will grow in rather dense shade, but much of its winter color is often lost in heavily shaded areas. My ideal sun/shade location would be 8 hours of full sun without reflected heat, along with shade from the hot afternoon sun. It may be used in masses as foundation plantings, stand-alone yard beds and backgrounds, and in confined areas such as planters.

HOW TO PLANT

N. domestica is a durable shrub tolerant of most Texas soil conditions, but it responds with great vigor to deep, fertile, moist soils. Remove weeds, turfgrass, rocks, and sticks from the planting area and till. Blend 4 to 6 in. organic matter such as compost, ground bark, and/or brown sphagnum peat moss into the native soil. Dig the planting holes soilball deep, set the plants in the holes, backfill, water thoroughly, apply root stimulator, and cover with 3 to 4 in. of bark.

CARE AND MAINTENANCE

Nandina has no pests. Prevent soil dryness and prune each spring. Fertilize with a premium-quality long-lasting slow-release 3:1:2 ratio lawn fertilizer such as 19-5-9, 21-7-14, or 15-5-10. Follow label directions, of course. Apply in the spring 2 weeks after the last killing frost in your area, 8 weeks later, again 8 weeks later during the growing season, and once in the fall. Remember to water thoroughly after each application.

ADDITIONAL INFORMATION

Nandina is a long-lived and oft-used shrub for Texas gardeners. It is second only to holly as my favorite shrub.

ADDITIONAL SPECIES, CULTIVARS, OR VARIETIES

Try some of these varieties: 'Compacta', 'Harbor Dwarf', 'Moon Bay', 'Nana', 'Gulf Stream', 'Ori-Hime', 'Wood's Dwarf', and 'Firepower'. Note: There are dwarf, semi-dwarf, compact, and tall-growing nandinas. I'm sure you will enjoy one or more varieties in your home landscape.

Oleander
Nerium oleander

EXPOSURE

F. Sun to Semi-

COLD HARDINESS

To 10° F.

WATER USAGE

Arid-Dry/Semi-Mst.

GROWTH RATE

Fast

AVG. HT × WIDTH

4–15' × 5–12'

SPACING

6–8'

Dense, multi-stemmed, upright, dark-green, narrow-leaved evergreen shrub. Blooms are white, pink, red, coral, and yellow.

Oleander is a blooming shrub that's so tough it's used in some highway medians (such as on I-35 south of Austin). You can see it in use all over Galveston. Oleander withstands intense heat and tolerates drought, salt, and neglect. This is a very adaptable blooming shrub where it is winter hardy. If you live in the areas of Texas where it is hardy, try one or more varieties or types in sunny locations. I'm currently growing and enjoying 'Little Red' inside a sunny enclosed area in zone 7B. The dwarf varieties may be used as foundation plantings, but they are often more showy as specimens. They are also good in large color beds.

WHEN TO PLANT

Plant in early spring after all danger of frost or freeze has passed, and almost anytime throughout the growing season, including early fall. I wouldn't plant in late fall or winter.

WHERE TO PLANT

The best locations are sunny, but it will grow in moderate shade. Oleander will tolerate almost any Texas soil, but it prefers a deep, moist, fertile, loose soil. It makes great natural screens in the landscape, from 8 to 15 ft. high and wide for the standard varieties, 5 to 7 ft. high and wide for dwarfs, and 4 to 6 ft. tall and wide for the petits. It also works well as natural hedges. Oleander may be clipped, but the plants are usually considered much more attractive when allowed to grow into their natural shapes and sizes. A tall-growing standard variety such as 'Hardy Red' may be trained into a "tree." Such "trees" may be used as patio plantings or in containers around pools, on decks, or other locations where relatively tall, upright, blooming tree form plants are desired.

HOW TO PLANT
Just because oleander will tolerate less-than-desirable conditions doesn't mean it likes them. To obtain optimum growth and bloom, the plants need a well-prepared soil. For bed plantings of all types, remove any debris, weeds, and grass, and till the area. Blend in 4 to 6 in. of organic matter such as compost, brown sphagnum peat moss, and/or ground bark. Till again and the bed will be ready for planting. After digging planting holes soilball deep, install the individual plants, backfill with the soil mix, water thoroughly, apply a root stimulator, and cover with 3 to 4 in. of your favorite bark mulch.

CARE AND MAINTENANCE
A caterpillar may visit, but it is easily controlled. Remember, read and follow label directions. Water sufficiently to prevent soil dryness; maintaining a thick mulch will greatly aid in moisture retention. Remove any dead stems or leaves by pruning during the early spring. Fertilize in the spring 2 weeks after your last killing frost, again 8 weeks later, and once in early fall according to label directions. Use a premium-quality slow-release granular rose fertilizer and water thoroughly after each application.

ADDITIONAL INFORMATION
In some years gardeners may experience damage or loss of oleander varieties that are usually hardy. CAUTION: All parts of oleander are *poisonous*, whether green or dry.

ADDITIONAL SPECIES, CULTIVARS, OR VARIETIES
'Hardy Red', a single red; 'General Pershing', a single dark red; and 'Sugarland', another single red, are all considered hardy in Zone 7B. Varieties hardy in Zones 8 and 9 include those in Zone 7 as well as 'Hardy Pink', 'Hardy White', 'Mrs. Roeding', 'Variegated Pink', and 'Cherry Ripe'.

Photinia
Photinia × *fraseri*

EXPOSURE

Full Sun

COLD HARDINESS

To 0° F.

WATER USAGE

Arid to Semi-Mst.

GROWTH RATE

Fast

AVG. HT × WIDTH

10–15′ × 8–10′

SPACING

5–8′

A large broadleaf evergreen shrub with many erect stems holding leathery, dark-green leaves. New leaf growth is brilliant red before turning green.

*P*hotinia is also known as red tips, Fraser's photinia, or *Photinia* × *fraseri*, the scientific name which often doubles as a common name. It is currently planted as a screen on the northwest side of our landscaped area. This is a full-sun location with excellent air movement in a rural setting. My soil is deep, loose, "doodle bug" sand, as we call it locally. The planting is irrigated by drip irrigation and is performing as expected. Because of red tips' size, it needs plenty of room to grow. When given the needed room, Fraser's photinia is excellent for reducing unwanted noise, and is good for all types of screens, including wind and privacy screens. Unless you have very wide beds and extra-tall walls, I would not recommend using red tips as a foundation planting.

WHEN TO PLANT
Photinia fraseri may be planted any time of the year, though the very best time is early fall, and second best is very early spring.

WHERE TO PLANT
Plant in full-sun locations with ample room, well-drained soils, and good air movement. Do not plant in front of standard windows or porches or near

walks or similar locations, because red tips will quickly outgrow these areas. Do not plant in poorly drained or wet soils, shady locations, or those without good air movement. These are top-notch plants when located in full-sun areas where they receive good air movement and can be grown as tall screens, hedges, or specimens.

HOW TO PLANT

Remove weeds and turfgrass and rocks, sticks, and other debris from the planting area, which should be at least 5 ft. wide. Till the area, then add 4 to 6 in. of organic matter such as compost, brown sphagnum peat moss, and/or ground bark. Till again, and the beds will be ready for planting. Dig the individual planting holes no deeper than soilball depth, set the plants in the holes, backfill with the mix, water thoroughly, apply a root stimulator, and cover with 3 to 4 in. of bark mulch. I usually use pine bark mulch.

CARE AND MAINTENANCE

Leaf spot disease may visit in locations where air movement is poor and the foliage is irrigated. To prevent this, place the plants in full-sun locations with good air movement, and water at the soil line. There are several products available to aid in the control of leaf spot. Remember, read and follow label directions. Minimal pruning is needed when growing the plants into their natural form; pruning at least every week is needed when growing them in relatively short-clipped or sheared hedges (I don't recommend this unless you really love to prune or shear). Water as needed to prevent soil dryness, applying water at the soil line. Maintain a 3-in. or deeper layer of mulch that covers the entire root system. Fertilize spring, mid-season, and fall with a premium-quality long-lasting slow-release 3:1:2 ratio lawn fertilizer. Follow label directions and water thoroughly after each application. 21-7-14, 19-5-9 and 15-5-10 are examples of 3:1:2 ratio lawn fertilizers.

ADDITIONAL INFORMATION

Fraser's photinia may be trained into "trees." In this form they work well as patio trees, specimens, and container plants for use in sunny areas such as pools and decks. You may want to check with your local nurseries to determine if Fraser's photinia is adapted to your soil and location.

ADDITIONAL SPECIES, CULTIVARS, OR VARIETIES

Photinia fraseri is a hybrid cross between *P. serrulata* and *P. glabra* and currently has no known additional varieties. I also enjoy *P. serrulata* or Chinese photinia, especially in "tree" form. It is usually more difficult to locate than red tips, but it is an interesting old-time plant.

Pyracantha

Pyracantha coccinea

EXPOSURE

Full Sun

COLD HARDINESS

All Texas

WATER USAGE

Arid to Moist

GROWTH RATE

Fast to Med.

AVG. HT × WIDTH

2–10 ′ × 2–10 ′ (v.)

SPACING

5–8 ′

Spreading groundcover to tall upright shrub with clusters of white blooms. Produces showy orange to red-orange berries. Evergreen to semievergreen to deciduous.

One of the most striking ornamental features of pyracantha or firethorn is the large clusters of berries which often give color into the fall and winter. The bloom clusters are nice, but the berries are much more colorful. This is an interesting tall, wide shrub when allowed to grow in its natural form, with compact branching and a spreading habit. Be sure to watch out for the plant's thorns when pruning. The thorns actually make firethorn more desirable in plantings designed to curtail passage. Pyracantha may be clipped into a relatively formal hedge, but it is usually best in its natural form when used for hedges or screens. Our feathered friends enjoy pyracantha berries during the winter.

WHEN TO PLANT

Early fall and very early spring are both good planting times, though firethorn may be planted successfully year-round.

WHERE TO PLANT

Plant in full-sun locations. Firethorn will grow in most Texas soils unless they are poorly drained or very wet, but it prefers fertile, moist, well-drained locations. Some very low-growing varieties work as groundcovers. Other varieties work as screens, accents, bank plantings, specimens, and espaliers. Pyracantha is usually not recommended for foundation plantings due to its size and growth pattern. Espaliers of pyracantha may be used on walls, fences, and landscape structures in various formal patterns in home and commercial landscapes. Be aware that prolonged pruning maintenance is necessary to keep an espalier of firethorn looking good.

HOW TO PLANT

In order for firethorn to perform its best for us, improve the soil before planting. Remove any weeds, turfgrass, rocks, and sticks from the planting area, and till. Add 4 to 6 in. of organic matter such as brown sphagnum peat moss, compost, and/or ground bark. Dig the planting holes soilball deep, insert the plants, backfill, water thoroughly, apply a root stimulator, and cover with 3 to 4 in. of bark. If planting in beds, make them a minimum of 5 ft. wide.

CARE AND MAINTENANCE

Lace bugs or spider mites may visit. Spider mites are especially likely to appear in hot, dry locations with poor air movement. Plantings in sunny locations with good air movement are much less likely to have any pest problems. If pests or diseases do visit, there are several possibilities for control. Remember, follow label directions. Firethorn require minimal pruning; espaliers may need pruning several times during the growing season to train and maintain their forms. Maintain a moist but not wet soil during the growing season. A 3- to 4-in. mulch layer will aid in moisture conservation. Fertilize 3 times a year, using a granular long-lasting slow-release rose fertilizer according to label directions. Apply 2 weeks after the last killing spring frost in your area, again 10 weeks later, and once in early fall.

ADDITIONAL INFORMATION

For good-looking results when using firethorn in your landscape, be sure to give it plenty of room to grow.

ADDITIONAL SPECIES, CULTIVARS, OR VARIETIES

Cold hardiness varies with pyracantha's species and cultivars. Here's a partial list including hardiness zones: *P. coccinea* 'Lowboy' (Zone 5), 'Lalandei' (Zone 6), 'Kasan' (Zone 5). Firethorn with red berries include *P. fortuneana* 'Graberi' (Zone 7), 'Cherri Berri' (Zone 7), 'Monelf' (Zone 7), *P.* 'Ruby Mound' (Zone 7), 'Red Elf' (Zone 7), *P. koidzumii* 'Victory' (Zone 7), 'Santa Cruz' (Zone 7), and 'Watereri' (Zone 7). Note: If hardy in zones 5, 6 or 7, they are also hardy in the Southern Texas zones.

Spiraea
Spiraea japonica

EXPOSURE

F. Sun to Semi-

COLD HARDINESS

All Texas

WATER USAGE

Semi-Moist

GROWTH RATE

Med. to Fast

AVG. HT × WIDTH

1–6 ′ × 3–5 ′

SPACING

5–8 ′

Deciduous shrub, a spreading mound form with dark-green dense foliage on slender stems. Very showy blooms in clusters of pink, rose-pink, purplish-pink, white, and red.

*I*f you live in the colder regions of Texas and are looking for an early spring-through midsummer-blooming shrub that will not be lost due to winter cold, take a look at *S. japonica* or Japanese spiraea, and try other spiraeas as well. They will dependably grow and bloom in all areas of Texas. They may be used in beds near your foundation or as hedges, screens, and specimens, depending on the varieties or species selected.

WHEN TO PLANT

Anytime is planting time for spiraea in Texas, though fall is the best time and very early spring is second best.

WHERE TO PLANT

Best bloom and growth is achieved in full-sun locations with moist, well-drained, fertile soils. These plants will tolerate almost any Texas soil and some shade. The lower-growing varieties will add color and interest to extra-wide foundation plantings. Their blooms stand out when planted in front of taller-growing broadleaf evergreens such as holly. Taller varieties may be used as informal hedges or screens. Spiraea specimens are often standouts in the landscape. When you are looking for a family of long-lived shrubs that are "sure to bloom" for little first-time gardeners, spiraea may be the answer. Children love their clusters of blooms.

HOW TO PLANT

While Japanese spiraea and its family members will grow in most Texas soils, this doesn't mean they prefer them. To obtain beat results, improve the soil. In your selected sunny location, remove any debris, weeds, and turfgrass, and till the planting area, which should be at least 5 ft. wide. Next add 4 to 6 in. of organic matter such as compost, brown sphagnum peat moss, and ground bark. Till again and the bed will be ready for planting. Dig the planting holes no deeper than soilball deep (being sure not to crowd), install plants, backfill, and water thoroughly. Apply a root stimulator and cover with 3 to 4 in. of bark. I usually use pine bark mulch.

CARE AND MAINTENANCE

This plant has no serious pests. Minimal pruning after bloom is completed may be necessary to aid in natural shaping. Fertilize in the spring 2 weeks after the last killing frost in your area, 10 weeks after that, and once again in the fall. Premium-quality long-lasting slow-release granular rose food applied according to label direc-tions works well. Remember to water thoroughly after each application. Water sufficiently to maintain a moist soil, espe-cially during growth and bloom periods. Prevent soil dryness during the remainder of the year. A 3- to 4-in. layer of mulch main-tained year-round will greatly aid in soil moisture conservation.

ADDITIONAL INFORMATION

One name often used by Texas gardeners when they are talking about spiraea is "Bridal Wreath," but that common name actually applies to S. prunifolia.

ADDITIONAL SPECIES, CULTIVARS, OR VARIETIES

Try some of these spiraeas: S. japonica 'Alpina' or Daphne spiraea, 'Little Princess', and 'Shirobana'. Other species and varieties are S. nipponica 'Halward's Silver' and 'Snowmound', S. dolchica' or pink spiraea, S. catoniensis 'Lanceata' or double bridal wreath and S. prunifolia or bridal wreath. The hybrids include S. × bumalda 'Anthony Waterer' or red spiraea, 'Crispa' or crisp leaf spiraea, 'Froebelli' or froebelli pink spiraea, 'Goldflame', and 'Norman'. Others are S. × 'Goldmound', S. thunbergii or 'Baby's Breath Spiraea', and S. × vanhouttei or Vanhoutte spiraea.

Viburnum
Viburnum spp.

EXPOSURE

Full to Semi-

COLD HARDINESS

All Texas

WATER USAGE
Semi-Moist

GROWTH RATE
Medium

AVG. HT × WIDTH

3–18' × 3–16' (v.)

SPACING
6–30'

Evergreen to semievergreen to deciduous. Compact to large shrubs with bright- to deep-green leaves. Clustered blooms are white, creamy, pink, pinkish-white, and rose-tinted white.

*T*he most frequently used common name in Texas for viburnum is snowball bush, and this usually applies to *V. opulus* 'Sterile'—but there are many other viburnums that merit our attention. In the viburnum family are selections that may be used as foundation plantings, tall or short hedges, screens, specimens, or mass plantings. We Texas gardeners sometimes overlook plants that have been in use for generations in Texas gardens, such as viburnum. If you want to know more about these plants, or haven't heard of them at all, let me suggest visits to nurseries and public gardens.

WHEN TO PLANT
Fall is the best viburnum planting time, and very early spring is second best. In Texas, they may be planted anytime.

WHERE TO PLANT
V. davidii or David viburnum's usual height is 2 to 3 ft. tall by 3 to 4 ft. wide, making it a candidate for a low, wide foundation planting or hedge. Japanese viburnum or *V. japonicum* may reach 18 ft. tall and 16 ft. wide. In nearly all

landscapes, this would not make a foundation planting at all, but it would function well as an outstanding specimen or very tall, wide screen. So the choice of where to plant really depends on the variety that has been selected. Most do best in sun with shade from the hot afternoon sun. *V. rhytidophyllum* or leatherleaf viburnum prefers partial shade to dense shade or dappled daylong sun and shade. So does *V. opulus* 'Sterile' or snowball bush. Some viburnums will grow in a rather wide range of Texas soils, but they all prefer a deep, fertile, moist, well-drained soil. Do not plant on wet or poorly drained soils of any type.

HOW TO PLANT

When planting in landscape beds, first remove any debris, turfgrass, and weeds, then till the planting area (even the smaller varieties should be planted in a bed at least 5 ft. wide). Add 4 to 6 in. of brown sphagnum peat moss, compost, ground bark, or other organic matter. Level, till again, and the bed will be ready for plants. Dig the planting holes rootball deep, place the viburnums in their new homes, backfill, water thoroughly, apply a root stimulator, and cover with 3 to 4 in. of your favorite bark.

CARE AND MAINTENANCE

Viburnum has no serious pests. Soil moisture is needed, but don't overwater. Prune as needed to shape. I prefer spring pruning for removing wild shoots and branches and dead or damaged parts. Major pruning is usually done after the main bloom flush and just as new growth begins. Fertilize 3 times a year with a premium-quality long-lasting slow-release granular rose fertilizer, according to label directions. Apply 2 weeks after the last spring killing frost in your area, again 10 weeks later, and once in the fall. Remember to water thoroughly after each application.

ADDITIONAL INFORMATION

Let me suggest that when viburnums are in bloom you visit arboretums such as the Stephen F. Austin State University Arboretum in Nacogdoches, as well as your area nurseries. Carry a camera to record their looks, and paper and pencil to write down information that will help you decide which ones to try at home.

ADDITIONAL SPECIES, CULTIVARS, OR VARIETIES

Give one of more of these a try: *V. opulus* 'Sterile'; *V. plicatum*; *V. rhytidophyllum*; *V. suspensum*; *V. tinus*; *V. plicatum tomentosum* 'Mariessii'; *V. lantana* 'Mohican'; *V. japonicum* 'Macrophyllus', 'Atrosanguinea', and 'Rosea'; *V. dentatum*; *V. nudum*; *V. rufidulum*; and *V. awabuki* 'Chindo'. There are also hybrids and additional varieties and species.

Wax Leaf Ligustrum
Ligustrum japonicum

EXPOSURE

F. Sun to Semi-

COLD HARDINESS

To 5° F.

WATER USAGE

Semi-Moist

GROWTH RATE

Fast

AVG. HT × WIDTH

10–14´ × 8–12´

SPACING

5–6´

Dark-green, shiny, waxy, thick foliage with clusters of showy, white, fragrant spring blooms. Large, upright, evergreen shrub.

L. japonicum, also known as *L. texanum*, 'Texanum', and wax leaf, is a tall, wide shrub ideal for making a natural screen. Our feathered friends, including cedar waxwings, enjoy the cover as well as the berries during the winter. Wax leaf is available just about everywhere in Texas, and it has been used for many years—though sometimes not in the best locations. Wax leaf planted in front of windows, porches, or other areas best left unobscured will give you a weekly or even more frequent workout with shears. Don't plant it in these locations! And unless you have a very tall, solid wall, don't use wax leaf as foundation plantings.

WHEN TO PLANT
Plant anytime in the zones in which it is hardy, though early fall is the best time, and early spring is second best.

WHERE TO PLANT
Wax leaf is a tough, rapid-growing shrub that will grow in almost any soil type, plants and transplants easily, tolerates drought, and will grow in sun or

shade. It is good for wind screens, privacy screens, and noise reduction screens. It lends itself well to horticultural training in forms such as patio trees, pyramids, and pom poms. In these forms it may be used as accents, specimens, or large container plants. Wax leaf is easily trained into various hedge shapes including square, round, and oval. When being trained as a hedge, wax leaf must be pruned weekly during the growing season.

HOW TO PLANT

Minimal soil preparation is needed to grow wax leaf, but if you want it to start off strong, soil improvement should be on your agenda. After removing any debris, weeds, and turfgrass and tilling the planting area, add 4 to 6 in. of compost, brown sphagnum peat moss, and/or ground bark. Spread the organic matter, till again, and the planting area will be ready for planting. Install individual plants in holes no deeper than the soilball, backfill, water thoroughly, apply a root stimulator, and cover with 3 to 4 in. of pine bark mulch.

CARE AND MAINTENANCE

This plant has no serious pests. Water as needed to prevent soil dryness. To aid wax leaf's color and growth, fertilize 4 times a year with a premium-quality slow-release 3:1:2 ratio lawn fertilizer (such as 15-5-10-, 19-5-9, and 21-7-14) according to label directions. Apply in the spring 2 weeks after the last frost, 2 times during the growing season approximately 10 weeks apart, and once in the fall. Prune as needed for your application, but don't prune in late fall or winter. Early spring is best for radical pruning.

ADDITIONAL INFORMATION

Wax leaf is widely sold throughout Texas. Just make sure you anticipate its ultimate size and the pruning frequency it will require.

ADDITIONAL SPECIES, CULTIVARS, OR VARIETIES

Wax leaf is a type of privet. You may want to try members of its immediate family or expanded family such as *L.* 'Suwannee River' or Suwannee River privet; *L. japonicum* 'Texanum Aureo-Marginata', variegated wax leaf ligustrum, 'Jack Frost', or Jack Frost ligustrum; *L. sinensis* 'Variegata' or variegated privet; *L. incidum* or tree ligustrum; *L. × vicaryi* or vicary golden privet; and *L. vulgare* 'Lodense' or lodense privet.

Winter Jasmine
Jasminum nudiflorum

EXPOSURE

Semi-Shade

COLD HARDINESS

All Texas

WATER USAGE

Semi-Moist

GROWTH RATE

Fast

AVG. HT × WIDTH
3–4′ × 4–6′

SPACING
4–6′

Deciduous. Unusual round form with weeping, arching green stems. Blooms are yellow.

During late winter to very early spring, when gardeners begin to think spring may never come, J. nudiflorum comes to the rescue with bright-yellow 1-in. flowers on green stems . . . and we are reassured that once again spring will arrive as usual. Winter jasmine is considered a fast grower, growing in areas of poor soil and full-sun locations. It is great for low shrub planting in the landscape. It works well cascading over walls, in masses, and on banks, and is good in spots where erosion may cause problems. When planted in very wide beds in front of tall-growing, dark-green, broadleaf evergreens, its early spring color really stands out. The contrasts between the greens and the leaf sizes of holly and winter jasmine are also interesting.

WHEN TO PLANT
Fall is the best time for planting, and spring is second best, but winter jasmine may be planted anytime.

WHERE TO PLANT
Plant on hillsides, in large wide beds with other colorful shrubs, or grouped together in masses in all sorts of sunny locations. Never plant in heavily

shaded spots. Winter jasmine requires at least 8 hours of full sun in order to do its best for us, and it prefers daylong full sun.

How to Plant

Make planting beds at least 5 ft. wide. Before bed construction, remove any rocks, sticks, weeds, and turfgrass, and till the area. You may stop at this point and plant if desired, but if you want good plant response, soil improvement is enhanced with the addition of 4 to 6 in. of organic matter such as brown sphagnum peat moss, compost, ground bark, and similar materials. I recommend that 4 to 6 in. of organic matter be added to the area and tilled in the beds. Never dig shrub planting holes deeper than soilball depth. After digging the holes, insert the shrubs, backfill with soil mix, water thoroughly, apply root stimulator, and cover with 3 to 4 in. of your favorite bark. I usually use pine bark.

Care and Maintenance

This is a minimum-care shrub that has no serious pests. It may be sheared to shape in spring after bloom is complete. While winter jasmine is tolerant of most soils, it will respond well to the increase in fertility that comes from a good fertilizing program. Fertilize in the spring after blooming is completed, twice more during the growing season, and once in the fall. Use a 3:1:2 ratio premium-quality slow-release lawn fertilizer such as 21-7-14, 19-5-9, and 15-5-10. Remember to follow label directions and water after each application. Water as needed to maintain a moist soil throughout the growing season and to prevent soil dryness the remainder of the year.

Additional Information

This shrub is most likely to be found at long-established full-service neighborhood nurseries.

Additional Species, Cultivars, or Varieties

J. nudiflorum or winter jasmine is a stand-alone plant. It has some family members you may wish to try such as *J. sambac* or Maid Of Orleans Sambac jasmine (hardy in Zones 8 and 9), *J. primulinum* or primrose jasmine (hardy in Zones 8 and 9), *J. polyanthum* or pink jasmine (hardy in Zones 8 and 9), *J. floridum* or showy jasmine (hardy in Zones 7, 8, and 9), and *J. nitidum* or angel wing jasmine, sometimes called Confederate star jasmine (hardy in Zone 10).

CHAPTER NINE

TREES

*T*REES CAN BE CONSIDERED MOTHER NATURE'S AIR CON-
DITIONERS—they actually do cool the air and climate for us. On
a hot Texas summer day, you may find the temperature under a nice
shade tree is 10 degrees cooler than the temperature in the open sun.

We have more trouble with heat than we do with cold in Texas.
Properly selected and placed shade trees can help cool our homes.
High-quality long-lived shade trees planted on the west side of a
home will help its inhabitants make it through the scorching Texas
summers. Certain deciduous varieties will provide great fall color
while allowing the sun to come through to warm our homes during
the relatively short, traditional winters.

It is a good idea to plant trees first in a home landscape. Many
gardeners don't plant their trees until they have finished the rest of
their landscape plan; but trees generally take longer to grow, and
they provide the framework for other landscape material. Draw a
landscape plan or have one created for you. When the plan is completed, plant your trees before you plant any other plants.

The very best time to plant trees is in the early fall. This will
allow the tree almost a full year of growth before the next July and
August heat wave. Trees may, however, be planted 12 months out of
the year. This is especially true of container-grown selections.

Properly selected and placed trees can break the wind. Wind-
breaks have been successful in reducing energy usage, saving valuable
topsoil, and helping to create a more enjoyable homesite environment.

Trees are generally classified as deciduous or evergreen. Most
shade trees we use are deciduous, and there are some great ones
which provide outstanding fall color. Among these are shumard red
oak, *Quercus shumardii*, Chinese pistachio, *Pistacia chinensis*, and
ginkgo, *Ginkgo bilboa*.

I am often asked for recommendations of fast-growing shade
trees for the home landscape. The most important thing to keep in
mind is that most of the "fast-growing" shade trees are weak-

Chapter Nine

wooded, problem-prone, and short-lived. Properly selected, planted, and cared for, high-quality long-lived shade trees grow almost as rapidly as those we consider "fast-growing"—and they will be around for decades.

Shade trees that reach particular heights may have to be shaped and pruned for various reasons. You may not feel comfortable doing this yourself. Here are some helpful tips and suggestions to use when hiring someone to prune your trees:

- Make sure the person you hire is a professional arborist with insurance. Ask for references and check them out.

- Put the agreement or contract for services in writing before any work begins. Both you and the contractor will benefit from having in writing exactly which services are to be performed and which are not, as well as total cost and when and how it's to be paid. No payment should be made before work is completed.

- Don't hire someone that calls on you with a pick-up, chain saw, and ladder, and without references, insurance, or a business site.

Trees are usually classified by height. Trees which grow less than 30 ft. tall are considered small. Medium trees grow 30 to 50 ft., and large trees grow over 50 ft. Ask the staff at Lowe's how tall and wide a particular tree will grow in your area. It is disappointing to plant a tree which looks as if it will remain relatively small but later obtains tremendous height and width. If planted too close to your home, foundation, drive, pool, or other structures, such a tree can cause damage. Gather your information *before* purchasing.

We Texans have a wide selection of trees from which to choose. In this chapter I have included nineteen tree families in which you will find interesting outstanding varieties.

Bald Cypress

Taxodium distichum

EXPOSURE

Full Sun

COLD HARDINESS

All Texas

WATER USAGE

Moist

GROWTH RATE

Fast

AVG. HT × WIDTH

50–100 ′ × 20–50 ′

SPACING

25–50 ′

Light-green fern- or feather-like leaves that turn a coppery/bronze shade in the fall. Deciduous, with a conical form that opens and spreads with age.

*B*ald cypress is a conifer, but unlike pine, fir, or other members of the conifer family, it is deciduous. I first noticed the bald cypress near the Stephen F. Austin State University library when Judy and I were students there. I thought they looked great then and 27 years later I still do today. They are often used in both urban and commercial landscapes. In the South we associate the bald cypress tree with swamps. It's true that they grow in these locations, but they also adapt well to less watery urban landscape locations.

WHEN TO PLANT
Fall is the best planting time; early spring is second best.

WHERE TO PLANT
Bald cypress prefers moist, full-sun areas, but they will grow in nearly any standard lawn area. I would not plant them in areas that are dry, difficult to water, or shady. They need room to grow—spacing of 25 to 50 ft. may be necessary to obtain an attractive result. If you want a tree in an area that is both sunny and a bit damp, bald cypress is a great choice. It also works well in waterscapes.

HOW TO PLANT

Loosen the soil in an area several times as wide and as deep as the rootball but no deeper. Dig the planting hole rootball deep. Install the tree and make sure it sits straight. Backfill with loosened soil, water thoroughly, and apply a root stimulator. Mulch with 3 to 4 in. of bark mulch. Temporary staking may be required.

CARE AND MAINTENANCE

Requires little care. No serious pests. No pruning required. Does best in deep, moist to damp soils. Bald cypress responds with vigor to fertilizer. Three times per season, apply a premium-quality long-lasting slow-release 3:1:2 ratio lawn fertilizer such as 19-5-9, 21-7-14, or 15-5-10 according to label directions. Make the first application just as new spring growth begins, again 10 weeks later, and again in the fall. Water thoroughly after each application.

ADDITIONAL INFORMATION

Once established, bald cypress will tolerate drought. In the short term, its fern-like foliage may change colors; in longer dry periods, leaf drop may occur. This rarely damages the tree.

ADDITIONAL SPECIES, CULTIVARS, OR VARIETIES

There are no cultivars of *T. distichum* readily available in Texas. *T. ascendens*, or pond cypress, has very narrow, almost string-like leaves. It is taller and more narrow than bald cypress, but is equally adaptable. Pond cypress may be more difficult to locate in Texas nurseries.

Cedar
Juniperus virginiana

EXPOSURE

Full Sun

COLD HARDINESS

All Texas

WATER USAGE

Arid-Dry

GROWTH RATE

Fast to Med.

AVG. HT × WIDTH

20–40′ × 20–30′

SPACING

20–30′

Usually upright conical form, but may become irregular with age. Foliage is medium- to dark-green to blue-green. Evergreen.

I grew up in the Woodland Heights section of Brownwood. Both of my parents came from "the farm." My father's parents were from the Bangs area while Mom's were from Indian Creek. Grandmother Groom was gone by the time I was 6 and Granddad Groom prior to that. I was fortunate to have Granddad and Granny Miller for many years. At Christmas time their plank home had minimum decorations, but when a tree was used it was *J. virginiana* or cedar tree. Judy and I also used them for several years in our own home as holiday trees. If you truly want to do a "country Christmas," a cedar tree (also known as Eastern red cedar) is the type to use. In Brown County, as well as other Texas counties, cedar trees are cut for fence posts and are also sawed into lumber for many uses.

WHEN TO PLANT
If they are in containers they may be planted anytime, but fall is best, followed by early spring. I've seen our state Highway Department successfully plant them in midsummer. It's not the best time, but it can be done.

WHERE TO PLANT

Cedar trees will grow in all types of Texas soil, as long as it is well drained. Don't plant in poorly drained or wet soils or in shady locations. Unless you select a named variety with known growth habits, cedar trees may vary widely in size and shape.

HOW TO PLANT

No special soil preparation is needed. Loosen the soil in an area 2 to 3 times wider than the plant's soilball, but dig the planting hole only soilball deep. Next, remove the plant from the container and place it in the planting hole. Backfill with loosened soil, water thoroughly, and apply root stimulator. Mulch with 3 to 4 in. of bark.

CARE AND MAINTENANCE

Spider mites, bagworms, Juniper scale or blight, and cedar apple rust could be problems. Check with your local nursery for available remedies. Follow label directions when applying any gardening aid. Cedar requires minimal watering—usually only when the tree is young and establishing itself. Prune to desired shape during the spring. Don't severely prune branches that have no foliage, or they will fail to produce new foliage. Cedar trees respond well to fertilizer. In most situations a 3-times-a-year program should work well. Apply long-lasting slow-release premium-quality 3:1:2 ratio lawn fertilizer such as 21-7-14 or 15-5-10 according to label directions. Apply the first treatment just as new spring growth begins, again 10 weeks later, and again during the fall season. Water thoroughly after each application of fertilizer.

ADDITIONAL INFORMATION

Female trees tend to be a bit more blue-green in color, and they are the only ones that produce berries. David Wade, "The Gourmet," uses juniper berries in cooking wild game and whatever he cooks is G-R-E-A-T!

ADDITIONAL SPECIES, CULTIVARS, OR VARIETIES

There are many, including 'Cupressifolia', 'Idyllwild', 'Manhattan Blue', 'Glauca', and 'Skyrocket'. Some are trees, while others are classified as shrubs; all are *J. virginiana*.

Chinese Pistachio
Pistacia chinensis

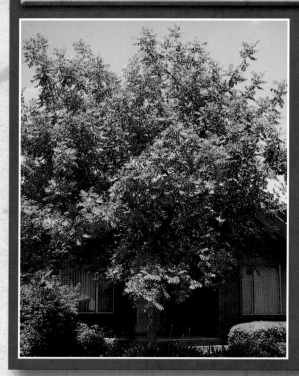

EXPOSURE	COLD HARDINESS
Full Sun	All Texas

WATER USAGE	GROWTH RATE
Arid to Semi-Mst.	Fast to Med.

AVG. HT × WIDTH	SPACING
25–40′ × 20–35′	35′

Medium-height deciduous tree with medium-green compound leaves. Fall color ranges from yellow to red-orange to brilliant red.

*C*hinese pistachio is an excellent small to medium-sized tree that is nearly perfect for Texas landscapes and should be used more often. It tolerates a wide range of locations (including confined urban areas and wide open rural areas) and soil conditions. Once it is firmly established, Chinese pistachio is very deep rooted and drought tolerant. It offers light shade that will allow you to grow other plants—like St. Augustinegrass—beneath it. We are currently growing two in the rocky areas around our deck and they are doing well.

WHEN TO PLANT
You can easily transplant container-grown stock in the fall or early spring.

WHERE TO PLANT
Plant in any sunny location where you want a low-maintenance, small to medium shade tree that will also provide outstanding fall color. The trees will also grow in confined or high heat areas. Due to their size and deep roots you may plant them close to your home, but do allow enough room so they can reach their normal rounded vase to umbrella canopy form.

HOW TO PLANT

I prefer planting from 7-, 10-, or 15-gallon containers. Smaller and larger container-grown plants are available in Texas. With your favorite shovel or digging fork, loosen the soil in the planting area. Dig the actual planting hole no deeper than the plant's soilball, remove from the container and plant. Backfill with loosened soil, water thoroughly, and apply a root stimulator. Mulch with 3 to 4 in. of bark mulch.

CARE AND MAINTENANCE

There will be no insects. Water as needed. Selective pruning may be desirable when the tree is young in order to train its growth, but pruning is usually unnecessary after this early stage. Chinese pistachio will grow quickly when fertilized and offered extra water during our typical July and August blast furnace conditions. Fertilize 3 to 4 times a year with a premium-quality long-lasting slow-release 3:1:2 ratio fertilizer such as 19-5-9, 21-7-14, or 15-5-10 according to label directions. Make the first application just as new leaf growth begins in the spring, 8 weeks later, again in 8 more weeks, and once during the fall. Water after each application.

ADDITIONAL INFORMATION

The wood from Chinese pistachio is very strong. Wind and ice usually do little, if any, damage.

ADDITIONAL SPECIES, CULTIVARS, OR VARIETIES

There are no known cultivars of Chinese pistachio. *P. vera* is the pistachio tree which produces nuts. It isn't hardy in Texas, except in the Zone 9 areas. It is much inferior to Chinese pistachio in terms of growth, shade, and overall durability in Texas. Two other family members you may want to try are *P. texana*, the Texas pistachio, and *P. atlantica*, which exhibits excellent drought tolerance.

Flowering Crab Apple
Malus spp.

EXPOSURE
Full Sun

COLD HARDINESS
All Texas

WATER USAGE
Arid to Semi-Mst.

GROWTH RATE
Fast to Med.

AVG. HT × WIDTH
10–25 ' × 15–30 '

SPACING
30 '

Deciduous, with a wide to oval crown. Foliage is bright to dark green or red to red-purple during the growing season. Showy blooms are white, pink, red, or a blend of them. Deep red fruit.

*I*f you are looking for showy trees, flowering crab apples will be hard to beat. They offer beautiful blooms, fruit, and foliage. They work well in small areas and are in scale with single story structures. Flowering crabapples may be planted singly, in groups or "groves," and in rows along drives or walkways. If you have an eating area with an outside view and like birds, plant one or more flowering crab apples. You will then get to enjoy the colors from the blooms, fruits, and foliage as well as the color from the birds.

WHEN TO PLANT

Fall is the best planting time; early spring is second best. You can plant container-grown nursery stock anytime.

WHERE TO PLANT

These are outstanding additions to gardens with decks or gazebos. Don't plant in heavily shaded areas; flowering crab apples require sunny locations in order to put on their best show. While tolerating most types of soil, they grow best in deep, fertile, moist soils. Groups of 3 or more trees, planted in triangular patterns, are great for sunny corners of the yard.

HOW TO PLANT
Measure the width of the soilball and loosen the soil in the planting area to 2 or 3 times wider than the soilball. Dig a hole as deep as the soilball, remove the tree from the container, and place in the hole. Backfill with the loosened soil, water thoroughly, and apply root stimulator. Mulch with 3 to 4 in. of bark mulch. The tree may need temporary staking.

CARE AND MAINTENANCE
There are usually no serious insect problems—although borers may attack unhealthy trees that are not growing properly. Maintaining a healthy tree is the best prevention. Fire blight, powdery mildew, and apple scab are potential problems. Control these by planting in sunny locations that have good air movement (for example: don't enclose in areas with a tall solid fence). Fertilize 3 times a year with a premium-quality, long-lasting, granular rose fertilizer. Follow label directions and water thoroughly after each application. Apply the first treatment after bloom drop, again approximately 10 weeks later, then once again in the fall. Prune as needed for shape in the spring after bloom drop. There is a wide selection of products for treating pest and/or disease problems. Follow label directions when using any aid. Your local County Agent's office has a fact sheet covering fire blight on landscape plants. Stop by or call for a copy.

ADDITIONAL INFORMATION
To help prevent problems, always plant disease-resistant plants.

ADDITIONAL SPECIES, CULTIVARS, OR VARIETIES
Nearly all flowering crab apples available at Texas nurseries are hybrids. The following are known to be disease-resistant: 'Sutyzam', 'Snowdrift', 'Jackii', 'Prairiefire', 'Robinson', and 'Centurion'.

Flowering Pear
Pyrus calleryana

EXPOSURE

Full Sun

COLD HARDINESS

All Texas

WATER USAGE

Arid to Semi-Mst.

GROWTH RATE

Fast to Med.

AVG. HT × WIDTH

30–50′ × 20–40′

SPACING

20–40′ (v.)

Dark-green, glossy leaves that turn gold, orange, deep mahogany, purple, reddish-purple and/or crimson. Deciduous.

*F*lowering pears originate from a tough and durable lineage: *P. calleryana* or callery pear. They grow well in all areas of Texas. Depending on the variety selected, some flowering pears are columnar in shape; they fit well in limited spaces, and can be used to frame structures or designate drives. Others have a more rounded shape and can be located near decks and gazebos, and in specialty gardens. In the spring, flowering pears are covered with masses of white spring blooms. Spring and summer foliage is shiny and dark-green. Fall color is outstanding.

WHEN TO PLANT
The best time to plant flowering pear is in the fall; early spring is second best.

WHERE TO PLANT
Flowering pears prefer sunny locations with deep, fertile, well-drained moist soil. They will tolerate a wide range of conditions, however, including poor soils, heavy clay, restricted root space, wind, drought, and limited water. All in all, flowering pear is a very adaptable tree for urban landscape uses. Flowering pears are used to line entrances to property, along driveways, and

as street trees. I would not plant them in poorly drained or wet locations, in shady locations, or where they will be crowded by other trees or structures.

HOW TO PLANT
No special soil preparation is needed for flowering pear. Simply loosen the soil in the planting area wider than the soilball. Dig the hole soilball deep and no deeper. Remove from the container and place in the planting hole. Backfill, water thoroughly, and apply a root stimulator. Mulch with 3 to 4 in. of your favorite bark mulch.

CARE AND MAINTENANCE
This plant has no serious pests. Water as needed to maintain a healthy tree, usually while the tree is establishing itself and during our July and August "oven times." Prune as needed to ensure strong branch/limb structure. This training is most needed during the early years of flowering pear's lifetime in the landscape. Failure to do the corrective pruning on some varieties, including 'Bradford', may result in a rather mature specimen splitting as a result of ice storms. My soil is deep, deep "doodle bug" sand, so I fertilize flowering pear 4 times per growing season. (In soils that hold nutrients better than mine, 3 or even 2 times a year is probably adequate.) I use a premium-quality long-lasting slow-release 3:1:2 ratio lawn fertilizer such as 15-5-10 or 18-6-12 according to label directions. Always make the first application after bloom drop just as new leaf growth begins. I fertilize again in 10 weeks and again in the next 10 weeks—plus one fall application. No matter how often you fertilize, always make the first spring and fall applications. Water thoroughly after each application.

ADDITIONAL INFORMATION
Container-grown selections can be planted successfully year-round.

ADDITIONAL SPECIES, CULTIVARS, OR VARIETIES
Try some of these in your home landscape: 'Capital', 'Cleveland Select', 'Redspire', 'Whitehouse', 'Bradford', 'Aristocrat', and 'Glens Form'.

Ginkgo
Ginkgo biloba

EXPOSURE

Full Sun

COLD HARDINESS

All Texas

WATER USAGE

Arid to Semi-Mst.

GROWTH RATE

Slow

AVG. HT × WIDTH

50–70′ × 20–50′

SPACING

50′

Deciduous. Upright columnar to round crown. Fan-shaped, medium-green leaves that turn golden-yellow in the fall.

I am 54, and my three children warmly refer to me as a fossil. But if you really want to see a living fossil, look no farther than ginkgo, which is sometimes called maidenhair tree. The maidenhair name is taken from the similarity in the ginkgo's leaf to the leaflets of the maidenhair fern (*Adiantum* species). Both are fan-shaped. Fossil records of ginkgo were found in North America, but the living plants were believed to be extinct. In the late 1700s, ginkgo was found growing in China. Subsequent propagation has made ginkgo available throughout our country, including Texas.

WHEN TO PLANT
Fall is the best planting time; spring is second best.

WHERE TO PLANT
Ginkgo will tolerate a wide range of urban conditions, including restricted space for root growth and pollution. It will also tolerate some drought. Ginkgo is considered a slow grower unless it is given ideal conditions. It prefers deep, fertile, moist soil and sunny locations. Given these conditions, ginkgo will

grow substantially every year after root establishment. Ginkgo is an outstanding lawn tree and a knock-out in the fall once sizable height and width is obtained. Don't crowd. Do not plant in areas of poor soil drainage, poor soils, shady locations, or spots that are difficult to water.

HOW TO PLANT
Loosen the soil wider than soilball width and dig the planting hole soilball deep. Remove from the container and place in the planting hole. Backfill with loose soil, water thoroughly, and apply a root stimulator. Mulch with 3 to 4 in. of bark mulch.

CARE AND MAINTENANCE
Ginkgo has no pests. Pruning is rarely needed. Water as necessary to maintain a moist soil, especially during early establishment. During our typical July and August heat and other periods of little rainfall, ginkgo may also benefit from a long, slow, deep drink. Beginning with the second year, fertilize ginkgo 4 times a year if you wish to obtain maximum possible yearly growth. Apply a premium-quality long-lasting slow-release 3:1:2 ratio lawn fertilizer such as 19-5-9, 15-5-10, or 21-7-14 according to label directions. Make the first application just as new buds break in the spring. Reapply in 10 weeks, again in another 10 weeks, and once during the fall. Always water thoroughly after each application.

ADDITIONAL INFORMATION
One of the most spectacular gingko trees I've seen in Texas is on the lawn of the Tyler City Hall in the downtown area of Tyler.

ADDITIONAL SPECIES, CULTIVARS, OR VARIETIES
There are male and female ginkgoes. Due to their foul-smelling fruits, the female selections are not desirable. Desirable male varieties include 'Autumn Gold', 'Princeton Gold', 'Fastigiata', and 'Pendula' (a relatively weeping form).

Golden Rain Tree
Koelreuteria paniculata

EXPOSURE

Full Sun

COLD HARDINESS

All Texas

WATER USAGE

Arid to Semi-Mst.

GROWTH RATE

Medium

AVG. HT × WIDTH

20–40 ′ × 20–35 ′

SPACING

45 ′

Deciduous. Small to medium-sized, open-branched, rounded crown. Medium-green to blue-green compound leaves with yellow fall color.

Our home is in a rural area, where we have loose, fine soil (known locally as "doodle bug" sand). We also have outcroppings of rusty-red sandstone. One of these outcroppings is located in the southwest corner of our yard, just off our back porch. People used to ask me, "What are you going to do around all these rocks?" My answer was, "Landscape around and with them." Today no one asks, "What are you going to do?" Instead the question is, "What is that and that?" Two of the trees in this area are golden rain trees. They are growing in the wide cracks of the large stones and doing well. People notice and remark favorably on their yellow blooms. I suggest you try one if you want an easy-to-care-for, small to medium tree that has bright-yellow fragrant blooms and attractive foliage during the growing season. The foliage turns golden-yellow in the fall, and—as a bonus—the tree has interesting seedpods.

WHEN TO PLANT
Fall is the best planting time; spring is second best.

WHERE TO PLANT

Golden rain tree requires full sun. Don't plant in shade or even semi-shady locations. It will grow in a relatively wide range of Texas soils (including loose sand and heavy clay), but it prefers relatively loose, moist, fertile soils. Don't plant in poorly drained areas or spots that are difficult to water. Golden rain tree is wonderful in areas where space is limited. It also works well along walkways.

HOW TO PLANT

I prefer to plant 7- or 10-gallon sizes. Larger and smaller sizes are also available. Whatever size you select, loosen the soil wider than soilball width and dig the planting hole no deeper than soilball depth. Remove from the container and place in the hole. Backfill with loosened soil, water thoroughly, and apply a root stimulator. Mulch with 4 in. of your favorite bark (I usually use pine bark). Stake temporarily if necessary.

CARE AND MAINTENANCE

This plant has no serious pests, though boxelder bugs may appear in the fall. If they become a nuisance, there are several control possibilities. Follow label directions on any product you use. Prune when young to help ensure strong branching. No additional pruning is usually required. Use a premium-quality long-lasting slow-release 3:1:2 ratio lawn fertilizer according to directions such as 21-7-14 or 15-5-10. In my loose sand, I fertilize 4 times a year. The first spring application is 2 weeks after the last freeze or just as new buds break, whichever comes first. I reapply in 10 weeks, again in 10 more weeks, and once during the fall. Water thoroughly after each application. Water as needed to prevent dry soil; be especially attentive during our famous July and August hot and dry months.

ADDITIONAL INFORMATION

Golden rain tree is sometimes written as goldenraintree or golden-rain tree. If a tree is a *K. paniculata*, it is the one described on these pages.

ADDITIONAL SPECIES, CULTIVARS, OR VARIETIES

'September' is a late-flowering variety. The variety 'Fastigiata' grows upright and narrow. *K. bipinnata* or Chinese flame tree is hardy in Zones 7 to 9 in Texas.

Green Ash
Fraxinus pennsylvanica

EXPOSURE

Full Sun

COLD HARDINESS

To -40° F.

WATER USAGE

Semi-Moist

GROWTH RATE

Fast

AVG. HT × WIDTH

40–70 ' × 30–50 '

SPACING

45 '

Deciduous. Round canopy with dark-green leaves. Fall color is golden yellow.

Green ash may be grown in most Texas soils, except for heavy clay. These trees grow naturally in soil with a high moisture content, but they adapt well to urban applications. When given reasonable care, they quickly provide excellent shade. If you want to drink iced tea under a shade tree, green ash may be the tree you need. Green ash will adapt to compressed growing areas and is relatively drought tolerant once established.

WHEN TO PLANT
Plant anytime, though the best time is fall and spring is second best.

WHERE TO PLANT
I would space green ash approximately 20 ft. from the foundation of my home. This will give it room to spread without causing foundation concerns. If you have a septic system, plant at the same distance or more from your field lines. This should prevent the roots from plugging the field lines. For maximum cooling benefits, plant on the west side of your home. The best soil is deep, moist, non-heavy clay.

HOW TO PLANT

It is easiest to plant trees grown in 5-gallon containers, but other sizes are also available. When planting trees grown in 15- to 20-gallon containers, it is advisable to have at least 2 people involved in the operation. If you decide to plant from containers larger than 20 gallons, have a landscape contractor do the planting. No matter the size of the tree you select, planting is always the same. Dig the planting hole no deeper than the plant's soilball, but as wide as desired. After loosening the soil and digging the planting hole, install the tree. Backfill with the loose soil, water thoroughly, and apply a root stimulator. Mulch with 3 to 4 in. of your favorite bark. (I usually use pine bark nuggets.) After planting, you may need to stake the tree temporarily.

CARE AND MAINTENANCE

Borers may visit unhealthy trees. The best way to prevent bore damage is to keep your green ash healthy. Should you decide to purchase and apply bore prevention aids, follow label directions. During the first year, applications of root stimulator may be advisable. At the beginning of the second season, apply a premium-quality long-lasting slow-release tree-and-shrub or 3:1:2 ratio lawn fertilizer such as 21-7-14, 18-6-12, or 15-5-10 according to label directions. Make your first application about two weeks after the last killing frost in your area or just as new spring growth begins—whichever comes first. Apply again in 10 weeks, and once more during the fall. Water thoroughly after each application. Remove any dead branches and/or twigs yearly, during very late winter. Supplemental irrigation may be needed in July and August.

ADDITIONAL INFORMATION

Green ash prefers a soil pH of 6.5 to 7.5. If your soil is highly alkaline and/or heavy clay, I wouldn't recommend planting green ash.

ADDITIONAL SPECIES, CULTIVARS, OR VARIETIES

F. pennsylvanica cultivars include 'Patmore' (40 to 50 ft. tall and 25 to 35 ft. wide), 'Summit' (40 to 50 ft. tall and 25 ft. wide), and 'Marshalls Seedless' (40 to 50 ft. tall and 30 to 40 ft. wide). Another ash is Texas ash or *F. texensis* (30 to 45 ft. tall and 30 to 35 ft. wide). Note: See native trees for more on Texas ash.

Japanese Maple
Acer palmatum

EXPOSURE

Full to Semi-

COLD HARDINESS

All Texas

WATER USAGE

Moist

GROWTH RATE

Slow

AVG. HT × WIDTH

2–20′ × 3–20′

SPACING

6–40′

Shrub-like to round-headed deciduous tree with finely cut or
divided leaves that range from
deep green to purple- and bright-
red during the growing season
and red or red-orange in the fall.

*J*apanese maple (often called Japanese red maple) is one super colorful small
landscape tree. The tall green varieties are also attractive. Their foliage is
often described as fern-like or lacy. While this is usually desirable, our July
and August furnace temperatures and southwestern winds may burn the
leaves. Don't plant in a western full-sun location. Eastern to northeastern locations usually work well because they usually offer protection from our hot
afternoon sun. Locations under the light shade canopy of larger trees should
also be acceptable. In most Texas locations where there are spring azalea
and/or spring flower trails, Japanese maple adds extra excitement to the
plantings. You will also find some great plantings in the various Texas botanical gardens. One example is inside the Japanese Garden section of the Ft.
Worth Botanic Garden.

WHEN TO PLANT

All Japanese maples are very hardy in Texas. If you are looking for something
to plant in your landscape in the winter, this tree is one possibility. The best

planting time is early fall; very early spring is second best. *Do not plant in midsummer.*

WHERE TO PLANT

Smaller varieties may be planted in groups near your foundation if the soil pH is acidic. You can find out the pH for any soil by having it tested through the soil testing laboratory at Stephen F. Austin State University or the Texas Agricultural Extension Service. If the soil test indicates an alkaline pH (above 7) you will need to make extensive bed improvements and commit to maintaining an acidic pH (below 7) to better ensure long term success. Plant groups of Japanese maple under the canopy of tall shade trees for a visual effect that will stop traffic. They also make great accent plantings. Remember: Japanese maples do not tolerate the full hot Texas sun.

HOW TO PLANT

The most spectacular Japanese maples I've ever seen were grown with beds around them. This is probably the best way to plant them in most geographical locations. In East Texas locations such as Tyler, Longview, Marshall, Nacogdoches, and Lufkin, the soils and climate are usually acceptable to individual plantings. For individual specimen plants, be sure your soil type and location are ideal. Loosen the soil several times wider than the soilball. Dig the planting hole no deeper than the plant's soilball, remove the plant from the container, and install. Backfill with loosened soil, water thoroughly, and apply root stimulator. Mulch with 6 in. of pine bark mulch. In beds, plant in the same type of bed mix as you do azaleas.

CARE AND MAINTENANCE

Aphids may visit new growth, but this isn't usually a problem. Prune only if needed to remove dead or damaged branches. Be sure to keep the soil moist during the growing season—maintaining a 6-in. layer of bark mulch will help. Fertilize 3 times a year with long-lasting slow-release granular azalea fertilizer according to label directions. Don't overfertilize. Water thoroughly after each application. Make the first application just as new leaves begin to emerge during the spring, reapply in 10 weeks, and again in the fall.

ADDITIONAL INFORMATION

Japanese maples may also be grown in various sizes and types of containers. They work well for the Oriental horticultural art of Bonsai.

ADDITIONAL SPECIES, CULTIVARS, OR VARIETIES

Some very interesting varieties include 'Bloodgood', 'Ever Red', 'Red Select', 'Viridis', 'Oshu-beni', 'Garnet', and 'Sango-kaku'.

Lacebark Elm
Ulmus parvifolia

EXPOSURE

Full Sun

COLD HARDINESS

All Texas

WATER USAGE

Semi-Moist

GROWTH RATE

Fast to Med.

AVG. HT × WIDTH

40–60′ × 30–50′

SPACING

60–100′

Leathery dark-green foliage on a round to oval crown. Deciduous with pale yellow fall color.

*L*acebark elm (*U. parvifolia*) is sometimes called the true Chinese elm. Do not get it confused with Siberian elm (*U. pumila*), which is a "trash tree"—one of those "I wouldn't plant it even if it were given to me" types. Lacebark elm is a very tough, durable, and drought-resistant tree for many Texas landscape applications. In locations where wind-resistant plants are important, lacebark elm does the job. Lacebark elms are great specimen yard trees to keep the afternoon sun off your house. They are also wonderful avenue or park trees and should be planted more often.

WHEN TO PLANT
These top-notch trees may be planted anytime from containers. The best time is fall; early spring is second best.

WHERE TO PLANT
They will grow almost anywhere, including parking areas and confined locations. They tolerate poor soils, including deep sand or heavy clay. This is a tree your little gardener can plant and be assured that it will grow for several

decades. These trees need room to grow, so don't crowd them. I'd place them 20 to 30 feet from the structure(s) to be shaded. Plant in sunny locations. They do best in deep moist soil.

HOW TO PLANT

Loosen the soil in the planting area several times wider than soilball width. Dig the planting hole as deep as the soilball and no deeper. Remove from the container and place in the planting hole. Backfill with loosened soil, water thoroughly, and apply root stimulator. Mulch with 3 to 4 in. of bark. (I usually use pine bark). The tree may need temporary staking.

CARE AND MAINTENANCE

This tree has no pests. Prune if needed to remove dead twigs any time of the year. Water if needed to maintain vigor. The young trees may need water in July and August. I fertilize my lacebark elms 3 times a year with a premium-quality long-lasting slow-release 3:1:2 ratio lawn fertilizer such as 18-6-12 or 15-5-10 according to label directions. Apply first at new spring growth, again approximately 10 weeks later, and once in the fall. Water thoroughly after each application.

ADDITIONAL INFORMATION

If you wish to plant lacebark elms from containers larger than 20 gallons, I suggest you call a landscape contractor to do the job. Lacebark or Chinese elm has a very fibrous root system. When planting, make sure you have spaced it far enough from landscape beds. I suggest 30 ft.

ADDITIONAL SPECIES, CULTIVARS, OR VARIETIES

Our lacebark elm is the 'Drake' variety, which is usually in the 30- to 35-ft.-tall by 40- to 45-ft.-wide range. 'Semervirens', 'True Green', and 'Prairie Shade' are other named varieties. *U. crassifolia* or cedar elm is a native Texan. It is usually taller and wider than lacebark elm. Note: For more information on cedar elm, check the native trees section.

TREES

371

Leyland Cypress

× *Cupressocyparis leylandii*

EXPOSURE
Full Sun

COLD HARDINESS
To 0° F.

WATER USAGE
Semi-Moist

GROWTH RATE
Fast

AVG. HT × WIDTH
20–60' × 15–20'

SPACING
30–40'

Pyramidal or conical with dark-green foliage. Evergreen.

I was introduced to Leyland cypress by our son, Aaron. One year we decided to pick a living Christmas tree to use through the season then plant outside. Aaron selected a Leyland from a nursery in Tyler. The tree worked great both indoors and later outside as an outdoor specimen lighted during additional holiday seasons. One reason it worked so well is because of its very soft foliage. Today we have a row of 6 on the southeastern corner of our landscaped yard area. They are being grown as a screen in this location. This hybrid between a cypress and a cedar is the most welcomed conifer in our landscape.

WHEN TO PLANT

Leyland cypress may be planted any time of the year, but fall is best. Spring is second best.

WHERE TO PLANT

While they will tolerate some shade, place in full-sun locations for best results. Don't plant in heavy-shade locations. They will grow in heavy clay to light sandy soils, but not in poorly drained or wet locations. They prefer well-drained, relatively loose, fertile, moist soils. Don't attempt to use as foundation plants, but do use as specimens. Because of their natural shape, color, and ability to shear, they are tops for use as a specimen. Leyland cypress is excellent as a wind, privacy, or noise screen. Because of their soft foliage they may be used in areas near pedestrian traffic.

CARE AND MAINTENANCE
Bagworms may visit, but Leyland cypress is not very susceptible to them. If some of these pests pay an unwelcome visit, hand pick them and discard in your trash inside sealed bags. (Don't just pick them off and drop on the ground because they can crawl out of their bags and go back up your tree.) If additional bagworm controls are needed, ask about your options. Follow label directions on any aid you use. Prune as needed to maintain desired shape. Spring is the best time to do pruning. These plants are drought tolerant once established, but they prefer a moist soil for best growth. Leyland cypress responds with vigor to a good fertilizing program. Here's what works for me: 4 applications a year of a premium-quality long-lasting slow-release 3:1:2 ratio lawn fertilizer such as 15-5-10 or 21-7-14. Apply just as new growth begins, reapply 10 weeks later, again in 10 weeks, and once during the fall. Water thoroughly after each application.

ADDITIONAL INFORMATION
In our typical July and August hot, dry oven conditions, Leyland cypress will enjoy a deep, slow, thorough drink.

ADDITIONAL SPECIES, CULTIVARS, OR VARIETIES
In addition to the original cross, there are some cultivars you can try: 'Castlewellan', 'Moncal', 'Naylor's Blue', 'Green Spire', and 'Silver Dust'.

Mimosa
Albizia julibrissin

EXPOSURE

Full Sun

COLD HARDINESS

All Texas

WATER USAGE

Semi-Moist

GROWTH RATE

Fast

AVG. HT × WIDTH

30–40 ' × 30–40 '

SPACING

30 '

Spreading relatively flattened top to umbrella crown. Deciduous tree. Light-green feathery leaves. Showy blooms range from pink to a red-rose tint.

*M*imosa is one of the longest-flowering and most-frequently-used summer-blooming trees in Texas landscapes and a favorite of many Texas gardeners including my grandparents. It is one of the last trees to leaf out in the spring, but then mimosa puts on a show. Mimosa will grow in loam, clay, or deep, loose, sandy soils. Mimosa is one of the very few ornamental blooming shade trees whose leaves fold up each evening. This trait is often interesting to children. Mimosa is relatively short-lived—its life span is approximately 25 years.

WHEN TO PLANT
The best planting time is early fall; early spring is second best. They are planted year-round in Texas.

WHERE TO PLANT
Don't plant mimosas near landscape beds unless you want large crops of mimosa seedlings in your beds. The seeds which are produced in their bean-like pods are viable and will germinate and grow. Swimming pools seem to attract fallen mimosa blooms like a magnet does iron filings. Provide plenty of room between a pool and mimosa to avoid this problem. I believe the best use

of mimosa is in full-sun locations. I've also seen them used success-fully to line both sides of driveways. This looks good, but could become a bit messy with bloom, seedpod, and fall leaf drop. They may also be used around yard structures. Be aware that if they are planted next to decks, gazebos, or similar structures they could become "messy" again. I'd avoid planting in poorly drained loca-tions, under the canopies of larger shade trees, or in soil that is too wet or too dry. Allow them room for full crown development. While they are tolerant of many types of soil, the best soil is well drained, fertile, and moist.

HOW TO PLANT

No special soil preparation is needed. Loosen the native soil wider than the width of the soilball. Dig the planting hole no deeper than the soilball. Remove from the container and place in the hole. Backfill with the loosened soil, water thoroughly, and apply root stimulator. Mulch with 3 to 4 in. of bark mulch. Stake if necessary.

CARE AND MAINTENANCE

Mimosa webworms may visit. There are several control possibil-ities available. Follow label directions when using any aid. Pruning may be needed for young trees to encourage strong branching. Don't perform radical pruning of limbs on a yearly basis—this is harmful to mimosa's long-term health and life span. Fertilize 30 days after the last killing frost in your area or just as new spring growth begins, again 10 weeks later, and once in the fall. Use a long-lasting, slow-release 3:1:2 ratio lawn fertilizer such as 19-5-9, 15-5-10 or 21-7-14 according to label directions. Water thoroughly after each application. Supplemental watering is usually needed only during establishment.

ADDITIONAL INFORMATION

Despite their rather untidy activities, mimosas are spectacular in full bloom when they are grown in sunny locations and allowed to reach their maximum size and bloom.

ADDITIONAL SPECIES, CULTIVARS, OR VARIETIES

Most retail nurseries will not have named cultivars or varieties, but some are available, including 'Charlotte' and 'Rosea'. Be sure to ask for the cultivar 'Union' if mimosa wilt is a problem in your area.

Oak

Quercus spp.

EXPOSURE

Full Sun

COLD HARDINESS

All Texas

WATER USAGE

Semi-Moist

GROWTH RATE

Fast to Slow

AVG. HT × WIDTH

20–120 ' × 15–80 '

SPACING

Varies

Evergreen to deciduous. Relatively small to large dark-green leaves, some changing to an array of fall colors on large upright to spreading crowns.

*O*aks are the most popular trees in the Texas landscape. Growth habits, structure, forms, leaf shape, and color vary, depending on the type of oak you choose. *Q. palustris* (pin oak), grows very well in the East Texas sandy acid soils but does very poorly in heavy alkaline clay soil. *Q. shumardii*, or shumard red oak, grows statewide in clay or sandy soils. If I had to choose just one tree for home landscape use, it would be a member of the oak family. We are currently growing shumard red oak, *Q. virginiana* (live oak), *Q. nuttallii* (nuttal oak), *Q. macrocarpa* (burr oak), and *Q. texana* (Texas red oak). Nuttal was the least familiar to me, but in our deep, loose, sandy soil they've done well. They have the potential of reaching 120 ft. tall—what a shade tree! Nuttal will tolerate a wide range of soil conditions. Our 3 shumards are growing on the west side of our home in a small "grove." We placed them to fully shade that side of our home, to provide partial shade to some ornamental plantings, and to provide cover for our feathered friends. Three Texas red oaks are placed in a much smaller "grove" or "clump" at the western end of our deck to provide shade. Two burr oaks are on the southeast side to provide shade in that location.

WHEN TO PLANT
Plant any time of the year. Fall is great and spring is good, but we have also successfully planted them during the summer.

WHERE TO PLANT
Oaks prefer full-sun locations with deep, fertile, well-drained soil. They are great as specimens, yard trees, or shade trees. Decide which oak(s) you wish to plant and determine their normal ultimate height and width in your area of Texas. Space from structures, drives, and walks, based on their normal spread.

HOW TO PLANT
Trees in containers larger than 20 gallons should be planted by a landscape contractor. Dig the planting hole wider than the soilball, but only soilball deep. Remove the tree from the container and place in the hole. Backfill with the loosened native soil, water thoroughly, and apply root stimulator. Mulch with 3 to 4 in. of bark mulch. Stake if necessary.

CARE AND MAINTENANCE
Pests rarely visit healthy oaks. Supplemental watering may be necessary during initial establishment—and they may appreciate a deep, long, slow drink in July or August. Prune to train, thin, or correct and remove dead limbs as needed. Oaks will respond with vigor to fertilizing. To obtain maximum healthy growth, fertilize in early spring just as new growth begins. Apply again 10 weeks later, again in another 10 weeks, and once during the fall season. Use a premium-quality long-lasting slow-release 3:1:2 ratio lawn fertilizer such as 21-7-14, 18-6-12, or 15-5-10. Water thoroughly after each application.

ADDITIONAL INFORMATION
Some people mistakenly call oaks "slow growing." If they are cared for properly, it isn't uncommon for them to grow 3 ft. or more each year.

ADDITIONAL SPECIES, CULTIVARS, OR VARIETIES
There are many. Visit your area nurseries to see what's available.

Palm
Washingtonia filifera

EXPOSURE

Full Sun

COLD HARDINESS

To 15° F.

WATER USAGE

Semi-Moist

GROWTH RATE

Medium

AVG. HT × WIDTH

30–45′ × 5–15′

SPACING

20–30′

Evergreen with typical fan-
shaped leaves that are gray-
green in color.

*A*long our Texas coast, palm trees are the best reminder that you are in a "tropical" or coastal area. Many people enjoy palm trees—and they some-times try to plant them in areas for which they are not suited. Washington palm is often listed as hardy throughout Zone 8, but it can be damaged by temperatures below 25 degrees Fahrenheit. Our USDA Plant Hardiness Zone Map says Zone 8 has winter temperatures of 10 to 20 degrees Fahrenheit. If temperatures drop only for a short time and rebound quickly, there usually isn't substantial damage. If the temperature drops into these ranges and remains there 24, 48, 72, or more hours, however, the Washington palm can be in big trouble. If you live in either Zone 8A or 8B, decide how badly you want a Washington palm and how much of a gamble you are willing to take.

WHEN TO PLANT

Plant in early spring—after any possible frost date has passed—or early summer.

WHERE TO PLANT

For planting in Zone 8, select sunny areas that are protected. In Zone 9, most sunny locations are acceptable. Washington palm requires a well-drained soil to do its best. It will adapt to a rather wide range of soil types, but do not plant in poorly drained spots. In suitable locations, Washington palm can be used for avenue plantings, for lining drives, for framing structures, as specimens, or in groups.

HOW TO PLANT

Washington palm may have a larger-than-normal rootball for its height. If your selection is in a container larger than 20 gallons—or if it is box balled—have it planted by a landscape contractor. I would plant the larger sizes in Zone 8. If you are going to plant smaller container sizes, select a sunny, well-drained location and loosen the soil in an area wider than the soilball. Dig the planting hole soilball deep and no deeper, and install the plant from the container. Backfill with loosened soil, water thoroughly, and apply root stimulator. Mulch with 3 to 4 in. of bark mulch (I usually use pine bark). Stake temporarily if necessary.

CARE AND MAINTENANCE

This plant has no serious pests. To prevent root rot and suffocation, make sure your selected planting location drains well. Water as needed to prevent total soil dryness, but don't overwater or keep wet. Prune to remove dead leaves only if desired. Fertilize twice a year, once in early spring as new growth emerges, and once in the fall. Apply a premium-quality long-lasting slow-release 3:1:2 ratio lawn fertilizer such as 15-5-10 or 21-7-14 according to label directions. Water thoroughly after each application.

ADDITIONAL INFORMATION

Palm trees are large dominant landscape plants, so place them carefully in the landscape.

ADDITIONAL SPECIES, CULTIVARS, OR VARIETIES

There is no known cultivar of *W. filifera*. Another species to try in Zone 9 *only* is *W. robusta* or Mexican fan palm. *W. filifera* is also known as northern or California Washington palm tree. A family member, *W. robusta*, is known as southern or Mexican Washington palm tree.

Pine
Pinus spp.

EXPOSURE

Full Sun

COLD HARDINESS

All Texas

WATER USAGE

Semi-Moist

GROWTH RATE

Fast to Slow (v.)

AVG. HT × WIDTH

4–100′ × 6–30′

SPACING

12–60′ (v.)

Needle-like leaves in various lengths, light- to medium- to blue-green. Conifer evergreen.

When you talk about pine trees, most Texas gardeners think of East Texas. While it is true that the area is great for growing several species, and the Texas pine lumber industry is located in East Texas, this isn't the only area for which pines are well adapted. Most soils are naturally acidic in East Texas and many pines are well adapted to this type of soil. Several pines will also grow in alkaline soils. The heavy clay soil in these areas are naturally alkaline. Slash pine (*P. elliottii*) grows well in the acidic soils of East Texas, but poorly in alkaline soils. Japanese black pine (*P. thunbergiana*) grows well in both acidic and alkaline soils. Ask your local nurseries or County Agent to help you determine the type of soil you have. Soil pH tests can be performed by the Soil Lab at Stephen F. Austin State University, the Texas Agricultural Extension Service, various private labs, and sometimes at nurseries. This information will help you select the type of pine you want to invite into your landscape. The first question to ask any nursery when seeking information on a specific tree is: "Should this tree do well (not merely survive) in my type of soil?" Then find out how tall and wide the specific pine tree you favor will grow in your area. With information on soil type, pH, and tree height and width, you should be able to make knowledgeable decisions about which trees to select.

When to Plant

Fall is the best planting time; early spring is second best.

Where to Plant

Planting location is species dependent, but all prefer sunny, well-drained spots. Don't plant in shady locations or poorly drained or wet soils. Pines make excellent windbreaks when planted in multiple rows. Some species, such as Japanese black pine (*P. thunbergiana*), make outstanding lawn and patio specimens in sunny locations. Mugo pine (*P. mugo*) grows so low in some Texas areas that it may be used as a foundation planting. Pines are also often used to line drives and can be planted in groups or groves.

How to Plant

No special soil preparation is needed. Loosen the native soil in an area wider than the soilball, but don't dig the planting hole any deeper than soilball depth. Remove from the container and place in the hole. Backfill with the loosened soil, water thoroughly, and apply a root stimulator. Mulch with 3 to 4 in. of pine bark mulch. Stake temporarily.

Care and Maintenance

Care and maintenance is species dependent. Some species may have visits from pine tip moth, pine bark beetle, or rust, while others are resistant. Ask about the various methods of controlling these pests. Follow label directions when using any aid. Water as needed to prevent dry soil while establishing, but don't keep wet or overwater, because root rot may occur under these conditions. Prune as needed to train when branches begin their new growth and are in the "candle" stage. Pines will respond to a good fertilizing program. Fertilize as their new spring growth begins, 10 weeks later, again in the next 10 weeks, and once during the fall. Apply a premium-quality long-lasting slow-release 3:1:2 ratio lawn fertilizer such as 21-7-14, 15-5-10, or 19-5-9 according to label directions. Water thoroughly after each application.

Additional Information

Pine is probably the best family of trees to plant if you desire multiples of the same tree.

Additional Species, Cultivars, or Varieties

Investigate these: *P. nigra* or Austrian pine, *P. taeda* or loblolly pine, *P. ponderosa* or ponderosa pine, *P. sylvestris* or Scots pine, *P. echinata*, known as shortleaf or yellow pine, and *P. brutia* spp. *eldarica* or eldarica pine. For additional pine selections review native pine in the native trees section.

Purple Leaf Plum
Prunus cerasifera

EXPOSURE

Full Sun

COLD HARDINESS

All Texas

WATER USAGE

Semi-Moist

GROWTH RATE

Fast to Med.

AVG. HT × WIDTH

15–25 ′ × 10–20 ′ (v.)

SPACING

15–25 ′

Small tree, deciduous upright vase to oval form, crown with soft red-purple to purple leaves. Blooms are light pink.

While living here before he left home to make his way, our son, Aaron, had a bedroom on the northeast corner of our home. Outside the east windows is a group planting of 3 purple leaf plums (also known as flowering purple leaf plum). Aaron selected and helped plant these trees that his little sister Ashley is currently enjoying outside of his former bedroom. This is one example of what you can do with purple leaf plum. By properly selecting, locating, planting and maintaining purple leaf plum you and your family can enjoy their beauty for many years. The neighbors, visitors and people passing by may also enjoy them because they put on a rather striking show all summer long with their leaf color displayed most intensely in full sun. As single specimens they offer great color to patios, decks, gazebos and other outside living areas or in the lawn. Purple leaf plum may also be grown in large containers or planters.

WHEN TO PLANT

Container-grown trees can be planted successfully year-round. The best planting time is fall; early spring is second best.

WHERE TO PLANT

While purple leaf plum will tolerate a wide range of growing conditions, it prefers moist, well-drained, fertile soil. Plant in full-sun locations with well-drained soil. Don't plant in shady spots, or in locations that are too wet or dry. Purple leaf plums may be used in almost any application where you want a small to medium ornamental tree in a sunny location. If you plant them in groups, be sure to space adequately to allow each plant to reach its usual maximum spread for your area. Due to their small size, they may be located rather close to structures, walks, and drives without damage to the latter. Be sure not to place so close to a structure as to deform the tree.

HOW TO PLANT

Loosen existing soil wider than rootball width, but dig the hole rootball deep and no deeper. Remove tree from the container and place in the hole. Backfill with the loose soil, water thoroughly, and apply a root stimulator. Mulch with 3 to 4 in. of bark. Temporarily stake if necessary.

CARE AND MAINTENANCE

Peach tree borers may pay an unwelcome visit to unhealthy trees. To prevent this problem, keep trees in a healthy condition. Water if necessary to prevent soil dryness. Prune to remove dead branches and twigs, or shape in very early spring. We fertilize our purple leaf plums 4 times a year: once as new growth begins, 10 weeks later, again the following 10 weeks, and once during the fall. Apply a premium-quality long-lasting slow-release 3:1:2 ratio lawn fertilizer according to label directions. Water after each application. 15-5-10, 18-6-12, and 21-7-14 are 3:1:2 ratio lawn fertilizers.

ADDITIONAL INFORMATION

If you are seeking spring-to-fall color for your landscape, take a look at purple leaf plum.

ADDITIONAL SPECIES, CULTIVARS, OR VARIETIES

When visiting gardens, look for name tags or ask which variety of purple leaf plum is being grown. Look for these: 'Newport', 'Thundercloud', 'Atropurpurea', and 'Krauterv Vesuvius'.

Redbud
Cercis canadensis

EXPOSURE

Full Sun

COLD HARDINESS

All Texas

WATER USAGE

Semi-Moist

GROWTH RATE

Medium

AVG. HT × WIDTH

15–30' × 15–25'

SPACING

35'

Irregular flat to round crown. Deciduous tree. Small white to pink-purple red blooms in clusters along twigs and branches. Heart-shaped, dark-green leaves that turn yellow during the fall.

*A*fter we Texas landscape gardeners have been indoors for what seems like long winters, we are ready to see some spring color. Redbud always does a great job of supplying this need! Unlike most blooming plants, redbud blooms early before it gets dressed for the summer in its heart-shaped leaves. *C. reniformis* 'Oklahoma' or Oklahoma redbud's foliage is soft pink when it emerges; then it changes to a rich shiny green. *C. canadensis* 'Forest Pansy' or forest pansy redbud's leaves are scarlet-purple while emerging, changing to maroon as they mature for the summer. I know it seems odd and perhaps it should be called something else, but there is a "white" redbud—*C. canadensis* 'Alba' or white-flowered redbud.

WHEN TO PLANT

Redbuds from containers may be planted anytime, but fall planting is preferable. Early spring is also good. I wouldn't plant in July, August, or even early September.

WHERE TO PLANT

For best results, plant in full-sun locations with moist, fertile, well-drained soil. Do not plant in heavily shaded areas or spots with poorly drained or wet soils. Redbuds may be used singularly as lawn trees, specimens, courtyard, or patio plantings. They also work well near yard swings, decks, gazebos, or other garden structures. In group plantings they provide a great spring show. They mix well with flowering dogwood trees (*Cornus florida*) in shady locations. Redbud also works well to line free-form drives and walks without damage to the latter. Their scale works well with single-story structures and they may be placed relatively close to those structures without damage to foundations. Be sure to leave sufficient space from structures to prevent the tree from becoming deformed.

HOW TO PLANT

No special soil preparation is needed for redbud. Loosen the soil wider than the soilball, and dig the planting hole no deeper than the soilball. Remove the tree from the container and place in the planting hole. Backfill with loosened soil, water thoroughly, and apply a root stimulator. Mulch with 3 to 4 in. of bark mulch. Stake temporarily if necessary.

CARE AND MAINTENANCE

Some unwelcome pests may visit, but they usually contribute only a less desirable appearance during the summer. If they become a problem for you, ask about various control possibilities. After redbuds are established, water only if desired during dry periods to help maintain healthy trees. I maintain a 4-in. layer of pine bark nuggets around my redbuds to help conserve soil moisture. Prune when young to prevent narrow, weakly angled branches. Very little pruning is needed afterwards. In my double-deep, loose, sandy soil, I fertilize 4 times a year with a premium- quality long-lasting slow-release 3:1:2 ratio lawn fertilizer such as 15-5-10, 18-6-12, or 21-7-14 according to label directions. Apply first when new spring leaves begin to emerge, then 10 weeks later, again in 10 more weeks, and finally during the fall. Water thoroughly after each application.

ADDITIONAL INFORMATION

Redbuds usually don't transplant successfully from the wild. To help ensure success, purchase high-quality container-grown selections.

ADDITIONAL SPECIES, CULTIVARS, OR VARIETIES

Check out these possibilities: 'Alba', 'Forest Pansy', 'Oklahoma', *C. canadensis* 'Texensis' or Texas redbud, and *C. canadensis* 'Mexicana' or Mexican redbud.

Sweet Bay Magnolia
Magnolia virginiana

EXPOSURE

F. Sun to Semi-

COLD HARDINESS

All Texas

WATER USAGE

Semi-Moist

GROWTH RATE

Slow

AVG. HT × WIDTH

20–40′ × 15–25′

SPACING

30–50′

Irregular in form. Semievergreen to almost evergreen with dark-green leaves. Blooms are fragrant and creamy white.

*I*n Texas, nothing beats the smell of magnolias blooming during late spring and summer. Texas gardeners have enjoyed sweet bay magnolia—along with its much larger cousin *M. grandiflora* or southern magnolia—for decades. Unlike southern magnolia, which often dominates the home landscape, sweet bay blends into the landscape. It works very well in limited spaces where an ornamental tree is desired. One question some callers to my radio shows ask is: "How do I grow grass under my southern magnolia?" The answer is: "You don't." With sweet bay magnolia, the answer is: "No problem—if it's St. Augustinegrass." Sweet bay is native to fertile, deep, moist soils along creeks and streams and in swamps and low woodlands. This is definitely not an ornamental tree for hot, dry locations. It works well in large beds of groundcover or low-growing shrubs. Cultural requirements are similar to azaleas, and sweet bay will do well planted among them.

WHEN TO PLANT
Container-grown selections may be planted anytime, but I wouldn't plant during our summers or midwinter. Early fall is a great planting time; early spring is also good.

WHERE TO PLANT

If you are using them as specimens, plant them in moist to damp areas. I prefer them used in beds with a drip watering system. Wherever you locate them, they are *not* drought tolerant. They tend to do better when protected from our hot afternoon sun and south-westerly summer winds. If I were asked to pick a specific directional location in the landscape for sweet bay, it would be in an eastern to northeastern full-sun location. Normally, this should provide adequate sun as well as afternoon protection. If you have a poorly drained spot, or one that tends to stay damp so that other trees die in the location, try sweet bay. You *may* be able to plant sweet bay magnolia in a full-sun location that is not naturally moist if you install drip irrigation and maintain a 6-in. layer of mulch.

HOW TO PLANT

When planted as a specimen, place in a well-watered location. Loosen the soil wider than the soilball and dig the planting hole soilball deep. Remove the plant from the container and place in the hole. Backfill with loose soil, water thoroughly, and apply a root stimulator. Mulch with 6 in. of pine bark mulch. Plant in beds the same way, but in improved soil. Stake if necessary.

CARE AND MAINTENANCE

There are no pests. Prune only if necessary to shape or remove dead or damaged branches. Maintain a moist soil—*do not* let the soil become dry. Maintaining a 6-in. mulch layer will help conserve soil moisture. Fertilize 3 times a year with a premium-quality long-lasting granular azalea fertilizer according to label directions. Make the first application as new leaves emerge. Reapply in 10 weeks and once again during early fall. Water thoroughly after each application.

ADDITIONAL INFORMATION

A moist soil is very important to successful long-term growth of sweet bay. It probably does best in the eastern half of Texas.

ADDITIONAL SPECIES, CULTIVARS, OR VARIETIES

Some varieties to try are 'Australis', 'Henry Hicks', and 'Havener'. Related species include M. grandiflora, M. macrophylla, M. × soulangiana, and M. × veitchii. There are many more hybrids and additional species.

Weeping Willow
Salix babylonica

EXPOSURE

Full to Semi-

COLD HARDINESS

All Texas

WATER USAGE

Moist

GROWTH RATE

Fast

AVG. HT × WIDTH

40–60´ × 30–40´

SPACING

45´

Round crown with very long weeping branches. Narrow, medium-green leaves turn yellow in the fall. Deciduous.

*T*he original home of weeping willow (sometimes called Babylon weeping willow) is northern China, but it has adapted to all areas of the United States. It is a striking tree that dominates both the spot it's growing in and the eye of those viewing it in the landscape. To many Texas gardeners, weeping willow speaks of moist places in the landscape, perhaps because *S. nigra*, or river willow, is very often seen growing near river banks, bayous, creek banks, stock pond dams, and lake shores. Weeping willow will grow in areas of poorly drained or damp soils where almost no other tree—with the exception of bald cypress—will grow. They aren't picky about soil types, as long as there is adequate moisture. This is considered a water-loving tree. Its root system is relatively shallow and voracious, which makes it a strong competitor for space and soil moisture in its vicinity. Because of this, weeping willow should not be located in areas where plants compete for moisture or space.

WHEN TO PLANT
Container-grown selections can be planted successfully year-round in Texas. The best planting time is fall; early spring is second best. I wouldn't plant in midsummer.

WHERE TO PLANT

Babylon weeping willow does best in full-sun locations and moist to damp soil. Do not plant in heavily shaded locations or spots that tend to dry or are difficult to water. Use this striking tree very sparingly in the landscape. Pick planting spots carefully, and don't locate near known sewage lines, homes, walks, or drives. They are best used as yard or feature trees. They may also be used as large screens where adequate water is available.

HOW TO PLANT

After selecting a full-sun location and determining that adequate moisture is normally available (including during July, August, and September), loosen the soil in the planting area wider than the soilball. Dig the planting hole no deeper than the soilball. Remove from the container and place in the hole. Backfill with loosened soil, water thoroughly, and apply a root stimulator. Mulch with 6 in. of bark. Stake temporarily if necessary.

CARE AND MAINTENANCE

Aphids and thrips may occasionally visit, but they usually aren't a concern. Borers may hit unhealthy trees. The best control is to keep your tree healthy. Pruning during establishment and in the early years may be required to produce a relatively straight trunk. Little pruning is needed thereafter. Remove dead wood as it occurs. Keep moist at all times; maintaining a thick mulch layer will greatly aid in soil moisture retention. Weeping willow responds with vigor to fertilizing. Apply a premium-quality long-lasting slow-release 3:1:2 ratio lawn fertilizer such as 21-7-14, 19-5-9, or 18-6-12 according to label directions. Begin your fertilizing program as soon as new growth begins in the spring. Reapply 10 weeks later, again in 10 weeks, and once during the fall season. Water thoroughly after each application.

ADDITIONAL INFORMATION

Be aware that weeping willow is a relatively short-lived tree, in the 15 to 25 year range. Take this into consideration when planning its use in your landscape.

ADDITIONAL SPECIES, CULTIVARS, OR VARIETIES

In addition to Babylon weeping willow, you may wish to investigate some other family members: *S. × blanda* or Wisconsin weeping willow, *S. caprea* 'Pendula' or weeping pussy willow, *S. alba* or golden weeping willow, *S. matsudana* 'Snake' or snake willow, 'Tortuosa' or corkscrew willow, and 'Umbraculifera' or 'Navajo', both known as globe willow.

CHAPTER TEN

VINES

MANY TEXAS GARDENERS DO NOT GIVE A SECOND THOUGHT to vines. When properly selected and placed, though, vines will accent locations, structures, and features in our landscapes. There's hardly anything more eye-appealing than vines growing over pergolas, fence posts, gazebos, arbors, or fences.

Certain vines provide springtime flushes of colors. Others offer season-long bloom. Still others, such as Virginia creeper, *Parthenocissus quinquefolia*, and Boston ivy, *Parthenocissus tricuspidata*, provide outstanding fall foliage color. Vines may be used as "groundcovers" to help hold the soil together, and they look great when cascading over embankments and walls.

Vines have energy-conservation possibilities as well. If you have a very narrow lot and no shade tree, vines placed on growing structures such as lattices can greatly reduce the heat load on your home. You will be more comfortable during the heat of the summer, and you will save your energy dollar.

Vines have interesting climbing mechanisms, including twining structures, holdfast structures, and tendrils. If you live in a town house, apartment, condo, zero lot line home, or other place that has limited growing space, try vines. You can grow a lot of them in small vertical spaces. Try growing interesting, colorful, fragrant, enjoyable plantings of vines on ornamental iron, cast aluminum, or wooden structures.

Screening is another use for vines. You may wish to screen for privacy, for ornamentation, traffic direction, or noise reduction. Try some vines on roughcut timber arbors for a secluded summertime spot. You can see an example of this usage on the campus of Stephen F. Austin State University, behind the Agricultural building in the SFA Arboretum. Roughcut heavy lumber has been used to create an interesting structure covered with vines. This pleasing combination works well in home landscapes.

Chapter Ten

Most vines perform nicely for us when planted in well-drained soils. If the soil is poorly drained, take the time to improve it before planting your first plant. The best material to improve any soil is organic matter: compost (purchased or homemade), brown sphagnum peat moss, and various aged wood by-products. Usually a combination of these three groups works best.

Tip: Make sure you understand a vine's growth habit, including how aggressive it may become, before inviting it into your landscape. For example, *Wisteria sinensis* is great when used by itself on a strong structure away from the house, but I wouldn't want it growing on my house or in my trees. It can overpower some locations, and the next thing you know, it's chain saw time!

I have included 6 families of vines or vining plants in my selections for this chapter. If your main vining interest is bloom, you will find some good ones on my list. You can probably find others.

Have a vining good time with vines in your landscape.

Boston Ivy

Parthenocissus tricuspidata

EXPOSURE

Full to Shade

COLD HARDINESS

All Texas

WATER USAGE

Semi-Moist

GROWTH RATE

Fast

AVG. HT × WIDTH

As Trained

SPACING

Varies

Tall deciduous vine. Relatively dark-green, maple-shaped leaves. Outstanding fall color.

*B*oston ivy is sometimes thought to grow only around Boston or the Ivy League schools. While it's true that this is the ivy of Ivy League schools, it also grows in Texas. It may be used as a groundcover, is excellent on trellises or other gardening structures, and may also be grown directly on brick walls. Boston ivy provides some relief from Texas sun and therefore reduces energy conservation. While it has bright-green maple leaf–shaped foliage throughout the growing season, it is most spectacular when it takes on its vivid shades of orange and red in the fall. As a fall color plant, it is outstanding.

WHEN TO PLANT

Boston ivy may be planted in the spring, summer, winter, or fall because it is extremely hardy in Texas. The best time to establish it is in very early spring; the second-best time is very early fall.

WHERE TO PLANT

My experience with Boston ivy has shown that it tends to do best where it has morning sun and some shade from the hot, west afternoon Texas sun; but I have seen some plantings that worked successfully in full sun, planted right on brick walls facing directly west. "Where to Plant" is entirely your decision.

How to Plant

Boston ivy can be grown in woodland locations as well as in prepared beds. If training it on structures, I suggest you prepare your soil well, blending approximately 3 in. of organic matter into the top 3 in. of the existing soil. Purchase your Boston ivy in 1-gallon containers and plant in the prepared bed no deeper than they were grown in their containers. Firm the mixed soil thoroughly around the new plants, water, and apply root stimulator according to label directions. Then cover with approximately 3 in. of bark mulch.

Care and Maintenance

In late summer, around July or August, spider mites may visit your Boston ivy in hot full-sun locations. If this does occur, consult your Lowe's customer service associate for the best control possibilities. Remember to read and follow label directions when using any lawn and garden aid. Prune as necessary, training your ivy to reach the shape or form you desire. If you plant Boston ivy on walls, pruning will be necessary to prevent it from growing into the wooden part of your home; this must be done every year if not more often. Water as necessary to prevent soil dryness. Fertilize in early spring as new growth begins; try a 3:1:2 lawn fertilizer such as 15-5-10, 19-5-9, or 21-7-14. Remember to use premium-quality long-lasting slow-release lawn fertilizer, follow directions, and water thoroughly after each application.

Additional Information

You may want to try Boston ivy in your home landscape. Understand that it can be overpowering if you put it in small locations; make sure there is adequate room for it to grow.

Additional Species, Cultivars, or Varieties

A cousin of Boston ivy is Virginia creeper or *P. quinquefolia*. The variety 'Engelmanni' has smaller leaves than the native Virginia creeper and is also less vigorous. It clings well to masonry walls. The fall color is basically a deep burgundy red and it has small fruits which a lot of birds like. The standard Virginia creeper will also work well, and will give outstanding fall color, generally a rich red. It will cling to walls or trellises.

Confederate Star Jasmine
Trachelospermum jasminoides

EXPOSURE

F. Sun to Semi-

COLD HARDINESS

To 10° F.

WATER USAGE

Semi-Moist

GROWTH RATE

Fast to Med.

AVG. HT × WIDTH

Vine

SPACING

3–5'

Small dark-green leaves. Blooms are masses of fragrant star shapes, typically blooming from April to May in Texas.

*J*asminoides is also known as star jasmine, Confederate jasmine, or Confederate star jasmine. However you see it listed, it is worth seeking out, especially if you are in Zone 8 or 9—and these two zones cover at least 50 percent of Texas. In Zone 7B, it is worth trying in protected locations. I have grown it in Zone 7B (in protected locations) and have enjoyed it for several years. Confederate star jasmine is good on trellises, making an excellent spring show that is quite fragrant. I have fashioned trellises with treated yellow pine and galvanized poultry netting. Confederate star jasmine may also be grown as a ground-cover, and I like it especially well on various garden structures. Try one or more plants in large containers planted at the base of a specialized structure on a deck, balcony, patio, or other sunny location.

WHEN TO PLANT
The best time to plant Confederate star jasmine is in the early spring.

WHERE TO PLANT

Plant in locations that have moist, well-drained soils. Full-sun to partial-shade spots work well, and make sure it receives a minimum of 6 hours of full sun for best results Do not plant in full-shade locations or difficult-to-water spots.

HOW TO PLANT

Plant Confederate star jasmine in well-prepared beds that you have enriched with organic matter, incorporating approximately 4 in. of organic matter into the top 4 in. of the existing soil. After the bed improvement is complete, remove your star jasmine transplants from their containers and install in the prepared bed no deeper than they were grown in the containers. Firm the mix, water thoroughly, and apply root stimulator according to label directions. After planting is complete, mulch with approximately 3 in. of bark mulch.

CARE AND MAINTENANCE

No pests or insects normally bother Confederate star jasmine. Prune and train as required to obtain a desired effect. Water as necessary to prevent soil dryness; mulching will help conserve soil moisture. Drip irrigation is beneficial. Fertilize as new growth begins in the spring with a premium-quality long-lasting slow-release rose fertilizer—other fertilizers may also be used. Remember to read and follow label directions when using any fertilizer.

ADDITIONAL INFORMATION

You may not be familiar with Confederate star jasmine, but its masses of fragrant flowers make it worth trying even for one spring season. Be sure to plant early.

ADDITIONAL SPECIES, CULTIVARS, OR VARIETIES

A cousin, Asian jasmine, *Trachelospermom jasminoides*, is not as cold tender as Confederate star jasmine. It is often used as a groundcover in Texas.

English Ivy
Hedera helix

EXPOSURE

Semi- to Full Shade

COLD HARDINESS

All Texas

WATER USAGE

Semi-Moist

GROWTH RATE

Fast

AVG. HT × WIDTH

Vine

SPACING

12"

Vigorous evergreen vine. Three-pointed leaves are usually dark green.

*E*nglish ivy is grown in all areas of Texas and is probably the most recognizable and commonly used vine in our home landscapes, though you will also see English ivy in commercial applications. It may be grown in espalier forms on many different types of growing structures including trellises, arbors, fences, and archways. English ivy typically performs best in a shady to semi-shady location. It will also grow in full-sun eastern locations where there is no reflected heat, the soil is well prepared, and adequate moisture is maintained. Many feel that English ivy is harmful to trees—if the ivy covers the canopy of a tree, blocking out all sunlight, the tree may no longer function properly. Another concern is that English ivy adds weight to the branches, which could result in damage to the tree during windstorms or ice storms. I prefer to grow English ivy on specialized structures and would not allow it to grow up into the branches of trees.

WHEN TO PLANT
English ivy is best planted in very early spring; very early fall is also an acceptable time.

WHERE TO PLANT

For best results, plant English ivy in well-prepared beds where it will receive morning sun and afternoon shade, or dappled sun throughout the day.

HOW TO PLANT

Incorporate approximately 3 in. of high-quality organic matter including brown sphagnum peat moss into the top 3 in. of the existing soil. After bed preparation is complete, remove your selections of English ivy from their containers and install into the bed no deeper than they were grown in the containers. Firm the soil well, water thoroughly, and apply root stimulator according to label directions. Mulch with approximately 2 in. of bark mulch.

CARE AND MAINTENANCE

Bacterial leaf spot may visit ivy in locations of high humidity where there is little air movement. Spider mites may visit in hot, dry locations. To prevent these problems, simply do not plant in such locations. If spider mites appear anyway, ask about control possibilities. Remember to read and follow label directions when using any gardening aid. Prune as necessary to maintain and train English ivy in the form you wish it to grow. Water as necessary to maintain a moist growing condition, but do not maintain a wet soil. Fertilize as new growth begins in the spring with a premium-quality long-lasting slow-release lawn fertilizer. The 3:1:2 ratio fertilizers such as 21-7-14, 18-6-12, or 15-5-10 will work well. Remember to water thoroughly after each application.

ADDITIONAL INFORMATION

There are many types and varieties of ivy on the market today. Should you decide to grow English ivy directly on your home, remember that it has been known to cause problems with the woodwork on homes.

ADDITIONAL SPECIES, CULTIVARS, OR VARIETIES

There are over 60 varieties of English ivy available. Among them are 'Aureo-variegata', which has a variegated creamy yellow foliage; 'Green Ripples', which has fan-shaped leaves; 'Hahn's Self Branching', which has smaller leaves and is very bushy; and 'Needlepoint', which has small 3-lobed leaves that are closely spaced.

Fig Ivy or Creeping Fig
Ficus pumila

EXPOSURE

F. Sun to Semi-

COLD HARDINESS

To 10° F.

WATER USAGE

Moist to Semi-

GROWTH RATE

Fast

AVG. HT × WIDTH

As Trained

SPACING

3–6 ′

Small vine that is evergreen where hardy.

*F*ig ivy makes a very interesting pattern if grown on structures, including rock and brick. I've seen it grown successfully on a stone wall around an older home in the Azalea District in Tyler, Texas. On some occasions there was some winter damage, but the plant always recovered rapidly. Try fig ivy if you are looking for a covering vine that does not require much room—that is, that does not get very wide. I'm currently growing a 3-year-old planting of fig ivy on a brick wall at the east end of our home. Each year I have some winter damage, but I like the looks of the plant where it is, and I'm willing to accept the damage. It recovers quickly in the spring, and we enjoy it till the next round of hard winter freezes. It should grow relatively well in protected areas of Zone 7B. Horticulturist Heith Hanson in Tyler confirms that it grows well in his area, which is 7B.

WHEN TO PLANT
Fig ivy does best planted in early spring, especially in locations where its hardiness is marginal.

WHERE TO PLANT

Fig ivy does best in full-sun to partial-shade locations. Do not plant in total shade.

HOW TO PLANT

To achieve best results, start your fig ivy in well-prepared beds. Incorporate approximately 3 in. of organic matter into the top 3 in. of the native soil. After bed preparation is complete, remove your selections of fig ivy from their containers and plant them in the improved bed no deeper than they were grown originally. Firm the soil well around your new transplants, water thoroughly, and apply root stimulator according to label directions. Mulch with 2 in. of bark mulch.

CARE AND MAINTENANCE

There are no serious pest or disease problems when growing fig ivy. Prune as necessary to achieve the desired results, and water as necessary to maintain a moist soil. Do not allow fig ivy to get totally dry, and do not keep it wet. Fertilize in the spring when growth begins. 3:1:2 ratio premium-quality long-lasting lawn fertilizers such as 21-7-7-14, 19-5-9 or 15-5-10 work well when applied according to label directions and watered thoroughly.

ADDITIONAL INFORMATION

Fig ivy is quite attractive in our landscapes. I think it is outstanding on native stone walls, but make sure that you prune it occasionally to help rejuvenate its new growth; this also helps to improve its appearance.

ADDITIONAL SPECIES, CULTIVARS, OR VARIETIES

Try one of these *F. pumila* varieties: 'Minima', 'Quercifolia', and 'Variegata'.

Japanese Honeysuckle
Lonicera japonica

EXPOSURE

F. Sun to Shade

COLD HARDINESS

To -30° F.

WATER USAGE

Arid-Dry to Mst.

GROWTH RATE

Fast

AVG. HT × WIDTH

As Trained

SPACING

8–10'

Climbing evergreen vine. Blooms are white, yellow, and red.

When I was growing up in Brownwood, Texas, my mother always had some honeysuckle growing on a trellis outside our bedroom windows. This was in the days before air-conditioning, and the fragrance from the honeysuckle was always enjoyed by my sisters and me. Today, it will be as wonderful in your home landscape as it was in mine. It works very well when grown on structures. Wherever you decide to plant Japanese honeysuckle, remember that it needs considerable room, for it is an aggressive vining plant. It can be contained in "islands" of concrete while serving as a groundcover. You often see it grown on chain link fences in Texas, as well as on other types of fences. It lends itself well to breaking up harsh structures, softening these areas. Japanese honeysuckle will also work as a groundcover, especially on steep slopes where erosion control is necessary. Keep in mind that it has in some areas escaped cultivation and has almost become a pest. This aggressive growth characteristic makes it desirable for fast and dense coverage of certain areas.

WHEN TO PLANT
Because it is extremely winter hardy in Texas, Japanese honeysuckle may be planted 12 months out of the year, though the best time to plant is in early spring.

WHERE TO PLANT
Plant Japanese honeysuckle where it will have room to grow yet not overgrow the location. It works great in full-sun locations on large arbors, giving you an opportunity to enjoy the shade, the fragrance, the blooms, and the ease of growth. It is also easier to maintain in such areas.

HOW TO PLANT
While Japanese honeysuckle will grow in almost any type of soil and soil condition, to achieve finest results, plant in prepared beds. The best way to improve your bed for Japanese honeysuckle is to incorporate 3 in. of organic matter into the top 3 in. of the existing soil. After bed improvement is complete, remove your selections from their containers. Install them in the bed no deeper than they were grown in the containers, and firm the soil well. Then water thoroughly, apply root stimulator according to label directions, and cover with 3 in. of bark mulch.

CARE AND MAINTENANCE
Normally no insects or diseases are a problem when growing Japanese honeysuckle. Prune and train as necessary to achieve the form that you desire. For best results, water as necessary to maintain a moist growing condition. Fertilize as new growth begins in the spring with a premium-quality long-lasting slow-release 3:1:2 ratio lawn fertilizer such as 15-5-10 or 18-6-12 and water thoroughly. Remember that Japanese honeysuckle is aggressive.

ADDITIONAL INFORMATION
Japanese honeysuckle is outstanding in open, full-sun locations, planted by itself or on large structures.

ADDITIONAL SPECIES, CULTIVARS, OR VARIETIES
The common Japanese honeysuckle is often called 'Hall's' or green honeysuckle, and you will find it listed this way. Other varieties are purple leaf honeysuckle or 'Purpurea' and *Lonicera heckrotti* 'Pink Lemonade™'.

Wisteria
Wisteria sinensis

EXPOSURE

Full to Shade

COLD HARDINESS

All Texas

WATER USAGE

Semi-Moist

GROWTH RATE

Fast

AVG. HT × WIDTH

20–35 ' As Trained

SPACING

10–12 '

Deciduous woody climbing vine. Groups of blooms in grape-like structures in white or shades of blue and purple. Lightly fragrant.

*W*isteria is a vining plant that has been long used in Texas landscapes. You will find wisteria growing in long-abandoned homesites as well as in some of the most current gardens in our state. In our environment, they will grow in all locations, including soils that are heavy as well as those that are extremely light. After establishment, they will grow with very little overall maintenance. Wisteria is an important part of our Texas spring flower shows along with azaleas, dogwoods, redbuds, and spring-blooming bulbs. Think about onstructing a free-standing arbor in your home landscape and covering it with one or more wisteria plants. It is spectacular when in bloom, and enjoyable the rest of the year. The best time to buy wisteria is when it is in bloom. You will be able to see the bloom color and you will know that it does, indeed, bloom.

WHEN TO PLANT
Because of its hardiness, wisteria may be planted 12 months out of the year, though the best time to plant is in early fall.

WHERE TO PLANT

Because wisteria has been known to literally take over other plant-ings, plant it on structures that are separate from other landscape locations. It will grow well in full sun or in dappled sun/shade.

HOW TO PLANT

Wisteria will grow in almost any soil, but to achieve best results, plant in well-prepared beds on strong structures. The best way to prepare your bed is to incorporate 3 in. of organic matter into the top 3 in. of the existing soil. After bed improvement is complete, remove your selections of wisteria from their containers and install in new beds no deeper than they were growing in the containers. Firm the soil well. Water thoroughly, apply root stimulator according to label directions, and cover with 3 in. of bark mulch.

CARE AND MAINTENANCE

Wisteria has no serious pest or disease problems in Texas. Water as necessary to prevent soil dryness. Usually no fertilization is required. Sometimes growing wisteria in alkaline soils results in chlorotic leaves; apply iron as necessary to correct this situation. Prune and train as necessary to achieve the desired form. Pruning may be necessary to prevent wisteria from taking over relatively confined locations and other plants. The best solution is to plant in areas where there is plenty of growing room.

ADDITIONAL INFORMATION

When properly trained, wisteria adds outstanding early-spring fragrance and a color blast to the home landscape. Remember that wisteria can get out of hand if not properly maintained by training and pruning. To achieve the "tree form" wisteria, it is necessary to prune severely for several years. Such forms will revert rather quickly to a vine if not maintained. I do not recommend planting wisteria for the purpose of growing up trees and spreading through-out their canopies.

ADDITIONAL SPECIES, CULTIVARS, OR VARIETIES

Varieties of *W. sinensis* include 'Alba', 'Caroline', 'Purpurea', and 'Rosea'.

SOURCES

BIBLIOGRAPHY
INFORMATION RESOURCES
MAPS
CHARTS

BIBLIOGRAPHY

Adams, William D. *Shrubs and Vines for Southern Landscapes*. Gulf Publishing Co. Houston, 1979.

————. *Southern Flower Gardening*. Gulf Publishing Co. Houston, 1980.

————. *Trees For Southern Landscapes*. Gulf Publishing Co. Houston, 1976.

Ajilvsgi, Geyata. *Wild Flowers of Texas*. Shearer Publishing. Fredericksburg, Texas, 1991.

————. *Wild Flowers of the Big Thicket*. Texas A&M University Press. College Station, 1979.

Alholm, Patricia, Mktg. Mgr. *Recommended Species of Wildflowers, Shrubs, Trees, Grasses and Vines for All Areas of Texas*. National Wildflower Research Center Clearing House. Austin.

Baker, M. L. "Marty." *Trees, Shrubs, Vines, and Groundcovers for North Central Texas*. Texas Agricultural Extension Service, 1987.

Blankenship, Allen G. *Personal Tips on Roses*. Denton, Texas, 1997.

Burke, Ken, ed. *All about Roses*. Chevron Chemical Co. San Ramon, California, 1983.

Carle, Mary, ed. *Everything's Coming Up Roses*. Dallas, Mid-Cities, and Fort Worth Rose Societies. 1986.

Classification of Roses Information Sheet. American Rose Society (ARS). Shreveport, Louisiana.

Clements, John K. Mac, ed. *Garden Color, Annuals and Perennials*. Lane Publishing Co. Menlo Park, California, 1981.

Cox, Jeff and Marilyn Cox. *The Perennial Garden*. Rodale Press. Emmaus, Pennsylvania, 1985.

Discover the Pleasure of Roses, All America Rose Selections (AARS). Chicago.

Duble, Richard L. *Fact Sheet: Lawn Establishment #L-188*. Texas Agricultural Extension Service. 1982.

Duble, Richard L. and A. C. Novosad. *Fact Sheet: Turfgrasses for Texas Lawns #L-1865*. Texas Agricultural Extension Service. 1981.

————. *Home Lawns #M P-1180*. Texas Agricultural Extension Service. 1978.

Ellefson, Connie Lockhart, Thomas L. Stephens, and Doug Welsh, Ph.D. *Xeriscape Gardening, Water Conservation for the American Landscape*. MacMillan Publishing Company. New York, 1992.

Engelke, M. C., Ph.D. *Research Reports on Crowne, Cavalier and Palisade Zoysia Grasses*. Texas A & M University and Research Center. Dallas, 1996.

Sources

Erwin, Howard S. *Roadside Flowers of Texas*. University of Texas Press. Austin, 1961. First paperback, 1975.

Ferguson, Barbara, ed. *Color With Annuals*. Chevron Chemical Co. San Francisco, 1987.

Ferguson, Rob, Gen. Mgr. *1995 Wholesale Catalog*. Hines Nurseries. Houston.

George, Stephen, Ph.D. *Recommended Landscape Plant Materials for North Texas*. Texas Agricultural Extension Service. Dallas.

Groom, Dale. *Color For Sun And Fall*. Dale Groom, The Plant Groom™. 1990.

———. *List of "Powdery Mildew Resistant" Crape Myrtles*. Dale Groom, The Plant Groom™. 1992.

———. *Plants For Shady Areas*. Dale Groom, The Plant Groom™, 1987.

———. *The Plant Groom's Lawn Fertilizing Time Table*. Dale Groom, The Plant Groom™. 1993.

———. *The Plant Groom's Trees for Texas*. Dale Groom, The Plant Groom™. 1995.

Hall, Dwight S. *Ornamental Plants for North and East Texas #LH4*. Texas Agricultural Extension Service. Overton, Texas.

———. *Up With Trees!* Texas Agricultural Extension Service. Overton, Texas.

Harris, Mrs. N. J., ed. *Dallas Planting Manual*. Dallas Garden Club of the Dallas Women's Club. Dallas, 1981.

Horton, Alvin and James McNair. *All About Bulbs*. Chevron Chemical Co. San Francisco, 1986.

Janne, Everette. *Fact Sheet, Annual Flowers in the Home Landscape #L-1848*. Texas Agricultural Extension Service. College Station, Texas, 1981.

Johnson, Eric A. and Scott Millard. *The Low-Water Flower Gardener*. Millard Publishing Services. Tucson, 1993.

Laughmiller, Campbell, Lynn Laughmiller, and Lynn Sherwood. *Texas Wildflowers, a Field Guide*. University of Texas Press. Austin, 1984.

Loewer, Peter. *The Annual Garden*. Rodale Press. Emmaus, Pennsylvania, 1988.

Miller, George O. *Landscaping With Native Plants of Texas and the Southwest*. Voyageur Press, Inc. Stillwater, Minnesota, 1991.

Nokes, Jill. *How to Grow Native Plants of Texas and the Southwest*. Texas Monthly Press. 1986.

Ogden, Scott. *Garden Bulbs for the South*. Taylor Publishing Co. Dallas, 1994.

Sources

Rosedale, Miles, Pres. *1996 Wholesale Catalog*. Monrovia Nursery Company. Azusa, California.

Sangster, Bruce, Pres. *Thompson & Morgan Seed Catalog*. 1997.

Scheider, Alfred F. *Park's Success with Bulbs*. Geo. W. Park Seed Co. Inc. Greenwood, South Carolina, 1981.

Scott, George Harmon. *Bulbs: How to Select, Grow and Enjoy*. H.P. Books, Inc. Tucson, 1982.

Simpson, Benny J. *A Field Guide to Texas Trees*. Gulf Publishing Co. Houston, 1988.

Sinnes, A. Cort. *All About Perennials*. Chevron Chemical Company. San Francisco, 1981.

Texas Agriculture Extension Service handbooks:
Efficient Use of Water in the Garden and Landscape, Revised 1990,
Integrated Pest Management of Texas Turfgrass, Reprinted 1993,
Texas Master Gardener's Training Manual, Vascular Plants of Texas, 1990

Thomas, John R., Pres. *A Grower's Guide to Wildflowers*. Wildseed Inc. 1988.

Turfgrass Tip Sheets from Turfgrass Producers International (TPI): Bermudagrass, Centipedegrass, Zoysia, Tall Fescue, St. Augustinegrass, and Rye.

Van der Voort, Henk. *Dutch Gardens 1992 Fall Planting Catalog*. Adelphia, New Jersey.

Wasowski, Sally, with Andy Wasowski. *Native Texas Plants, Landscaping Region by Region*. Texas Monthly Press. Austin, 1988.

Welch, William C., Ph.D. *Perennial Garden Color for Texas and the South*. Taylor Publishing Co. Dallas, 1989.

Whitcomb, Carl E., Ph.D. *Know It and Grow It, II*. Lacebark Publications. Stillwater, Oklahoma, 1983.

White Flower Farm, The Garden Book, Southern Edition. Litchfield, Connecticut, 1997.

Wonderful World of Roses, All America Rose Selections, Inc. (AARS). Chicago.

Zangger, James M., Pres. *1996 Wholesale Catalog*. Greenleaf Nursery Company. Parkhill, Oklahoma.

INFORMATION RESOURCES

American Hemerocallis Society (Daylily), 3803 Graystone Drive, Austin, TX 78731.

American Iris Society, 7414 East 60th St., Tulsa, OK 74145.

American Rose Society, 8877 Jefferson-Paige Road, Shreveport, LA 71130; mailing address, P.O. Box 30000, Shreveport, LA 71130.

Austin Area Garden Council, 220 Barton Springs Road, Zilker Park, Austin, TX 78746.

Bayou Bend Gardens, 1 Wescott St., Houston, TX 77219.

Botanical Resources Institute of Texas, 509 Pecan St., Ft. Worth, TX 76102.

Carleen Bright Arboretum at Woodway, 924 Estates Drive, Woodway, TX 76712

City of Tyler Municipal Rose Garden, 420 South Rosepark Drive, Tyler, TX 75710.

Corpus Christi Botanical Garden, 8510 South Staples, Corpus Christi, TX 78413.

Corpus Christi Botanical Society, P.O. Box 8113, Corpus Christi, TX 78412.

Dale Groom, The Plant Groom™, P.O. Box 365, Eustace, TX 75124, e-mail plantgrm@cleaf.com and website www.cleaf.com/~plantgrm.

Dallas Arboretum and Botanical Garden, 8617 Garland Road, Dallas, TX 75218.

El Paso Native Plant Society, 6804 Tolvea, El Paso, TX 79912.

Fort Worth Botanical Garden, 3220 Botanic Garden Blvd., Ft. Worth, TX 76107.

Friends of the Ft. Worth Nature Center and Refuge, P.O. Box 11694, Ft. Worth, TX 76109.

Heritage Roses Group, 810 East 30th Street, Austin, TX 78705.

Houston Arboretum and Botanical Society, 4501 Woodway Drive, Houston, TX 77024.

McMurray College, Iris Garden, Sayles Blvd. and South 16th St., c/o Abilene Chamber of Commerce, 325 Hickory St., Abilene, TX.

Mercer Arboretum and Botanical Garden, 22306 Adline Westfield, Humble, TX 77338.

Moody Gardens, 1 Hope Blvd., Galveston, TX 78739.

National Wildflower Research Center, 4801 La Crosse Blvd., Austin, TX 78739.

Native Plant Society of Texas, P.O. Box 891, Georgetown, TX 78627.

Native Prairies Association of Texas, Texas Woman's University, P.O. Box 22675, Denton, TX 76204.

Sources

San Antonio Botanical Garden, 555 Funston Place, San Antonio, TX 78209.

Society for Louisiana Irises, 1216 Cedar Pine Lane, Little Elm, TX 75068.

South Texas Plant Materials Center, Caesar Kleberg Wildlife Research Center, Texas A&I University, P.O. Box 218, Kingsville, TX 78363.

Stephen F. Austin State University Arboretum, P.O. Box 13000, Nacogdoches, TX 75962.

Texas Association of Nurserymen, Inc., 512 East Riverside Drive, Suite 207, Austin, TX 78704.

Texas Botanical Garden Society, P.O Box 5642, Austin, TX 78763.

Texas Department of Agriculture, P.O. Box 12847, Austin, TX 78711.

Texas Department of Highways, Landscape Division, 11th at Brazos, Austin, TX 78701.

Texas Garden Clubs, Inc., 3111 Botanic Garden Road, Ft. Worth, TX 76107.

"The Plant Groom"™ half-hour TV series on FamilyNet, America One Television Network, and American Independent Network.

"The Plant Groom"™ lawn/garden/landscape column.

Another great source of information is the local representative of the Texas Agricultural Extension Service in your county. We typically call these folks the "County Agent." Their offices are usually located in the County Courthouse, Annex Buildings, or other county properties. Look for their numbers in the phone directory under listings for your county's offices.

TEMPERATURE MAP

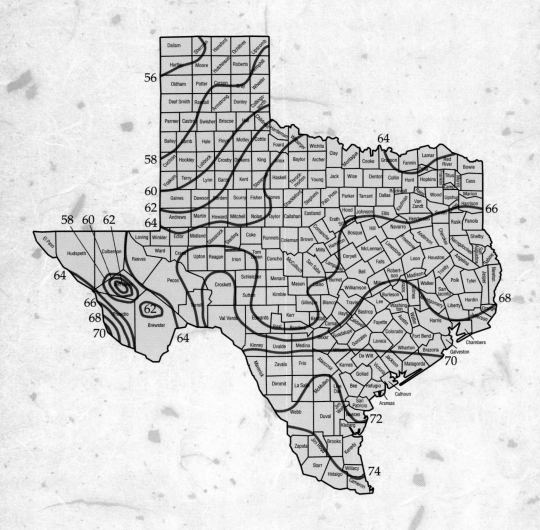

Mean annual temperature (°F.)
Adapted from Griffiths and Orton (1968).

VEGETATION MAP

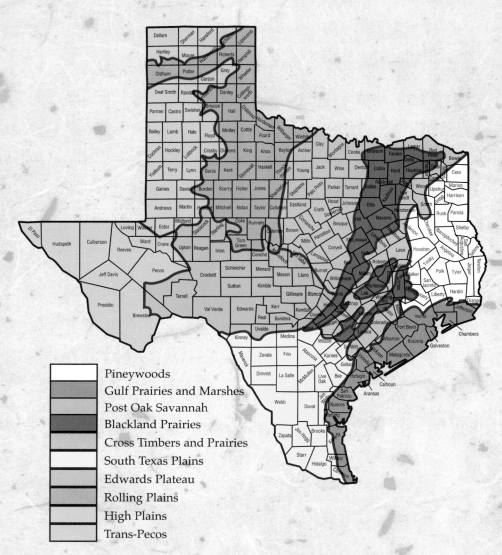

Pineywoods
Gulf Prairies and Marshes
Post Oak Savannah
Blackland Prairies
Cross Timbers and Prairies
South Texas Plains
Edwards Plateau
Rolling Plains
High Plains
Trans-Pecos

Vegetational areas of Texas.
Adapted from Griffiths and Orton (1968).

VEGETATION CHART

Summary of the physical and climatic characteristics of the vegetation area of Texas.*

	Million acres (million hectares)	Annual precipitation (inches)	Frost-free days	Typography	Elevation (feet)	Major soil orders	Month of peak precipitation (secondary peak)
1. Pineywoods	15.80 (6.4)	40-56	235-265	Nearly level to gently undulating	200-700	Utisols, Alfisols	Even distribution
2. Gulf Prairies and Marshes	10.00 (4.1)	26.56	245-320	Nearly level	0-250	Vertisols, Entisols	September (May)
3. Post Oak Savannah	6.85 (2.8)	30-45	235-280	Nearly lvel to gently rolling	300-800	Alfisols, Vertisols, Utisols	May (September)
4. Blackland Prairies	12.6 (5.1)	30-45	230-280	Nearly Level to rolling	250-700	Vertisols, Alfisols	May (September)
5. Cross Timbers and Prairies	15.3 (6.2)	25-35	230-280	Gently rolling	500-1500	Mollisols, Alfisols	May (September)
6. South Texas Plains	20.9 (8.5)	18-30	260-340	Nearly lvel to rolling	0-1000	Mollisols, Vertisols, Alfisols, Entisols	September (May)
7. Edwards Plateau	25.45 (10.3)	12-32	220-260	Deeply dissected hilly, stony plain	1200-3000	Entisols, Mollisols, Alfisols	May (September)
8. Rolling Plains	24.0 (9.7)	18-28	185-235	Nearly level to rolling	1000-3000	Mainly Mollisols, secondarily Alfisols	May (September)
9. High Plains	19.4 (7.9)	14-21	180-220	Nearly level high plateau	3000-4500	Alfisols, Mollisols	May (September)
10. Trans-Pecos	17.95 (7.3)	8-18	220-245	Mountain ranges, rough, rocky land, flat basins and plateaus	2500-8751	Aridisols, Entisols, Mollisols	July, August, September (November)

* Adapted from Godfrey et al. (1973).

FROST-FREE MAP

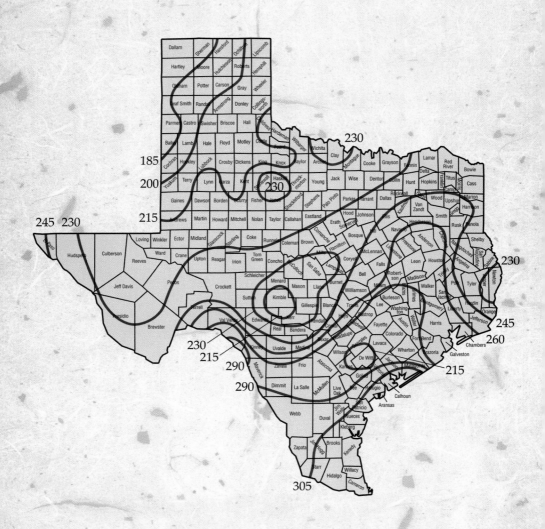

Mean length (days) of frost-free period.
Adapted from Griffiths and Orton (1968).

PRECIPITATION MAP

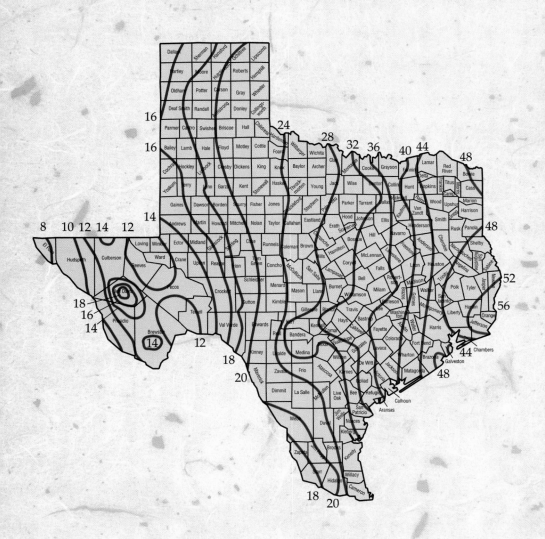

Mean annual total precipitation (inches) in Texas.
Adapted from Griffiths and Orton (1968).

SOIL TEXTURAL TRIANGLE

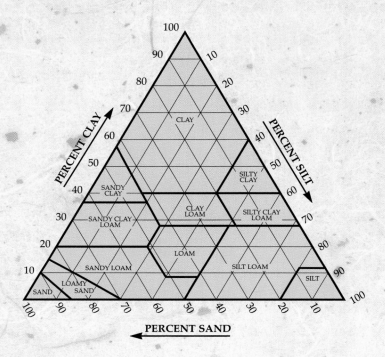

Principal Surface Soil Classes Found in Texas

1. **Loam** — When rubbed between the thumb and fingers, approximately equal influence of sand, silt, and clay is felt.

2. **Sandy loam** — Varies from very fine loam to very coarse; feels quite sandy or rough, but contains some silt and a small amount of clay. The amount of silt and clay is sufficient to hold the soil together when moist.

3. **Silt loam** — Silt is the dominant size particle in silt loam, which feels quite smooth or floury when rubbed between the thumb and fingers.

4. **Silty clay loam** — Smooth to the touch when dry. When moist it becomes somewhat slick or sticky, or both. Noticeable amounts of both silt and clay are present in silty clay loam, but silt is a dominant part of the soil.

5. **Clay loam** — Clay dominates a clay loam, which is smooth when dry and slick and sticky when wet. Silt and sand are usually present in noticeable amounts in this texture of soil, but they are overshadowed by clay.

6. **Clay** — Fine texture with absence of sand or silt; holds form when wet and ribbons when pressed with fingers; hard when dry.

Reprinted from:
The Texas Agricultural Extension Service Training Manual

Determination of Soil Moisture Content

Soil Moisture Level	How Soil Feels and Looks			
	Coarse (sand)	Light (loamy sand, sandy loam)	Medium (fine sandy loam, silt loam)	Heavy (clay loam, clay)
No available soil moisture. Plants wilt. Irrigation required. (First Range)	Dry, loose, single grained, flows through fingers. No stain or smear on fingers.	Dry, loose, clods easily crushed and flows through fingers. No stain or smear on fingers.	Crumbly, dry, powdery, barely maintains shape. Clods break down easily. May leave slight smear or stain when worked with hands or fingers.	Hard, firm baked, cracked. Usually too stiff or tough to work or ribbon* by squeezing between thumb or forefinger. May leave slight smear or stain.
Moisture is available, but level is low. Irrigation needed. (Second Range)	Appears dry; will not retain shape when squeezed in hand.	Appears dry; may make a cast when squeezed in hand but seldom holds together.	May form a weak ball** under pressure but is still crumbly. Color is pale with no obvious moisture.	Pliable, forms a ball; ribbons but usually breaks or is crumbly. May leave slight stain or smear.
Moisture is available. Level is high. Irrigation not yet needed. (Third Range)	Color is dark with obvious moisture. Soil may stick together in very weak cast or ball.	Color is dark with obvious moisture. Soil forms weak ball or cast under pressure. Slight finger stain but no ribbon when squeezed between thumb and forefinger.	Color is dark from obvious moisture. Forms a ball. Works easily, clods are soft with mellow feel. Stains finger and has slick feel when squeezed.	Color is dark with obvious moisture. Forms good ball. Ribbons easily, has slick feel. Leaves stain on fingers.
Soil moisture level following an irrigation. (Fourth Range)	Appears and feels moist. Color is dark. May form weak cast or ball. Leaves wet outline or slight smear on hand.	Appears and feels moist. Color is dark. Forms cast or ball. Will not ribbon but shows smear or stain and leaves wet outline on hand.	Appears and feels moist. Color is dark. Has a smooth mellow feel. Forms ball and ribbons when squeezed. Stains and smears. Leaves wet outline on hand.	Color is dark. Appears moist; may feel sticky. Ribbons out easily; smears and stains hand; leaves wet outline. Forms good ball.

* Ribbon is formed by squeezing and working soil between thumb and forefinger.
**Cast or ball is formed by squeezing soil in hand.

Reprinted from:
The Texas Agricultural Extention Service publication #B-1496

INDEX

Abelia, 278
Abelia × grandiflora, 278
Acalypha wilkesiana, 34
Acer palmatum, 368
Achillea cultivars, 250
Agarito, 184
Ajuga, 126
Ajuga reptans, 126
Albizia julibrissin, 374
Algerita, 185
Althea, 280
American Beautyberry, 186
Annuals 26-67
Annual Vinca, 50
Antigonon leptopus, 230
Antirrhinum majus, 58
Aralia, 282
Aralia japonica, 282
Aralia seboldi, 282
Arborvitae, 284
Artemisia abrotanum, 248
Artemisia absinthium, 249
Artemisia dracunculus, 249
Artemisia ludoviciana, 249
Artemisia schmidtiana, 249
Artemisia vulgaris, 249
Asian Jasmine, 128
Astilbe, 228
Astilbe chinensis, 229
Astilbe spp., 228
Aucuba, 286
Aucuba japonica, 286
Azalea, 288
Babylon Weeping
    Willow, 388
Bachelor Buttons, 28
Bald Cypress, 352
Barberry, 290
Bearded Iris, 84
Begonia × Semperflorens-
    Cultorum Hybrids, 64
Berberis buxifolia, 291
Berberis swaseyi, 185
Berberis thunbergii, 290
Berberis trifoliolata, 184
Berberis × gladwynensis, 291
Berberis × mentorensis, 291
Bermudagrass, 98
Black-eyed Susan, 148, 164
Bleeding Heart, 192
Blue Fescue, 112
Bluebonnet, 150
Border Phlox, 242
Boston Ivy, 392
Boxwood, 292

Brassica oleracea, 38
Brown-eyed Susan, 148
Buchloe dactyloides, 100
Buddleia davidii, 296
Buddleia spp., 196
Buddleia nanhoensis, 297
Buffalograss, 100
Bugle Weed, 126
Bulbs, Corms, Rhizomes
    and Tubers, 68-91
Burning Bush, 294
Busy Lizzie, 42
Butterfly Bush, 296
Buxus harlandii, 293
Buxus microphylla, 292
Buxus sempervirens, 293
Caladium, 70
Caladium × hortulanum, 70
Callery Pear, 360
Callicarpa americana, 186
Callicarpa americana cv.
    Lactea, 187
Camellia, 298
Camellia japonica, 298
Camellia oleifera, 299
Camellia sasanqua, 299
Canna, 72
Canna × generalis, 72
Cape Jasmine, 316
Carolina Jasmine/
    Jessamine, 214
Carpet Bugle, 126
Carya illinoensis, 204
Castilleja integra, 157
Castilleja latebracteata, 157
Castilleja purpurea, 157
Castilleja sessiliflora, 157
Castilleja indivisa, 156
Catharanthus roseus, 50
Cedar Elm, 198
Cedar Tree, 354
Celosia, 30
Celosia cristata, 30
Cenizo, 190
Centaurea cineraria spp.
    cineraria, 232
C. gymnocarpa, 233
Centipedegrass, 102
Cercis canadensis, 384
Cercis reniformis, 384
Chaenomeles japonica, 312
Chaenomeles speciosa, 313
Cherry Laurel, 300
Chinese Arborvitae, 284
Chinese Junipers, 328

Chinese Pistachio, 356
Chrysanthemum, 236
Clasping-Leaf
    Coneflower, 152
Cleyera, 302
Climbing Rose, 256
Clump Fescue, 112
Cockscomb, 30
Coleus, 32
Coleus × hybridus, 32
Common Hyacinth, 82
Confederate Jasmine, 394
Confederate Star
    Jasmine, 394
Copper Plant, 34
Coral Honeysuckle, 216
Coral Vine, 230
Coreopsis basalis, 160
Coreopsis
    cardaninaeforlia, 160
Coreopsis enuecensis, 160
Coreopsis grandiflora, 160
Coreopsis lanceolata syn.
    grandiflora, 161, 168
Coreopsis longipes, 160
Coreopsis tinctoria, 160
Cornus florida, 200
Cortaderia selloana, 122
Cotoneaster, 304
Cotoneaster acutifolius, 305
Cotoneaster adpressus, 305
Cotoneaster apiculatus, 304
Cotoneaster congestus, 305
Cotoneaster dammeri
Cotoneaster divaricatus, 305
Cotoneaster
    glaucophyllus, 305
Cotoneaster horizontalis
    'Perpusilla', 304
Cotoneaster salicifolius
    'Repens', 304
Cotoneaster spp., 304
Crape Myrtle, 306
Creeping Fig, 398
Crimson Fountain
    Grass, 114
Crinum, 74
Crinum spp., 74
Cupressocyparis
    leylandii, 372
Cynodon dactylon, 98
Daffodil, 86
Daylily, 76
Dendranthema
    cultivars, 236

Index

Dianthus barbatus, 36
Dianthus chinensis, 36
Dianthus spp., 244
Dusty Miller, 232
Dutch Hyacinth, 82
Eastern Arborvitae, 284
Echinacea augustifolia, 178
Echinacea pallida, 179
Echinacea purpurea, 179
Echinacea sanguinea, 179
Elaeagnus, 308
Elaeagnus macrophylla, 309
Elaeagnus pungens, 308
Elaeagnus × *ebbengi*, 309
English Ivy, 396
English Laurel, 300
Eremochloa ophiuroide, 102
Eriobotrya japonica, 330
Erythraea beyrichii, 163
Euonymus, 310
Euonymus alata, 294, 311
Euonymus fortunei, 144, 311
Euonymus japonica, 310
Euonymus kiautschovica, 311
Eustoma grandiflorum, 162
Evening Primrose, 166
Exaltatum, 163
Fatsia, 282
Fatsia japonica, 282
Ferns spp., 134
Festica ovina, 112
Festuca arundinacea, 108
Ficus pumila, 398
Fig Ivy, 398
Fig Seed, 160
Fig Weed, 160
Firethorn, 340
Firewheel, 154
Floribunda, 258
Flowering Cabbage, 38
Flowering Crab Apple, 358
Flowering Dogwood, 200
Flowering Pear, 360
Flowering Purple Leaf
    Plum, 382
Flowering Quince, 312
Forsythia, 314
Forsythia × *intermedia*, 314
Fountain Grass, 114
Four-o-Clocks, 234

Fraser's Photinia, 338
Fraxinus americana, 213
Fraxinus pennsylvanica,
    213, 366
Fraxinus texensis, 212, 367
Gaillardia aristata, 155
Gaillardia pulchella, 154
Garden Hyacinth, 82
Garden Mum, 236
Gardenia, 316
Gardenia jasminoides, 316
Gelsemium
    sempervirens, 214
Geranium, 40
Ginkgo, 362
Ginkgo biloba, 362
Gladiolus, 78
Gladiolus alatus, 79
Gladiolus byzantinus, 79
Gladiolus sp., 78
Gladiolus × *colvillei*, 79
Glads, 78
Globe Amaranth, 28
Gold Dust Plant, 286
Golden Rain Tree, 364
Golden Wave, 160
Gomphrena, 28
Gomphrena globosa, 28
Grandiflora, 260
**Grasses: Lawn and
    Ornamental**, 92-123
Gray Santolina, 130
Green Ash, 366
Green Santolina, 130
Groundcovers, 124-145
Groundcover Junipers, 132
Hardy Ferns, 134
Hardy Hibiscus, 318
Hardy Phlox, 242
Hardy Red Amaryllis, 80
Heavenly Bamboo, 334
Hedera helix, 396
Helianthus annuus, 60
Hemerocallis spp., 76
Hibiscus coccineus, 319
Hibiscus moscheutos, 318
Hibiscus syriacus, 280
Hippeastrum × *johnsonii*, 80
Holly, 320
Hosta, 136

Hosta spp., 136
Hyacinth, 82
*Hyacinthus orientalis
    albus*, 83
Hyacinthus orientalis, 82
Hybrid Tea, 262
Hydrangea, 322
Hydrangea paniculata, 323
Hydrangea macrophylla, 322
Hydrangea quercifolia, 323
Ilex cornuta, 321
Ilex crenata, 321
Ilex spp., 320
Ilex vomitoria, 321
Ilex × 'Nellie R.
    Stevens', 321
Impatiens, 42
Impatiens walleriana, 42
Indian Blanket, 154
Indian Hawthorne, 324
Indian Paintbrush, 156
Ipomoea alba, 47
Ipomoea nil, 47
Ipomoea tricolor, 47
Ipomoea purpurea, 46
Iris, 84
Iris spp., 84
Japanese Honeysuckle, 400
Japanese Lawn Grass, 110
Japanese Maple, 368
Japanese Red Maple, 368
Japanese Yew, 326
Japonica, 312
Jasminum floridum, 349
Jasminum nitidum, 349
Jasminum nudiflorum, 348
Jasminum polyanthum, 349
Jasminum primulinum, 349
Jasminum sambac, 349
Jonquil, 86
Juniper, 328
Juniperus chinensis, 328
Juniperus conferta, 132, 329
Juniperus horizontalis,
    132, 329
Juniperus procumbens,
    132, 329
Juniperus sabina, 329
Juniperus scopulorum, 329
Juniperus spp., 132

Index

Juniperus squamata, 329
Juniperus virginiana,
    329, 354
Koelreuteria bipinnata, 365
Koelreuteria paniculata, 364
Korean Lawn Grass, 110
Lacebark Elm, 370
Lady Bank's Rose, 264
Lagerstroemia indica, 306
Lanceleaf Coreopsis, 168
Lantana, 238
Lantana camara, 181, 239
Lantana horrida, 180, 239
Lantana macropoda, 181
Lantana montevidensis,
    181, 238
Leucanthemum ×
    superbum, 246
Leucophyllum frutescens, 190
Leatherleaf Mahonia, 332
Leyland Cypress, 372
Ligustrum incidum, 347
Ligustrum japonicum, 346
Ligustrum japonicum
    'Texanum Aureo-
    Marginata', 347
Ligustrum sinensis
    'Variegata', 347
Ligustrum 'Suwannee
    River', 347
Ligustrum texanum, 346
Ligustrum vulgare
    'Lodense', 347
Ligustrum × vicaryi, 347
Lily Turf, 118
Liquidambar styraciflua, 210
Liriope, 120
Liriope muscari, 120
Lolium multiflorum, 104
Lolium perenne, 104
Lonicera japonica, 400
Lonicera sempervirens, 216
Loquat, 330
Lupinus havardii, 151
Lupinus perennis, 151
Lupinus plattensis, 151
Lupinus subcarnosus, 151
Lupinus texensis, 150
Lycoris radiata, 89
Lycoris spp., 88

Lycoris squamigara, 89
Lycoris traubii, 89
Magic Lily, 88
Magnolia grandiflora,
    208, 387
Magnolia macrophylla, 387
Magnolia virginiana, 386
Magnolia × soulangiana, 387
Magnolia × veitchii, 387
Mahonia, 332
Mahonia aquifolium, 333
Mahonia bealei, 332
Mahonia fortunei, 333
Mahonia repens, 333
Maidengrass, 116
Maidenhair Tree, 362
Malus spp., 358
Malvaviscus arboreus var.
    drummondii, 192
Marigold, 44
Mari-Mums, 45
Maypop, 218
Mealy Blue Sage, 170
Mexican Hat, 172
Mexican Love Vine, 230
Mexican Petunia, 240
Mimosa, 374
Miniatures, 266
Mirabilis jalapa, 234
Miscanthus sinensis, 116
Mondo Grass, 118
Monkey Grass, 120
Morning Glory, 46
Moss Rose, 54
Myrica cerifera, 194
Myrica pussila, 195
Nandina, 334
Nandina domestica, 334
Narcissus, 86
Narcissus jonquilla, 87
Narcissus
    pseudonarcissus, 87
Narcissus, spp., 86
Narcissus tazetta, 87
Native Texas Plants,
    146-223
Nerium oleander, 336
Oak, 202, 376
Oenothera drummondii, 166
Oenothera hookeri, 166

Oenothera lamarckiana, 166
Oenothera missouriensis, 166
Oenothera spp., 166
Oenothera triloba, 166
Old Garden, 268
Oleander, 336
Ophiopogon, 118
Ophiopogon japonicus, 118
Oriental Arborvitae, 284
Ornamental Cabbage, 38
Ornamental Fescue, 112
Ornamental Kale, 38
Palm Tree, 378
Pampas Grass, 122
Pansy, 48
Parthenocissus quinquefolia,
    222, 393
Parthenocissus tricuspidata,
    223, 392
Passiflora incarnata, 218
Passiflora lutea, 219
Passion Vine, 218
Passionflower, 218
Pecan, 204
Pelargonium × hortorum, 40
Pennisetum
    alopecuroides, 114
Periwinkle, 50, 138
Perennials, 226-251
Petunia, 52
Petunia × hybrida, 52
Phlox, 158, 174, 242
Phlox divaricata, 174
Phlox drummondii, 158
Phlox paniculata, 242
Phlox nana, 174
Phlox nivalis, 175
Phlox pilosa, 174
Phlox spp., 174
Photinia, 338
Photinia glabra, 339
Photinia serrulata, 339
Photinia × fraseri, 338
Pine, 206, 380
Pinks, 36, 244
Pinus brutia spp. *eldarica*, 381
Pinus cembroides, 207
Pinus echinata, 207, 381
Pinus elliottii, 380
Pinus nigra, 381

Index

Pinus palustris, 207
Pinus ponderosa var.
    Scopulorum, 207, 381
Pinus spp., 206, 380
Pinus sylvestris, 381
Pinus taeda, 207, 381
Pinus thunbergiana, 380
Pistacia atlantica, 357
Pistacia chinensis, 356
Pistacia texana, 357
Pistacia vera, 357
Plains Coreopsis, 160
Podocarpus, 326
Podocarpus
    macrophyllus, 326
Polyantha, 270
Portulaca, 54
Portulaca grandiflora, 54
Prairie Verbena, 176
Prostrate Rosemary, 140
Prunus caroliniana, 301
Prunus cerasifera, 382
Prunus laurocerasus, 300
Purple Coneflower, 178
Purple Fountain Grass, 114
Purple Leaf Plum, 382
Purple Sage, 190
Pyracantha, 340
Pyracantha coccinea, 340
Pyracantha fortuneana, 341
Pyracantha koidzumii, 341
Pyrus calleryana, 360
Queen's Wreath, 230
Quercus macrocarpa,
    203, 376
Quercus muehlenbergii, 203
Quercus nuttallii, 376
Quercus palustris, 376
Quercus phellos, 203
Quercus shumardii, 203, 376
Quercus spp., 202, 376
Quercus texana, 203, 376
Quercus virginiana, 202, 376
Raphiolepis indica, 324
Raphiolepis umbellata, 325
Ratibida columnaris, 172
Red Salvia, 56
Red Tips, 338
Redbud, 384
Resurrection Lily, 88

Rhododendron spp., 288
Rosa, 256, 258, 260, 262,
    266, 268, 270, 272, 274
Rose Moss, 54
Rose of Sharon, 280
Rosea banksiae, 264
Rosa banksia 'Alba
    Plena', 275
Rosa banksia 'Lutea',
    265, 274
Rosa centifolia, 275
Rosa eglanteria, 275
Rosa foetida, 275
Rosa gallica, 275
Rosa laevigata, 275
Rosa moschata, 275
Rosa multiflora, 275
Rosa palustris, 275
Rosa roxburghii, 275
Rosa setigera, 275
Roses, 252-275
    Climbing Rose, 256
    Floribunda, 258
    Grandiflora, 260
    Hybrid Tea, 262
    Lady Bank's Rose, 264
    Miniatures, 266
    Old Garden, 268
    Polyantha, 270
    Shrub, 272
    Species, 274
Rosmarinus officinalis
    'Prostratus', 140
Rudbeckia amplexicaulis
    syn. Dracopis
    amplexicaulis, 152
Rudbeckia grandiflora, 165
Rudbeckia hirta var.
    'Angustifolia', 149, 164
Rudbeckia hirta var.
    'Pulcherrima', 148
Rudbeckia laciniata, 165
Rudbeckia missouriensis, 165
Rudbeckia nitida, 165
Ruellia, 240
Ruellia brittoniana, 240
Ruellia caroliniensis, 183
Ruellia humilis, 183
Ruelliamalacosperma, 183, 241
Ruellia metzae, 183

Ruellia nudiflora, 183
Ruellia occidentalis, 183
Ruellia pedunculata, 183
Ruellia spp., 182
Ryegrass, 104
Sabatia campestris, 163
Salix alba, 389
Salix babylonica, 388
Salix caprea, 389
Salix matsudana, 389
Salix nigra, 388
Salix × blanda, 389
Salvia, 56
Salvia coccinea 'Lady In
    Red', 57
Salvia coccinea, 171
Salvia farinacea, 170
Salvia Greggii, 188
Salvia greggii, 171, 188
Salvia roemeriana, 171
Salvia Splendens, 56
Salvia splendens, 56
Salvia texana, 171
Santolina
    chamaecyparissus, 130
Santolina neapolitana, 131
Santolina pinnata, 131
Santolina rosmarinifolia, 131
Santolina virens, 130
Scarlet Paintbrush, 156
Scarlet Sage, 56
Scented Geraniums, 40
Sedum, 142
Sedum spp., 142
Shasta Daisy, 246
Shrubs, 276-349
Shrub, 272
Siberian Elm, 370
Silver Leaf, 190
Snapdragon, 58
Snowball Bush, 344
Southern Magnolia, 208
Southernwood, 248
Species Roses, 274
Spider Lily, 88
Spiraea, 342
Spiraea catoniensis, 343
Spiraea dolchica, 343
Spiraea japonica, 342
Spiraea nipponica, 343

Index

Spiraea prunifolia, 343
Spiraea thunbergii, 343
Spiraea × 'Goldmound', 343
Spiraea × *bumalda*, 343
Spiraea × *vanhouttei*, 343
St. Augustine, 106
St. Joseph's lily, 80
Standing Phlox, 242
Star Jasmine, 394
*Stenotaphrum
   secundatum*, 106
Sultana, 42
Summer Petunia, 240
Summer Phlox, 242
Sunflower, 60
Sweet Bay Magnolia, 386
Sweet Gum, 210
Sweet William, 36
Tagetes erecta, 44
Tagetes patula, 44
Tall Fescue, 108
Tarda, 91
Taxodium ascendens, 353
Taxodium distichum, 352
Ternstroemia japonica, 302
Texas Ash, 212
Texas Bluebells, 162
Texas Lantana, 180
Texas Paintbrush, 156
Texas Sage, 190
Texas Wisteria, 220
Thuja occidentalis, 284
Thuja orientalis, 284
*Trachelospermum
   asiaticum*, 128
*Trachelospermum
   jasminoides*, 394, 129

Trailing Lantana, 238
Trees, 350-389
Tulip, 90
Tulipa clusiana, 91
Tulipa fosterana, 91
Tulipa greigii, 91
Tulipa kaufmanniana, 91
Tulipa kuschkensis, 91
Tulipa linifolia, 91
Tulipa lutea, 91
Tulipa montana, 91
Tulipa saxatilis, 91
Tulipa spp., 90
Tulipa undulatifolia, 91
Turk's Cap, 192
Ulmus alata, 199
Ulmus crassifolia, 198, 371
Ulmus parvifolia, 199, 370
Ulmus pumila, 370
Verbena, 62
Verbena bipinnatifida, 176
Verbena brisiliensis, 177
Verbena canadensis, 177
Verbena halei, 177
Verbena rigida, 177
Verbena × *hybrida*, 62
Viburnum, 344
Viburnum awabuki, 345
Viburnum davidii, 344
Viburnum dentatum, 345
Viburnum japonicum, 345
Viburnum lantana, 345
Viburnum nudum, 345
Viburnum opulus, 344
*Viburnum plicatum
   tomentosum*, 345
Viburnum plicatum, 345

*Viburnum
   rhytidophyllum*, 344
Viburnum rufidulum, 345
Viburnum spp., 344
Viburnum suspensum, 345
Viburnum tinus, 345
Vinca major/minor, 138
Vines, 390-403
Viola × *wittrockiana*, 48
Virginia Creeper, 222
Washingtonia filifera, 378
Washingtonia robusta, 379
Wax Leaf, 346
Wax Leaf Begonia, 64
Wax Leaf Ligustrum, 346
Wax Myrtle, 194
Weeping Willow, 388
Wild Petunia, 182
Winter Jasmine, 348
Wintercreeper, 144
Wisteria, 402
Wisteria macrostachya, 220
Wisteria sinensis, 402
Wooly Butterfly Bush, 196
Yarrow, 250
Zinnia, 66
Zinnia elegans, 66
Zinnia linearis, 67
Zoysiagrass, 110
Zoysia japonica, 110
*Zoysia matrella
   'Cavalier'*, 111

ABOUT THE AUTHOR

*H*ORTICULTURIST AND NATIVE TEXAN, DALE GROOM is nationally known as The Plant Groom™ through his far-reaching television shows, radio shows, and newspaper columns. The Plant Groom™ television series has aired on Family Net, ACTS, America One Television and America Independent Networks, helping many viewers become gardeners—including children. The father of three, Groom has launched a national campaign "How to Grow . . . a Gardener" to encourage America's families to garden together.

The author's radio program is heard coast to coast on the USA Radio Network, American Forum Radio Network and Salem Radio Network. His newspaper column, The Plant Groom™, is syndicated throughout Texas.

A native of Brownwood in Brown County, Groom comes from several generations of farmers and gardeners. The author received his Bachelor of Science degree in agriculture from Stephen F. Austin State University and a Master of Science from East Texas State University. Groom also established the Ornamental Horticultural program at Tyler Junior College.

As a member of the Texas Association of Nurserymen, Groom has served as the group's regional director and as a reporter for its trade publication. The author belongs to several other professional organizations including the Agriculture Honor Society, Men's Garden Club of America, and the Garden Writers Association of America. In addition, Groom is a certified professional nurseryman and plant/flower show judge.

The author and his wife of more than 30 years, Judy, live with their youngest child on their farm in northeast Texas.